HISTORY
OF THE
PRESBYTERY
OF
ERIE

EMBRACING IN ITS ANCIENT BOUNDARIES THE
WHOLE OF NORTHWESTERN PENNSYLVANIA
AND NORTHEASTERN OHIO

WITH

BIOGRAPHICAL SKETCHES OF
ALL ITS MINISTERS

AND

HISTORICAL SKETCHES
OF ITS CHURCHES

S. J. M. Eaton

Pastor of the Presbyterian Church, Franklin, Pa.

HERITAGE BOOKS
2012

HERITAGE BOOKS
AN IMPRINT OF HERITAGE BOOKS, INC.

Books, CDs, and more—Worldwide

For our listing of thousands of titles see our website
at
www.HeritageBooks.com

A Facsimile Reprint
Published 2012 by
HERITAGE BOOKS, INC.
Publishing Division
100 Railroad Ave. #104
Westminster, Maryland 21157

Entered according to Act of Congress, in the year 1868, by
S. J. M. Eaton,
in the Clerk's Office of the District Court for the
Eastern District of Pennsylvania

— Publisher's Notice —
In reprints such as this, it is often not possible to remove blemishes from the original. We feel the contents of this book warrant its reissue despite these blemishes and hope you will agree and read it with pleasure.

International Standard Book Numbers
Paperbound: 978-0-7884-2646-9
Clothbound: 978-0-7884-9263-1

TO THE MEMORY

OF THE

FATHERS AND BRETHREN OF THE PRESBYTERY OF ERIE,

WHO REST FROM THEIR LABORS:

AND TO

THOSE WHO YET LABOR IN THE GREAT FIELD,

DOING THE MASTER'S WORK,

This Volume

IS RESPECTFULLY DEDICATED BY THEIR

FELLOW SERVANT,

THE AUTHOR.

PREFACE.

The Presbytery of Erie, although small in its present membership and territory, has a most interesting history. It is substantially the history of Presbyterianism in the early settlement of Northwestern Pennsylvania and Eastern Ohio. Being the third Presbytery organized west of the Mountains, its history is connected with the recital of enterprise and self-denial and energetic endeavor, such as have characterized the histories of few Presbyteries, east or west.

But the early records are brief, and in many respects unsatisfactory. There is no record of the organization of churches for the first thirty years of its history, and it is often impossible to distinguish between regularly organized churches and mere preaching points. At the first, the names of places seem to have been recorded just as they petitioned for supplies, and were permitted to change to the more important relation of organized churches without any record being made.

The authorities chiefly relied on in this work, are the Minutes of the Presbytery, of the Synod of Pittsburgh, and of the General Assembly. Aid has also been received from the "Western Missionary Magazine," "Evangelical Intelligencer," Gillett's "History of the Presbyterian Church," Wilson's "Presbyterian Historical Almanac," "Old Redstone," Elliott's "Macurdy,'² "History of Western Pennsylvania," Dr. Smith's "Sketches," and an extended correspondence with brethren, to whom thanks are here tendered. Added to this, familiarity from childhood with the relation of the stirring scenes and incidents connected with the early history of the Presbytery, by those who mingled in its affairs, has greatly assisted in filling up what had else been but dim outline.

In the biographical department, sketches have been given of all the ministers who have been at any time connected with the Presbytery, together with brief historical notices of all the living ministers whose names have been upon its roll. The numbers prefixed to the names denote the order in which they became members of Presbytery; and these numbers affixed in the history proper, refer to the biographical sketches, in Part II. The sketches of churches are designed to embrace all connected with the history of the Presbytery. They necessarily embrace churches now under the care of the Presbyteries of Beaver, Alleghany, Alleghany City, and St. Clairsville; also, the Presbyteries of Erie, Meadville, Buffalo, and Trumbull, of the other branch. These sketches are brief and meagre, even where much matter was at hand, as extended notices would have swelled the volume to an undue size.

The work was undertaken at the request of the Presbytery of Erie. The task of collecting and arranging the materials has been the labor of years; and the completed work is now offered to the Church as an humble memorial of the past, and to perpetuate that which else had soon been forgotten forever upon earth.

FRANKLIN, PA., *February*, 1868.

CONTENTS.

PART I.

CHAPTER I.

PRELIMINARY.

The Times. — Peace with the Indians. — Spirit of Enterprise. — Spirit of Revival. — Great Prosperity. — The Territory extended; uncultivated. — Eager calls for Laborers. — Boundaries. — The Ministers: Hardy; inured to Labor; Enterprising; Educated in the West; adapted to the Field; Advantages; Character; their Labors; Missionary Toilers. — Churches to be organized. — Difficulties to be settled. — Anecdote. — Hardships. Mode of Travelling. — Stockton. — Eaton. — Successes. — Anecdote of Rice. — Presbyterianism. — Revivals. — Young Men. — The People: Scotch; Irish. — Frolics. — Primitive Houses. — McGarraugh's House; Eaton's. — Church Buildings. — Middlebrook. — Seeking Supplies. — Edward Johnston. — Domestic Manufacture. — Supplies. — Manners. — Church Service. — Lining Out. — Tedious Service. — Communion Service. — Tokens. — Fencing the Tables. — Catechism 3

CHAPTER II.

FROM THE ERECTION OF THE PRESBYTERY TO THE FIRST DIVISION.

1801–1808.

Redstone and Ohio. — Act of Synod. — Boundaries. — First Meeting. — Members. — Officers. — Mr. Hughes and Mr. Wick. — Mr. Tait's First Church. — Mr. Stockton's Youth. — Satterfield, Wylie, Plumer, Dodd. — First Supplies. — Prayer. — Education. — Academy. — Statistical Report. — First Preaching. —

xii   CONTENTS.

Dickson's Journal. — Wood. — John and Abraham Boyd ordained. — Cook and Patterson. — Books sought. — Elements of Boards. — Badger. — Supplies. — Patterson's Journal. — First Licensure. — First Pastoral Relation Dissolved. — Missions to Indians. — History of Presbytery. — Plan of Union. — Division of Presbytery. — Protest. — Stated Clerk's Bill. — Academy. — Licensures. — Division of Presbytery. — Minute of Synod. — New Presbytery of Hartford 27

CHAPTER III.

FROM THE FIRST TO THE SECOND DIVISION OF PRESBYTERY.

1808–1820.

New Roll. — Settlements. — Territory. — Houses of Worship. — Barns. — Forest Worship. — Tradition. — Dismissions. — Matthews. — Riggs. — Fire in Churches. — Missionary Ground. — Matrimony. — Synod's Action. — Hilands'. — Early Experience. — Butler. — Salem. — Serious Question. — Chaplains. — Temperance. — Redick and Chase. — Offense. — Troubles. — Psalmody. — Music. — Alden and Missions. — Theological Seminaries. — Candidates. — Camp. — Complaint. — Division of Presbytery. — Results. — Revivals. — Presbytery of Alleghany . . . 66

CHAPTER IV.

FROM THE SECOND DIVISION OF PRESBYTERY TO THE GREAT DIVISION.

1820–1837.

Contracted Limits. — Small Number of Ministers. — Churches. — Discouragements. — Energy. — First Meeting. — Van Liew. — Narrative. — Sunday-schools. — Meadville. — Missionary Circular. — Springfield Controversy. — New Members. — Erie. — Mercer. — Franklin. — Increase. — Revival. — Incidents. — Temperance. — Four Days' Meetings. — Sacraments. — Evangelists. — Revival. — Baptism. — Fast Difficulties. — New Members. — Act and Testimony. — West. — Slavery. — Elders' Convention. — Franklin. — Troubles in the Distance 100

CHAPTER V.

THE GREAT DIVISION.

1837-1838.

The Storm. — Action of General Assembly disapproved of. — Vote. — Complaint and Appeal. — Action of Synod. — Last Meeting. — Members Present. — McCready's Resolutions. — Report of Commissioners. — Motion to postpone and refer to Synod. —Vote. — Withdrawal of Minority. — Rule of General Assembly. — Officers. — Records. — Synod. — Decision. — Presbytery of the other Branch 135

CHAPTER VI.

FROM THE GREAT DIVISION TO THE PRESENT.

1838-1867.

Numbers. — Division. — Feeling. — New Members. — Education. — Missionary. — Sabbath. — Slavery. — Proposition of Reunion. — 1845 to 1855. — Revival. — Death of Mr. Eaton. — Death of Glenn and McCullough. — 1859 to 1861. — State of the Country. — 1865. — Exchange of Delegates with New School. — State of the Country. — President. — 1867. — Revivals . . . 143

CHAPTER VII.

SUPPLEMENTAL.

Changes. — Short Settlements. — Causes. — Roll. — Longevity. — Oldest Ministers. — Nativity. — Places of Study. — Chaplains. — Christian Commission. — Stated Clerks. — Influence. — Example. — Lessons 169

PART II.

BIOGRAPHICAL.

BIOGRAPHIES OF DECEASED MINISTERS.

Thomas Edgar Hughes	177	John Redick		288
William Wick	183	Timothy Alden		290
Samuel Tait	185	John Munson		296
Joseph Stockton	191	Phineas Camp		299
Robert Lee	195	Bradford Marcy		302
James Satterfield	199	Giles Doolittle		303
William Wylie	203	Nathan Harned		308
John Boyd	211	Wells Bushnell		311
Abraham Boyd	213	Thomas Anderson		315
William Wood	216	Pierce Chamberlain		319
Joseph Badger	218	Edson Hart		323
Alexander Cook	230	Robert Glenn		324
Robert Patterson	233	John McNair		328
Robert Johnston	240	Nathaniel West		331
Nicholas Pittinger	249	Charles Danforth		334
John McPherrin	251	John Limber		336
Benjamin Boyd	255	Alexander Boyd		339
Cyrus Riggs	256	John Kinkead Cornyn		341
Reid Bracken	261	Lewis W. Williams		343
Johnston Eaton	265	Lemuel P. Bates		349
James Boyd	269	Charles V. Struve		351
John Matthews	271	Nathaniel M. Crane		352
Robert McGarraugh	275	William McCullough		356
Ira Condit	277	Robert Taylor		361
Amos Chase	282			

NOTICES OF LIVING MINISTERS.

John Van Liew	369	James G. Wilson		377
David McKinney	370	Robinson S. Lockwood		378
Absalom McCready	371	Reuben Lewis		378
Peter Hassinger	372	William Fuller		379
James Alexander	373	David Waggoner		380
George A. Lyon	374	Daniel Washburn		380
George W. Hampson	374	John V. Reynolds		381
William A. Adair	375	Edmund McKinney		381
Simeon Peck	376	Cyrus Dickson		381

CONTENTS.

Edward S. Blake	382	John R. Findley ... 393
Hiram Eddy	382	John R. Hamilton ... 394
Joseph T. Smith	383	John D. Howey ... 394
James Coulter	383	Ira M. Condit ... 395
Henry Webber	384	Anthony C. Junkin ... 395
James W. Dickey	384	Huey Newell ... 396
Alexander Cunningham	385	George Scott ... 396
John M. Smith	385	James H. Spelman ... 396
Miles T. Merwin	386	John G. Condit ... 397
Lemuel G. Olmstead	386	John H. Sargent ... 397
James H. Callen	387	Newell S. Lowrie ... 398
Samuel J. M. Eaton	387	James H. Gray ... 398
Michael A. Parkinson	388	William T. Hamilton ... 398
John Sailor	388	William P. Moore ... 399
Robert S. Morton	389	George F. Cain ... 399
William Wilson	389	William M. Robinson ... 399
John W. McCune	390	Luther M. Belden ... 400
David Grier	390	John Rice ... 400
George W. Zahniser	390	Henry B. Lambe ... 401
Robert F. Sample	391	James J. Marks ... 401
James I. Smith	391	Robert S. Van Cleve ... 401
James M. Shields	392	John J. Gridley ... 402
William J. Alexander	392	James J. Smyth ... 402
Charles A. Behrends	393	David Patton ... 403
William M. Blackburn	393	

PART III.

HISTORICAL NOTICES OF CHURCHES.

Sketches of Churches, either now or at any former time under the care of Presbytery 407

PART I.

HISTORY.

HISTORY

OF THE

PRESBYTERY OF ERIE.

CHAPTER I.

PRELIMINARY.

THE Presbytery of Erie was erected under most auspicious circumstances. The dark clouds that had lowered so heavily over the church and over the country for a quarter of a century were rapidly rolling away, and everything betokened prosperity and peace. General Wayne's treaty with the Indians had opened the way for the occupation of territory that had hitherto been locked up. A tide of emigration had set in from Eastern Pennsylvania, Maryland, and Virginia, that bade fair to occupy the country that had hitherto been but the hunting ground of the Indian; or at least neutral ground in the great conflict between civilization and barbarism. There was a spirit of enterprise, now greatly stimulated by the love of adventure, that was spreading over the older settlements, and that promised to bring into the new territory just opening up, the better class of the population of the East. Hitherto the region north and west of the Ohio, and extending to the great Northern Lakes, had been comparatively an unknown land. It had been partially explored for half a century, but up to this time had been all unsettled and unsafe. About the year 1750–52, the French had set up their claim to its possession, and were in some degree in alliance with the Indians, rendering the work of exploring even unsafe and unprofitable. After the departure of the French, there was a bitterness and a jealousy in the minds of the Indians, who claimed the territory, that effectually closed up the country against actual settlement. At the beginning of the present century, all these difficulties were surmounted and the gates opened that invited the westward march of civilization, bearing in its train the blessings of evangelization.

The religious influence at this time was most blessed and happy. The terrible scourge of skepticism and infidelity that seemed as though it would sweep over the entire country, after the war of the Revolution, was rapidly abating. The stamp of French influence that at one time seemed fixing itself upon the religious institutions of the country was vanishing, and a pure Christianity fast assuming its place. Added to this, the spirit of revival was making itself felt with wondrous power and efficacy. The Spirit of God had been poured out most copiously upon the older Presbyteries of the West, and the infant churches recently planted in the new territory had been largely blessed. These revivals had commenced in 1778, in Vance's Fort,[1] into which the settlement had been driven by the incursions of savages. "From 1781 to 1787, a most extensive work of grace was experienced in the churches of Cross Creek, Upper Buffalo, Chartiers, Pigeon Creek, Bethel, Lebanon, Ten Mile, Cross Roads, and Millcreek, during which *more than a thousand* persons were brought into the kingdom of Christ."

"From 1795 to 1799, another series of gracious visit-

[1] Rev. Joseph Stevenson.

ations were enjoyed by the churches generally throughout Western Pennsylvania, extending to the new settlements north of Pittsburgh."

These gracious visitations continued into the beginning of the new century, filling the minds of many with the conviction that the very dawn of the Millenium had come. Even in the midst of the labors and watching peculiar to the founding of new settlements, and sometimes without the labors of the stated ministry, this spirit of revival was present, stimulating the hearts of the settlers with hope and courage, and inviting others who were looking for some new place of settlement to cast in their lot with them. Says a venerable father,[1] lately fallen asleep: "My mother was pious, and hearing of the revival of religion in Western Pennsylvania, felt a great anxiety that her family might enjoy the benefits of such a season. Accordingly we removed to Beaver County in 1806." Others were influenced, no doubt, in the same way, and thus the spiritual attractions of the new territory added to its temporal prosperity.

In the mean time all fear of hostility on the part of the Indians being removed, settlers pushed their way northward to Lake Erie, and westward into Ohio, forming settlements, and laying the foundation of the dense population that now occupies what was the original territory of the Presbytery of Erie.

The territory that was occupied by the old Presbytery of Erie was widely extended. It embraced all the churches and settlements north and northwest of the Ohio and Alleghany rivers. It extended from Beaver, Pa., on the Ohio River on the south, to Lake Erie on the north, and from the Alleghany River on the east to Canfield, Ohio, on the west, embracing the whole of

[1] Rev. John Munson.

what is now the Synod of Alleghany with portions of the Synods of Wheeling, Buffalo, and Pittsburgh. The field was almost wholly uncultivated by ministerial labor. The population was mainly Presbyterian. They had brought with them a few books from the East. The Bible, the Westminster Confession, the Hymn Book, and some works on practical religion — these were their spiritual pabulum during the intervals of their labor and toil. They often met together on the Sabbath and held what they called "Society Meetings." The exercises consisted of singing, prayer, and reading a sermon from Burder or some other standard work. But the parents felt that, much as they delighted in those social meetings, they needed the minister of Christ. Their children had many of them been baptized in their infancy but were now growing up, and they felt the deepest interest in their spiritual welfare. Says the same father already quoted:[1] "They saw the importance of having the standard of the gospel planted at the commencement of their new settlement. In all their meetings for prayer they earnestly sought the Lord that he would send them a godly man, to break to them the bread of life, and be the instrument of laying the foundation of a rising church in the wilderness. Their prayers were heard, and thus God in a short time selected out of these and other families materials for the organization of a church."

This remark has reference to the settlement in Beaver County, Pa., which afterwards constituted the congregation of Mount Pleasant; but was also characteristic of other portions of the territory constituting the Presbytery of Erie. There was therefore an eager call for laborers that went up with an earnestness almost

[1] Munson to Plumer, *Pres. Mag.* vii. 463.

Macedonian, and was responded to by many of the ministers in the older settlements with a zeal and self-denial well-nigh apostolical. The people had no great inducements to offer; certainly very few of a temporal kind. There was labor and self-denial, with little in the way of salary or worldly fame. But there were opportunities for doing good, seldom exceeded. There was the way opening for planting the church in the wilderness, and of gathering immortal souls into its safe and peaceful inclosure.

And so the early fathers of the Presbytery of Erie girded themselves for the work and the warfare, and went forth with manly hearts to labor as best they might in the Lord's cause.

These fathers were a hardy set of men, modeled after a type peculiar to their day, and eminently adapted to the performance of the great work to which they were called. They had been educated mainly in the West. Of the first twenty-eight on the roll, embracing a period of twenty years of its history, twenty-three were educated at Cannonsburg, and at the Academies that sprung up and were fostered under the influence of the Presbytery. And of the same twenty-eight, twenty-two pursued their theological studies in the west, and no less than eighteen at Dr. McMillan's log-cabin. These men had been inured to labor. Almost every one of them had been accustomed to the work of subduing the forest, and of cultivating the soil from childhood. Even during his studies at Cannonsburg, Robert Lee was engaged in clearing land from forest trees, and in order not to trench upon the hours of study and recitation had labored at rolling logs and kindling fires at night. As a general thing then, they came to the duties of the ministry with physical constitutions matured and indurated by labor and exercise. They were enabled at once to endure the hardships and privations that were peculiar to frontier life. Not only did they make long and fatiguing journeys in the work of organizing and supplying churches in remote places, but were obliged also to labor with their hands in securing a support. This may also account for the longevity that characterized these early fathers. They were enterprising men, too. They saw the field spreading before them, with its labors and its promises; they had girded themselves for the work, and neither labor nor peril appalled them. Whether they set out for the shore of Lake Erie, or plunged into the wilderness seeking the red man of the forest in his wild haunts, it mattered not. It was the Lord's work. It was for this they had entered the service; and they took the labors and the privations as matters of course.

If they lacked the polish and accomplished education that pertain to more modern times, they possessed that furniture that better fitted them for the then rude contact with Nature, and with the hardy race of pioneers that were felling the mighty forests and opening up the pathway for the progress of Empire in its mighty Western march.

Concerning these early ministers, there yet linger amongst us aged fathers and mothers, who tell us wondrous things of their power and eloquence, and many imagine that there are no such preachers and no such preaching at the present day, even amid the most effective preachers of modern times. But we are to remember the times, and the circumstances in which they lived. The men and women who constituted their hearers, were not educated as hearers are educated now. The Bible and Psalm Book, lying on the window-sill, as a general thing, constituted their library. And although these are prime sources of theology, they were read as books of devotion — as daily, spiritual bread — rather than as furnishing the mind with any regular system of theology.

They were thinking men and women, yet was their range of thought circumscribed within narrow bounds. Hence the preachers labored in a virgin soil. Grand new truths seemed to be constantly making their impression upon the minds of the audience. The preacher seemed to be dispensing blessings fresh from the treasury of the Lord. His warnings and reproofs and expostulations fell like fiery barbed arrows upon consciences not yet seared by constant familiarity with the awful truths of God's word. And the sweet and precious consolations of the gospel — its promises, its hopes, and its encouragements — were healing balm and living waters to the faint and weary soul not familiar with these sacred things from childhood. Added to this, there was that profound reverence, amounting almost to awe, for the gospel minister, that lifted him up above the sphere of the common, and elevated him almost to the height of the angels. All these things conspired to give the old fathers an influence that was most important, and that they used for the carrying forward of the great work committed to their care. But it is possible that these circumstances gave their people an exaggerated estimate of their power and ability. They were, many of them, no doubt men of ability, and circumstances were calculated to call out all their strength and energy; yet there were also adverse circumstances connected with their life and ministry. They entered upon their preparatory studies, as a general thing, late in life, when their habits of thought and elasticity of mind had become somewhat fixed. They entered upon the labors of the ministry after the active powers of the intellect had begun to settle down so as not to be readily moved: circumstances certainly not favorable to the full development of the mind and the efficient exercise of the powers of thought. Their education, too was oftentimes defective. A few years in the academy, and a brief period with some hard-working pastor in the study of theology, was all they could hope to obtain in the way of education. They had access to very few text books, and those perhaps none of the best. The only system of theology that the great majority of them had was Dr. McMillan's "Lectures." These they copied carefully and laboriously, and bore with them to their labors for future reference and authority. Many copies of these "Lectures" are still in existence in many parts of the church, all of which were copied in the seclusion and quiet of the old log-cabin that constituted the first Theological Seminary of the West.

Again, these primitive ministers, whatever their thirst for knowledge might have been, had not access to books after entering upon their labors. Books were rare treasures then. They had not found their way into the wilderness of the West. And even if they had, the minister had neither money to purchase nor time to read. Other and more pressing duties would have crowded them out. Nor had they leisure for that close, patient study, that is favorable to the highest development of mind. Their time was spent either in the saddle or in the field. Samuel Tait, the pioneer of Mercer County, made his preparation for the pulpit whilst following the plough. His Bible, which he carried with him to the field, was his library; and as he turned over the furrows, and scattered the seed, he thought of God's husbandry, and wrought out his sermons as best he might. And in addition to this, there was the almost constant travelling to and fro connected with missionary work, that could afford but little time for systematic study.

But these men did a wondrous work. They stood in their lot, and their memory should be revered and loved to the remotest generations. They laid the foundations of Zion broad and deep, and the results remain unto this present time. The remarks just made are not designed to take a single leaf from the chaplet of their fair fame, but simply to arrive at the truth in estimating their character and influence. The great wonder is, that with their intellectual furniture and widely extended labors, they were able to make so broad and deep an impression upon the times as they did.

The labors of these men were most arduous. When the Presbytery was organized, there were but seven ministers to enter upon the work. The field embraced what now constitutes ten or twelve counties in Pennsylvania, Ohio, and New York. There were a few churches organized, perhaps eight or ten. But they did not confine themselves to these. The whole field must be brought under cultivation. New churches must be organized. Those already organized must be visited, supplied, and strengthened. Difficulties must be removed, discipline administered, and the ordinances dispensed. Oftentimes, long missionary tours were undertaken, sometimes singly, sometimes two and two, for the purpose of exploring the country, and preaching the gospel to the destitute. Sometimes this preaching continued day after day, for weeks. The services would be held in private houses at first, and after the progress of settlement had advanced, in school-houses; — just where a few neighbors could be gathered together. Occasionally the minister must be content to lay him down at night under the shadow of a spreading tree, with the stars of heaven for his canopy, and the song of the nightingale for his lullaby, with no evening repast but the thought of God's goodness and mercy and faithfulness to those who lean on his hand.

At the time of the organization of the Presbytery of Erie, there was not a bridge from the Ohio River to Lake Erie. In passing to and fro, the streams must be forded, or if this was impracticable the horse must swim and bear his rider on his back. Often has the missionary been obliged to swim the creek or river on the Sabbath morning, preach in his dripping garments, and hasten on to fulfill some other appointment. Instances are on record where the missionary, after travelling perhaps two day's journey to fulfill an appointment, found on Sabbath morning a swollen stream between him and his place of preaching, that could not possibly be crossed, and so returned without delivering the message. Nor was it an unfrequent thing for the missionary to lose his way in the wilderness. One of the earlier ministers, in his peregrinations through what is now the "Oil region," losing his way, finally came upon an Indian camp, and sought shelter for the night. Some bear meat and coarse hominy was his repast, and dried skins his bed. In the morning he took his way down Oil Creek to the Alleghany and thence to Franklin. Sometimes these pioneers on their missionary journeys took with them some of what were then called the luxuries of life, not expecting to find these in the cabins of the settlers. On one occasion, Mr. Wood (10) placed a small package of tea in his saddlebags, thinking that a cup of the beverage that "cheers but not inebriates" would be grateful after a weary day's ride. Finding refuge at night-fall in the cabin of a settler, he inquired of the hostess if she had any tea. She replied, "No, I never had any in my house." He then produced his little package and asked her to prepare him some. He busied himself about his own thoughts, until supper was announced. Seating himself at the little table by the wall, he looked for the tea-pot, and not seeing anything that looked like it he inquired of the woman for his tea. She pointed to a broad earthen dish, where the entire paper of tea stood, dished up in the form of greens.

The ministers shared with the people all the hardships incident to the settlement of a new country. They built their cabins of the rough unhewn logs that were cut from the forest, often chinked and daubed them with their own hands, and as far as time would allow, cleared and worked their own fields. Indeed the probabilities are, that without this manual labor they could not have been sustained by the people. Lands were cheap, and almost every minister for the first twenty years in the history of the Presbytery, procured a farm and proceeded to prepare it for cultivation. In process of time these farms became valuable, and were of use to the minister's family, and as a resource against old age. Occasionally the people would assemble and assist the minister in his logging, ploughing, and harvesting, and thus lighten his labor and afford him more time to devote to labor of a spiritual kind, as well as show their appreciation of him and sympathy in his pursuits.

The mode of travelling was on horseback. All the journeys of the early ministers were performed in this way, not only in their missionary expeditions, but in journeys more remote, such as to meetings of Synod, General Assembly, and occasional visits to the older settlements. When Joseph Stockton with his young wife moved to Meadville to settle, in 1801, the journey was made on horseback. And when his household effects were packed up it was with reference to being borne on the backs of horses. And when Johnston Eaton with his wife removed six years later, from near Uniontown, Pa., to the shores of Lake Erie, everything that was necessary to the comfort or convenience of the family must be packed in long boxes or trunks and slung upon opposite sides of horses, and be in this way transported through the woods and across streams, a distance of nearly two hundred miles.

Yet the success of these hardy pioneers was very great. No doubt they often felt sorely cast down, as they sat beneath the shadows of the evening, crying out "Who hath believed our report, and to whom is the arm of the Lord revealed," but withal they had much to encourage them. There was a willing heart on the part of the people to hear. Though poor, they were willing to share their labor in building a cabin for the minister and a house for public worship, and when necessary, to give the hard earned silver dollar to support the institutions of religion. Says an old father [1] who yet lingers amid the scenes of the church militant: "The first dollar I ever gave to the Lord in the support of his worship, was the only one I possessed at the time; and it was given as cheerfully as I have ever given one since." This was in 1800. Samuel Tait (3), then a young licentiate, had gone out to what is now Mercer County, to preach. He found a settlement [2] five

---

[1] Thomas Rice.   [2] Cool Spring.

miles from the present site of Mercer, and made an appointment to preach on the Sabbath. This young man, Thomas Rice, had worked the week before at making rails on the very spot where Mercer now stands, cutting the first tree that was felled, and had received a silver dollar as the proceeds of his labor. He carried it with him to the place of preaching to insure its safety. Mr. Tait preached from the words, "And they all with one consent began to make excuse." The sermon was blessed to the conversion of several persons, amongst them Thomas Rice. He thought he then and there was enabled to give his heart to God. After sermon the hat was passed around to take up a collection for the minister, when Thomas Rice, showing his faith by his works, put in his silver dollar.

It is astonishing to notice the amount of labor that was performed by these men during the first years of their labor in the new territory. Churches seemed to spring up everywhere. Many of them became self-sustaining in a very short time, and soon began to send out colonies, forming new churches that in turn became self-sustaining. The foundations of Zion were firmly laid, and the peculiar and distinctive type of their teaching became deeply impressed upon society. In many portions of the territory this distinctive character of doctrine and practice remains clearly traceable to the present time.

In many cases the harvest seemed to succeed the sowing with wondrous rapidity. Gracious ingatherings were common in almost all the churches, and in some cases where the regular ministrations of the gospel were not enjoyed. Sometimes the spirit was poured out so copiously that a large proportion of the hearers were brought into the church. Robert Johnston (14) relates that during a revival in Scrubgrass congregation, whilst he was pastor there, fully one half of the adult members of the congregation were hopefully converted. In other cases the seed was sown, that afterwards germinated and sprung up, producing "some thirty fold, some sixty, and some an hundred."

Another feature in the policy of these early fathers was, that they constantly sought out promising young men, and encouraged them to make preparation for the ministry. Sometimes they instructed them at their own houses, sometimes they were sent to Cannonsburg or Greersburgh; and in this way a constant succession of ministers were raised up, adapted to the wants of the country and prepared for labor in the great field.

The people that settled this new territory were mainly from the eastern counties of Pennsylvania, Maryland, and Virginia. As a general thing they were of the Scotch-Irish descent, and had been taught the great principles of the gospel at home, in the East. They naturally inclined to Presbyterianism and were attracted to Presbyterian forms of worship. They were at first poor in this world's goods, living plainly and quietly, and generally supplying their wants from their own resources. Their manners and customs were most primitive. Articles of luxury were not often thought of, as utility was the great thought. The land must be cleared. The mighty giants of the forest must be felled, and their trunks burned up, to allow space for the plough. Houses must be built to accommodate the family. Food and clothing must be furnished for all. To bring about these ends, labor and toil must be endured. The neighborhood combined its efforts to bring about many of these results. The neighbors would assemble for chopping, logging, and husking frolics, as they were termed. When a house was to be erected, they would come together with their axes and other implements, cut down trees of a suitable size, reduce them to a proper length, and bring them to the ground selected as the site for the house, notch the ends for the corners, and place them in position. Others would prepare clapboards, by splitting them from the trunk of a solid oak, for the roof. These were kept in position by logs laid upon them, keeping them down by their weight. The floors were made of puncheons split from smooth-grained chestnut or oak. The places for doors and windows were then cut out, and doors made of puncheons, with wooden hinges and latches, completed the outside of the building. The furniture on the inside was at first equally primitive. Bedsteads were made of rough poles. Benches and tables rudely constructed with the axe and auger, answered the purpose admirably. In such houses as these, the early ministers lived and raised their families. When father McGarraugh (23) came to what is now Clarion County, in 1804, he lived for one year in a cabin about fifteen feet square, with a door made of chestnut bark, that had been first dried in the sun. And an old elder,[1] yet living, relates that calling once in about 1807 at the cabin of Johnston Eaton (20) on the Lake shore, he found the minister and his wife trying to keep themselves protected from the beating rain. And when the offices of hospitality required that a fire should be kindled, the minister pulled the bark from the inner walls of the house, which was of dry logs, for that purpose.

In such houses there was no fire-place with jambs, but simply a hearth and back wall. The chimney com-

[1] Wm. Dickson.

menced at about the height of the ceiling, and was constructed of sticks split out like laths, and plastered over with moistened clay. The house usually consisted of a single room. Sometimes two cabins were built about ten or twelve feet apart, when a common roof extended over both, leaving a kind of open area between. Church buildings were built in the same manner as the dwellings. Oftentimes they worshipped in the open air, with what was called a tent for the accommodation of the minister. Generally such a building was completed in a single day, with all its appointments. Frequently there was not a single nail or scrap of metal in the whole building. Weights kept the clapboards in place, and pins made of wood furnished the arrangements for the doors and windows.

In Upper Greenfield, afterwards called Middlebrook, in Erie County, such a church was erected. The people had formed a little settlement; had built cabins for themselves, and were beginning to feel comfortable in a worldly point of view; but they remembered the churches in Eastern Pennsylvania from which they had come, and resolved to build a house for the Lord. The neighborhood assembled one morning in the opening summer, with axes and oxen. Trees were cut down for logs and clapboards, the logs drawn to the proper place, notched and laid in position, the roof and floor laid, and the house completed by sundown.

These churches were usually furnished with seats made of round logs. Sometimes they lay upon the ground, at other times they were raised up to the proper height by rude legs. Upon these logs the people sat and listened to the word, sometimes relieving their weariness by rising and standing upon their feet for a time, or walking about. They were not punctilious about their dress, so that it was clean. Very frequently, in summer, the men went to church without coats. When Mr. Porter returned to Westmoreland County, after visiting Mr. McPherrin's congregation near Butler, Pa., "He stated that Mr. McPherrin had settled amongst a very poor people; that very few of the men wore coats; and that these coats were of the coarsest kind." [1]

The people manufactured all the material for their own clothing. Flax was extensively grown. This was broken and scutched by the family, and afterwards spun and woven, and made up into shirts and pantaloons. The female members of the household also wore clothing made from it; and from the same staple, table and bed linen was prepared. Woolen cloth was manufactured likewise by the household. Sometimes a mixture was formed of wool and flax combined, making an article known as "linsey woolsey." When the flannel was woven it was colored in a strong decoction of butternut bark, and for the fulling process, soap and water were placed on the cloth, and the feet of the young men brought into requisition, tramping and kicking it until fulled and thickened. All kinds of manufacturing were carried on at home, so that even in the depth of the forest a good degree of independence was obtained.

Leather was tanned in large troughs cut from the trunks of trees, and manufactured into shoes by the families themselves. Hats were made of straw and leatherwood bark, and caps from the skins of furred animals. Much of the cabinet and chair making was performed at home. The frame of the chair was made of wood, unpainted and unturned, and the seat formed

[1] Dr. Young's Sermon.

of the bark of the slippery elm, or of splits separated from the wood of the black ash, by pounding.

Domestic supplies too were simple, and luxuries few. The field supplied grain and vegetables. Coffee was made from rye, first boiled, and then roasted like the genuine article. Tea was sometimes made from the boughs of the hemlock, and sometimes from the roots of the sassafras, while sugar was manufactured from the maple trees that grew in the forest. For a time, the great want was mills to grind the grain. It was carried great distances to the older settlements, and much of the corn was pounded in mortars for hominy. Salt and iron were carried on the backs of horses from the eastern side of the mountains.

Travelling in those days was on horseback. The mode of going to church was to bring all the horses that were at the command of the family into requisition, and then supplement the want of horse-power by walking. A family of six might frequently be seen coming to church mounted upon two horses. The father would be mounted upon one horse, with the oldest child behind him, and the third one before him; whilst the mother would be upon the other horse, with the infant in her arms, and the second in age behind her. Sometimes the mother and two children would be mounted on a solitary horse, whilst the father walked by her side with his coat hung over his arm. Young ladies often walked a distance of several miles to church, and in summer would carry their shoes in their hands until they approached the place of worship, when they would stop by the wayside and place them upon their feet, and be prepared to present a respectable appearance at the sanctuary. In the early days the services of the Sabbath were usually all in the day-time. They consisted of two sermons, with a recess of about half an hour between. During this half hour the congregation eat the biscuits they had brought in their pockets, walked to the spring for a drink of water, or wandered into the burial ground, that was then usually connected with the church, to think of the loved ones whose dust was slumbering there. At the expiration of the half hour, the congregation would assemble as though by a similar impulse, seat themselves reverently, and engage in the worship of God.

In those days the singing of the praise of God was always on the congregational plan. After the hymn had been announced, one, two, or three persons, called clerks, took their position in front of the pulpit, and "lined out," as it was termed, the hymn. The name of the tune proposed to be sung was then announced, when the clerk led the way, and the whole congregation joined in the singing. This lining out consisted in reciting one and sometimes two lines of the hymn at a time, before singing them. The origin of the custom arose, perhaps, in part from the scarcity of books, and in part from the inability of many of the people to read; but it was continued long after both of these difficulties had been removed. In fact, it became actually a matter of conscience with many of the old fathers, who insisted that the lining out was as much a part of worship as the singing and praying. The change from lining out to the regular singing of the hymn was attended with many difficulties and disturbances as years rolled by. This lining out, too, had many grotesque features connected with it, that were not perhaps observed by the fathers. It was not simply reading the lines in a sober, decorous tone of voice; but a whining, nasal, intoning of the words, marvelously like the very poorest class of singing that could be executed. Yet the people became accustomed to this kind of performance, and not only tolerated it, but considered it a desideratum, so that the ability to "line out" properly became quite an accomplishment.

In those days the Sabbath services were long and tedious. The whole day was usually devoted to the service. Soon after ten o'clock in the morning the people began to assemble, and it was nearly night when they returned home. Long psalms or hymns were sung; long prayers were offered up; and very long sermons were preached. If the day was warm the minister laid off his coat and cravat, and proceeded deliberately from firstly to twelfthly. The ancient mode of sermonizing was perhaps formal, yet it was so arranged that the hearers could readily retain it in their memories. The text was announced; then followed a general, easy introduction to the whole subject. The matter was usually divided into three general heads, and these subdivided into three or four branches, and the whole wound up with the application. The sermon often occupied an hour and a half, making some three hours of preaching, besides the other parts of the service. Yet the people did not complain of weariness. If sleepy or weary of sitting, they could stand up, or walk about, until rested.

Sacramental occasions were great days in the history of the fathers. They usually embraced the services of four days. The first day was usually Thursday, and set apart as a "Fast Day." It was observed precisely as the Sabbath. No work was done, and everything was quiet throughout whole neighborhoods, as the Sabbath itself. In some cases it was observed as a literal fast day by abstaining from food, but when this was not done, there was abstinence from labor. The second day of the service was Saturday, and after the preaching the session of the church met for the purpose of receiving applications for membership in the church. "Tokens" were also distributed to the members of the church, admitting them to the communion the following day. These "tokens" were simple bits of lead, with the initial letters of the name of the congregation upon them; as "F. C.," denoting "Fairview Congregation." These bits of lead were distributed by the pastor and elders on Saturday and Sabbath mornings to all who wished to unite in communion, or who were in good standing in the church. After the communicants had seated themselves at the table, the elders collected these tokens, when the services proceeded. This practice of distributing tokens was evidently brought from Scotland and Ireland. Its object, no doubt, was to exclude unworthy communicants, especially at times when a large number present were strangers. But it is extremely doubtful whether it was ever of any practical advantage. After their use began to be discontinued, a good old elder who had never even dreamed that a communion could be held without them, was dreadfully horrified by a facetious minister advising him to put his tokens in his gun and shoot them at the crows.

The communion Sabbath, as it was observed by our fathers, has been thus aptly described by the author of "Old Redstone"[1]: —

"The *action sermons*, as they were called, on communion Sabbaths, were generally preached by the pastors, or resident ministers; this was considered peculiarly proper. And we must remember that perhaps fully one half of the audience were not his ordinary hearers. Then followed what was called *fencing the*

[1] Page 158.

tables. This was often tedious, occupying an hour or more. Not unfrequently there was a regular review of all the sins forbidden in each of the Ten Commandments. And it was remarked by the profane, that the preacher never stopped until he had solemnly debarred from the ordinances every one of his people, and himself besides. Our old ministers, however, seldom indulged in such lengthened details as the *Seceders* were said to be in the practice of doing, forbidding and debarring various classes of offenders, that were not to be found among them, such as stage-players and visitants of theatres; and yet it must be confessed that our venerable fathers took this occasion to pour out a great deal ' de omnibus rebus, et quibusdem aliis.' "

Concerning this same matter of fencing tables, there was no doubt call for admonition and warning, yet withal it savored of harshness and severity. It must have been oftentimes gall and wormwood to the trembling, fearful Christian, needing, instead of such words, encouragement and assurance. One who remembers those old scenes, makes the remark that on such occasions there were usually two ministers, one of whom debarred every person from coming by the strictness of his charge; when the other would censure, and upbraid, and reproach every one for not coming, when the invitation was so free. It must be confessed that in those days the spirit of John the Baptist seemed to characterize the preaching, more than that of John the beloved disciple.

The ordinance was in those days always connected with the literal use of tables. Sometimes there was accommodation for all to partake at the same time; if not, there were two or more tables just as circumstances might require. In this way the services became often very tedious and even exhausting. There were usually two or more ministers in attendance, who divided the labors between or amongst them. Still the exercises on such occasions were exhausting.

Oftentimes these services were held in the woods. Indeed this was usually the case in the summer season, for no house of worship, then in use, would have contained the people. This woods' service was in connection with what was called a tent, for the accommodation of the ministers. The tent was simply a stand, such as is used at political and Fourth of July meetings at the present time. The seats were simple logs raised to the proper height, with intervening aisles for the accommodation of the people.

The fourth day of the service was Monday following the Sabbath, when the services were concluded. To these old-fashioned communion services, the people came from far and near. It was nothing unusual to come a distance of ten or twelve miles. It was also usual for strangers to spend the evenings of Saturday and Sabbath in the congregation, and many a house in near proximity to the place of worship was literally packed with guests ; and these guests expected to enact the part of host to their entertainers on some similar occasion. In this way sociability was cultivated, as well as practical godliness.

Great attention was paid to the Shorter Catechism. All parents were expected to have it taught to their children, and to retain it likewise in their own memories. No one was supposed to be too old to be called on to repeat his " Questions." Indeed it was customary to have the catechism taught in the common schools. Nor was it common to find any objections raised to the practice in the schools. It was the custom to have the questions asked in families every Sabbath evening, in the assembled household. In addition to this, the minister examined the entire congregation once in each year. Usually during one year, whilst making pastoral visitations, the catechism was reviewed in each family, separately; during the next year public examinations were held in certain districts of the congregation, when all had an opportunity of showing their promptness and diligence in this matter.

It was under these circumstances, and in these times, that the Presbytery of Erie, the mother Presbytery of the Synod of Alleghany, set up its gates and entered upon its great work. From feeble beginnings, it gradually extended its influence until it became the mother of Presbyteries, and sent its missionaries to the aborigines of our own country, to the far distant nations of heathenism, as well as to every State and Territory of the Great West.

CHAPTER II.

FROM THE ERECTION OF THE PRESBYTERY, TO THE FIRST DIVISION.

1801–1808.

THE Presbytery of Erie was erected by the Synod of Virginia, in 1801. It was the third Presbytery that was organized, west of the Alleghany Mountains. Redstone had been organized in 1781, and Ohio in 1798. The territory of these latter Presbyterians was large, and the way opening for the rapid spread of population; and material seemed abundant for a new Presbytery. Presbyterianism was aggressive as regarded the world and Satan, and its founders here were fully up to the times and to its spirit. So they desired a new Presbytery, that the new and promising field might be more readily occupied. There was probably another reason for its formation. The territory was within the bounds of the Synod of Virginia. The journey to meetings of Synod was laborious and burdensome. The Western members must cross the mountains and be exposed not only to fatigue but actual danger in accomplishing it. Besides, the great work of keeping the institutions of religion abreast with the extending settlement of the country could be best attended to by erecting a Synod upon the new territory. This could only be done by first erecting a third Presbytery. Accordingly, on petition of the members of the Presbyteries of Redstone and Ohio, the new Presbytery was erected. The following is the minute of Synod in the matter : —

"At a meeting of Synod held at Winchester (Va.), October 2d, 1801, at the unanimous request of the members present from the Presbyteries of Redstone and Ohio, the Synod did and hereby do erect the Rev. Messrs. Thomas [Edgar[1]] Hughes (1), William Wick (2), Samuel Tait (3), Joseph Stockton (4), and Robert Lee (5), together with all the congregations north and northwest of the Ohio and Alleghany rivers, unto the place where the Ohio River crosses the western boundary of Pennsylvania, into a separate Presbytery, to be called the Presbytery of ERIE, and appointed their first meeting to be held at Mount Pleasant, on the second Tuesday of April next. William Wick was appointed to open the Presbytery with a sermon, and to preside until a new Moderator be chosen."

In obedience to this order of Synod, the Presbytery of Erie met at Mount Pleasant in Beaver County, Pennsylvania, at the time appointed, April 13, 1802, and was opened with a sermon by Mr. Wick, on the words, "And the government shall be upon his shoulder" (Isaiah ix. 6).

After constituting with prayer, the following persons were found present to be enrolled, namely : Thomas Edgar Hughes, William Wick, Samuel Tait, Joseph Stockton, and Robert Lee, ministers, with three elders, William Plumer, John Menteith, and William Waddell. James Satterfield (6) and William Wylie (7) having settled within the bounds of Presbytery since the ac-

[1] The middle name does not occur in the minute.

tion of Synod, and having been dismissed from the Presbytery of Ohio for the purpose, were considered as members, and their names enrolled. Elder Ithiel Dodd was enrolled on the second day of the session.

Mr. Hughes was chosen Moderator, and Mr. Tait Clerk for the ensuing year. Mr. Wick was the first stated clerk of Presbytery. The territory embraced by the new Presbytery was taken from that of Redstone and Ohio, although all the original members were ordained by the Presbytery of Ohio. This territory was large, embracing what are now the counties of Beaver, Butler, Mercer, Crawford, Erie, Lawrence, and Venango, with portions of Warren and Clarion, in Pennsylvania, the whole of the Western Reserve in Ohio, with Chautauque County, New York.

The seven ministers who were now upon the roll of Presbytery were all settled at this time. Mr. Hughes was pastor of Mount Pleasant and New Salem. He had been ordained and installed on the 28th of August, 1799, by the Presbytery of Ohio. Mr. Wick was pastor at Hopewell, now in Lawrence County, Pa., and Youngstown, now in Mahoning County, Ohio. He had been ordained and installed on the 3d day of September, 1800, by the same Presbytery. Mr. Tait was pastor of Cool Spring and Upper Salem, in Mercer County, Pa., ordained and installed November 19, 1800. Mr. Stockton was pastor at Meadville and Sugar Creek (now Cochranton), Crawford County, Pa., ordained and installed June 24, 1801. Mr. Lee was pastor at Rocky Spring and Amity, Mercer County, Pa. He had been ordained and installed June 26, 1801. Mr. Satterfield was pastor at Moorfield, and Neshannock, Mercer County, Pa., ordained and installed March 3, 1802. Mr. Wylie was pastor at Fairfield and Upper and Lower

Sandy, in Mercer and Venango counties, ordained and installed March 5th, 1802.

Mr. Hughes, who heads the long roll of this Presbytery, was the first minister settled in the territory north and northwest of the Ohio and Alleghany rivers. The nucleus of his charge was constituted of several families that had emigrated from Washington and Westmoreland counties, and settled on the Beaver River, some ten or twelve miles above the town of Beaver.[1] The war-whoop of the Indian was still heard and his war-path still traced, at the time of their coming. There were a number of pious families in this settlement, and feeling the importance of the regular ministry, they applied to Dr. McMillan and other of the pioneer ministers to send one of their young men to settle among them as their pastor. Mr. Hughes, a graduate of Princeton College, who had just completed his theological studies at Dr. McMillan's log seminary, was sent to visit them. "He was," says Mr. Munson (28), "a young man of good address, of ardent feelings, and of genuine piety. I subsequently became a member of his church, and well remember the searching nature of his preaching. He labored much to remove all false confidence, and to shake to the foundation all deceptive hopes."

Mr. Hughes continued the pastor of the church of Mount Pleasant more than thirty years. Many interesting incidents are related in connection with his life and labors at this place. The following was communicated by a member of the church, who was present at the time of the occurrence. The congregation had assembled in a grove on a communion occasion. The communicants were about going to the tables, when the heavens became overcast. The clouds rolled their

[1] Munson's letter to Dr. Plumer, *Pres. Mag.* vii. 463.

sombre folds athwart the sky, and there was every appearance of a great rain. Mr. Hughes arose and prayed most earnestly, that, if consistent with the Divine will, the rain might be stayed, and his people permitted to commune in peace. After this, it was noticed by the whole assemblage, that the clouds quickly dispersed, and there was no rain.

Mr. Wick was the pioneer missionary in the Western Reserve, or New Connecticut, as it was then called. For some time he labored alone, serving his people at Youngstown and Hopewell, and making occasional tours amongst the Indians. He retained his first charge until his death in 1815.

Mr. Tait had much of the missionary spirit. He was endued with great physical strength and endurance, and used them well in the Master's cause. Having been sent out by the Presbytery of Ohio in the spring of 1800, to preach where he could find hearers, he came to a settlement called Cool Spring, in Mercer County, Pa., and about five miles from where the town of Mercer now stands. Having preached on the Sabbath, he told the people that if they would procure a lot and build a church, he would come and preach to them. A lot was at once promised, and the next Thursday appointed as the day when the people would assemble to build a meeting-house. On the day appointed they assembled with their axes. The site was selected. "Axes were lifted up upon the thick trees," the forest resounded with the blows made by sinewy and willing arms. The bodies of the rough logs were cut off the proper length, but were too heavy to be brought into position, although near to the site of the building. There was but one team in all the settlement, and that was a yoke of oxen belonging to a professed infidel. It would not do to ask him to bring his team for such a purpose. Just as the necessity became pressing, Mr. S. was seen approaching with his oxen, crying out with his great merry voice, "Here comes the devil with his oxen, to help you build your meeting-house." The work then went gayly forward.

The next important thing was the appearance of Thomas McLean, with a small flat keg of whiskey under his arm. This was placed in Mr. Tait's hands, when all took a drink, beginning with the minister and ending with the donor himself. Three cheers were then given for Thomas McLean, with the promise that when the church was organized he should be the first elder. This promise was afterward fulfilled and Mr. McLean was the first elder that was elected.

By sundown, the church was built, covered with clapboards, floored with puncheons, and round logs rolled in for seats. The house was so located that a huge stump answered the purpose of a pulpit, with two puncheons set upright in front, and one across secured to the uprights with pins, on which the Bible might be placed. A puncheon seat for the minister completed the arrangement. Here was a building that afforded the people ample room and abundant comfort in the worship of God.

But luxury soon began to creep in to trouble the church. After a time one of the members of the congregation had a bench made and set in the church for his family to sit upon. During the recess on the next day of worship, little groups might have been seen discussing the matter of the new bench; some affirming that such pride should not be tolerated, and that if his neighbors could sit on a log to hear the gospel preached, William McMillan could do the same, as neither he nor his family were better than others. Others affirmed that if William McMillan could afford a bench with legs to it, he had a right to have one. The contention, like that between Paul and Barnabas, waxed exceeding sharp, but was finally settled by the minister declaring for the largest liberty, each one being permitted to provide such a seat as he chose.

Soon the first house was found too small to contain the people. The difficulty was remedied by cutting out the logs from one side of the building and erecting a kind of shed as an addition. Subsequently, as the congregation increased, another shed was erected on the other side.

Joseph Stockton was probably the youngest man ever ordained in the bounds of the Presbytery. He was but a few months past twenty at the time of his licensure, and a little past twenty-two at his ordination. His pastorate of ten years, at Meadville, was succeeded by labors in teaching and the preparation of school books.

Robert Lee was twenty-nine years of age when he entered the ministry. His was a life of labor, accompanied with a calm patience and patriarchal dignity that was peculiar to his age.

James Satterfield, with his tall, erect form and self-denying labor, won a respect that was remarkable even in his day. He was a godly man and lived very near to Christ.

Dr. William Wylie, the last of those who constituted the first Presbytery, was a zealous pastor and a most earnest preacher. His letters that are extant, and written during his last days, possess a wondrous savor of piety and a richness of unction that would place them on a level with those of Rutherford.

Of the four elders at this meeting, William Plumer

was the father of Rev. W. S. Plumer, D. D., and Ithiel Dodd belonged to a family for two centuries remarkable for two characteristics — piety, simple and childlike, and a talent for mathematics.

The first two licentiates that were taken under the care of the Presbytery, were John (8) and Abraham Boyd (9). They were two Irish boys, educated in this country and licensed by the Presbytery of Redstone. In those days, "supplications" for supplies were the constant order of the day. At the first meeting, there were supplications from "Slippery Rock, Westfield, Lower Neshannock, Breakneck, Thorn's Tent, Concord, Franklin, Big Sugar Creek, Oil Creek, Gravel Run, Upper and Lower Greenfield, Middlebrook, Presque Isle, Powers' Mills, Crossings of Cussawaga and Pymatuning."

The infant Presbytery seems to have set up its banners in the name of the Lord. Almost the first resolution passed was, to seek God's help in the great work :

"Presbytery taking into consideration their infant state, and the growing prospects of the new settlement under their care, and the necessity of Divine influence to aid and direct them in their arduous work, do resolve to spend part of to-morrow in supplication and prayer."

The matter of education, and facilities for the preparation of young men for the gospel ministry, occupied the attention of Presbytery at its first meeting. Their resolution is to this effect: "Presbytery proceeded to take into consideration the necessity of a seminary of learning being instituted within their bounds for the education of youth ; *Resolved*, To give their aid to erect an academy at Greersburgh, and to solicit the aid of their respective charges." Greersburgh is now known as Darlington, in Beaver County, Pa. This academy was long an efficient aid in the great work of fitting young men for the ministry. Sometimes they pursued their studies there preparatory to Jefferson College, but many received all their classical education within its walls.

It was commenced in 1806. The legislature of the State appropriated six hundred dollars towards it, when the charter was granted. The first teacher was Mr. Hughes; afterwards it was taught by Rev. Robert Dilworth, D. D. This academy was the result, principally, of the labors of Mr. Hughes, who travelled over the New England States, soliciting funds for its establishment. Before the erection of the academy building, he built a log cabin near his own residence that served as a school-room.

At this meeting the Boyd brothers, having accepted calls to settle within the bounds of Presbytery, were examined with a view to ordination, and were assigned subjects for trial sermons to be delivered at the next meeting.

Messrs. Tait and Satterfield were the first Commissioners to the General Assembly. Presbytery adjourned to meet at Union, Armstrong County, on the 15th of June, 1802, with the following order: " That members endeavor to bring forward, at our next fall meeting, an account of the time of their settlement, state of religion, number of families and communicants, and the number of baptisms in the congregations under their care."

And thus the Presbytery commenced its labors, few in number yet strong in faith. There was much land to be possessed, yet they trusted in God, and went forward.

In addition to the preaching of Mr. Hughes in the

southern portion of the territory, perhaps the first in the extreme north was during the celebrated tour of Elisha McCurdy and Joseph Stockton. This was in 1799. They preached at Sandy (perhaps the present Georgetown), Meadville, Waterford, Erie, North East, and other places.[1] In 1802 another missionary tour through the same region was undertaken by McCurdy, Satterfield, and McPherrin (16), with McCurdy's "praying elder," Philip Jackson, organizing churches and strengthening the brethren.

At this time the churches of Upper and Lower Greenfield were organized in Erie County, Pa. There were many people scattered through this region who had come from the counties east of the Alleghany Mountains, and some from Washington and Westmoreland, west of the mountains. They remembered the God of their fathers, and welcomed the pioneer ministers most gladly. There was a large Presbyterian element in all their early settlements, and for very many years the great religious element of the country was of this type of faith.

The organization of a church there was a most important era in the history of the people, and the dispensing of the ordinances made them feel that the trials and privations of the new settlements were passing away.

And when the people of what is now Venango Township, Erie County, Pa., met together to build a house of worship, it was a matter of more interest to them than they had felt in the erection of their own houses. It was with the thought that God would be with them, and be their God.

We have a minute account of the building of this

---

* Dr. Elliott's *Life of McCurdy*, p. 29.

house, and the circumstances attending it, in an old journal written by William Dickson, Esq., formerly of Erie County, Pa., but now of Camden, Illinois. An extract follows: —

"Some time in August, 1801, a notice was sent to Mr. James Hunter, an old man, who the spring previous had emigrated to what is now Venango Township, Erie County. He had been an elder in Dr. Bryson's church in Northumberland County, and was to notify the people that the Rev. James Satterfield (6), a missionary, would preach at a place designated by them, on the following Sabbath. The notice was given, I believe, to every individual in the township; and the place fixed upon for the meeting was at a 'chopping' made by Robert Donaldson, on the bank of French Creek, near the centre of the town. Four or five of us, all young men, went on the ground on Saturday, to prepare a place for worship. We selected a spot under a large beech-tree; we split a large log, turning the split sides up, and raising them a little from the ground made a platform. We then squared a block for a seat, placing it on the platform near the tree, which made a good stiff backing; we then drove two stakes into the ground in front, pinning and nailing a clapboard across the top, to lay the Bible and Psalm Book on. I am thus particular in describing the first pulpit from which I ever heard the gospel in Erie County.

"Sabbath morning came, and every man and woman within our township was gathered, I believe, around the beech-tree. About the hour appointed, the minister came; he had lost his way the evening previous, having nothing but marked trees for a guide, and had lain out all night. In the morning he found a cabin where two young men lived; they gave him a good breakfast of indian bread and potatoes, and having his inner man strengthened, he appeared to come unto the work in the *Spirit,* and preached two sermons, and administered the ordinance of baptism. He stated it was possible the Synod of Pittsburgh would send us some more preaching that Fall. After preaching, and before the people dispersed, Mr. Hunter called several of us young men around him, and said, 'Boys' (for by that name he always called us), 'I want you all to meet me at a certain land corner (naming it) on next Thursday morning early, and bring your axes and dinners with you.' That was enough; we all knew what was wanting, and at the time appointed we were there almost to a man. The old man then stated the reasons for calling us together. He said the Lord had been mindful of us in that wilderness, and had sent us the gospel by the mouth of one of his servants, and we had no house to meet in, but heard it, as you know, under the beech-tree, in the open air. Now, if we wish to prosper, while we build houses for ourselves, we must build one for God; and he had selected that spot, as it was the centre of the township.

"As the large hemlock-tree which marked the corner stood in a swamp, — a place by no means suitable for our purpose, — a young man, whose name was Warren, said that if we would agree to go a half or three quarters of a mile north, he would show us a good place on his land, where there was a fine spring of water, and he would give us a deed of two acres, if we chose that spot.

"As it would shorten Father Hunter's distance in coming to meeting, which was no small consideration with us, we at once shouldered our axes and followed our leader to the spot; and that day, before sundown, we had cleared the ground, and built a habitation for the Most High to dwell in.[1] In the evening, before we parted, Father Hunter called us around a large stump, and explained the propriety of supporting the gospel. He said that those men who came to preach to us, suffered so much in travelling through the wilderness that they ought to be well paid, and it would be best for us to have a fund on hand for that purpose. He also said that he had made a calculation of the amount required to begin with, and it would be best to appoint a treasurer, and each one pay twenty-five cents. We all stepped up to the stump and laid down our money, mostly fifty cents; when we had all paid, the good old man laid down a dollar; and on seeing him do so, one of the party said: 'Father Hunter, you shall not go ahead of me,' and took up the fifty cents he had paid and laid down a dollar. Thus commenced a fund which never failed during my residence in that congregation of over twelve years, and I never knew a minister to preach in that place (who was a Presbyterian) but was paid promptly. A few days after we had built our house of worship, notice came that the Rev. James Satterfield and Rev. Elisha McCurdy were expected to preach, and organize a church in our new meeting-house. They came, and each brought his wife with him. They came on horseback, picking their way through woods, in many places only by lines marked on the trees; encountering swamps, and every other obstacle imaginable, all without complaining. Here I will relate a little circumstance about Mrs. McCurdy. In passing through, they lodged for a night with one of my neighbors, whose cabin was very small and had but

[1] This house is still standing. A drawing of it may be seen in Miss Sanford's *History of Erie County.*

one bed (that used by the man and his wife), and a bunk in the corner for three or four children. Mrs. McCurdy saw that her hostess was preparing the bed for the strangers, and said, 'I perceive that you are giving yourself unnecessary trouble for us. Is not that the bed which you and your husband occupy?' 'Yes,' was the reply. She said, 'Then sleep in it; all we ask is room in your house, and I will provide a bed for me and Mr. McCurdy; the floor will do for us.' The woman insisted that they should take the bed. 'Where will you sleep?' was the next question. 'O, somewhere here,' she replied. 'You shall not leave your bed for me' said Mrs. McCurdy; 'my Master had not where to lay his head, and we have saddle-bags and blankets, and a house to shelter us.' By this time I found there was no room for me, so I went out to a stack where there was some straw, and made a nest under the side of it, where I slept comfortably.

"From thence they went to Lower Greenfield, now North East, and organized a church, and returned to our log meeting-house, and organized a church, and called it Middlebrook. Mr. McCurdy preached the sermon from these words, 'My sheep hear my voice, and I know them, and they follow me.'"

At the second meeting of Presbytery, another licentiate was taken under its care. This was William Wood (10), a licentiate of the Presbytery of Ohio. At this meeting, John and Abraham Boyd were both ordained and installed, the former June 16, 1802, as pastor of Union and Slate Lick; the latter on the following day, as pastor of Bull Creek and Middlesex. All these churches are in what is now Armstrong County, Pa.

The ordination of John Boyd was the first act of that kind performed by the Presbytery. There is one feature connected with these early ordinations that is worthy of our attention. They were always accompanied by "fasting," as well as prayer, and the imposition of the hands of the Presbytery.

At a *pro re nata* meeting of Presbytery held at Pittsburgh, September 30, 1802, Robert Patterson, a licentiate of the Presbytery of Ohio, was received under its care, and accepted calls from the churches of Erie, and Upper and Lower Greenfield.

The next meeting was at Plaingrove, November 2, 1802, when William Wood was ordained and installed as pastor of the churches of Plaingrove and Centre, in Mercer County, Pa.

At the meeting held at Rocky Spring, April 12, 1803, Alexander Cook (12), a licentiate of the Presbytery of Ohio, was received under the care of Presbytery. At the same time it was resolved to solicit from the General Assembly a donation of religious books, to be granted to such inhabitants as may not be able to supply themselves. This appeal was successful, and the Assembly granted them the following list of books: twenty Bibles, forty copies Doddridge's "Rise and Progress," thirty Janeway's "Token," eight "Russell's Sermons," eight Boston's "Crook in the Lot," and eight Willison's "Sacramental Meditations."

This grant was followed by the following order: —

"That the Treasurer take charge of the books, pay the carriage on them, and distribute as follows: the Bibles given gratis to such poor people as need them, the others to be divided equally amongst the ministers, and by them circulated amongst such people as need them, until they are called for by Presbytery." [1]

Here we find cropping out the germs of many of the

[1] *Min. of Pres.* vol. i. p. 15.

Boards that are now the glory and crown of the Church, missions to the Indians, missions at home, education and publication — all are found in the bud and ready to be developed.

On the 13th of April, 1803, Presbytery received the first ordained minister into its bounds. This was Joseph Badger (11), the famous missionary from Connecticut. His life was one of romance, and yet one of sternest reality. Born and reared in poverty, struggling always with adversity and discouragements, he yet performed labor and achieved results, such as few men even of his day were able to accomplish. His famous journey from Connecticut to Ohio, during the depth of winter, with his four-horse team, sometimes on wheels and sometimes on runners, will long be remembered as one of the heroic labors that characterized the early settlements of the West. His wonderful versatility of genius, admirably adapted him to the peculiar work in which he was engaged. He was at home equally in his cabin, on horseback swimming the rivers, in the Indian wigwams preaching Christ, and in the depth of the forest, sleeping at the root of a tree, his head pillowed upon a stone like Jacob's, or hiding from beasts of prey in the tree-tops. He was a remarkable man, and lived to see fourscore and ten years.

As an instance of the demand for supplies, the following minute, made in 1803, is reproduced: "Fairview, Westfield, Poland, Warren (O.), Trumbull, Beula, Pymatuning, Conneautee, Outlet of Conneaut, Hilands, Saltspring, Concord, Gravel Run, Middlebrook, Beavertown, Franklin, Titus's, Hugh McGirl's on Pithole, Andrews' on Brokenstraw, Jackson's on Conewango, Robert Miles', Major Gray's on French Creek, Mount Nebo, Sugar Creek, Smithfield, and Canfield (O.)." Here is a region of country extending along Lake Erie for thirty miles, thence south to Beaver one hundred and thirty miles; and from Warren, Pa., on the east, to Warren and Canfield, Ohio, on the west, and embracing territory and points that are still, after the lapse of sixty-five years, considered as missionary ground. And at this time the whole force of the Presbytery consisted of but twelve ministers.

On the 22d of June, 1803, Alexander Cook was ordained and installed as pastor of the congregations of Slippery Rock and New Castle, formerly called Lower Neshannock. The former church was in what is now Beaver County, and the latter Lawrence County, Pa. On the same day Robert Johnston (14), a licentiate of the Presbytery of Ohio, was received under the care of Presbytery. On the 31st of August following, Robert Patterson was ordained and installed as pastor of the congregations of Upper and Lower Greenfield. These churches are now known, the former as Middlebrook and the latter North East. They are in Erie County, Pa., and at present in the New School connection.

Mr. Patterson was the first settled minister in Erie County. He took frequent missionary tours, in the region along the shore of Lake Erie. A brief journal, kept during one of these tours, will convey some idea of the character of the work : —

"*Saturday*, Nov. 5, 1803. Set off from the place of my residence, at the mouth of the Twelve Mile Creek, below Presque Isle. Rode thirty miles to the house of Thomas Miles, on Elk Creek.

"Nov. 6, *Sabbath*. Rode nine miles to Lexington, on the Great Conneaut. Met this morning, at different places on the road, one man carrying a hoe, shovel, and basket, going into his potato field; another carrying a log chain ; and a third a cutting knife. Besides these met several others on their return from a Saturday night's lodging in a tavern, after having attended at the office of a justice, whose custom it is to transact law business on Saturdays, and so late that those who are obliged to appear before him are under the necessity, some with and a few against their will, of staying all night in a place where drunkenness, profanity, and obscenity too frequently introduce the Sabbath.

"Preached at the house of —— ——, from John iii. 19, 20, to eighteen hearers, some not very attentive, and no appearance of solemnity. Rode in the evening three miles to the house of C. Woods and Dr. Hastings, near the Great Conneaut.

"Nov. 7, *Monday.* Preached from Joshua xxiv. 15, to eleven persons, attentive and serious. Rode in the evening three or four miles to John Saton's, near Great Conneaut.

"Nov. 8, *Tuesday.* Rode eight or nine miles to Samuel Holliday's on the lake, near the mouth of Crooked Creek. Preached from Matt. iii. 9, to seven persons.

"Nov. 9, *Wednesday.* Rode eleven miles to Widow McCreary's, near Walnut Creek. Preached from Acts iii. 19, to twenty persons. Received $1.37. Rode in the evening two miles to Mr. McCoy's.

"Nov. 10, *Thursday.* Rode twenty miles home.

"Nov. 12, *Saturday.* Set out for Waterford, alias Le Bœuf, on French Creek, distant twenty-two miles, the road solitary, swampy, and in some places covered with deep snow. . . . . Towards evening, when within five or six miles of my destination and near Le Bœuf Creek, was led astray by the devious track of two travellers, who had wandered themselves, and were the cause of my wandering. . . . . Two or three hours after night, came to a watercourse, seen by snow-light, which was too broad and miry to cross. Prepared to pass the night as well as I could. All in a perspiration, my feet wet with walking and wading, for the place did not admit of riding, hungry and fatigued, I lay down on the slushy snow, somewhat afraid of wild beasts, but more of perishing with the chilling cold, though it did not freeze. About midnight the cold in my feet became excessive. Rose and walked for about an hour on a path which I made in the snow for the purpose. My feet were somewhat relieved from the cold. Lay down again and passed the night sometimes awake but mostly asleep.

"Nov. 13, *Sabbath*. In the morning, after having spent eleven or twelve hours in this dreary place, and after having suffered severer hardships than I ever before endured in travelling, and feeling some sense of my obligation to God for His preserving mercy, took my track backward, and between nine and ten o'clock reached the house of John Bundle. Preached from Acts ii. 38, to ten persons.

"Nov. 14, *Monday*. Rode eighteen miles home.

"Nov. 16, *Wednesday*. Rode ten miles to the house of John Culver. Preached to six persons — home in the evening.

"Nov. 19, *Saturday*. Rode seventeen miles to Adam Reed's, on French Creek.

"Nov. 20, *Sabbath*. Rode nine miles to Matthew Gray's, and preached from Eph. vi. 4, to eighteen persons.

"Nov. 21, *Monday*. Rode nine miles to Adam Reed's. Lectured to twenty persons on the parable of the sower, Matt. xiii. Received one dollar. In the evening rode seven miles to Thomas McGahan's.

"Nov. 22, *Tuesday*. Rode ten miles to Wilson Smith's, in Waterford, alias Le Bœuf.

"Nov. 23, *Wednesday*. Preached in the town at the house of Esquire Vincent, to eleven persons, from Acts xvii. 18. Rode in the evening eight miles to John Philips'.

"Nov. 24, *Thursday*. Set out about sunrise, having appointed to preach at the house of P. Clooke, distant eleven or twelve miles. The road, however, was so extremely bad with mud, frost, and snow, and the day wet, that at twelve o'clock I found that I could not reach the place until two or three hours after the time appointed; and not being well since the night I lay in the snow, rode home from John Philips', seventeen or eighteen miles.

"Nov. 26, *Saturday*. Rode twenty miles to the house of James McMahan, living in a new settlement in the State of New York, situated about Chautauque Creek, that empties into Lake Erie.

"Nov. 27, *Sabbath*. Preached on 1 Cor. iv. at Widow McHenry's, to fifteen grown persons and a greater number of children. Received one dollar.

"Nov. 28. *Monday*. Rode twenty miles from James McMahan's house.

This journal gives a mere sample of the every-day labors of these early missionaries. As a general thing the study and preparation were confined to the saddle and the brief tarrying at the log-cabins by the wayside, whilst the preaching was often of daily occurrence — in the forest, in the dwelling-house, or wherever a few people could be assembled.

On the 19th day of October, 1803, Robert Johnston was ordained and installed as pastor of the congregations of Scrubgrass and Bear Creek, in Venango County, Pa.

This was a most interesting field of labor. The first, or at least amongst the first families, that came to settle in Scrubgrass, was that of Mrs. Abigail Coulter, a pious woman from Washington County, Pennsylvania. She came out in 1797. The first sermon ever heard in this neighborhood, was delivered by Rev. William Moorhead, a son-in-law of Rev. Dr. McMillan (see "Old Redstone," page 330), in the year 1800, at Mrs. Coulter's house, that was about forty rods from the site of the present church building. This was the first sermon ever heard by her son John,[1] then sixteen years of age. He had never before even seen a minister, and was, as he expressed it, more afraid of a minister than of an Indian. After this, was an occasional sermon by Rev. A. Boyd, and Mr. Gwynn. The first communion was conducted by Mr. Johnston, assisted by Mr. Cook, in 1803. It was held in a grove. The people assembled from a great distance. Thirty persons came from Slate Lick, thirty miles distant. Snow fell on Sabbath night, and at the services on Monday the logs used as seats were thickly covered with snow; but the people brushed it off, and sat down, and listened gladly and contentedly to the preached Word.

At the meeting in June, 1804, Nicholas Pittinger (15), a licentiate of the Presbytery of Ohio, was received under the care of Presbytery. At the next meeting, October 24, 1804, he was ordained and in-

---

[1] Afterwards Rev. John Coulter, of the Presbytery of Alleghany. Born June 26th, 1784; licensed by Presbytery of Ohio; ordained by that of Alleghany, April 21st, 1823; died December 6th, 1867. He was pastor of Concord Church forty-one (41) years. He was the father of Rev. J. R. Coulter, now pastor of Scrubgrass.

stalled as pastor of the congregations of Westfield and Poland. The former of these charges was in what is now Lawrence County, Pa., and the latter, Trumbull County, Ohio.

At the same meeting the first licensure took place in the Presbytery. Hitherto the new accessions had been from the licentiates of the mother Presbyteries; now they began the work of licensing candidates for themselves. The first licentiate was Benjamin Boyd (17), a brother of John and Abraham, who were already members of Presbytery.

On the 5th of December, 1804, the first pastoral relation was dissolved, and the first members dismissed from the Presbytery. This was the case of William Wylie. His pastoral relation was dissolved for a reason that has since been the prominent one in such changes for a half a century and more — failure to comply with stipulations, and consequent want of support. Mr. Wylie was dismissed to the Presbytery of Redstone.

A singular instance of the punctilious observance of forms occurs in the matter of the church of Bull Creek. The calls for the labors of Abraham Boyd, on which he had been installed, were accidentally consumed by fire. Commissioners appear in Presbytery with papers signed by the trustees of the congregation, obliging themselves to pay the pastor the sum promised in the call, together with subscriptions for the amount. These were accepted by the pastor instead of the original call.

In the matter of supplies, it was usual at this time to send two ministers where the Lord's Supper was to be celebrated. The services were usually protracted, and several days occupied on the occasion, so that much labor was imposed.

There is another feature in the polity and practice of these early fathers that is interesting. It is the great frequency of occasions on which committees were appointed to visit congregations and even individuals, to reconcile difficulties and remove complaints. Were difficulties reported by pastor or people, a committee of Presbytery was appointed to visit the place, call the people together, preach to them, pray with them, secure mutual concessions, and as a general thing restore harmony and peace. The influence of the ministry over the people was then very great. The ministers were much like diocesan bishops. Their advice was potent, their word was almost like law.

But the labor connected with these things was onerous. The question arises, too, with this large amount of travel in reconciling belligerent churches and individuals, in supplying vacancies, and in assisting brethren on communion occasions, where was the time for study and attention to the minister's own field? The complaint must often have been made, "They made me a keeper of vineyards, but mine own vineyard have I not kept."

At this time much attention was paid to the Indian Mission at Sandusky. Mr. Badger was commissioned by the "Board of Trust" of the Synod of Pittsburgh to conduct the mission. He met with many difficulties, and was confronted by obstacles. Whiskey then, as now, was in the way of the red man's elevation and prosperity. He arrived among them in May, 1806. The plan proposed was to combine religious instruction with the arts and humanizing influences of civilized life. Mr. Badger was accompanied by three laborers, with oxen and farming implements, who were to instruct the Indians in agriculture.

Mr. Badger was to have a salary of four hundred and fifty dollars, with any extra expenses that should appear reasonable. The laborers were two white men at twelve dollars per month, and one colored man and his wife, at one hundred dollars per year. He was also furnished a horse at forty-five dollars, and farming utensils, carpenter's tools, and household furniture, to the amount of one hundred and forty-five dollars and eighty-six cents.[1]

But the discouragements were very great. The missionary life was not all rose-colored. During Mr. Badger's temporary absence, Mr. McCurdy took his place. He writes as follows of the Indians: "Their houses, when they have any, are wretched huts, almost as dirty as they can be, and swarming with fleas and lice; their furniture, a few barks, a tin or brass kettle, a gun, pipe, and tomahawk. Such is their ingratitude, that whilst you load them with favors they will reproach you to the face, and construe your benevolent intentions and actions into intentional fraud or real injury. They will lie in the most deliberate manner, and to answer any selfish purpose."[2]

At this juncture, a committee was appointed to prepare a history of the Presbytery. They reported progress the next year, and were directed to send their manuscript to Dr. Ashbel Green. The subsequent fate of this history is unknown.

The Missionary Society of Connecticut at this time had many missionaries in the Western Reserve of Ohio, which was settled mainly by families from Connecticut. They occupied in common with the Presbytery of Erie a large extent of country. The Presbytery

[1] Minutes, Synod of Pittsburgh, 1806.
[2] Dr. Elliott's *McCurdy*, p. 120.

seemed disposed to cultivate friendly relations with them. A minute was passed advising the ministers to exchange professional services with them, and the people to commune with them in their churches. This grew out of the celebrated " Plan of Union " entered into between the General Assembly and the General Association of Connecticut in 1801 and 1802.

In April, 1805, John McPherrin (16) was received from the Presbytery of Redstone, and soon after became pastor of the congregations of Concord, Muddy Creek, and Harmony, in Butler County, Pa.

In October, 1806, Presbytery received Johnston Eaton (20), a licentiate of the Presbytery of Ohio, under its care, and on the following month ordained Benjamin Boyd, and installed him as pastor of the congregations of Trumbull, Beula, and Pymatuning. The first two of these congregations were in Ohio.

In April, 1807, Cyrus Riggs (18), a licentiate of the Presbytery of Ohio, was received under the care of Presbytery, and at the same meeting Robert Patterson was released from the charge of Upper and Lower Greenfield in Erie County, Pa. At this meeting also, James Boyd (21), the fourth of the Boyd brothers, was licensed to preach the gospel.

In July, 1807, Robert Lee (5) was dismissed, on the ground of ill health, from the pastoral charge of Rocky Spring and Amity.

About this time the matter of a division of Presbytery was first agitated. The minute recorded is in these words: " Presbytery agreed to petition the Synod at its next meeting to erect Rev. John McPherrin, Thomas E. Hughes, William Wick, James Satterfield, Robert Lee, John Boyd, Abraham Boyd, William Wood, Robert Johnston, Alexander Cook, and Nicholas

Pittinger, into a separate Presbytery, to be known by the name of the Presbytery of Harmony, to hold their first meeting at Concord."

Against this action there was the following

PROTEST.

" We, the undersigned members of Erie Presbytery, do protest against the decision of said Presbytery in favor of the proposed division, inasmuch as we believe it will prove inimical to the interests of religion in many respects. "SAMUEL TAIT,
"JOSEPH STOCKTON,
"BENJAMIN BOYD."

On the 20th day of October, 1807, Reid Bracken (19), a licentiate of the Presbytery of Ohio, was received under the care of Presbytery, and on the same day Cyrus Riggs was ordained and installed as pastor of the congregations of Fairfield and Mill Creek, the former in Mercer County, and the latter in Venango County, Pa.

A note appended to the minutes, here shows that whilst the weightier matters were attended to, the smaller were not neglected: "Stated Clerk paid for writing for two preceding years, three dollars and twenty-five cents."

In January, 1808, Mr. Hughes reported that he had collected four hundred and forty-four dollars and forty-six cents for Greersburgh Academy. It was resolved, that this money should be appropriated to the use of young men preparing for the gospel ministry, and be under the control of Presbytery; that it be furnished only to such young men as shall be recommended by Presbytery, to be by them refunded at the rate of twenty dollars per annum, to commence as soon as they shall have been settled one year, "in any profession or line of business."

Supplies at this time were granted to "Sewickly, Gravel Run, Canfield, Boardman, Upper Salem, West Unity, New Salem, Second Presbyterian Congregation, Pittsburgh,[1] Hilands, Indiana, Amity, Upper Greenfield, Middlebrook, Waterford, Major Gray's, Oil Creek, Brokenstraw, Conewango, Upper and Lower Sugar Creek, and Erietown."

On the 20th of April, 1808, Reid Bracken was ordained and installed as pastor of the congregations of Mount Nebo and Plain, in Butler County, Pa. Mr. Wood (10) preached on the occasion, and Mr. Pittinger (15) delivered the charges. This pastoral charge continued until Oct. 7, 1819, when he was released from Plain, and in 1844 from Mount Nebo.

On the 30th of June, 1808, Johnston Eaton (20) was ordained, and installed as pastor of the congregations of Fairview and Springfield, in Erie County, Pa. Mr. Johnston (14) preached on the occasion, and Joseph Stockton (4) delivered the charges. This ordination took place in a barn belonging to William Sturgeon. The relation continued with the congregation of Fairview until the death of the pastor in 1847.

On the 19th day of October, in the same year, James Boyd (21) was ordained and installed as pastor of the congregations of Newton and Warren, Ohio. Mr. Wick (2) preached on the occasion, and Mr. Hughes (1) delivered the charges. This relation continued until the death of Mr. Boyd in 1813. He was the last of the four brothers that was licensed, and the first called to his rest.

[1] Special request, by permission of Presbytery of Ohio.

On the day following this ordination, Presbytery licensed three young men to preach the gospel. They had passed through all their preparatory exercises under the direction of Presbytery, and were commissioned together to go into the great field. Their names were, Edward Johnston, Daniel Heydon, and Joshua Beer. Their names will not be found again in this record, as they were transferred the next spring to the roll of the new Presbytery of Hartford. Mr. Johnston was an older brother of Robert Johnston (14). After accepting calls from the congregations of Brookfield and Hubbard, Ohio, he was called away from his earthly labors, to a higher sphere of service, on the very day that had been set apart for his ordination. His death took place September 20, 1809.

Daniel Heydon was afterwards settled in the bounds of the Presbytery of Miami, and still later in those of the Presbytery of Cincinnati. Joshua Beer was settled first at Springfield, in the Presbytery of Hartford, and subsequently at Middle Sandy and Bethesda.

The little church of Middlebrook was still keeping up its fund for the support of the gospel, and William Dickson, afterwards an elder at North East, was sent to Presbytery to ask for supplies. The Presbytery sent to them one of their licentiates, Edward Johnston, who preached to them on the Sabbath ; and on Sabbath night the stream between him and the man who kept the money arose to such a height that there was no possibility of crossing it. So Mr. Johnston went home without his money. To the next meeting of Presbytery Mr. Dickson went with the money, but found that in the mean time Mr. Johnston had been called home to his rest and his reward. The money was placed in the hands of Presbytery, to be disposed of as was fitting and best.

The project of a new Presbytery to be erected from a portion of the territory of the old, that had been agitated for a year previous, now assumed a definite form. The bounds were large, and the churches multiplying in the region extending into the State of Ohio. The request does not appear to have proceeded from the Presbytery of Erie as such, but from a Convention, called on the minutes of the Synod of Pittsburgh, " The Convention of New Connecticut." The eastern portion of the State of Ohio was known at this time as New Connecticut, and this Convention was probably made up of the ministers and elders residing in that region. The first minute of Synod is to this effect : —

" A petition was handed in by the Committee of Bills and Overtures, from the Convention of New Connecticut, praying that such arrangements might be made in the division of Presbyteries, as that they might be embraced within the bounds of a Presbytery."

On this petition a committee of five, John McMillan, William Wick, Thomas E. Hughes, Clement Valandingham, and Johnston Eaton, was appointed, which reported the following minute : —

" The committee to whom was referred the memorial from the Ecclesiastical Convention of New Connecticut, reported, that they were of opinion that the welfare of the church and the interests of religion may be promoted by the erection of a new Presbytery, bounded by a line beginning at the mouth of Big Beaver Creek, thence up said creek, and up Neshannock, to the mouth of Little Branch ; thence northerly to the mouth of Walnut Creek, on Lake Erie ; thence along the line of the lake to the west line of New Connecticut ; thence to the southwest corner of the Connecticut Reserve ; thence east along the south line of the Connecticut Reserve to the Tuscarawa branch of the Muskingum River; thence in a direct line to the Ohio River, at the mouth of Yellow Creek; thence up the Ohio River to the place of beginning: including the Rev. Messrs. Thomas Edgar Hughes, William Wick, Joseph Badger, James Satterfield, Benjamin Boyd, Nicholas Pittinger, Clement Valandingham, and Johnston Eaton,— to be known by the name of the Presbytery of Hartford." [1]

The report was adopted, and the new Presbytery ordered to meet at Hartford, Ohio, on the second Tuesday of November, 1808.

In process of time the territory of the new Presbytery was divided, until the town after which it had been originally named was no longer within its bounds. In the year 1833, the name was changed by act of Synod to Beaver. From the territory of this Presbytery and its expansion was formed, in 1814, the Presbytery of Grand River; and from this, in 1818, Portage; and from this, in 1823, Huron; and from this, in 1830, Cleveland. From Beaver Presbytery was also formed, in 1838, the Presbytery of New Lisbon.

The Presbytery of Erie had now been in existence eight years. The general result had been most encouraging. Its roll had increased from five to nineteen members, with one licentiate and six candidates. Of these, seventeen were pastors. The churches had increased in number and in strength. At the last meeting of Synod, previous to the division, there were reported the following congregations able to support a pastor: "Warren and Newton, Amity and West Unity, Gravel Run and Conneaut, Oil Creek and Sugar Creek, Hartford, Smithfield, and Kinsman."

[1] Minutes, Synod of Pittsburgh, 1808.

HISTORY. 57

There were also reported, as unable to support a pastor: "Upper Salem, New Salem, Erietown, Waterford, Brokenstraw, Conewango, Vienna, Bristol, Beavertown, Bear Creek, Upper and Lower Greenfield, Mesopotamia, Middlefield, Hilands, Middlebrook, Miles' Settlement, Franklin, Cleveland, East Unity, Sewickly, Boardman, Indiana, Center, Austinburgh, and Morgan."

What number of these were regularly organized churches, and what were merely preaching points, it is impossible to determine. The early records rarely if ever give any account of the date and circumstances of the organization of particular churches. They seem to have been enrolled just as they sought supplies, and became known as places desiring the public ordinances of religion.

Much missionary labor had been performed by the Presbytery through its members, and some enterprises had been undertaken by the Synod and General Assembly within its bounds.

The first years in the history of the Presbytery were marked and rendered eternally memorable by the wonderful revivals of religion that were enjoyed. The great awakening of 1801 and 1802 commenced in the Presbytery of Ohio, but soon extended into what became the territory of the Presbytery of Erie. The first notice of it is found in the history of the charge of Mr. Hughes (1) at Mount Pleasant, Beaver County, Pa. Mr. Munson, who was a member of that charge, tells us [1] many of the particulars of it. It was preceded by a spirit of prayerfulness and anxiety for God's blessing. The people met together for prayer. The female members of the congregation met for prayer. Individuals

---

[1] Letter to Dr. Plumer, *Pres. Mag.* vii. 463.

wrestled with agony and weeping. They laid hold on the strength of Jehovah. They watched and waited for the blessing. They brought the tithes into the store house, and God poured them out a blessing. People came together as with one heart and one mind, to seek the Lord. No business was so pressing, no cares so urgent, as to interfere with these solemn assemblies. Oftentimes they could not be persuaded to retire after the benediction had been pronounced, but lingered around the door of the church, or the tent, as though by some unusual fascination. In some cases, under such circumstances, the services were renewed, and continued all night. Great numbers were brought to the knowledge of Christ; the hearts of God's people were refreshed, and the churches greatly enlarged.

An extract from the "Western Missionary Magazine," describing the work as witnessed in the Congregation of Cross Roads, will convey an idea of the manifestation of God's Spirit during these times. It was during the exercises of a communion season. Nine ministers were present. Great feeling had been manifested during the services. The communicants had retired from the tables: " A great many were affected, and some had to be assisted to move out. Ministers still preached successively in the hours throughout the day. Prayers and exhortations were continued all night in the meeting-house, except at short intervals, when a speaker's voice could not be heard for the cries and groans of the distressed. On Monday three ministers preached at different places, one in the house, and two out in the encampments. This was a very solemn day, particularly in the house. After public worship, when the people were preparing to remove, the scene was very affecting; the house was thronged full, and when some of those without were about to go away, they found that part of their families were in the house, and some of them lying in distress unable to remove. This prevented a general removal; and although a number went away, the greater part remained. About the time of the departure of those who went away, the work became more powerful than it had been at any time before, and numbers who had prepared to go were constrained to stay. It was a memorable time of the display of Divine power and grace through the whole night. Many of the young people were remarkably exercised, and frequently addressed others about the condition they were in, the glories of the Saviour, the excellency and suitableness of the plan of salvation; and warned and invited, and pressed sinners to come to Christ; all this in a manner quite astonishing for their years. Numbers of old, experienced Christians, also, were particularly exercised, were much refreshed and comforted, and affectingly recommended the Lord Jesus and his religion to those around them. About sunrise, after a time of solemn, sweet exercise, the congregation was dismissed, and soon after dispersed." [1]

Another account describes the work in a different congregation: "The administration of the Word and ordinances was accompanied with an extraordinary effusion of divine influences on the hearts of the hearers. Some hundreds were, during the season, convinced of their sin and misery; and many of them sunk down and cried bitterly and incessantly for several hours. Some fell suddenly; some lost their strength gradually; some lay quiet and silent; some were violently agitated; and many sat silently weeping, who were not exercised with any bodily affections." [2]

[1] *Western Miss. Mag.* i. 334–35.   [2] *Ibid.* 338.

The work extended throughout all the region round. All classes, all ages, all conditions in life were affected. The hoary-headed sinner, who had looked unappalled on scenes of human and elemental strife, and had been unmoved by any appeals to reason or to conscience before, was bowed and subdued. Eyes that seldom wept, poured out their tears like rain, and hearts that were like the adamant were melted beneath the Spirit's power. Lips that had curled with scorn at the name of Jesus, uttered cries for mercy or lisped the praises of redeeming love. Many who came from mere curiosity, or to show, as they expressed it, that strong men could not be influenced by such things, were crushed in the dust and made to cry for mercy. Little children were the subjects of this work. In one instance, some children spent the whole night in prayer, a young man, without their knowledge, being stationed near to guard them against danger.

From the accounts as given above, it is evident that the work of divine grace was accompanied by remarkable and unusual circumstances. The body was affected as well as the mind. These affections were different in different individuals. Sometimes the body was affected with feebleness and languor, so that the person seemed to faint away. Sometimes there were apparent convulsions, or as the people then termed it, "jerks," or spasmodical contortions of the muscles. In some, the body became quite powerless and without motion for a length of time; the breathing became very weak, animation was almost suspended, and the pulse almost still. But no pain was experienced, nor did any injurious consequences follow to the most delicate constitutions. Yet all this time there was an entire consciousness of all that was passing. The mind was not in a comatose state, although the body seemed often slumbering. "It is no unusual thing," says Dr. McMillan, " to see persons so entirely deprived of bodily strength that they will fall from their seats, or off their feet, and be as unable to help themselves as a new-born child."[1] "There was," says Dr. Anderson, "in some cases gradually, and in others instantly, a total loss of bodily strength, so that they fell to the ground, like Saul of Tarsus — and with oppression of the heart and lungs, with suspension of breath, with sobs and loud cries."[2]

This wondrous affection of the bodily powers was not confined to the place of religious worship : it came upon men in the wood, in the fields, in the workshop, at home, and in bed. It was altogether involuntary, and in spite of every effort of the will to prevent it. The strong and the weak, both in body and mind, were equally its subjects. Sometimes it came upon those who were professing Christians and who had given undoubted evidences of piety. On the other hand, many who were its subjects, received no spiritual benefit, but went on careless as ever.

These affections seem generally, though not always, to have followed some mental exercises, or anxiety and concern about the soul's salvation. In some instances, however, they followed where there was a determination to avoid any outward exhibition of feeling and interest in the great concern. Yet as the hearers lay apparently unconscious of all that was passing around them, their minds were active. They could hear and reason, and feel even more intensely than under ordinary circumstances.

Rev. Robert Johnston (14), whilst pastor of the congregation of Scrubgrass, in Venango County, Pa., relates

[1] *Western Miss. Mag.* ii. 354.   [2] *Ibid.* 464.

many of the circumstances connected with this work in his own congregation. On a certain occasion, after the benediction had been pronounced at the close of the Sabbath evening service, a remarkable state of feeling presented itself. The circumstances are related in his manuscript autobiography: "While a solemn awe was visible in every face, five or six appeared to be awakened to a sense of their undone condition, among whom were two of the most unlikely persons in the house. One of them was the largest man in the assembly, and full of self-importance; the other a file-leader in the devil's camp, who attempted to escape by flight, got entangled in the bushes, and was forced to come back for a light to find his path, and who, the moment he set his foot inside the door, fell prostrate on the floor, under a sense of self-condemnation." As a result of this revival one half of the adult persons in the congregation were brought into the church.

In a letter to Rev. Dr. Elliott of the Western Theological Seminary, Mr. Johnston relates more minutely the circumstances connected with this "Bodily Exercise," as it was then called:[1] "The effects of this work on the body were truly wonderful, and so various that no physical cause could be assigned for their production. I have seen men and women sitting in solemn attitude, pondering the solemn truths that were presented, and in a moment fall from their seats, or off their feet, if they happened to be standing, as helpless as though they had been shot, and lie from ten or fifteen or twenty minutes, and sometimes as long as half an hour, as motionless as a person in a sound sleep. At other times, the whole frame would be thrown into a state of agitation so violent as seemingly to endan-

[1] *Life of McCurdy*, p. 82.

ger the safety of the subject; and yet in a moment this agitation would cease, and the persons arise in the possession of all their bodily powers, and take their seats composed and solemn, without the least sensation of pain or uneasiness. . . . Another fact that I ascertained beyond doubt, was, that those who lay for a considerable length of time, apparently insensible, and sometimes without one discernible symptom of life, except the natural warmth and color of the skin, could hear, understand, and reflect on what they heard as well as, or better than, when in possession of all their natural powers. Nor was there that kind of uniformity in the occurrence of their different effects on the body as to allow them to be ascribed to corresponding exercises of the mind. Some have been agitated in body, under pleasing exercises of mind, and others have lain motionless under the anguish of a wounded spirit. Some were under deep and pungent conviction for weeks before they felt any effect on the body; whilst some passed through the whole course of awakening and conviction, and became hopefully pious, who never felt any symptoms of bodily agitation. Of the former class, was a very intelligent young man, now a minister of the gospel, who told me that he had more pungent distress of mind before than after he became affected in body. From these, and many more similar facts that occurred under my own observation, I became satisfied that no natural cause could be assigned, sufficient to account for the extraordinary effects on the bodies of a large majority of the subjects of the revival."

"The physical effects of the excitement on the body, was by no means a desirable appendage, in the view of the sensible part of the community, but they were evidently irresistible, and persons were as liable to be affected in the very act of resisting, as in any other circumstances; and many who came to mock and oppose remained to pray, and returned, inquiring what they must do to be saved."

This state of feeling and action was not encouraged by the ministers. It was something they could not understand, and they took circumstances as they found them. Mr. Johnston states that at the beginning of the revival in his congregation, he cautioned his people against any outcries, or bursts of feeling. This seemed to have had a good effect, for although the work was very powerful, yet this bodily exercise was no interruption to the exercises. "I have preached," says he, "to a crowded assembly, when more than one half of the people were lying helpless before me during the greater portion of divine service, without the least noise or disturbance of any kind, to divert or interrupt the attention of any individual from the word spoken."

The character of the preaching at these times was plain and practical. The terrors of the law were often set forth with peculiar pungency. Says Mr. Munson, in speaking of Mr. Hughes' preaching at Mount Pleasant during one of these revivals: "He took the ground that Boston and Rutherford and Edwards had done, to cut them off stroke by stroke from the Old Covenant. He thought the case of these anxious sinners required the exhibition of the requirements and threatenings of the law. This method was calculated to increase the distress which was already insupportable." Afterwards his thoughts took a different channel. "These distressed souls were directed to the Cross; Christ was held forth in his ability, willingness, and sufficiency; as suited in all his offices to relieve the distressed souls before Him of their heavy burdens. The new course had the desired effect; a favorable change was soon apparent, so that that was the beginning of days to a goodly number."

The character of the preaching was largely doctrinal. Man's total depravity and corruption was largely dwelt upon. The awful penalty of the law was set forth, at times, with dreadful severity and terror; the utter helplessness of the sinner without the assistance of divine grace was insisted upon; and then the blessings of the Atonement of Christ were spread before the convicted sinner as his only hope and peace.

During the first years of the history of the Presbytery this grand and wonderful work of God spread over its bounds, and extended with greater or less power to almost every pastoral charge. It was a baptism of the early days of the Presbytery that was a prophecy of great and glorious things for days to come. And whilst there were peculiarities connected with it that have not been seen in modern times, yet there can be no doubt that it was a genuine work of God. Its results show this. Its subjects dwelt in the church as sincere Christians. They died in peace and now stand before the Throne.

CHAPTER III.

FROM THE FIRST TO THE SECOND DIVISION OF PRESBYTERY.

1808–1820.

THE first meeting of the Presbytery, after the erection of the Presbytery of Hartford, was at Concord, in Butler County, Pa., on the 18th day of April, 1809. The number of its members was much reduced, and its territory greatly curtailed. But there were men of energy and zeal and courage yet left, and there was territory left more than sufficient to occupy all their time and attention. The roll at this time contained the names of Samuel Tait, settled at Cool Spring and Mercer; Joseph Stockton, settled at Meadville and Little Sugar Creek, or Cochranton; Robert Lee, who was without a pastoral charge; John Boyd, settled at Union and Slate Lick, Armstrong County, Pa.; Abraham Boyd, settled at Bull Creek and Middlesex; William Wood, settled at Plaingrove, Mercer County, Pa.; Alexander Cook, settled at Slippery Rock and New Castle; Robert Patterson, who was without charge, and not residing within the bounds of Presbytery; Robert Johnston, settled at Scrubgrass, in Venango County, Pa.; Cyrus Riggs, settled at Fairfield and Mill Creek, in Mercer and Venango Counties; Reid Bracken, settled at Mount Nebo and Plain, in Butler County, Pa., and John

McPherrin, settled in Concord and Harmony, also in Butler County, Pa.

At the following meeting of Synod they reported the following vacant congregations, as "able to support a pastor : West Unity and Amity, Gravel Run and Waterford. Vacant congregations, not able to support a pastor : Erie, Upper and Lower Greenfield, Oil Creek, Brokenstraw, Conewango, Middlebrook, Franklin, and Unity."

The territory with which they had parted was about as great as that which they retained. But its boundaries were now more definitely determined. Heretofore the western boundary had been rather mythical than real, extending as far as civilization had advanced, and consequently rather migratory than permanent. It was deprived also of its Indian missionary ground, although, as will be seen, its interest in Indian missions did not abate in the least.

At this time the accommodations for religious worship began to improve. The "tent," as the little covered platform on which the ministers stood was called, was used only on sacramental occasions, or in times of great religious interest. Comfortable log-houses with glazed windows had been erected in almost all the congregations. In some of the congregations, sacramental services were held in barns, and with great comfort and satisfaction. There was at this time an occasional frame barn throughout the settlements. Before harvest these could be comfortably occupied. The barn was carefully swept out. Seats of rough wood were arranged in the threshing-floor and in the haymows, and sometimes in the stables, with a long tier out in front of the open doors. A platform in the further end of the threshing-floor served for a pulpit.

But it is doubtful whether this worship in barns and mills was any improvement on that of the forest. In summer, with pleasant weather, and a delightful site, under the great trees, and the sweet breath of God all around in its purity, the worship was most delightful and inspiring.

> "The groves were God's first temples. Ere man learned
> To hew the shaft and lay the architrave,
> And spread the roof above them, — ere he framed
> The lofty vault, to gather and roll back
> The sound of anthems, — in the darkling wood,
> Amidst the cool and silence, he knelt down
> And offered to the Mightiest, solemn thanks
> And supplication."

There was a freedom too about those forest sanctuaries that was most inviting to the earlier settlers. It suited their ideas of propriety to come together on common ground, where every one was alike at home, and where the accommodations were unlimited, save by the extent of the forest. Many scenes of melting interest were witnessed at such times and under such circumstances.

A single picture of this forest worship will convey some idea of the early worship of the fathers. It is in the month of June. It has been announced far and near that a stranger from the old settlements is to preach on the following Sabbath in the woods near the Big Spring. A great congregation has assembled; and it is a motley assemblage. Every variety of costume and habit and expression of countenance is there. One is habited in a suit brought from his early home, but since unused, save on special occasions like the present. The texture is still good, but the changing fashions have left it far in the background. Another, perhaps, has a single garment of this kind, whilst the remainder of his costume is manufactured in the wilderness. Still another has a costume that is nondescript in its character. His hunting-shirt is of deerskin, whilst his lower extremities are cased in garments of the same material, shrunk by the weather, until they completely adapt themselves to the form they were designed to protect.

The wives and daughters of the settlers are in as good trim in their outward adornment as circumstances would permit; where a bonnet was wanting a cotton handkerchief supplies the deficiency; where shoes were wanting, they manifest their sense of propriety by coming without these appendages of modern refinement.

It is an imposing place, too. The tall trees have stood there for centuries, witnesses of the power and wisdom of the God of creation; and now in the midst of their deep solitude, the love of the God of Redemption is to be set forth.

The preacher appears and takes his stand under the shadow of a venerable elm. He is a mere youth, and bears a cast of care. He is thin and sallow, almost cadaverous, yet with an eye full of the fire of thought. As he proceeds with his subject, his form becomes erect, and his ideas flow forth in a torrent of burning eloquence. He sways that untutored multitude as the passing breeze sways the unreaped grain. Many a brown cheek is moist with tears; many a heart hard as the adamant, is melted beneath the burning power of truth.

When he commenced, the congregation were seated upon fallen logs, leaning against the trees, or carelessly lounging upon the ground. But as he proceeds and warms with the subject, and the truth begins to fall upon their consciences, they gradually draw nearer until all are standing around the speaker. Every eye is riveted upon him; they hang upon his lips. Upon those upturned countenances are plainly visible the deep emotions that are struggling within. "Is not my word like as a fire? saith the Lord ; and like a hammer that breaketh the rock in pieces ?"

In some of the churches at that day, in the summer time, it was not unusual for some thoughtful man to carry a brand of fire from his home, and apply it to a dry stump in the neighborhood of the church. To this fire the men would resort for the purpose of a quiet smoke. Occasionally, even during the sermon, a staid deacon would quietly withdraw, light his pipe, smoke to his satisfaction, and return, perhaps even before the minister had taken up a new head of discourse.

On the 14th of June, 1809, Mr. Cook (12) was released from the charge of Slippery Rock and New Castle, and on the 6th of March following was dismissed to the Presbytery of Hartford, and soon after went on his missionary tour to South Carolina and Georgia.

April 17, 1810, John Boyd was released from the pastoral charge of Slate Lick, Armstrong County, Pa., when he began to labor as a stated supply at Amity and West Unity. On the 27th of June, 1810, Mr. Stockton was released from the charge of Meadville and Little Sugar Creek, and dismissed to the Presbytery of Redstone.

On the 4th of October, 1810, Mr. John Boyd (8), having relinquished his position as stated supply at Amity and West Unity, on account of ill health, was dismissed to the Presbytery of New Lancaster, now Zanesville.

On the 26th of June, 1810, John Matthews (22), a licentiate of the Presbytery of Ohio, was received under the care of Presbytery, and on the 17th of October following, he was ordained and installed as pastor of the churches of Waterford and Gravel Run.

Discouraging circumstances had arisen in Scrubgrass, as they frequently do after great revivals, and Mr. Johnston was constrained to sunder his connection with a people he loved. His field there had been, as it has been since, a remarkable one. Old John Lowrie, his principal elder, had been a host in himself, in the church. His family have been remarkable since in the influence they have exerted on Presbyterianism. Walter Lowrie, his son, was at one time a candidate for the ministry under the care of the Presbytery of Erie, but has since, as the Secretary of the Presbyterian Board of Foreign Missions, been, perhaps, of more service to the church than though he had been in the ministry. Three sons of Walter Lowrie, John C., Walter M., and Reuben P., have been foreign missionaries. Another son of John Lowrie, Matthew B., was long a valuable elder in the church. A son of Matthew B., Hon. Walter H. Lowrie, is also an elder, and another son, the late Rev. John M. Lowrie, D. D., was a prominent man in the church. Judge Lowrie has also a son in the ministry. A daughter and two grandchildren of John Lowrie are missionaries to the Indians in the Northwest, and a grandson, Rev. W. L. Lyons, is a member of the Presbytery of Iowa.

On the 2d day of January, 1811, Mr. Johnston (14) was released from the pastoral charge of the church of Scrubgrass, and calls placed in his hands from the congregations of Meadville, Sugar Creek (Cochranton), and Conneaut Lake (Evansburgh), with an injunction to these congregations. " To augment their stipulated salary for the whole of Mr. Johnston's time, to at least four hundred dollars for the whole of his time."

At this meeting "The Presbytery, taking into view the gloomy and shattered state of the churches under their care, appointed the first Thursday of February next, to be observed as a day of fasting, humiliation, and prayer to Almighty God, that He would remove the clouds of separation between Him and us."

April 9, 1812, Mr. Riggs (18) was dismissed from the pastoral charge of the congregation of Fairfield, and commenced his labors, soon after, in the congregations of Scrubgrass and West Unity. In this latter charge, he found many of the prejudices of the times in his way. But he was a quiet, unpretending man, and yet had his own ideas of propriety; and in addition to this, had the faculty of carrying out his own plans, in spite of the prejudices of the times and the unreasonableness of many of his people. His strategy was simple and yet effective. It was to approach new subjects gradually, and undermine foolish prejudices by degrees, until his object was accomplished. His people were not probably more unenlightened than others at that day, and their operations may be taken as a specimen of the spirit of the times.

One of their peculiar notions was that fire was not necessary in the church edifice, even in the coldest weather. When he went to Scrubgrass, the people were in the habit of coming to church from distances of from one to seven miles. They would then hitch their horses, and sit in the cold church during the two hours of divine service, and return home, without seeing fire. When they erected a new house of worship, Mr. Riggs proposed putting in it two ten-plate stoves, in order that the people might worship with comfort. This prop-position met with a most strenuous opposition. They argued that their fathers had never had fire in the church, and they were no better than their fathers. Moreover they said, the house would be so warm they could not occupy it. The spirit of improvement prevailed, however, and the stoves were placed in the new church; yet it was observed that an old father, who could not be convinced against his will, gave up a pew he had occupied near the pulpit, and took one near the door, with a window at the back of it, which he regularly opened a little lest he should be suffocated.

Churches were not generally heated in any way, in these times, even during the long winters that characterized the country. Occasionally an old foot-stove that had done service in New England was found in some household, and was filled with coals and embers and carried to church. Yet even this was considered effeminate, and none but the aged would condescend to use them. Nor were the services abridged on account of the cold. There was the regular routine — two services, and the intervening recess, during which the people eat their biscuits, and shook hands with the minister. Nor were the people warmly clad in those days. Overcoats were rare, and overshoes almost wholly unknown. During the service there was often an audible sound of shuffling feet, that was produced in the attempt to quicken the circulation and so restore warmth to the system. But this was never excepted to on the part of the minister. It was justified by circumstances.

About this time an improvement was introduced in the Church of Fairview, a portion of Mr. Eaton's charge, The little log church, which overlooked Lake Erie, was exposed to the bleak winds that sometimes raged with great fury; and the idea was suggested that as the people had fire in their cabins at home, a little would improve the temperature of the meeting-house. But there was neither fire-place nor chimney. So a large iron kettle, that had been used in boiling sugar, was set in the middle of the floor, half filled with charcoal, and the mass ignited. This moderated the cold somewhat; yet the ladies would sometimes approach the kettle so near as to inhale the carbonic acid gas that arose from the coal, faint away, and be carried out into the open air to revive. Subsequently a large ten-plate stove, that had been brought from Eastern Pennsylvania by some enterprizing settler, was obtained, and added greatly to the comfort and satisfaction of the worshippers.

In the spring of 1812, Rev. John McPherrin (16) was invited to preach in Erie County, and remained some six months, preaching in North East and Middlebrook. The journal of William Dickson, already quoted, mentions an incident of interest.

"In the spring of 1812, Rev. John McPherrin accepted a call from North East and Middlebrook congregations, and came and preached six months. As war was declared that year, and we were on the frontier, he declined staying with us, and returned to his former charge in Butler County. While he was with us, we had an election for elders, and he was not pleased with the choice, as politics had something to do with it. Two men were elected who were never known to pray in their families, and the time was appointed for their ordination ; but they had first to pass an examination that was like a refiner's fire, and he declared from the pulpit that they were not qualified for members of any church, and he would never ordain such men ; if we must have elders, we must elect praying men. One of these men repented, and became an elder; the other like Judas, went to his own place."

At the meeting of Presbytery on the 9th of April 1812, the attention of Presbytery was called to missionary ground, near Pittsburgh, now the site of Alleghany City. The minute is in these words: "An indigent and needy neighborhood, situated on the Alleghany, opposite to Pittsburgh, having applied to Rev. Messrs. Herron and Hunt of the Presbytery of Redstone, for supplies of preaching from them and the Rev. Robert Patterson, of Erie, as frequently as convenient; it was deemed proper by them to lay the case for consideration before the Presbytery of Erie. On motion, *Resolved*, That they, with discretion, attend to this application."

At the same meeting a resolution was offered, but afterwards negatived, looking to the continuance of the practice of publishing the bans of matrimony in the congregation on the Sabbath. This practice had been of long standing. The custom had been to set forth the intentions of matrimony in something like the following words: "There is a purpose of marriage between John Smith and Hannah Brown of this congregation; whereof this is the first publication." The next Sabbath it would be the second publication, and the following the third; when it would be proper to celebrate the marriage. The publication was read by the clerk, as he was called, or the leader of the singing, as he stood in front of the pulpit, and was done with as much gravity and unction and sing-song tone as he would line out the psalm preparatory to singing. Sometimes there would be a disposition to smile on the part of the younger portion of the congregation, at the first publication of the bans, but usually it was received with gravity and decorum such as were fitting to the worship of the Sabbath.

At the date referred to, the Presbytery did not feel like insisting on the observance of the old rule. Against this laxity, Mr. McPherrin enters his solemn protest, giving four reasons as grounds of his protest. The protest is spread upon the minutes.[1]

At the meeting of the Synod, the year previous, the same question had come up, when it was decided, first, "That the Synod do not approve of their members celebrating marriage, without publishing the purpose of marriage, or license." And secondly, that it is not a breach of the Sabbath to publish a purpose of marriage on that sacred day.[2]

At the meeting of Synod in 1811, Robert McGarraugh (23), with his congregations, New Rehoboth and Licking, was detached from the Presbytery of Redstone, and annexed to that of Erie. The territory so annexed was determined by the boundary line between the two Presbyteries, thus defined by Synod: "*Ordered*, that the Redbank Creek from the mouth up the southern branch to the boundary line of the Synod, shall hereafter be the line of division between the Presbyteries of Erie and Redstone."[3]

Mr. McGarraugh was a laborious minister, and suffered a full share of the privations and difficulties incident to the new settlements. He was a plain, humble man, intent only on the great work of preaching the gospel and leading souls to Christ. His field once embraced the whole of what is now Clarion Presbytery. A few sermons had perhaps been preached in that region before his arrival, yet he was the first minister that came permanently into the field. He did not content himself with preaching in his own particular charge, but extended his labors in all directions, wherever there

---

[1] Vol. ii. 10.   [2] Min. of Synod, 1811.   [3] *Ibid.*

were people to hear, or needy souls to be sought out. During one year of his labors, he visited every family, without regard to denomination, in the whole of what is now the Presbytery of Clarion. Without being a fluent preacher, he was an earnest worker, and probably no person in all his region of country doubted either his sincerity or his piety. He was the only Presbyterian minister in all this region up to the year 1824, when John Core came into the bounds.

Mr. McGarraugh was pastor of the churches of New Rehoboth and Licking from 1807 to 1822, when he resigned his charge, but continued to labor in the congregations of Concord and Calensburgh, up to the time of his death in 1839. A detailed record of his labors, and the struggles of himself and family during the early years of his ministry, would seem more like romance than reality. Yet his experience, probably, did not differ much from that of our early ministers generally during the first quarter of a century of the history of the Presbytery.

In June, 1812, Mr. Wood (10) became pastor for the whole of his time over the congregation of Plaingrove. At the meeting of Synod in October of this year, the congregation of Hilands was detached from the Presbytery of Erie, and annexed to that of Redstone. At the same time a remarkable action was had by the Synod, defining the boundaries of this congregation: "That the first point be at the Alleghany River, opposite the mouth of Puckety Creek; thence westerly until it intersects the Franklin road twelve miles from Pittsburgh; thence southwest, until it strikes the Ohio River, eight miles from Pittsburgh; and thence up the river to the town of Pittsburgh."[1]

[1] Minutes of Synod, 1812.

At the same meeting of Synod, Johnston Eaton (20), with his pastoral charge, Fairview and Springfield, on the shore of Lake Erie, was detached from the Presbytery of Hartford, and annexed to the Presbytery of Erie. This was an extensive charge. It extended from the Ohio State line to that of New York. Sometimes he supplied at Erie, and sometimes at Lower Greenfield or North East. He had begun the work in 1805. In 1807 he moved with all his worldly effects from Fayette County, Pa., on horseback. There was no road for wagons, and all the fixtures for housekeeping and domestic comfort must be "packed," as it was then termed, or lashed on the backs of horses, and these horses led single file, one being tied behind another. A portion of the furniture was manufactured by the minister himself; a small table was constructed out of a walnut log, by laboriously hewing down split puncheons, until they were of the proper thickness. For the children's comfort the minister made shoes with his own hand, and his wife braided hats from the bark of the leatherwood that grew plentifully in the forest. They manufactured coffee from rye; and good Mr. Blair furnished all the sugar that was wanted, made from the trees that grew on his broad acres. Sometimes the bread was made from "sick wheat,"[1] and caused a terrible agitation of the stomach, but venison and bear-meat and fish were plenty, and the little family lived in comparative comfort. During the absence of the minister on his preaching tours, the log-cabin parsonage was lonely and often visited by Indians, but a neighbor was usually at hand for company and protection. Twice during these years, Mr. Eaton was a Commissioner to the General Assembly at Philadelphia,

---

[1] A peculiar disease that affected the wheat in that day.

and on both occasions performed the journey to and from on horseback. The road led by the way of Pittsburgh, and required about two weeks to complete the journey each way.

April 7, 1813, Mr. McPherrin was installed as pastor of the congregation of Butler. On the same day, Mr. Lee (5) was dismissed to the Presbytery of Redstone. In June, 1813, an arrangement was made by which Mr. Tait (3) became pastor once more at Salem, the people of Cool Spring agreeing to worship at Mercer. Salem had been a portion of Mr. Tait's original charge in 1801. Joseph Stockton (4) had preached the first sermon to this congregation in 1799; it was on the banks of the Shenango, about half a mile from where Greenville now stands. He was a candidate at the time Mr. Tait was elected pastor. In this congregation a singular question arose in regard to the ruling eldership. Amongst the elders elected was William Beatty, who was a bachelor. The mothers in Israel doubted the propriety of ordaining such a man. The question was warmly debated at several "frolics" in the neighborhood, and the conclusion arrived at was, that an elder "should be the husband of one wife, and rule his household well." The difficulty was mentioned to Mr. Tait, who at first humored the joke, as he considered it, but finding the matter growing serious, it required quite an effort on his part to remove their doubts; and they only yielded their opinion in deference to that of their minister. Mr. Beatty was ordained and installed into office, and thenceforward scrupulously devoted one tenth of his income to religious purposes.

In the year 1813, during the war with Great Britain, Johnston Eaton was appointed chaplain by the government. His people were generally in the army, as was the case throughout the Presbytery, and his feelings and sense of duty induced him to desire to go with them. Joseph Badger and Benjamin Boyd, former members of the Presbytery, were also in this service under the government.

During a portion of this war, the congregations along the Lake Shore were in great fear and often terror. After Hull's surrender, it was reported that a British fleet was coming down the Lake, and a body of British and Indians by land at the same time. On one occasion the land forces were reported as coming, when heroic John Sturgeon commenced casting bullets, declaring he would "Make them stand off, or he would send the lead at them." The British and Indians did not come. On another occasion the fleet was reported landing, when an old gentleman, with commendable zeal, but doubtful judgment, set off on foot at full speed for the shore, taking off his old hat and filling it with stones as he ran, with the avowed intention of sinking the fleet. The fleet proved to be a single boat with a few fishermen in it, from the neighborhood.

During the war there was a circumstance that should be recorded to illustrate the general religious influence that prevailed in at least some portions of the Presbytery. In Mercer County a company was raised to go to Erie, for the defense of the border. This company was under the command of Captain Joseph Junkin.[1] During the entire campaign, family worship was kept up daily, in every tent but two, by their respective inmates, and in these two, it was kept up by the officers volunteering to attend to the duty for those who occupied them.

In October, 1813, Ira Condit (24), a licentiate of the

[1] Brother of Rev. Drs. George and David X. Junkin.

Presbytery of Ohio, was received under the care of Presbytery, and on the 8th of November following, was ordained and installed as pastor of the congregations of Fairfield and Big Sugar Creek.

On the 20th of October, 1813, John Redick (26) was licensed to preach the gospel. On the same day it was urged upon all the churches, notwithstanding their poverty, to contribute to the fund for educating young men for the gospel ministry.

On the 6th of April, 1814, Mr. Riggs was installed at Scrubgrass. At the meeting of Presbytery, September 29, 1814, there was a movement that reveals the incipient dawn of a great moral enterprise. It contains the prophecy of the temperance reformation. Its voice now seems faint and feeble; yet it was the bud wrapped up in its cerements, out of which grew the great work in which Presbytery, in later days, has taken such an active part. The minute and resolution are couched in the following words: —

"The Presbytery, taking into view the pernicious effects of ardent spirits on the peace and good morals of society, and the necessity of testifying, by example as well as precept, against the common and excessive use of them at public meetings and social visits: *Resolved*, To make no use of them at their various ecclesiastical meetings."[1]

Mr. Eaton was released from the pastoral charge at Springfield, and Mr. Matthews from Gravel Run, in November of this year. In June, 1815, Amos Chase (25) was received from the South Consociation of Litchfield. He at once engaged in missionary work, and was for many years an untiring laborer in what has since become the great oil-field of Pennsylvania, trav-

---

[1] Min. ii. 41.

elling from neighborhood to neighborhood, and from house to house, bearing the great message. At this meeting Mr. Eaton was permitted to supply the churches of Erie and North East. At this time the monthly concert of prayer for missions, was recommended to be observed on the first Monday evening of each month.

At the same time the question of "moral societies" was discussed, and the following minute passed : —

" Presbytery being informed by their commissioner to the General Assembly that moral associations have been formed in many parts of our church, and have been successful in checking immorality, and that the assembly at their late sessions have earnestly recommended the formation of such societies, deem it their duty to make known to the churches under their care the wish of the Assembly on this subject, confidently believing that they will cheerfully give their united aid in endeavoring to suppress Sabbath-breaking, drunkenness, profane swearing, gambling, and all immoralities, within their bounds." [1]

At this meeting a complaint was brought against one of the pastors, for having violated a fast day, by going on that day to purchase whiskey. The investigation showed that the alleged offense was committed on a Thursday that had been set apart previous to the Lord's Supper. The offense, as urged, consisted solely in performing a secular work on a fast day, and not in the quality of the work itself. The Presbytery unanimously agreed that the delinquent pastor should be admonished by the moderator.

On the 28th of September, 1815, John Redick was ordained and installed as pastor of the congregations of

[1] Min. ii. 51.

Slate Lick and Union. April 2, 1816, Timothy Alden (27) was received from the Presbytery of Jersey. At the same meeting a committee was appointed to draw up a petition to the Legislature in behalf of "Common English Schools."

June 26, 1816, the congregation of Erie requested one third of the ministerial labors of Mr. Eaton. The request was granted.

In September, 1816, the following resolution was adopted:—

"Whereas, vice and immorality abound to the destruction of the souls of men, and of the peace and happiness of the church; therefore, the Presbytery resolve to bear a more public, decided, and unanimous testimony against vice in general, and particularly against the sins of drunkenness, Sabbath-breaking, swearing, gambling, dancing, etc., than formerly, and enjoin it on the ministers and sessions under their care to pay special attention to this resolution."[1]

The pastoral relation between William Wood and the congregation of Plaingrove was dissolved October 7, 1816, and on the 1st of April, 1817, he was dismissed to the Presbytery of Hartford.

On the 2d of April, 1817, the pastoral relation between Mr. Matthews and the congregation of Waterford was dissolved. On the same day the pastoral relation existing between Mr. Johnston and the congregations of Meadville, Little Sugar Creek (Cochranton), and Conneaut Lake (Evansburg), was also dissolved. The congregation of Meadville then requested that Mr. Alden might be appointed as a stated supply; but as there were arrearages still due Mr. Johnston, from a part of the charge, Presbytery declined the request.

[1] Min. ii. 65.

This was the source of serious difficulty in these congregations. They felt that they were treated unjustly, and the result was that the church of Little Sugar Creek eventually withdrew from the Presbytery, and connected with the Presbytery of the Associate Reformed Church.

On the 24th of June, 1817, John Munson (28), a licentiate of the Presbytery of Hartford, was received under the care of Presbytery. He was a native of New Jersey, a man of uncouth exterior, but of a genuine earnest nature, with a heart to work, and a physical constitution that peculiarly adapted him to the wants of the times. For a time he labored as a missionary. He would take his horse and set out on a tour of two hundred miles, seeking his way at times through cow-paths, over lofty hills, swimming rivers, fording streams, sleeping on the floors of log-cabins, eating corn-bread and bear meat, and all this that he might preach the gospel to the scattered settlements that were on the verge of the great forest. For a time the Upper Alleghany, and from that to Lake Erie, was his favorite resort. He would find the people, gather them together on Sabbath and on week-days, and preach the gospel to them. Sometimes his congregations were numbered by hundreds, and sometimes by half dozens. It mattered not; one soul was precious, and a small company had the same promise of the Master's presence as a large one. His early habits of labor and toil in assisting in the support of the home family, and his custom of self-dependence in the great struggle with the world, from boyhood up, were of great use to him in the labors of the Lord's vineyard. And these early missionary labors fitted him for entering upon pastoral work, upon which he entered a year or two later.

The question of psalmody is an interesting one in

this connection. The minutes of Presbytery throw no light upon it. They are silent in regard to the ancient practice of the churches, and the gradual transition from the old version of the Psalms of David, to the imitations of the Psalms and the Hymns of Dr. Watts, and thence to the more improved hymnology of the modern church. That these changes took place without any jarring or discord or contention, we can hardly suppose. Human nature is by far too stern and rugged in its constitution to undergo such changes without conflict, even though they be connected with the worship of God and the spiritual enjoyment of the heart. And so the traditions that have come down to us from the fathers and mothers that have fallen asleep, and the recollections of fathers and mothers who yet linger amongst us, assure us of the troubles and contests that were connected with this subject.

The records of the old Synod give us an idea of the feelings of the fathers in this matter. As far back as 1765, we find this action passed by the Synod: —

"After some consideration of the query concerning the use of Dr. Watts' imitation of the Psalms, the Synod judged it best, in present circumstances, only to declare that they look on the inspired Psalms of Scripture to be proper matter to be sung in divine worship, according to their original design and the practice of Christian churches, yet will not forbid those to use the imitation of them whose judgment and inclination leads them to do so."

Twenty-two years later, 1787, the liberal feeling had greatly increased. "The Synod did allow, and hereby do allow, that Dr. Watts' imitation of David's Psalms, as revised by Mr. Barlow, be sung in the churches and families under their care." At the same meeting they advised care and caution in regard to the troubles that this subject had gathered around it. Charity and forbearance and mutual conciliation, were earnestly enjoined upon the people and upon the ministers, so that no undue burdens might be laid upon either.

In regard to the practice of the early fathers of the Presbytery of Erie, we have sufficient light to induce us to believe that from the very first they were in favor of a New Testament psalmody. But they were in advance of the people generally. As a general thing, they used Watts' Psalms and Hymns, in family worship at home and in social worship, where it would not greatly offend the prejudices of the people. But on the Sabbath day, and in public worship, the old version of Rouse was generally used. There were exceptions, however, in regard to some of the old ministers. It was long before they could give up the idea of an "Inspired Psalmody," in public worship. It is related of good old Samuel Porter, of the Presbytery of Redstone, that being at a prayer meeting, where the people were singing with great animation —

> "Let them refuse to sing
> Who never knew our God;
> But children of the Heavenly King
> May speak their joys abroad;"

he was greatly troubled, and distressed even, for he had not felt at liberty to sing words of human composure; yet after hearing these lines, he joined in, saying to himself, as he afterwards remarked, — "If my conscience won't let me sing, I'll wring its neck."

But there were almost intolerable prejudices in the minds of many of the people against the use of anything but Rouse. Some who did not appear to have much conscience in regard to other things of greater importance, were here immovable. They could not sing words of "human composition" in the Lord's worship. They were wedded to the rough, jagged lines of Rouse, and could as readily be diverted from them as from the Holy Book itself. And the Synod acted reasonably and well in the matter, to urge charity, tenderness, and forbearance toward the people. These old psalms had been hallowed in their minds as being connected with the blessed memories of early years, as associated with the family altar, as having been sung by lips voiceless now upon earth, but tuneful on the heights of Mount Zion.

But it is evident that the early fathers generally were anxious for a fuller liberty in the praises of the Lord. They felt limited and constrained, and longed for a service of song that would be adapted to all times and circumstances. From introducing the use of Watts at home and in pastoral visitations, they gradually began to sing an occasional psalm or hymn from Watts in the social prayer-meeting, just as the feelings and prejudices of the people rendered it proper or expedient. This could very readily be done, as the use of books was not then a necessity in worship. The psalm or hymn was invariably "lined out" by the clerk. Sometimes one line at a time, and sometimes two, according to custom. One book in the congregation, then, would suffice for all. After the people became accustomed to the sound of Watts, and their prejudices began to soften, the pastor would occasionally introduce a hymn during the service of the Sabbath; and thus the transition was passed, until in the course of years the use of hymns became the rule instead of the exception.

But this change was not accomplished without a struggle. Men's feelings, passions, prejudices were sometimes all in the way. Sometimes the sound of a hymn, or even the sight of a hymn-book, would overcome all devotional feeling and all desire for worship, and induce a speedy departure from the house of God.

There was a large admixture of Scotch-Irish element in all the churches there, and although eminently conservative and Presbyterian, yet they remembered the green banks of Ireland, and the gay heather of Scotland, and albeit they had sung paraphrases as well as psalms in the fatherland, yet they still looked upon these as having a kind of inspiration. Hymns had a doubtful look and a doubtful rhythm about them, and they could not at once fall in with them. Besides, they inherited something of the spirit of the Covenanters of old, and resolved to "contend earnestly for the faith once delivered to the saints." And so, sometimes, rather than give up what they considered the right of conscience, they preferred to leave the old church of their fathers, and find a home where old psalms were the rule.

When Mr. Riggs took charge of Scrubgrass and Unity churches, they used Rouse's version of the psalms exclusively in divine service. This continued for some time, when the pastor, having scruples against this exclusive use, began to labor in private to prepare the people for a change. He used the version of Watts, together with his hymns, in social meetings, and occasionally sung one before divine service. When he thought the people were ripe for the change, a vote was taken at Unity Church, when it was directed that one of Rouse's psalms should be sung at the opening of the morning service, and Watts' the remainder of the time. This vote was passed with but three or four dissenting voices. Accordingly, on the next Sabbath, one of

Rouse's psalms was sung; and at the second singing one of Watts' psalms was announced, and the pastor commenced reading it, when a certain tall, broad-shouldered, brusque-looking man, with a rich Milesian accent to his voice, having looked in vain for the psalm in his own thin volume, and thinking perhaps that the speech of the psalm bewrayed it, arose from his seat, stepped into the aisle, and addressing the minister, cried out: " Quut that;" and receiving no attention from any source, proceeded up the aisle toward the pulpit, crying, "If you dunno quut that, I'll go up and pull ye doon by the neck."

One of the elders here interposed between the belligerent psalm-singer and the pulpit. Mr. Riggs spoke a few mild, soft words of rebuke, with a reference to the protecting power of the civil law; when the irate Milesian turned suddenly about, and striding rapidly out of the house returned no more. Henceforward the congregation had no further trouble on the score of psalmody. This was the last roar of the storm that seemed so threatening.

In other congregations there were difficulties of a similar kind. Some of the good fathers who had been nurtured upon the psalms, were disposed to consider anything else in the hour of worship as an innovation not to be tolerated for a moment. One such zealous worshipper was mortified and grieved at suddenly dropping a pocket Bible on the floor, under the belief that it was a "Methodissy Hymn-Book," as he had named Watts' Hymns. But these days passed away. Many, no doubt, left the Presbyterian Church and found a home in other branches of the church on account of psalmody, yet peace and harmony on this question at length prevailed.

The matter of music in churches was another source of trouble. Formerly the "Seven Sacred Tunes," as some facetious individuals expressed it, were used to the exclusion of all others. They were the grand old airs of Scotland, that had resounded over brake and burn in times of peace, and struggled faintly through crevice and cranny of dens and caves where God was worshipped in days of persecution. Nothing like lightness or undue rapidity was tolerated in church music. At first, nothing like a repetition of the words was supposed to be proper or decorous or lawful; yet in the course of years, the mellowing influence of time was felt in softening prejudices and in reconciling the people to new things. In the lapse of time, the style of the music used in church became greatly changed. It became even more complicated and involved than that used at the present day. Fugue tunes became very popular. A glance at the music books that were in use forty years ago, shows us that this style of music was very common. And yet with all their defects in harmony and arrangement, there was a richness and exuberance about that music that renders many of the tunes very attractive even at the present day. The music then was by the congregation. A clerk "raised the tune," as they called it, and the people followed after, until the house and the grove and the hill-side were flooded with the strains of melody that gushed forth in praise to God.

On the 25th of June, 1817, the pastoral relation existing between Mr. Abraham Boyd and the congregation of Middlesex was dissolved, on the ground of the inadequate support of the pastor. Measures were taken to organize a Missionary Society, agreeably to the recommendation of the General Assembly, and the matter of contributions to this purpose urged upon the churches. A day was set apart at the close of the June meeting, 1817, by the following action: "Presbytery, taking into view the prevalence of vice and immorality and the declining state of vital piety, together with the threatening aspect of Divine Providence with respect to the church in their bounds, appointed the first Monday of September next to be observed as a day of humiliation, fasting, and prayer."

Mr. Alden had never been settled as pastor in the bounds of Presbytery. His work was connected with Alleghany College at Meadville, Pa., of which he was President. This college was then under Presbyterian influence. But Mr. Alden had a love for missionary labor, and often took tours into the Indian Reservation lying along the Alleghany River, and within the bounds of the Presbytery. He had a great regard for the Indians, and loved to visit them, not only for the opportunity of preaching the gospel to them, but of studying their character in their native habits and customs. These Indians were remains of the once powerful and ferocious Six Nations; but were now known as the Senecas and Munsees. They led an indolent and inactive life, and were, from the circumstances of the case, exposed to all the vices, and very few of the virtues, of the white man.

For years Mr. Alden was in the habit of paying them a visit during the summer, as he could find time from his college engagements. At first, these excursions were undertaken on his own account and at his own charges. Afterwards they had the sanction of the Presbytery. At one time, on representations being made to the proper authorities, he received an appointment from the Society for Propagating the Gospel among the Indians.

These labors were not regular or protracted, but occupied what time could be spared from the duties of the college.

In these labors he came in contact with the famous Seneca chief Cornplanter, whose head-quarters were on the Alleghany River, in Warren County, Pa. In a letter dated November, 1816, he gives an account of an interview with this famous chief: —

"Last year, at a council of the tribe, Cornplanter made an eloquent speech of two hours' length, in which he gave a lucid history of his life. He stated that his father was a white man from Ireland, and that his mother was a Seneca; that he had always been attached to the tribe; that he had been zealous in their way of worship; but that now he was convinced they were all wrong; that he was determined to devote himself to the way in which the ministers walk — meaning the Christian religion. 'I know,' said he, 'that we are wrong; I know that they are right. Their way of worshipping the Great Spirit is good. I see it; I feel it; I enjoy it.'

"In this happy and persuasive manner did he, with his imperfect knowledge, plead the cause of Christ. In one part of his animated address, while speaking of his former views and habits, his language seemed to be like that of Paul, giving an account of his Pharisaic zeal in opposition to Christianity. In another part, it was like that of Joshua, stating his pious resolutions to the tribes of Israel at Shechem."[1]

This old chieftain, the last of a line of heroic braves, lived to the patriarchal age of one hundred and five years, and lies buried by the side of the Alleghany,

[1] Sprague's *Annals*.

whose waters he had been familiar with from his childhood.

On the 15th of February, 1818, Mr. Matthews was dismissed to the Presbytery of Missouri. The missionary spirit was largely developed in his nature; and as he looked out upon the inviting fields of the great West, he longed to explore them and do what he could in their evangelization.

In these days frequent inquiries were instituted as to the matter of collections for "the Theological Seminary." This was, of course, the seminary at Princeton, for no other was then established. Although these early fathers had not enjoyed the advantages of such an institution themselves, they felt its value, and desired that those who were preparing for the sacred office might have every facility in their preparation for the work.

It was also strictly enjoined on the churches to be careful in examining the credentials of travelling ministers, as they were called, passing through the Presbytery or tarrying within its bounds. A standing committee of Presbytery was appointed, to whom all strange ministers were referred for examination; and until approved by them, it was considered disorderly for vacant churches to countenance them. This was rendered necessary from the fact that numerous adventurers from the East were at that time drifting westward, and seeking that standing amongst strangers they could not obtain at home.

On the 28th day of February, 1818, John Munson was ordained and installed as pastor of the united congregations of Plaingrove and Center. In these exercises Mr. Chase preached the sermon, and Mr. McPherrin delivered the charges. On the same day Mr. Johnston was dismissed to the Presbytery of Redstone. He had been a member of Presbytery fifteen years, and one of the most successful pastors within its bounds. At this meeting the question of the relation of persons baptized in infancy was discussed, when " It was moved and seconded, that those ministers and sessions who exercise discipline upon baptized members, and censure such as are guilty of any immorality, be considered as justifiable." This action was passed as the voice of the Presbytery.

The matter of educating candidates for the ministry still pressed earnestly upon the Presbytery. New measures were adopted and new efforts put forth. The matter was brought individually before each congregation, and in order that vacant churches might have the same opportunity of contributing as those with pastors, a layman was sought out and appointed in each congregation within the bounds of Presbytery. There was at this time no general education board for the whole church. The Presbytery conducted the matter of education in its own way. Funds were collected throughout the congregations and paid into the treasury of Presbytery, and by it supplied to the students under its care, as circumstances seemed to justify. These students generally commenced their studies with the pastors. Sometimes their entire classical studies were pursued in this way; and in all cases at the first, they pursued their theological course either with Dr. McMillan or some pastor at home. In this way the funds of Presbytery, though small, were made to go a great way in preparing young men for the field. The rule then, as in more modern times, was that no promising young man, desirous of entering the ministry, should be discouraged for want of funds. The pastors did a great work in this way. They generally lived on farms, and were always ready to receive young men into their families as students, furnishing them books, instruction, and a quiet home free of expense. In these days there was scarcely a minister in the Presbytery who was not instrumental in introducing one or more young men into the ministry, not only in the way of advice and encouragement, but in actually undertaking their instruction and maintenance, either in whole or in part. In this way every pastor's cabin in the early days was made a miniature college or theological seminary. Sometimes the pastor could say, as Dr. McMillan did, in regard to the accommodations: " Sometimes we had no bread for weeks together; but we had plenty of pumpkins and potatoes and all the necessaries of life; and as for luxuries, we were not much concerned about them."[1] But what they had was freely shared with the student. And many a time did the pastor's wife deny herself some great convenience, in order that the student might not want for hose, and that his wardrobe in other respects might be maintained in a presentable appearance. And in order to assist in the same matter, the mothers in Israel formed what they called " Cent Societies," the object of which was to collect funds mainly through their own labor, as well as to provide clothing, socks, collars, handkerchiefs, and other articles pertaining to wearing apparel, for the comfort and convenience of the young candidates for the ministry. There is a long record of self-denying labors and secret sacrifices, made by these early mothers in behalf of God's church and ministry, that will be found written only in God's Book of Remembrance, and concerning which it has already been said, "Inas-

[1] Sprague's *Annals*, vol. iii. p. 352.

much as ye did it unto the least of these, my brethren, ye did it unto me."

On the 29th of June, 1819, Phineas Camp (29) was received from the Presbytery of North River. He was from the State of New York, and the first minister received into the Presbytery who had been a student at a theological seminary. He had been through a full course at Princeton, and was a most zealous and fervid minister. To a warm, impassioned nature, he added a zeal and energy that were remarkable, and that adapted him peculiarly to missionary labor. He delighted to go from church to church and from house to house urging and entreating souls to trust in Christ. His labors in Erie County, Pennsylvania, and Chautauque County, New York, were peculiarly blessed. During his labors in this region, there were many cases of the "bodily exercise," spoken of in a preceding chapter. This was considered by Mr. Camp as of very great importance, as a manifestation of the divine Spirit, and a most encouraging feature connected with his labors. Perhaps Mr. Camp was the first member of the Presbytery who was known technically as a "revival minister." He seems to have been more successful in his labors as an Evangelist than as a settled pastor. On the 8th day of September, 1819, he was installed as pastor of the congregation of Westfield, New York. In these services Mr. Riggs preached the sermon, and Mr. Tait delivered the charges.

At this meeting, a complaint was brought against the session of the church of North East, for inviting members of the Methodist Church "To be active with them at the Monthly Concert of Prayer." The Presbytery "*Resolved*, That we deem it wrong that members of the Methodist Church, a church that holds doctrines contrary to our confession of faith, be invited to be active members in our prayer meetings." This activity consisted in leading in prayer. Against this action Thomas Robinson complained to Synod. A reference to the action of this latter body shows that whilst the Synod approved of the zeal of Presbytery for the purity of the church, they yet feared that in this particular case the zeal was not altogether according to knowledge, and intimated kindly that the record was not judicious or charitable.

On the 7th of October, 1819, Reid Bracken was released from the pastoral charge of the congregation of Plain; and on the same day calls from the congregation of Middlesex were placed in his hands and accepted by him.

On the 15th of February, 1820, the Congregational church of Lottsville asked to be taken under the care of Presbytery. The request was granted, and Deacon Fox enrolled as a member. On the 28th of September following, on petition of the inhabitants of Lawrenceburg, the congregation of Ebenezer was recognized as under the care of Presbytery; and on the same day Mr. Bracken was installed as pastor at Middlesex for half his time.

The Presbytery at this time began to consider the propriety of another division of its boundaries. The labor of travelling to meetings of Presbytery was great, and that of supplying vacancies and performing missionary work was still more arduous. Accordingly, at a meeting held at Middlesex, Butler County, Pa., on the 28th of September, 1820, a committee, consisting of Mr. Boyd and Mr. Eaton, was appointed to propose a division line of Presbytery. On the following day they presented the following report, which was embodied in a request to the Synod of Pittsburgh for the necessary action: —

"*Resolved*, That the Presbytery of Erie request the Synod of Pittsburgh, at its next meeting, to set off a new Presbytery by a line commencing at the mouth of Little Neshannock Creek; thence up Big Neshannock to the mouth of Yellow Creek; thence up Yellow Creek to Hosack's Mill; thence along the Mercer Road to Franklin, and north of Franklin to the mouth of French Creek; thence up the Alleghany to the State line; to include the Rev. Messrs. John McPherrin, Abraham Boyd, Robert McGarraugh, Cyrus Riggs, Reid Bracken, John Munson, and John Redick; and all the congregations south of that line, to be known by the name of Alleghany Presbytery."

This request was granted by the Synod; and the new Presbytery was directed to hold its first meeting "at the town of Butler, on the first Tuesday of April, 1821, at twelve o'clock; to be opened with a sermon by the Rev. John McPherrin, and in case of his absence, by the next senior minister present, who is to preside until a moderator be chosen."

At that meeting of Synod the Presbytery reported thirteen ministers and forty-seven congregations. Of these ministers Mr. Chase was without charge; Mr. Tait settled at Mercer and Salem; Mr. McPherrin at Butler and Concord; Abraham Boyd at Bull Creek and Deer Creek; Mr. McGarraugh at New Rehoboth and Licking; Mr. Riggs at Scrubgrass and Unity; Mr. Eaton at Fairview and Erie; Mr. Bracken at Nebo and Middlesex; Mr. Condit at Fairfield, Big Sugar Creek, and Sandy; Mr. Redick at Slate Lick and Union; Mr. Munson at Plaingrove and Center; and Mr. Camp at Westfield. Mr. Alden was President of Alleghany College.

It was now twelve years since the previous division of the Presbytery; the territory had been more fully occupied, and although the number of ministers on the roll had not been largely increased, yet the general results were encouraging. Revivals of religion had not been so numerous nor so powerful as during the first period of the history of Presbytery; yet the churches were not without the presence and refreshing influences of the Holy Spirit. During these years the narrative of the state of religion was not recorded; yet in 1818, the minutes record this testimony: "The Presbytery are of opinion that the evidences in favor of God's visiting most of our congregations with his grace, are more hopeful than they have been for years past." Again, the next year, after "a free conversation," as they term it, in which they bewail carelessness and lukewarmness, they say: "The Presbytery are of opinion, that there are evidences of God's having graciously visited several of our congregations and vacancies especially, in a manner not witnessed for some years past."

It was during these years that the revivals connected with Mr. Camp's labors are reported, in which the "bodily exercise" was prevalent.

CHAPTER IV.

FROM THE SECOND DIVISION OF PRESBYTERY TO THE GREAT DIVISION.

1820–1837.

By the late organization of the new Presbytery of Alleghany, the bounds of Presbytery were very much reduced. It now consisted of the counties of Erie and Crawford, with portions of those of Mercer, Venango, and Warren. The territory was reduced about one half in its extent.

Its members numbered but six, one less than when it held its first meeting in 1802. Samuel Tait was settled at Salem and Mercer; Johnston Eaton at Fairview and Erie; Ira Condit at Fairfield, Big Sugar Creek, and Sandy; Amos Chase without charge; Timothy Alden, President of Alleghany College; and Phineas Camp at Westfield, New York. At the next meeting of Synod, they reported twenty-nine congregations, the names of which, in addition to the pastoral charges given above, are: Westfield, Poland, Springfield, North East, Ripley, Conneaut, Waterford, Middlebrook, Cussawago, Gravel Run, Union, Oil Creek, Great Brokenstraw, Lottsville, Beachwoods, Warren, Tidioute, Alleghany, Conneaut Lake, Harmonsburg, and United Christian Society.

The circumstances under which the Presbytery were now situated, were somewhat discouraging. There were but four pastoral charges, leaving over twenty vacant churches to be supplied and nurtured. And these vacancies were generally weak. With the exception of Meadville, not one, or even two combined, seemed able to support a minister. Still the Presbytery do not seem disheartened, but give themselves to the work, and set forward as though they meant to accomplish the work set before them.

The first meeting of Presbytery, after bidding farewell to the brethren who were to set up the gates of the Presbytery of Alleghany, was at Gravel Run, Pennsylvania, on the 17th day of April, 1821. Mr. Tait was chosen moderator, and Mr. Alden clerk. John Van Liew (30), a licentiate of the Classis of New Brunswick, being present, was received under the care of Presbytery. Mr. Van Liew was a licentiate of the Reformed Dutch Church. He was licensed by the Classis of New Brunswick, N. J., and had preached but a short time before coming into the bounds of the Presbytery. The prospect was promising for his settlement at Meadville, and he was willing to change his ecclesiastical relation in order to enter this field of usefulness. He was a young man, and while in the dew of youth, entered zealously upon the work.

As a part of the minutes of this meeting of Presbytery, the narrative of the state of religion is recorded. It is the first instance in which this was done. It is reported that "there is an increasing attention to the means of grace. Our vacancies are earnestly soliciting ministerial labors. Several congregations have been organized during the year, and some are preparing for, and are uncommonly anxious to settle, a minister."

"Our benevolent societies have felt the general pressure of the times; but, unwilling to relax in their exertions, have, in some cases, given their mites in clothing and books for the Indian schools.

"In some congregations, there have been a number of hopeful additions. The most general awakening has been in Mercer and Salem, which were visited last summer with the special influences of the Spirit of God. The fruits of these gracious influences have been sixty added to the church."

"The number of Sabbath-schools has been increasing, and their efforts flattering. The monthly concert of prayer is attended, and in some of our churches the pious are in the habit of spending Wednesday evening for the effusion of the Divine influence on the ministers and churches with which they are in connection."

This is the first mention of the Sabbath-school enterprise. It is not probable that schools were organized generally through the country churches. The people generally were scattered over a large extent of country, and could not conveniently meet for that purpose. But in the towns and villages the matter seems to have been generally attended to. Mr. Alden was the great apostle of Sabbath-schools in the Presbytery. When not engaged in his Indian missions, he spent his available time in going through its bounds, organizing schools, visiting those already organized, and encouraging the enterprise by his counsel and his efforts. The facilities for carrying on schools were not good. Books were scarce and unsuitable in character. The Bible, the Catechism, and oral instruction must be the chief dependence. And these, with an earnest prayerful heart on the part of teachers and superintendent, were blessed to great good by the Head of the Church.

On the 21st day of August, 1821, John Van Liew was ordained and installed as pastor of the congregation of Meadville. In these services Mr. Eaton preached from these words: "How shall they hear without a preacher?" Rom. iii. 10; and Mr. Chase presided and delivered the charges.

This settlement of Mr. Van Liew was the dawn of better days to the church of Meadville. For the last three or four years they had been dependent mainly on supplies. During a portion of that time, by a private arrangement, they had enjoyed the labors of Mr. Alden and Allan D. Campbell,[1] then in connection with the Associate Reformed Church. These brethren supplied on alternate Sabbaths. But there was dissatisfaction in the church. At one time they were on the eve of calling Mr. Campbell, and putting the church under the care of the Associate Reformed Presbytery. But this intention failed. The people became united in Mr. Van Liew; the feeling of dissatisfaction with the Presbytery ceased, and the church began to prosper. The whole of Mr. Van Liew's time was taken, and the congregation was thenceforward self-sustaining.

On the 21st of August, 1821, Mr. Camp's pastoral relation to the church of Westfield, N. Y., was dissolved. The pastoral work was not so congenial to him as the work of an Evangelist. He felt most at home when travelling from place to place, and seeking out destitute points, and preaching the Word of Life.

In February, 1822, Presbytery, after considering the destitution of the vacant churches under its care, sent a pastoral letter to each vacant church, proposing a plan for their relief, and stimulating them to exertion on their own part. After reminding them of their delinquencies in the matter of remunerating their supplies, they say: "The plan we have adopted for the pur-

[1] Born in England, 1791; licensed, 1815; ordained, 1818; died, 1861.

pose of remedying this defect, is as follows: Every vacant congregation shall become responsible by its proper officers, or otherwise, for as large a sum as can be raised with certainty within the bounds. The sum thus raised, with the aid expected to be obtained from missionary societies, will probably be sufficient for the support of a missionary the whole year. As an inducement for exertion, we hold out the assurance that every congregation shall receive its quota of missionary labor in proportion to the moneys raised within its bounds. Let it be also understood that the service of the missionary in each place will, with the expected aid from abroad, be nearly double the amount subscribed."

This appeal was responded to at the next meeting of Presbytery by eleven churches, reporting in the aggregate two hundred and eighty-two dollars and fifty cents.

In the autumn of 1822, Mr. Tait was appointed by Synod as superintendent, *pro tem.*, of the mission family about to be located among the Ottowa Indians on the Maumee River, and the Presbytery was directed to supply his pulpit during his absence. This position he held for about seven months.

In the mean time trouble was brewing in Springfield, in Erie County, Pa. A Presbyterian church had been organized there by Mr. Eaton in the year 1806. Of this church he had been the pastor for many years. About the year 1821, a Congregational church was formed. The consequence was, that the efforts of the people were divided. Bickerings and heart-burnings were engendered, and the matter was brought to the notice of Synod. The Congregational wing of the church had applied to the Presbytery of Grand River to be taken under its care. This Presbytery was advised by Synod not to take the church under its care, and a committee appointed to visit Springfield to endeavor to reconcile difficulties, and recommending the two congregations of Springfield to observe the 15th of the following November as a day of *fasting and prayer*.

The committee, consisting of Thomas Edgar Hughes, an old member of the Presbytery of Erie, E. T. Woodruff, and Randolph Stone, visited Springfield, held a "free conversation" with the people of the two congregations, and heard statements from both parties. The Presbyterian brethren were then requested to withdraw, when the committee proposed to the Congregational brethren a union with the Presbyterians, on condition of being present at the examination of candidates for membership in the church, and asking such questions as conscience might dictate, and also of attending all cases of trial and discipline. This was agreed to. The Congregational brethren then withdrew, and the Presbyterian brethren were called in. The terms of union on the part of the former were laid before them and agreed to, and the Congregationalists were called in, when the following resolution was mutually adopted: —

"*Resolved*, That the present ruling elders in the Presbyterian Church, namely, Charles Manly, Isaac Miller, James Blair, Robert Porter, and Allen Law, and the present acting deacon in the Congregational church, namely, William Branch, be, and are hereby constituted, the standing committee of the United Church of Springfield, according to the principles of union recommended by the General Assembly of the Presbyterian Church, and the General Association of Connecticut."[1]

Against this action of the committee, the Presbytery complained. The elders of the church at Springfield

[1] Minutes of Synod, 1823.

wrote to Presbytery for advice in the matter. After discussing the action of the committee, Presbytery resolved that said committee had "assumed a stretch of power not authorized by the constitution or usages of the Presbyterian Church, in setting aside the eldership of the Presbyterian Church of Springfield, as the said Synodical committee virtually did, by appointing a committee that was to supersede the elders of that church; and therefore that the act of said Synodical committee, and thus setting aside the eldership of that church, is null and void." [1]

They further resolved that the elders of said church were the constitutional officers.

At the next meeting of Synod the matter was compromised and settled by Synod declaring that the action of the committee did not affect the standing or position of the session, but simply added Deacon Branch to their number.

On the 8th of April, 1823, Rev. William Kennedy was received from the Presbytery of Huntington, and at the same meeting dismissed to the Presbytery of Alleghany. He seems to have passed from that Presbytery to some other the same year or the next, as his name does not appear on the roll after the next meeting of Synod.

On the 1st of October of the same year, John Barrett, a licentiate of the Andover Association of the Congregational Church, was received under the care of Presbytery. He labored for a time in the vacant churches, but was never settled, and was eventually dismissed to the care of the Presbytery of Grand River, in 1826.

At this meeting also, Presbytery received under its

[1] Min. ii. 142.

care three candidates for the gospel ministry,— Thomas Anderson (37), a graduate of Washington College, and Absalom McCready (36), and John C. Tidball, graduates of Jefferson College. The first two were eventually licensed and ordained by the Presbytery; the latter was dismissed to another Presbytery. Mr. Judah Ely, a licentiate of the Presbytery of Niagara, was permitted to labor for a time within the bounds, but was never received under the care of Presbytery.

On the 13th of April, 1824, Bradford Marcy (31), was received from the Presbytery of Long Island. He had been living for some time in Crawford County, but had turned his attention to agricultural pursuits. In these he was successful. He had no pastoral charge in the Presbytery. Although a man of some learning and zeal, yet his success in the pastoral work was confined to his earlier fields of labor at Islep, on Long Island, and in New Jersey.

On the 21st of June, 1824, the pastoral relation between Mr. Van Liew and the church of Meadville was dissolved. Mr. Van Liew's health had been feeble for some time, and feeling that it might be improved by returning to the sea-board, asked to be released for that purpose. On the following day he was dismissed to the Presbytery of Jersey.

On the 9th of February, 1825, Mr. Camp was dismissed to the Presbytery of St. Lawrence; and on the same day David McKinney (32), a licentiate of the Presbytery of Philadelphia, was taken under the care of Presbytery, and accepted calls from the congregation of Erie, Pa. At this meeting Presbytery assigned to Mr. McCready, as a theme for a Latin exegesis: "Non ignari mali miseris, sucurrere disco;" and to Mr. Anderson: "Auri sacra fames."

On the 2d of March, 1825, Nathan Harned (34), a licentiate of the Presbytery of Philadelphia, and Giles Doolittle (33), a licentiate of the Presbytery of Oneida, were received under the care of Presbytery.

On the 13th of April, 1825, David McKinney was ordained and installed as pastor of the 1st Presbyterian congregation of Erie. In these services Mr. Alden preached, and Mr. Tait delivered the charges. This was the first pastoral settlement in the church at Erie. Mr. Patterson had first labored statedly for a time, and a call was made out for his pastoral labors in connection with North East and Middlebrook, but he was never installed. Afterwards Mr. Eaton labored for some five years from one third to one half of his time, but it was simply as a stated supply. They worshipped at this time in the "Yellow Meeting-house." Mr. Colt was the principal ruling elder and prime patron of the church. He had been converted under the ministrations of Mr. McCurdy of Cross Roads, and had connected with the church at Upper Greenfield, on Middlebrook, and was always a consistent, earnest Christian and efficient ruling elder. Now a pastor was called, and the church began to gather strength, and has since exerted a most important influence in the community. The session of the church had been in correspondence with Dr. Archibald Alexander in relation to a student of Princeton. The doctor states in a letter dated June 3, 1823: "We are not able to meet the demands for missionaries; not more than a tenth of the calls can be answered." Dr. Alexander had first recommended to Mr. Colt, Joseph H. Jones,[1] speaking of him as "a graduate of Harvard University, of respectable talents and acquirements, and very amiable in

[1] Now Dr. Jones of Philadelphia.

his manner and disposition." The salary spoken of was "thirty-three dollars per month." Mr. Jones visited Erie, travelling on horseback, and spent some weeks, making a most favorable impression. He afterwards declined the call to Erie. Dr. Alexander then wrote under date of January 16, 1824: —

"I have concluded to advise that David McKinney, now in the seminary, should pay you a visit in the Fall. He is a young man, not of showy, but of solid talents. As a student, he is indefatigable, and possesses a sound judgment, with an excellent character for piety."

Under these circumstances, Mr. McKinney entered upon the work, and was rewarded with a good degree of success. If the thirty-three dollars per month was not sufficient, it was eked out by teaching and other arrangements.

On the 14th of April, 1825, Giles Doolittle (33) was ordained and installed as pastor of the united congregations of North East and Ripley, the former in Erie County, Pa., the latter in Chautauque County, N. Y. In these services, Mr. Eaton preached, and Mr. Tait delivered the charges. North East had been formerly known as Lower Greenfield, and had constituted a part of the pastoral charge of Mr. Patterson, and from which he had been released in 1807. Ripley had not heretofore engaged the labors of a pastor. Mr. Doolittle was a most excellent pastor. Accustomed from childhood to exertion and effort, he labored most assiduously for the building up of his congregations. He was successful. His people enjoyed several revivals during his pastorate. In some things he differed from his brethren, yet he always had the glory of God in view, and labored earnestly for the good of souls. Although he found many difficulties in his way, he yet, by precept and example sought to lead the erring, the opposing, and the indifferent in the way of life.

In the year 1825, Messrs. Tait and Eaton were appointed to prepare a history of Presbytery, and the members enjoined to grant them such aid as might be in their power. One year from this time the committee reported progress, and were directed to continue their labors.

On the 20th of April, 1825, Nathan Harned was ordained and installed as pastor of the united congregations of Warren, Sugar Grove, Great Brokenstraw, and Lottsville. Mr. Tait preached on the occasion, and Mr. Chase delivered the charges. Here was a wide field, and one that has continued, with the exception of Warren, missionary ground for more than forty years.

On the 28th day of December of the same year, Mr. Condit was released from the charge of the congregation of Big Sugar Creek, and devoted the one third of his time to that of Amity, in the Presbytery of Alleghany. On the same day, Absalom McCready (36), and Thomas Anderson (37), were licensed to preach the gospel.

On the 28th of December, 1825, Mr. Tait was released from the pastoral charge of Salem, where he had been laboring for the third of his time; and a call was put into his hands for the whole of his time from the congregation of Mercer. This call was accepted on the following month, when the whole of his time was given to Mercer, until the period of his death.

The first place of preaching in Mercer was the upper room of the jail, an old log building that stood near the Diamond. The first effort towards the erection of a house of worship, was made by drawing logs and putting up the body of a house, but the building was never covered. After this a brick building was erected, but so frail was the construction, that it was never considered safe, and was finally abandoned. It was not until the year 1830, that a comfortable house was erected.

On the 18th of January, 1826, Mr. Harned was released from the pastoral charge of Great Brokenstraw; and at the same time the organization of a church at Randolph, in Crawford County, was reported.

On the 11th of April, 1826, Mr. Condit accepted calls from the congregation of Upper Sandy, now Georgetown. This call was for one third of Mr. Condit's time. On the 24th of May following, Mr. Chase was installed as pastor of the congregation of Oil Creek, for half his time. This church is now known as Titusville. Mr. Chase had for the last ten years acted as a missionary through the country now known as the "Oil Region." He had gathered this church, and established a preaching-point at Centerville, in which he was installed the following year, a church having been organized by Mr. McKinney, and wished for a little relief from the constant travel; yet he reserved still one fourth of his time for the regions beyond.

On the 24th day of May of this year, Wells Bushnell (35), a licentiate of the Presbytery of New Brunswick, was received under the care of Presbytery, and accepted calls from the congregation of Meadville. His ordination took place on the 22d of June following, when he was regularly installed as pastor of the congregation. In these services, Mr. Stockton, the first pastor of the church, being present by invitation, preached the sermon. Mr. Tait delivered the charge to the pastor, and Mr. Eaton the charge to the people.

On the 24th of May, 1826, Mr. Harned was released from the pastoral charge of the congregations of Warren and Sugar Grove, and on the 22d of June following, he was dismissed to the Presbytery of Hartford. In June of this year the congregation of North Bank, in Crawford County, was organized.

On the 14th of September, Absalom McCready (36) was ordained and installed as pastor of the united congregations of Middlebrook and Beaverdam, in Erie County. Mr. McKinney preached the sermon, Mr. Tait delivered the charge to the pastor, and Mr. Doolittle the charge to the people.

Middlebrook was formerly known as Upper Greenfield, and had constituted a part of Mr. Patterson's charge as early as 1803. It was in fact one of the oldest churches in the bounds of the Presbytery.

On the 19th day of September following, Thomas Anderson (37) was ordained and installed as pastor of the united congregations of Big Sugar Creek, Concord, and Franklin, in Venango County. Mr. Bushnell preached the sermon, Mr. Chase delivered the charge to the pastor, and Mr. McKinney the charge to the people. Previous to this time Franklin had been under the care of the Presbytery of Alleghany, but was about this time, at the request of the congregation, set over to the Presbytery of Erie. It was an arduous charge upon which Mr. Anderson entered. Concord was twenty miles distant from either of the other two congregations, and they were seven miles asunder. The roads were bad, and the weather often stormy. The congregations too, were weak, and the salary small. Once whilst living in Franklin, the barrel of meal and the cruse of oil were just about failing. The family sat down to breakfast on bread and molasses, and coffee. The usual blessing was sought. The bread and molasses were discussed. The minister betook him to his study, telling the family that God would provide for them, as He fed even the little birds; the mother sat down to her toil until the evening, when two sons of good Mrs. Bowman appeared with a basket filled with comforts and even luxuries. That night the pastor thanked God for "friends, food, and raiment."

The church of Franklin consisted at the time of Mr. Anderson's settlement of but fourteen members. The first communion was held on the bank of French Creek, under the shade of the trees. He was the first pastor, and always afterward spoke of it as his first love.

On the 11th of January, 1827, Pierce Chamberlain (38), a member of the Presbytery of New Castle, was received as a member of Presbytery. He was a meek, quiet, good man, who had devoted much time and labor to missionary work. From the prisons and almshouses of Philadelphia, he had come to the missionary territory of Northwestern Pennsylvania. And he did good service in this work. He was constantly going from point to point, preaching, organizing Sabbath-schools, and encouraging the vacant churches.

On the 11th of January, 1827, the people of Cool Spring petitioned Presbytery for a new organization. They had been disbanded now for some years, and had generally been identified with Mercer. But the settlement was filling up. It was some distance to Mercer, and they thought their interests required a separate organization. The measure was opposed by Mr. Tait with all his accustomed warmth and energy, and the consideration of the petition was postponed until the next meeting of Presbytery. At this meeting Mr. Bushnell was appointed to organize the church, who at a subsequent meeting, April 29, 1828, reported that he had organized the church.

On the 10th of October, 1827, Mr. Condit was installed as pastor of the congregation of Georgetown. This was formerly known as Upper Sandy congregation. Mr. Condit labored here for one third of his time.

On the 9th of April, 1828, James Alexander (40), a member of the church of Mercer, was licensed to preach the gospel.

On the 24th of June, 1828, Peter Hassinger (39), a licentiate of the Presbytery of New Castle, was taken under the care of Presbytery. On the 1st of October following, Mr. Hassinger was ordained and installed as pastor of the congregation of Gravel Run, in Crawford County. Mr. Doolittle preached on the occasion. Mr. Chase delivered the charge to the pastor, and Mr. McKinney to the people. In the mean time Mr. Chamberlain had been called to the church at Springfield. His feeling and desire were to accept, but feebleness of health compelled him to return the call, and devote himself to missionary work.

On the 13th of October, 1828, James Alexander was ordained and installed as pastor of the united congregations of Salem, Greenville, and Big Bend. Mr. Chamberlain preached. Mr. Eaton delivered the charge to the pastor, and Rev. H. Coe, who was present from the Presbytery of Grand River, the charge to the people.

April 22, 1829, Mr. Condit was dismissed from Amity.

During these last years some interesting revivals of religion had occurred. In Mr. Doolittle's charge the Spirit of God had been poured out with power. Some interesting cases are reported of the manner in which these manifestations were at first noticed. In North East, an elder [1] was awakened in the middle of the night by

[1] William Dickson.

a messenger from the country. On inquiry as to his desire, he cried out, —

"O, do come out and see —— ——, he is in a most dreadful way."

"But what is the matter?"

"He is suffering everything. Come out quickly and do something for him."

"Go for the doctor if he is sick; I am not the one to send for on such an occasion."

"But it is not the doctor he wants. He complains of his sins, and is afraid he will be lost forever; and we thought you could come and pray for him, and maybe do him some good. We did not know what else to do."

The elder went out and prayed, and counseled with the young man. This was the beginning of a good work. Soon after, during the progress of some meetings, a strong, honest man from the country, known as Billy Wilson, was at the church on the Sabbath. God's Spirit was stirring the hearts of the people, and many, who had hardly a religious conviction before, were moved and melted by his power. Wilson felt troubled and anxious without fully comprehending his feelings. They were new to him. During the recess between sermons he stepped over to the hotel, and was standing before the fire, doubtful as to the cause of his strange feelings. At length, stepping up to the bar, he said, addressing the proprietor: "Lem, I feel most dreadful bad to-day; I guess I'll take a little whiskey; the day is raw, and it may help me." The bar had been partially closed, out of respect to the Sabbath, but a small pigeon-hole was left open for the accommodation of an occasional visitor. The proprietor set down the bottle, but still holding the glass in his hand, seemed for a moment in a brown study. At length he said: "Billy, where is it that you feel bad?"

"O, Lem; I feel monstrous bad about my heart; I never felt so before."

The bottle and glass were immediately returned to the shelf, with the curt advice: "Billy, it is not whiskey you want; it's the minister. Go to him at once, for you're under conviction."

The result was that Wilson became a Christian, and the Lord remembered Lemuel Brown for his good deed done to one who was under conviction, for many years had not rolled by, before he too was brought into the church.

On the 22d of April, 1829, the following paper on Temperance was adopted: —

"*Resolved* — 1. That Presbytery view with much satisfaction the efforts now making in the cause of temperance, and hope to see them crowned with great success.

"2. That we recommend to the congregations under our care, the formation of societies for the promotion of temperance.

"3. That as we have derived great aid from the female friends of Zion in the cause of benevolence, we would now recommend to them the formation of societies, to aid, not only by an example, but also by the whole weight of their influence, the cause of temperance.

"4. That the ministers of the Presbytery form themselves into a temperance society, on the plan of rigid and entire abstinence from the use of ardent spirits, except for medicinal purposes."[1]

By this time the bud, spoken of in chapter second, as having presented itself in 1814, had expanded into the full-blown flower. Public opinion had made rapid

[1] Min. ii. 241.

strides in the course of fifteen years, and no doubt the fruit that followed was good and wholesome.

On the 22d of April, 1829, Mr. McKinney was released from the pastoral charge of the church of Erie. At the same meeting the Commissioners to the General Assembly were directed "to purchase sixty copies of the 'Confession of Faith' of our Church, for our congregations, for the payment of which, Presbytery will be responsible."

On the 24th of June of the same year, Mr. Condit was installed as pastor of the congregation of Cool Spring, for one third of his time. This relation continued until his death in 1836.

On the same day, George A. Lyon (41), a licentiate of the Presbytery of Carlisle, was received under the care of Presbytery, and accepted calls from the congregation of Erie. This action was followed by the ordination and installation of Mr. Lyon at the next meeting of Presbytery, September 9, 1829, as pastor of the congregation of the 1st Presbyterian Church, Erie, Pa. In these services Mr. Doolittle preached the sermon, Mr. Tait presided, Mr. Bushnell delivered the charge to the pastor, and Mr. Anderson the charge to the people. Mr. Lyon entered upon his work with every encouragement. He was in the strength of youth, the congregation was enlarging its boundaries, and the people were unanimous in sustaining him. The old "Yellow Meeting-house" had been abandoned, and a large, comfortable brick house was now occupied as the place of worship.

At the same meeting of Presbytery, the church of Harmonsburg was enrolled. This church is in Crawford County. A day of fasting and prayer was also appointed, "for the purpose of unitedly calling upon God for the outpouring of his Spirit upon that section of his church with which we are more especially connected, as well as upon the church at large."

On the 13th of January, 1830, Mr. Chase was released from the pastoral charge of the congregation of Centerville, in Crawford County.

On the 14th of April, of the same year, George W. Hampson (43), a member of the church of North East, was licensed to preach the gospel. On the same day Mr. Chase was released from the pastoral charge of the congregation of Oil Creek, and Mr. Doolittle from that of Ripley. Mr. Doolittle then accepted a call from North East, for the whole of his time.

On the 21st of September, 1830, Mr. McKinney was dismissed to connect himself with the Presbytery of Huntington. He had been a member of Presbytery five years.

On the next day, Edson Hart (42), a member of the Presbytery of Trumbull, was received as a member of Presbytery.

On the 2d day of February, 1831, Robert Glenn (44) was licensed to preach the gospel. He had been a student of Mr. Tait, a man of no pretension to brilliancy, yet a genuine, earnest worker in the cause of Christ; and his record was marked with the seal of God's approval throughout his ministry.

On the 23d of the same month, Mr. Hassinger was released from the pastoral charge of the congregation of Gravel Run, and on the 14th of April following, Mr. Anderson was released from the pastoral charge of Concord.

There was a recommendation at this time that throws light upon the practice of the church at this period of its history: " Presbytery, taking into consideration the destitute state of the vacant congregations under their care, recommend to its members and such vacancies, to adopt the practice of holding two, three, or four days' meetings during the week, and administering the Lord's Supper; and that two or three ministers go together on such occasions."[1] These days were usually observed in the following order: On Thursday, a fast day was observed. It was not usually observed as a day of literal fasting, but simply as a day of abstinence from worldly labor. On Saturday, divine service was held as preparatory to the Communion. On Sabbath the communion service was attended to; and this was followed by service on Monday. It was also usual to hold evening service at school-houses in different parts of the congregation, in the evenings during these days. Sometimes two, and sometimes three, ministers were present during these meetings. The services, particularly of the Sabbath, were protracted, and the addresses at the communion table were long and varied.

Whilst these meetings were being held, the people of the congregation, and others, expected to give all their attention to the matter. Business was so arranged that the families could attend without distraction. This extended in a greater or less degree to neighboring congregations. In these days the service was usually known as "The Sacrament." Such a meeting was known far and near, and people thronged thither from distances of ten or twelve miles or more. Families living near the place of meeting always expected to accommodate strangers at their houses. Sometimes their houses were crowded for two or three days in succession. Where the ordinary accommodations were not sufficient, cots and blankets were laid upon the floors. Everything was free and welcome as the provisions of

[1] Min. iii. 37.

the gospel they came to receive. And for such occasions, families made provision for weeks beforehand; and looked upon it as a matter of course.

At this time houses of worship were generally provided, yet on sacramental occasions they often resorted to the grove. There was more room. The air was fresh and pure. The heart was more cheerful. Sometimes storms would come up, and summer showers pour down, but it did not seem to disturb the people. They would sit unmoved in the driving rain, and the ministers would preach in the storm as though they knew not of its presence. Nor were the services abridged by these unfavorable circumstances. The ministers came to preach and administer the ordinances; and the people came to hear; and so they fulfilled their intentions, without regard to the clouds or the rain.

To these meetings as of old, people came on foot where there were not conveniences for riding. Sometimes the oxen were attached to the farm-wagon, and this sufficed for the entire family. But young women often walked from two to five miles to "meeting," as the service was called. Sometimes they walked barefooted, and carried their shoes to within a short distance of the meeting-house, and then put them on; sometimes they wore coarse shoes, and exchanged near the place of worship, leaving their coarse shoes in some place of concealment.

These "four days' meetings," in some parts of the Presbytery, about the year 1831, became remarkable for a new feature. This was the presence of ministers who were called revival men, or Evangelists, as they sometimes styled themselves. They went from place to place, devoting themselves entirely to this kind of work. In many of these meetings the pastor of the church acted quite a subordinate part, leaving all to the evangelist, who preached on day after day, exhorting, entreating, and persuading men to turn to the Lord.

About this time, too, a new feature in Presbyterianism was introduced, called the "Anxious Seat." It was simply a certain seat or seats set apart, to which persons anxious about the concerns of the soul were invited to come, as an expression of their feelings, and for the purpose of being conversed with and made the subject of special prayer. Sometimes such persons were simply invited to come; at others they were urged and entreated to take this as the most important step of their lives. Like almost every other good work, this was sometimes carried to an extreme. Sometimes too great stress was laid upon the simple matter of going to the anxious seat. Sometimes, possibly, persons were persuaded to go there who had no heart conviction, and were disappointed or deceived. But many of the ministers of that day considered that they were drawing the gospel net, and that all were to be gathered in, where at the last the good would be gathered into vessels and the bad cast away. Others opposed these measures. They could not think them necessary, but rejected them as innovations, and having a dangerous tendency. And the records of the churches show that the revivals of that day were not confined, by any means, to those congregations where the new measures were adopted. As a general thing the older ministers hesitated about countenancing them. Such men as Father Tait, although their hearts were always warm, and the spirit of revival always glowing in their preaching, felt that "the old paths" were safest and best. In the good old days of 1802, powerful revivals were enjoyed without them. Souls flocked to Christ under the simple preaching of the Word, and the irresistible influences of the Spirit of God; and they thought these the best means that could be used.

On the other hand the younger ministers, at least many of them, adopted the new measures, conscientiously believing them best adapted to accomplish the great object. Something was needed to attract attention and fix the mind. Something was wanted to induce inquirers to commit themselves to the great work, and thus take the first step toward the service of God. Something was needed by way of example, to induce others to go in the same direction. Thus they reasoned, and thus they pursued the course that to them seemed right. Great good was done, no doubt, and many brought into the Church.

But in many cases disastrous results followed. Some of these revival men were not men after God's own heart. Whilst some of them were earnest, conscientious men, others were moved only by excitement, if not by a more unworthy motive still. And at times the hurt of the daughter of God's people was healed but slightly. The building was daubed with untempered mortar. Desolation was found in the track of what the pious, earnest people of God thought was the chariot of salvation.

Nor is this strange or unusual. Satan strives to counterfeit every good work. In the midst of the wondrous works that Moses did in the presence of Pharaoh, we read: "These things did the magicians with their enchantments." When the Apostles wrought miracles, and such wondrous scenes were witnessed of divine power and efficacy, Simon Magus offered them money that he might take part in the glorious work. And an hundred years ago, when wondrous revival scenes were witnessed in Eastern Pennsylvania, Maryland, and New Jersey, disorders crept in that marred and blighted the beautiful work of God. And during the powerful outpouring of the Spirit that occurred during the founding of the Presbytery of Erie, the wheat and the tares were seen springing up together. So it is, and so it will be in all the imperfect scenes of time. The good and the evil dwell together. The rose and the violet are found side by side with the deadly nightshade. The poison ivy is found clasping to the death the flowering magnolia.

The summer of 1831 was a harvest season in the Presbytery. God's presence was most sensibly felt, and his power most signally displayed. Thus it is recorded, in the narrative of the state of religion sent up to Synod: "Many of our congregations, through the reviving power of the Holy Ghost, wear an aspect which has hitherto been new to them. The Lord has poured down upon them the influences of his Spirit, quickening his own people, and convincing and converting the ungodly. The churches at Meadville, Erie, North East, Forks of French Creek, Fairview, Springfield, Salem, and Warren, have been specially favored. These vines have produced fruit, some thirty, some sixty, some an hundred fold. Other churches have been quickened, and many sinners brought to inquire what they must do to be saved."

"And while the Presbytery unite in blessing and adoring God, that through the special influences of the Holy Ghost near six hundred souls have been added to their churches within the last year, they would acknowledge their unfaithfulness, and implore the continuance of his kind regard and blessings."

That year Meadville reported fifty-five; Erie seventy-five; North East, sixty-nine; Fairview, twenty-seven; Mr. Condit's charge, thirty; Springfield, eighty-two; Salem, Greenville, and Big Bend, forty-three; Franklin and Big Sugar Creek, twenty-three; Middlebrook, Beaver Dam, and Union, twenty-seven. Warren and Brokenstraw, thirty-three. This was the largest report that was made by any Presbytery to the Synod that year. And it is doubtful whether, either before or since, there has been as great a number gathered into the churches, in one year, during the entire history of the Presbytery. So that the year 1831 may be considered the great harvest year in the history of the Presbytery.

At the meeting in September, 1831, the question of baptism was brought to the notice of Presbytery. It was reported that one of the members had recently baptized fourteen or fifteen persons by immersion. After mature deliberation, Presbytery declared their "unanimous opinion that this practice is not in accordance with our standards, and is altogether inexpedient."[1] From the above date, Mr. Anderson gave half his pastoral labors to the congregation of Big Sugar Creek, and the remaining half to Franklin.

On the 26th of May, 1832, the church of Harbor Creek, in Erie County, was organized. It was a colony from the church of North East.

On the 11th of April, 1832, Mr. Alden was dismissed to connect himself with the Presbytery of Cincinnati. He had been a member of the Presbytery sixteen years, and although at no time a pastor, yet he had done a noble work for the cause of education and Sabbath-schools. He had also performed a large amount of missionary work, and retired to another field with the respect and love of all his brethren.

[1] Min. iii. 46.

On the 27th day of June, 1832, George W. Hampson (43) was ordained and installed as pastor of the united congregations of Oil Creek and Concord. In these services Mr. Doolittle preached the sermon, Mr. Eaton delivered the charge to the pastor, and Mr. Anderson the charge to the people.

The year 1832, being the year in which the Asiatic cholera made its appearance in the United States, Presbytery sent down to the congregations the following recommendation: "In view of the threatening aspect of Divine Providence toward our guilty land, particularly that scourge of nations, the Asiatic cholera, which has already reached our country, Wednesday, the 11th of July, is recommended to be spent as a day of humiliation and prayer." [1]

At the meeting of Presbytery June 28, 1832, notice was called to a sermon, published by Mr. Doolittle, upon the words "To every man according to his several ability." It was resolved to review this sermon at the next meeting of Presbytery. Accordingly, at the next meeting, the matter was brought up, and the following order fixed for the discussion: "Each member, in the order of the roll, shall have opportunity of stating what erroneous doctrines, if any, are contained in the discourse. If errors are alleged, they shall be definitely stated, and the part of the discourse in which they are contained pointed out." After discussing the discourse at some length, a committee, consisting of Messrs. Eaton, Chamberlain, and Elder John Lytle, was appointed to bring in a minute on the subject. The committee subsequently reported that they could not agree, and were discharged. A motion was then made to postpone the matter indefinitely, which was carried by a majority of one.

[1] Min. iii. 59.

"Coming events cast their shadows before." Here was the beginning of differences of opinion that ere long were to involve the Presbytery in trouble, and result in changes disastrous to the peace of Zion.

At the same meeting, Mr. Doolittle, at his own request, was released from the pastoral charge of the congregation of North East. This was on the 13th of September, 1832. On the 10th of April following, he was dismissed to the Presbytery of Portage. He had found a home at Hudson, Ohio, and thither he removed to enter upon a new field of labor. Both his friends and himself were afterward of opinion that he made a mistake in removing from North East. His labors had been abundantly blessed there; he had many devoted friends there; yet the path of duty to him seemed to lead elsewhere; he was a man of decision, and for him to decide was to act.

On the 12th day of September, 1832, Robert Glenn (44), was ordained and installed as pastor of the congregations of Mill Creek and Amity. In these services Mr. McCready preached the sermon, Mr. Tait delivered the charge to the pastor, and Mr. Hassinger the charge to the people. Mr. Glenn labored in these churches one third of his time in each; the remaining third was given to Sandy Lake, although he was never installed there. The church of Sandy Lake was not really organized until October 3, 1835. Mr. Glenn preached for some time at the house of Theodore Bailey, and in the school-house in the vicinity. The house of worship was not erected until 1846.

On the 11th of April, 1833, Morgan D. Morgans was licensed to preach the gospel. He had been a preacher in Wales in some independent branch of the Church, and had given satisfaction as to his experimental acquaintance with religion, but had not received a liberal education. Against this action Synod entered its protest.' Mr. Morgans did not prove an acceptable preacher, and being about to remove from the bounds, Presbytery recalled his license after he had preached one year. He subsequently engaged in teaching.

On the 10th of April, 1833, Benjamin J. Wallace,[1] a licentiate of the Presbytery of Carlisle, was received under the care of Presbytery.

On the 25th of June, 1833, Mr. Bushnell was released from the pastoral charge of the congregation of Meadville. The Western Foreign Missionary Society had been organized, having its centre of operations at Pittsburgh; and missionaries were called for to go to India, to Africa, and to our Western Indians. Mr. Bushnell's ardent missionary spirit impelled him to devote himself to the work, and after much thought and prayer he resolved to offer himself as a missionary to the Indians. He was designated as a laborer amongst the Weas, in Missouri, but did not sunder his connection with the Presbytery. The result showed that he had overestimated his strength and endurance. After struggling for a year and a half, he resigned and returned to the bounds of the Presbytery of Indianapolis, to which he was dismissed on the 3d of February, 1836, having been a member of the Presbytery ten years.

On the 26th of June, 1833, James G. Wilson (49), was licensed to preach the gospel. During this year

[1] Son of William and Eleanor (McClay) Wallace; born in Erie, Pa., June 10, 1810. Cadet at West Point. Studied theology at Princeton; licensed by Presbytery of Donegal. Ordained by Presbytery of Muhlenburg; Professor of Languages in Newark College, Delaware. Editor *Presbyterian Quarterly Review;* also of *American Presbyterian.* Died of neuralgia, July 25, 1862, in the fifty-third year of his age. — Wilson's *Presbyterian Historical Almanac.*

Mr. Hassinger was installed as pastor of the congregations of Harmonsburg, Evansburg, and North Bank, in Crawford County.

On the 11th of September, 1833, William A. Adair (46), a licentiate of the Presbytery of Hartford (Beaver), was received under the care of Presbytery, and accepted calls from the congregations of North East and Harbor Creek. On the 6th day of the following November, he was ordained and installed as pastor of this charge. In these services Mr. Eaton preached the sermon, Mr. Anderson delivered the charge to the pastor, and Mr. Chamberlain to the people. At this meeting, John NcNair (45), a licentiate of the Presbytery of Philadelphia, was taken under the care of Presbytery and ordained with Mr. Adair, as an evangelist, with the view of laboring as a missionary in Warren County.

On this occasion, Presbytery cordially endorsed the Western Foreign Missionary Society, and resolved to support one missionary in the foreign field. It was further resolved, that Mr. Bushnell be the missionary to be supported by Presbytery. After Mr. Bushnell returned from the field, Presbytery still resolved to continue their support of a missionary. At this meeting, Wattsburg was reported and enrolled as an organized church.

On the 25th of June, 1834, Mr. Alexander was released from the pastoral charge of Salem, Greenville, and Big Bend. On the 9th day of the following month B. J. Wallace, licentiate, was dismissed, to place himself under the care of the Presbytery of Muhlenburg; and Mr. Adair released from the pastoral charge of the congregation of Harbor Creek.

On the 25th of June in this year, a paper, called the

"Act and Testimony," drawn up by a number of the members of the last General Assembly, was brought to the notice of Presbytery, a portion of it read, and committed to a committee consisting of Messrs. Tait, Hampson, and Alexander Brown, elder, to report upon at the next meeting of Presbytery.

At the meeting on the 9th of October following, the committee presented the following report:—

"The circumstances of your committee being so different as to location, and the various sources of information from those who framed the 'Act and Testimony,' they consider it inexpedient for them to express an opinion on the document, taken as a whole, but they freely acknowledge that a document, framed and signed by men of such known integrity and worth, and whose attachment to the standards and doctrines of our church is highly to be regarded, they would therefore recommend the following resolutions, namely:—

"1. That this Presbytery do solemnly protest against the conduct of any claiming the right to interpret the doctrines of our standards differently from the sense in which our church has always held them, or preaching or publishing Arminian or Pelagian errors, while they profess to adopt and approve our doctrine and order, and retain a standing in our church.

"2. That Presbytery solemnly protest against the following errors, namely, our relation to Adam, etc., etc.

"3. That we will not knowingly countenance such ministers, elders, editors, or teachers, who hold or propagate such errors as are referred to.

"4. That we protest against the erection of Presbyteries or Synods on the elective affinity plan, as a departure from our form of government, and the usages of our church, and also as opening a wide door for the spread of errors.

"5. That all the sessions under the care of this Presbytery take order, and express their opinion, on the said Act and Testimony."

This report was adopted by the following vote: Samuel Tait, Johnston Eaton, Ira Condit, Peter Hassinger, James Alexander, G. W. Hampson, Robert Glenn, ministers; and elders Alexander Brown, Robert Clark, John Melon, W. Beatty, S. Wade, Washington Tait, and Robert Mann: *yeas*, 14. In the negative, Thomas Anderson and Pierce Chamberlain, ministers; and elders John McCord, John Reynolds, George Reznor, and Lansing Wetmore, 6. Mr. Eaton and Elder Alexander Brown were appointed to attend the Convention called by the signers of the Act and Testimony at Pittsburgh, to take into consideration the state of the church. Here was another indication of the struggle that was coming upon the church. The low mutterings of the coming storm were becoming portentous, and all things were assuming the appearance of danger.

On the 28th of January, 1835, Mr. Alexander was dismissed to connect himself with the Presbytery of Ohio. On the following day, Mr. McCready was released from the pastoral charge of the congregations of Beaver Dam and Union, in Erie County, and advised to accept a call from that of Warren, Pa. On the 15th of April following, Mr. Adair accepted a call, for the whole of his time, from the congregation of North East. On the same day Rev. Nathaniel West (47), a foreign minister formerly connected with an independent church in Edinburgh, Scotland, presented a certificate of dismission from the Second Presbytery of Philadelphia, showing that he had been taken on trial as a foreign minister. Mr. West was accordingly received on further trials as a foreign minister.

The narrative of the state of religion, that is recorded during the year 1834-35, does not indicate that there was much of the spirit of revival in the Presbytery. Good attendance is reported, as being paid to catechetical instruction and Sunday-school effort; but no general revivals of religion.

At a former meeting the Presbytery had resolved to support Mr. Bushnell as their missionary in the foreign field, and now as Mr. Bushnell had retired from the work on account of feeble health, it was resolved still to continue the aid of Presbytery to the Western Foreign Missionary Society.

At the October meeting of Presbytery, it was "*Resolved*, That the members of this Presbytery give their efficient aid in circulating and procuring signatures to petitions to the next session of Congress to abolish slavery in the District of Columbia."[1]

On the 19th of April, 1836, Mr. Hassinger was released from the pastoral charge of the congregations of Evansburg, Harmonsburg, and North Bank. At the same time, the organization of the churches of Conneautville and Sandy Lake was reported. At this meeting the approval by Synod of the action of Presbytery in receiving Mr. West as a member of Presbytery, was reported, and Mr. West's name was placed upon the roll.

Mr. McNair (45) was, on the 20th of April, dismissed to connect himself with the Presbytery of Vincennes. On the 11th of May, 1836, Mr. West was installed as pastor of the congregation of Meadville. On the following day Rev. Simeon Peck (48) was received on

[1] Min. iii. 122.

certificate from the Presbytery of Buffalo. At the same time Presbytery approved the reorganization of the church of Warren, Pa.

On the 15th of September, of the same year, Mr. Hassinger was dismissed to the Presbytery of Washington. At this meeting Mr. Chamberlain was installed as pastor of the congregations of Waterford and Union. On the 12th day of October, 1836, James G. Wilson (49), was ordained and installed as pastor of the congregations of Greenville and Salem. In these services, Mr. Anderson preached the sermon, Mr. Tait delivered the charge to the pastor, and Mr. West the charge to the people. At the same time the name of the church at Elk Creek, in Erie County, was changed to Girard.

The report of a convention of elders at Meadville having been laid before Presbytery, was approved, and the object commended. The convention seems to have been composed of elders from Crawford County, and its object to have been to devise means to promote the spiritual interests of the people of that county.

On the 3d day of February, 1836, Mr. Bushnell was dismissed to the Presbytery of Indianapolis. On the 11th day of January, 1837, Robinson S. Lockwood (50), a licentiate recently received from the Presbytery of St. Lawrence, was ordained and installed as pastor of the congregation of Girard. In these services Mr. West preached the sermon, Mr. Eaton delivered the charge to the pastor, and Mr. Lyon the charge to the people.

The matter of slavery was again noticed, by the adoption of the following resolutions : —

" 1. That it is the duty of the ministers of this Presbytery to preach against the sin of slave-holding.

" 2. That it be earnestly recommended to each of the

churches under our care, to address a memorial to the next General Assembly, imploring that body to use all its influence for the expulsion of slavery from our church."[1]

The organization of the churches of McKean and Cherrytree, was reported April 11, 1837. On the following day Reuben Lewis (51), a licentiate of the Presbytery of Blairsville, was received under the care of Presbytery; and on the same day Mr. McCready was installed as pastor of the congregation of Warren; Mr. Hampson was also released from the pastoral charge of the congregation of Concord in Venango County, and was permitted to labor for two thirds of his time at Oil Creek.

At this meeting it was resolved, that for members of the church to sign petitions for the licensing of taverns, is wrong, and subjects them to the censure of the church.

On the 12th day of September, 1837, Mr. Anderson was released from the pastoral care of the congregation of Franklin, Pa., and on the 1st of November following Reuben Lewis (51), a licentiate, who had been received the previous year from the Presbytery of Blairsville, was ordained, and installed as pastor of the congregation of Harbor Creek. In these services, Mr. Lyon preached the sermon, Mr. Adair delivered the charge to the pastor, and Mr. Hampson the charge to the people.

On the 11th of April, 1838, Rev. Wells Bushnell (35), who had formerly been a member of Presbytery, was received from the Presbytery of Indianapolis, and on the following day, Rev. William Fuller (52) and Rev. Charles Danforth (53) were received from the

[1] Min. iii. 146.

Presbytery of Grand River. On the next day Mr. Adair was released from the pastoral charge of the congregation of North East. On the same day John Van Liew Reynolds (56) was licensed to preach the gospel. On the 26th day of June following, Mr. West was released from the pastoral charge of the congregation of Meadville.

This chapter closes with dark forebodings of trouble. Clouds had been gathering that foretokened a storm of greater magnitude than any that had yet swept over the church. Differences had sprung up that could not be reconciled. In many cases these differences were really serious and important; in some perhaps wholly imaginary. But the brethren were divided either in sentiment or in heart, or in both, and the consequences were most lamentable. The hearts of good men on either side were ready to fail them for fear; for schism if not open revolution seemed unavoidable; and the church, that had for so many years been expanding and prospering and overshadowing the land with its blessed influences, bid fair to be shorn of its splendor, and weakened in its influence.

CHAPTER V.

THE GREAT DIVISION.

1837–1838.

THE shock came at last. The storm burst forth in its fury, leaving for a time little but desolation in its path: alienated hearts, sundered ties, riven churches, and the exultation of the foes of Zion. The General Assembly of 1837 had passed resolutions declaring certain Synods no longer portions of the Presbyterian Church, and dissolving the Third Presbytery of Philadelphia. With reference to this action, at a meeting of Presbytery held September 12, 1837, the following resolution was passed by a majority of one: "*Resolved*, That in the opinion of this Presbytery, the act of the late General Assembly, which dissolved the Third Presbytery of Philadelphia without previous citation or notice, was unconstitutional, and therefore null and void."[1] Yeas, 13. Nays, 12.

This was followed by another resolution, —

"*Resolved*, That in the opinion of this Presbytery the act of the late General Assembly, by which the four Synods of Utica, Geneva, Genesee, and Western Reserve were declared to be no longer a part of the Presbyterian Church in the United States of America, without previous citation or notice, is unconstitutional, and therefore

[1] Min. iii. 158.

null and void." This resolution was also decided in the affirmative, by a vote of fifteen to ten. The ayes and nays were as follows: Ayes: Ministers, Amos Chase, Thomas Anderson, Robinson S. Lockwood, Edson Hart, George W. Hampson, George A. Lyon, and William A. Adair, with elders Andrew Bowman, D. H. Chapman, William Miller, S. Heimbaugh, T. Reid, J. Kinkead, George Kellogg, and Samuel Kingsbury — 15.

Noes: Ministers, Samuel Tait, Johnston Eaton, Absalom McCready, and James G. Wilson, with elders John Hackney, Eliab Axtell, James Jagger, William White, James McCracken, and Homer Bailey — 10.[1]

After the recess the following complaint and appeal was offered by Mr. Tait in behalf of himself and others, and directed to be entered on the minutes: —

"WARREN, (PA.), *September* 13, 1837.

"WE, the undersigned members of the Presbytery of Erie, protest against the decisions of this Presbytery in declaring the acts of the General Assembly unconstitutional, null, and void, which dissolved the Third Presbytery of Philadelphia, and declared the Synods of the Western Reserve, Genesee, Utica, and Geneva no longer a part of the Presbyterian Church, for the following reasons, namely —

"1st. Although we admit that Presbyteries have a right to complain, and petition our higher courts for redress of supposed grievances, yet for a Presbytery to declare the acts of our General Assembly null and void, we deem unconstitutional and disorderly.

"2d. We believe that these acts of the General Assembly were the only means left to correct the evils, and restore peace and purity to our church.

[1] Min. iii. 159, 160.

HISTORY. 137

"3d. We believe the General Assembly, acting in a legislative capacity, had a right to repeal its own acts."[1]

This complaint was signed by Samuel Tait, Johnston Eaton, Absalom McCready, and James G. Wilson, ministers: and by John McCracken, James Jagger, John Hackney, and Homer Bailey, elders.

In regard to these resolutions the Synod of Pittsburgh, in reviewing the Records of Presbytery, took the following exception:

"The resolutions recorded on the pages 158 and 159 of the Records, whereby the acts of the last General Assembly, in reference to the Third Presbytery of Philadelphia, and the Synods of Western Reserve, Utica, Geneva, and Genesee are declared to be unconstitutional, null, and void, are, in the judgment of Synod, incorrect, as to matter of fact.

CHARLES C. BEATTY, *Moderator.*"
PITTSBURGH, *October* 25, 1837.

This was the state of affairs, when the Presbytery met at Meadville, Pa., on the 26th day of June, 1838. There were present at this meeting, the following members: Ministers, Samuel Tait, Amos Chase, Johnston Eaton, Bradford Marcy, Pierce Chamberlain, Wells Bushnell, Absalom McCready, Thomas Anderson, Nathaniel West, George A. Lyon, George W. Hampson, Robert Glenn, William Fuller, Charles Danforth, James G. Wilson, Robinson S. Lockwood, and Reuben Lewis. Elders: Alexander Brown, George G. Foster, John Reynolds, George Reed, James McClanahan, Cyrus Mansfield, Moses Logan, James Gilleland, Noah Town, Robert Stockton, David Brackenridge, John C. Robinson, John Wilson, John Hackney, Calvin Martin, James Campbell, D. H. Chapman, Pros-

[1] Min. iii. 160, 161.

per A. Booth, James Smedley, George Kellogg, Samuel Kingsbury, Francis Gray, John Carson, John N. Miller, J. Fritz, John McCracken, and Ninian Irwin.

It was known that the late General Assembly had divided, and that the Commissioners from this Presbytery, Rev. Pierce Chamberlain and Elder George Kellogg, had given in their adherence to the Assembly known popularly as "The Other Branch," and had identified themselves with it; and the consideration of this matter was to be the great question before the Presbytery.

Soon after the organization of Presbytery, the following preamble and resolution were offered by Mr. McCready: "Whereas, it is a time of great conflict, corruption, and difficulty in the Presbyterian Church in the United States and whereas the General Assemblies of 1837 and 1838 have entered upon reform measures, agreeably to our standards, to promote the peace, purity, and orthodoxy of said church, which have hitherto proved successful; and whereas, they enjoin it upon all the Presbyteries under their care to pursue the same measures of reform, in all their boundaries; and whereas it is publicly reported that Pierce Chamberlain and George Kellogg, our delegates to the last Assembly, after giving in their commissions to the Assembly, did absent themselves from the true Assembly, and associate themselves with a number unknown to the General Assembly to form a new Assembly, and are officially reported as being absent from the true Assembly without cause: Therefore —

"*Resolved*, That the roll be now called to take proper order in regard to the Commissioners for neglect of duty according to the resolution of the last Assembly; and also that the members of this Presbytery be now called, individually, to sustain the reform measures of the General Assemblies of 1837 and 1838; and that the answers be given yea or nay."[1]

The consideration of this paper was made the order of the day for the next morning.

The next morning "The order of the day was taken up, and after some discussion was postponed for the purpose of hearing the report of our Commissioners to the General Assembly, who being called upon informed Presbytery that they gave in their commissions to the General Assembly, but that before the roll was completed they united with a number of ministers and elders, in organizing another body, calling itself the General Assembly of the Presbyterian Church in the United States, and which our Commissioners acknowledged as the lawful General Assembly; after which they withdrew: whereupon, it was moved that their conduct be approved.

"And while this motion was under discussion, a postponement of it was moved, for the purpose of taking up a resolution, the object of which was to refer the whole matter to Synod. During the pending of these motions, the whole subject of the constitutionality of the two Assemblies was fully discussed; after which the motion of postponement was taken by calling the roll."[2]

The following was the result of the vote: Amos Chase, Bradford Marcy, Nathaniel West, Pierce Chamberlain, Thomas Anderson, George A. Lyon, George W. Hampson, Robinson S. Lockwood, William Fuller, and Charles Danforth, ministers, with John Reynolds, James McClanahan, Cyrus Mansfield, Noah Town, Robert Stockton, David Brackenridge, John Wilson, Calvin Martin, James Campbell, David H. Chapman, James Smedley, George Kellogg, Samuel Kingsbury, Francis

[1] Min. iv. 21-23.   [2] Min. iv. 24, 25.

Gray, John Carson, J. N. Miller, J. Fritz, and Ninian Irwin, elders, voted in the affirmative, being ten ministers and eighteen elders — twenty-eight in all.

In the negative there were seven ministers, namely, Samuel Tait, Johnston Eaton, Wells Bushnell, Absalom McCready, Robert Glenn, James G. Wilson, and Reuben Lewis, with nine elders, namely, George Reed, Moses Logan, James Gilleland, George G. Foster, Alexander Brown, John McCracken, John C. Robinson, Prosper A. Booth, and John Hackney, sixteen in all.[1]

It will be seen that the actual vote was not on the merits of the case, but on the reference of the whole matter to Synod. It is also obvious, however, that the majority of Presbytery were in opposition to the reform measures of the late General Assembly. The minority, seeing that there was now no other resource, quietly withdrew to another house, and continued the business of Presbytery, according to the order of the General Assembly adapted to circumstances like the present. This order is in the following words: "In case the majority of any Presbytery shall refuse or neglect to take proper order in regard to its seceding Commissioners, or shall approve their conduct, or adhere to the new sect they have created, or shall decline, or fail to adhere to the Presbyterian Church in the United States of America, upon the basis of 1837 and 1838, for the reform of the Church, then, and in that case, the minority of said Presbytery shall be held and considered to be the true Presbytery, and shall continue the succession of the Presbytery by its name and style, and from the rendition of the erroneous and schismatical decision, which is the test in the case, be the Presbytery; and if sufficiently numerous to perform Presbyterial acts, shall

[1] Min. iv. 25, 26.

go forward with all the proper acts and functions of the Presbytery." [1]

The Moderator and Stated Clerk being among the minority, the Presbytery was already organized, and lacked but a temporary clerk to proceed with its regular business. The Records of Presbytery also remained in the keeping of the minority.

Two ruling elders, David Brackenridge and Robert Stockton, who had voted with the majority, appeared before Presbytery and declared their approval of the reform measures of the General Assembly, and requested seats in Presbytery, which request was granted. The conduct of the Commissioners to the General Assembly was then formally disapproved.

At the next meeting of the Synod of Pittsburgh, several members of the majority of Presbytery appeared and claimed seats. Those who thus claimed seats, were: ministers George W. Hampson, Nathaniel West, and William A. Adair; elders John McCord and Samuel Kingsbury. Synod refused to admit them to seats, and their case was referred to a committee consisting of Rev. Drs. David Elliott and Charles C. Beatty, and Rev. T. D. Baird, to consider and report thereon. These brethren were fully heard in regard to their claim. The committee reported adversely to their claim, which report was adopted. A protest against the decision of the Synod was presented, signed by Rev. David H. Riddle, D. D., Rev. Aaron Williams, and elders John Herron, Richard Edwards, John Wright, and Matthew F. Champlin. A committee consisting of Dr. Elliott, Rev. William Jeffrey, and Rev. James Hervey, was appointed to answer the protest. This committee presented a long paper, which was adopted, as the answer of Synod.

[1] Baird's *Digest*, 758.

The other branch of the Presbytery of Erie has enjoyed a good degree of prosperity. After occupying the same territory substantially as before the division, for a few years, their Presbytery was divided by an act of the Synod of Pennsylvania into two Presbyteries. This division was ordered on the 25th of October, 1842. All the ministers and churches within the County of Erie, were to be considered as the Presbytery of Erie, and all the ministers and churches outside the County of Erie were to be constituted into a Presbytery, to be called the Presbytery of Meadville. This new Presbytery of Meadville consisted of six ministers, four of whom had been members of the old Presbytery of Erie.

These two Presbyteries, together with one that had been organized in the region of Pittsburgh, and called Pittsburgh, constituted the Synod of Western Pennsylvania.

CHAPTER VI.

FROM THE GREAT DIVISION TO THE PRESENT.

1838–1867.

The storm had come and gone. The noise and the strife were over. But the consequences remained. The first meeting of the Presbytery was a sad and painful one. The officers and the records were there, but brethren beloved and respected were absent. Those present looked around to see who were present and who were absent. It was like the meeting of Æneas and his comrades after the storm that Juno's wrath had excited; counting the ships that were safe, and lamenting over those that had been stranded on the great deep. Here were fast friends for years, separated forever upon earth. Brethren who had taken sweet counsel together, and walked to the house of God in company, who had labored and wept and prayed together, and whose sympathies had been in common for nearly a lifetime, were to meet no more together. Henceforth they were to pass at life's meeting-places, like ships upon the ocean, with nought but the ordinary signal of recognition, bringing up the love and esteem many of them felt for each other in the secret chambers of their own hearts.

But like Æneas of old in another respect, they girded themselves for new labors and new perils. With sad thoughts at the division of the Presbytery, and separation from cherished brethren, they prepared to gather up the fragments of what remained, and go forward with the labor and the toil as best they might. New churches must be organized as new fields were explored. Divisions must be expected in churches already established. The evil consequences of these divisions must be met, and the injury to Zion must, as far as possible, be repaired.

And so they went on, the two divisions; two Presbyteries, bearing the same name, occupying substantially the same territory, and to all intents and purposes one in design and one in faith and polity, yet separate in organization and in feeling; and yet withal striving to do their own appropriate work, not walking together, nor talking together, yet dealing only in charity, and feeling, if not expressing, confidence in each other's piety and zeal in the Master's cause. It was Paul and Barnabas, contending so sharply that they had "departed asunder one from the other," yet both striving to do the Lord's work.

The vote recorded in the preceding chapter shows the relative numbers of the two Presbyteries. The minority, that now constituted the Presbytery called by way of distinction " Old School," consisted of Samuel Tait, Johnston Eaton, Wells Bushnell, Absalom McCready, Robert Glenn, James G. Wilson, Simeon Peck, and Reuben Lewis.

Of the congregations, some remained entire with one division and some with another, whilst some were divided. In many cases these divisions were most disastrous to the congregations, weakening and disheartening them and rendering them unable to support the gospel. Of those remaining entire, with the Old School branch, were Fairview, Fairfield, Georgetown, Cool

Spring, Franklin, Big Sugar Creek, Mill Creek, Harmonsburg, Evansburg, Salem, Greenville, Sugar Grove, Concord, Deerfield, Warren, Amity, Irvine, and Big Bend. Of those remaining entire with the other branch, were Erie, North East, Springfield, Girard, Middlebrook, Beaver Dam, Union, McKean, Centerville, Oil Creek, Pine Grove, Cherrytree, Randolph. Of those divided were, Meadville, Mercer, Harbor Creek, Washington, Gravel Run.

In the division of Presbytery, there was no property held by the Presbytery directly that was calculated to bring the constitutionality of either body before the civil courts; so that happily, for the present, the authority of Cæsar was not invoked, and each branch pursued its own course in comparative peace and quietness. There was not much sociability between the members of the different Presbyteries, who had once been on the kindest terms of fellowship, yet there was nothing like warfare. They agreed to differ, and whilst in their hearts they respected and loved each other, there was no demonstration of this feeling — it was buried up amongst the sacred things of the past.

On the 27th of June, 1838, Mr. McCready was released from the pastoral charge of the congregation of Warren, Pa., and on the same day, David Waggoner (54), a licentiate of the Presbytery of Ohio, was received under the care of Presbytery, and accepted calls from the congregations of Georgetown and Fairfield.

On the 28th of the same month, William McMichael[1] was licensed to preach the gospel.

On the 11th of July following, Daniel Waggoner was ordained and installed as pastor of the churches of

---

[1] Transferred to the Presbytery of Clarion. Pastor of the churches of Richland and Rockland, in Venango County, Pa.

Georgetown and Fairfield, dividing his time equally between them. In these services Mr. Bushnell preached the sermon, Mr. McCready delivered the charge to the pastor, and Mr. Glenn the charge to the people.

On the 17th of April, 1839, Rev. Daniel Washburn (55) was received on certificate from the Presbytery of Beaver, and Rev. Wells Bushnell dismissed to the Presbytery of Beaver.

At this time a committee was appointed to report what action should be taken in regard to persons withdrawing themselves from the churches to connect with churches of the other branch. This committee reported recommending that when such withdrawals are ascertained, a simple record be made of the fact in the sessional records, and no further action be taken.

On the 14th of October, 1839, Mr. McCready was installed as pastor of the church of Neshannock, which had been set over from the Presbytery of Beaver. On the same day, Mr. Peck was dismissed to the Presbytery of Philadelphia, and Edmund McKinney (57), a licentiate of the Presbytery of Carlisle, received under the care of Presbytery.

On the 15th of October of this year, Cyrus Dickson (58) was licensed to preach the gospel.

On the 13th of November, John Van Liew Reynolds (56) was ordained and installed as pastor of the congregation of Meadville, and at the same time Edmund McKinney was ordained as an evangelist. In these services Mr. McCready preached the sermon, Mr. Tait delivered the charge to the ministers, and Mr. Eaton delivered the charge to the congregation.

On the 24th of June, 1840, Cyrus Dickson was ordained and installed as pastor of the congregations of Franklin and Sugar Creek, half his time at each. In these services, Mr. Eaton preached the sermon, Mr. McCready gave the charge to the pastor, and Mr. Wilson the charge to the congregation.

On the 9th of September following, Mr. Lewis was dismissed to the Presbytery of Ohio. On the 27th of January, 1841, Edward S. Blake (59), a licentiate of the Presbytery of Ohio, was received under the care of Presbytery, and on the 14th of April following, ordained and installed as pastor of the churches of Gravel Run and Evansburg. In these services, Mr. Waggoner preached, Mr. Eaton delivered the charge to the pastor, and Mr. McCready the charge to the people. On the same day Joseph T. Smith (61) was licensed to preach the gospel.

On the 14th of June, 1841, Rev. Hiram Eddy (60), of the Congregational Association of Western New York, was received as a member of Presbytery. On the 15th of September following, Daniel Washburn and Edmund McKinney were dismissed from Presbytery, the former to the Presbytery of Wooster, and the latter to Carlisle. Mr. Blake was also released from the pastoral charge of the congregations of Gravel Run and Evansburg, on account of feeble health.

About this time a zealous effort was made by Presbytery to seek out and encourage pious and hopeful young men to turn their attention to the gospel ministry. It was made the direct duty of each member of Presbytery to give attention to this matter; although the result does not seem to have been encouraging.

The matter of missionary effort within its own bounds was during this year pressed upon the churches. In January, 1842, Presbytery resolved to sustain a missionary in its vacant churches.

At the same meeting the churches were all enjoined

to unite in memorializing Congress for the better observance of the Sabbath.

On the 19th of April, William McMichael, a licentiate under our care, was dismissed to put himself under the care of the Presbytery of Clarion. On the following day, Joseph T. Smith was ordained and installed as pastor of the congregation of Mercer. In these services Mr. Reynolds preached the sermon, Mr. Dickson delivered the charge to the pastor, and Mr. Waggoner the charge to the people. In this congregation Mr. Smith had been born and raised, all his associations were connected with it, and his father was a member of the session. On the same day Mr. Wilson was released from the pastoral charge of the congregation of Greenville.

Sometime during the month of May of this year, the church of Mount Pleasant was organized. On the 28th of June, James Coulter (62), a licentiate of the Presbytery of Alleghany, and Henry Webber (63), a licentiate of the Presbytery of Elizabethtown, were received under the care of Presbytery. On the 14th of September following, Mr. Coulter was ordained and installed as pastor of the congregations of Concord and Deerfield; at the former, one half his time, and at the latter, one fourth, leaving a remaining fourth for missionary labor. In these services Mr. Reynolds preached, Mr. Dickson delivered the charge to the pastor, and Mr. Waggoner the charge to the people. On the same day, Alexander Cunningham (65) was licensed to preach the gospel. On the next day, John H. Townley,[1] a licentiate under the care of the Presbytery of Elizabethtown, was received under the care of Presbytery.

On the 20th of January, 1843, Henry Webber was ordained and installed as pastor of the church of Green-

---

[1] Returned soon after to New Jersey. Pastor of the church of Hacketstown, N. J. Since deceased.

ville. Mr. Glenn preached on the occasion, Mr. Reynolds delivered the charge to the pastor, and Mr. Dickson the charge to the people. The name of the church of Big Bend was stricken from the roll, the church having become extinct. Mr. Hart was dismissed to the Presbytery of Muhlenburg. On the 9th of August, James W. Dickey (64), a licentiate of the Second Presbytery of Philadelphia, was received under the care of Presbytery. In September of this year, Mr. Wilson was installed as pastor of the church of Cool Spring. On the 4th day of October, Mr. Dickey was ordained and installed as pastor of the congregations of Conneautville, Harmonsburg, and Evansburg. Mr. Dickson preached the sermon, Mr. Coulter delivered the charge to the pastor, and Mr. Waggoner the charge to the people. On the same day, John Limber (66) was licensed to preach the gospel.

On the 5th day of October, Mr. Cunningham was ordained and installed as pastor of the congregations of Gravel Run and Washington. Mr. Reynolds preached the sermon, Mr. Smith delivered the charge to the pastor, and Mr. Wilson the charge to the people. At the same time Lemuel G. Olmstead (73), a licentiate of the Presbytery of Beaver, was received under the care of Presbytery. In April of this year the church of Irvine was organized.

In April, 1844, Presbytery petitioned the General Assembly to devise some means to purge the church of "the enormous evil of slavery." On the 16th of October, of the same year, John Limber was ordained as an evangelist, with the view of laboring amongst the Indians. On the 22d of January, 1845, Mr. Webber was dismissed to connect himself with the Presbytery of Beaver. On the 12th of February following, an overture was sent to the Presbytery of Meadville, of the other branch, with reference to a union of the Presbyteries. This overture was replied to by the Presbytery of Meadville, in a kind and conciliatory manner, expressing a wish for reunion, yet expressing doubts whether the time had fully come for such reunion. They also suggested that the practice of some of the results of union should be first brought to bear, such as inter-communion, exchange of pulpits, and other mutual labors. This reply is noticed on the minutes, with the recommendation that the suggestions in it be carried out, that ministers and members use their discretion in regard to occasional inter-communion.

On the 26th of August, Mr. Eddy was dismissed to the Presbytery of Buffalo City. At this meeting the organization of the church of Sturgeonville was reported, as a colony from the church of Fairview. On the 22d of October, John M. Smith (67), of the Presbytery of Ohio, and Alexander Boyd (68), formerly a minister in the Associate Reformed Church, were received as members of Presbytery, and at the same time an elaborate paper was passed on the subject of slavery, bearing its testimony against slavery, dissenting against the fanaticism of men, North and South, in their war against the church of God, hoping for the time when this great evil shall be removed from the country, and declaring themselves free from all participation in the crime of oppression.

Mr. Dickson was permitted to give the whole of his labors to the congregation of Franklin, and Sugar Creek was declared vacant. At the same time Mr. Boyd was dismissed to the Presbytery of Steubenville.

During the year 1846, there were not many changes in the Presbytery. Peace and quietness reigned, and prosperity prevailed, although there was no special outpouring of the Holy Spirit. On the 28th of January, Mr. Smith was installed as pastor of the church of Warren; and on the same day Miles T. Merwin (69), a licentiate of the Presbytery of New York, was received under the care of Presbytery, and on the 24th of June ordained and installed as pastor of the church of Irvine. On the 22d of April Mr. Coulter was released from the charge of the congregations of Concord and Deerfield. On the same day Rev. John Matthews (22), who had formerly been a member of Presbytery, was received from the Presbytery of Coshocton. On the 26th of August, Mr. Dickey was released from the pastoral charge of the congregations of Harmonsburg and Conneautville, and at the following meeting, from that of Evansburg; and on the 28th day of October, John F. Kean,[1] a licentiate of the Presbytery of Blairsville, was received under the care of Presbytery.

During the year 1847 two ministers were received into the Presbytery, one was dismissed, and one removed by death. On the 23d of June, Mr. Matthews was dismissed to the Presbytery of Saint Louis, and on the same day, John K. Cornyn (70), a licentiate of the Presbytery of Alleghany, was received under the care of Presbytery, and on the 10th of August ordained and installed as pastor of the churches of Girard, Sturgeonville, and Harbor Creek.

On the 17th day of June, Johnston Eaton (20), the oldest minister then on the roll, departed this life. He had been for forty years and upward pastor of the church of Fairview, and had spent the whole of his ministerial life in the pastoral relation to that church.

[1] Born in Westmoreland County, Pa. Graduated at Jefferson College and Western Theological Seminary. Died December 20, 1846.

On the 10th day of August, Mr. Dickey was dismissed to the Presbytery of Richland, and on the same day Mr. Smith was released from the pastoral charge of the congregation of Warren; and on the 27th day of October, Lewis W. Williams (71) was received from the Presbytery of Blairsville.

There were more changes in the year 1848. On the 15th of March Mr. Smith was dismissed to the Presbytery of Muhlenburg, and on the next day Samuel J. M. Eaton (76) was licensed to preach the gospel, and Lemuel P. Bates (72) received from the Presbytery of Michigan. Mr. Dickson was also released from the pastoral charge of the congregation of Franklin, and dismissed to the Presbytery of Washington. On the 20th of April Mr. Olmstead was ordained as an evangelist, and on the 28th of June Charles V. Struve (74), a minister of the Baptist Church, was received as a member of Presbytery. On the 25th of October, James H. Callen (75), a licentiate of the Presbytery of Washington, was received under the care of Presbytery; and on the same day Mr. Coulter was installed as pastor of the congregation of Sugar Creek, and Mr. Merwin dismissed to the Presbytery of Huntington.

In the year 1849, there was one death in the ministry of the Presbytery, — that of Mr. Struve, that occurred at St. Louis in October. One ordination, that of S. J. M. Eaton (76), as pastor of the churches of Franklin and Mount Pleasant, February 7. On the 18th of April, Mr. J. T. Smith was released from the pastoral charge of the congregation of Mercer, and dismissed to the Presbytery of Baltimore. On the 26th of June, Mr. Williams was dismissed to the Presbytery of Huntington, and Mr. John M. Smith to the Presbytery of Ohio. On the same day, Nathaniel M. Crane (77) was received from the Presbytery of Buffalo. Mr. Crane had been a missionary to India, under the auspices of the American Board, and had done most excellent service in that benighted land. Enervated and enfeebled by the climate, he had returned to spend such days as God might give him in preaching the gospel. Of a meek and quiet and lovely disposition, he seemed, like the evangelist John, to be always leaning upon the Master's bosom, and reflecting the quiet expression of his countenance in his daily life.

During the year 1850, the Presbytery held its own in point of numbers. On the 18th of June, Michael A. Parkinson (78), a licentiate of the Presbytery of Ohio, was received under the care of Presbytery, and on the 11th of September, ordained and installed as pastor of the congregations of Concord and Deerfield, the former in Venango, and the latter in Warren County, Pa. On the same day, John Sailor (79) was received from the Presbytery of Pennsylvania, of the other branch. On the 3d of April, Mr. Glenn was released from the pastoral charge of the congregation of Amity, and on the next day, Mr. Cornyn was released from his charge of Girard, Sturgeonville, and Harbor Creek. On the 19th of June, Mr. Glenn was installed as pastor of Sugar Creek for half his time. On the 11th of September, Mr. Bates was dismissed to the Presbytery of Michigan, from which he had been originally received, and on the same day, Mr. Wilson was released from the pastoral charge of Cool Spring and Salem, and dismissed to the Presbytery of Iowa.

In 1851, one minister was dismissed from the Presbytery — Mr. Cornyn, to the Presbytery of Wyoming, April 9; and one received. This was Robert S. Morton (80), who was received from the Presbytery of Beaver,

June 10, and installed pastor of the church of Mercer on the 10th of September.

On the 10th of April, George Wright Zahniser (84) was licensed to preach the gospel; and on the same day William Willson (81), a licentiate of the Presbytery of Ohio, was received under the care of Presbytery; and Alexander Cunningham released from the pastoral charge of the congregation of Washington. On the next day, Mr. Willson was ordained and installed as pastor of the congregations of Girard, Sturgeonville, and Fairview.

The year 1852 presents few changes. On the 14th of April James Young [1] was licensed to preach the gospel. Mr. Cunningham was released from the pastoral charge of Gravel Run, and dismissed to the Presbytery of Alleghany. On the 22d of June, Mr. Callen was released from the pastoral charge of Greenville, and John Wesley McCune (82), a licentiate under the care of the Presbytery of Carlisle, was received and ordained and installed as pastor of the congregations of Cool Spring and Sandy Lake. Mr. Coulter was installed as pastor over the congregations of Harmonsburg and Conneautville on the 14th of September, and the following day over that of Evansburg.

On the 15th of September, Mr. Morton was released from the pastoral charge of the congregation of Mercer, and dismissed to the Presbytery of Beaver; and William McCullough (85) licensed to preach the gospel.

During the year 1853, Presbytery dismissed two of its members, and received an addition of three. On the 12th of January, Mr. Callen was dismissed to the Presbytery of Redstone. On the 4th of May, Mr. Waggoner was released from the pastoral charge of the

---

[1] Graduated at Washington College, Pa., and Western Theological Seminary; member of the Presbytery of Sydney.

congregations of Georgetown and Fairfield, and Mr. Sailor installed at Warren, Pa. On the 7th of September, David Grier (83) was received from the Presbytery of Wyoming, and George W. Zahniser ordained and installed as pastor of the congregation of Conneautville; and at the same time William McCullough was ordained as an evangelist; and on the next day James Irvine Smith (87) was licensed to preach the gospel. On the 22d of June, Robert F. Sample (86), a licentiate of the Presbytery of Northumberland, was received under the care of Presbytery, and on the 18th of October, ordained and installed as pastor of the congregation of Mercer. On the 20th of October, Mr. Parkinson was released from the pastoral charge of the congregations of Concord and Deerfield, and dismissed to the Presbytery of Steubenville; at the same time Mr. Young, licentiate, was dismissed, to put himself under the care of the Presbytery of Greenbrier.

In the year 1854, two new churches were enrolled: Waterloo, in Venango County, with a membership of twenty, and two elders, was organized on the 8th of March; and Greenfield, in Crawford County, on the 22d of June, with eleven members and two elders. On the 18th of January, Mr. Dickey (64), who had formerly been a member of Presbytery, was received from the Presbytery of Richland, and on the 19th of April, installed as pastor of the congregations of Gravel Run and Washington. On the 18th of January, Mr. Waggoner was dismissed to the Presbytery of Beaver, Mr. Grier was installed as pastor of the church of Greenville, and William J. Alexander (89), a member of the church of Mercer, licensed to preach the gospel. On the 27th of June, Mr. Crane was dismissed to the Presbytery of Clarion; and on the 25th of September, James Irvine

Smith was ordained as an evangelist, with the view of laboring as a missionary in the region of Lake Superior.

In 1855, the usual changes took place, pastoral relations formed, and others broken up; members received and others dismissed. On the 7th of February, Mr. McCune was released from the pastoral charge of Sandy Lake, and gave all his time to Cool Spring. On the 2d of May, James M. Shields (89), a licentiate of the Presbytery of Blairsville, was received under the care of Presbytery, and on the 29th of August, ordained and installed as pastor of the congregations of Georgetown and Fairfield. On the 2d day of May, Mr. Willson was released from the pastoral charge of Girard, Fairview, and Sturgeonville; and Mr. Eaton from the pastoral charge of Mount Pleasant, giving all his time to Franklin. On the 28th of August, Mr. Sailor was dismissed to the Presbytery of St. Joseph's, of the other branch. On the 19th of December, Mr. Alexander was ordained and installed as pastor of the congregations of Concord and Deerfield, and John D. Caldwell licensed to preach the gospel. On the 28th of June, Park Church, Erie, was organized.

In 1856, there were fewer changes than usual. The church of Milledgeville was organized; Mr. Caldwell, licentiate, was dismissed to the Presbytery of Dubuque on the 7th of May. On the same day, Mr. Sample was released from the pastoral charge of the congregation of Mercer, and dismissed to the Presbytery of Carlisle. On the 13th of August, Charles A. Behrends (90), a German minister, was received into the Presbytery from the United Evangelical Synod of North America.

During the year 1857, there were still fewer changes, as regards the reception or dismission of members. But the Presbytery, during the year, were called to lament the death of Robert Glenn, the oldest minister on the roll. He was not old in years, yet he had been a faithful laborer in the vineyard of the Lord. He died whilst yet pastor of the church of Mill Creek, where he had been ordained on the 12th of September, 1832. He died with the harness on, trembling as a sinner, yet rejoicing and triumphing as a Christian, in the grace of our Lord Jesus Christ. His death took place on the 6th of September, 1857, after having preached the gospel for a quarter of a century, and leaving behind him a record of piety and Christian consistency that is far more valuable than that of the heroes and conquerors, whose deeds are chronicled in story and in song.

On the 6th of January, William M. Blackburn (91) was received from the Presbytery of Lake, and on the 25th of May, installed as the first pastor of Park Church, Erie. On the 7th of January, Mr. Eaton was released from the pastoral charge of the congregation of Franklin, but continued as a stated supply, and Mr. Alexander from that of Concord and Deerfield. On the 29th of April, John Ross Findley (92) was received from the Presbytery of Sydney, and installed as pastor of the congregation of Mercer; and the name of Charles A. Behrends stricken from the roll, and on the 26th of September Mr. Willson was dismissed to the Presbytery of Kansas.

During the year 1858, there were few changes, but it was a year of rich mercy and blessing to many of the churches. The spirit was poured out in many places, reminding the attentive reader of the early years of the history of Presbytery. In the narrative of this year we read: "Sinners, not by twos and threes, but by scores, have been hopefully converted. One narrative (church) reports one hundred and fifteen precious souls as brought to Christ, another seventy-five, another forty, another twenty-five, another twelve."

On the 13th of April, Mr. Alexander was dismissed to the Presbytery of Washington. Mr. Coulter was released from the pastoral charge of Harmonsburg and Evansburg, and on the next day Ira Miller Condit (95), a member of the church of Georgetown, was licensed to preach the gospel. During this year the hearts of the brethren were made sad by the death of Mr. McCullough, who went to rest on the 1st day of February. He was anxious to labor, yet the call to rest was welcome and joyous.

In the year 1859, there were two dismissions from Presbytery, and three ordinations. On the 13th of April, Mr. Zahniser was released from the pastoral charge of Conneautville and dismissed to the Presbytery of Huntington; and on the same day, Mr. Grier was released from the pastoral charge of Greenville. On the next day, Mr. Coulter was dismissed to the Presbytery of Alleghany. Also, John R. Hamilton (93), a licentiate of the Presbytery of Blairsville, and John Dagg Howey (94), a licentiate of the Presbytery of Steubenville, were received under the care of Presbytery. On the 15th of June, Mr. Hamilton was ordained and installed as pastor of the congregation of Fairview, and on the 20th, of that of Sturgeonville. Half his time was employed in each congregation. On the 21st of September, Mr. Howey was ordained and installed as pastor of the congregations of Mill Creek and Sugar Creek — time divided equally. On the 24th of the same month, Mr. Condit was ordained as an evangelist, with the view of laboring as a missionary in China. The Presbytery had already sent two of its members to labor as missionaries amongst the Western

Indians, but Mr. Condit was the first to go to foreign lands. The occasion of his ordination was one of great interest. Rev. E. P. Swift, D. D., by invitation, preached the sermon, Dr. Reynolds offered the ordaining prayer, and Mr. Eaton delivered the charge to the missionary.

In the year 1860, two ordained ministers were received into the Presbytery and one dismissed. One licentiate was received and one candidate licensed. Rev. Anthony Canon Junkin (96) was received from the Presbytery of Baltimore on the 10th of April, and on the following day, Rev. Huey Newell (97), from the Presbytery of Iowa. On the same day, John Gordon Condit (100), a member of the church of Fairfield, and nephew of Rev. Ira Condit (24), one of the fathers of the Presbytery, was licensed to preach the gospel. On the 26th of June, George Scott (98), a licentiate of the Presbytery of Washington, was received under the care of Presbytery, and on the next day ordained and installed as pastor of the congregations of Greenfield and Evansburg, and afterwards of Harmonsburg. On the 27th of June, Mr. Grier was dismissed to the Presbytery of Carlisle. On the 19th of June, the church of Mount Vernon, a colony from the old church of Concord, in Venango County, was organized. This church consisted of eleven members with two elders.

In 1861 there were few changes. On the 8th of May, Rev. James Hilliar Spelman (99) was received from the Presbytery of Hudson of the other branch. On the same day, John Haskell Sargent (101), a licentiate of the Presbytery of Philadelphia, was received under the care of Presbytery, and on the 26th of June, ordained as an evangelist. On the 8th of May, Robert Taylor (102), a member of the Mercer County Bar-was licensed to preach the gospel, and on the 13th of November ordained and installed as pastor of the congregation of Warren, Pa. On the 26th of June, Mr. Condit was ordained as an evangelist. Both Mr. Condit and Mr. Sargent were ordained with reference to missionary work in the bounds of Presbytery. On the 26th of June, the name of the Fairview church was changed to Westminster. Fairview church had been gathered by Rev. Johnston Eaton, and was one of the oldest churches on the roll of Presbytery. But the changes of the times had placed it wholly outside of Fairview Township, and the name was consequently changed. On the 8th of April, Mr. J. M. Condit was dismissed to the Presbytery of Canton, China.

It was during this year that the Presbytery first placed upon record its deliverance on the state of the country, in connection with the war of the Rebellion. After approving of the conduct of its commissioners [1] to the General Assembly, in sustaining the "Spring Resolutions," they further say: "Presbytery, moreover, desires to express its hearty concurrence in the action adopted by the General Assembly, declaring it to be the duty of the Presbyterian Church, loyally to support the Government of the United States in its present struggle, regarding said action as being consistent with the patriotic devotion to the principles of civil and religious liberty, which said church has never failed to manifest, and which said government is so well and wisely adapted, as its organization was designed, to secure.

"Looking upon the present conflict as being, substantially, for the maintenance and preservation of what our revolutionary struggle was waged to establish (for

[1] Rev. S. J. M. Eaton, and Elder Elias Alexander, of Mercer.

the success of the present rebellion would go far, we believe, to endanger republican institutions themselves, by destroying confidence in them), we would be unfaithful to our noble record as a church, if now we should fail, in every proper way, to show our attachment to those institutions, to help to give us which, its ministers, ruling elders, and members, were amongst the first in offering treasure and blood, together with their prayers to the God who giveth the victory to whom He will." [1]

In 1862 there were the usual changes. On the 10th of June, Mr. Scott was released from the pastoral charge of the congregations of Greenfield, Evansburg, and Harmonsburg, and Mr. Junkin installed at Greenville. On the same day, Newell S. Lowrie (103), a licentiate of the Presbytery of Saltsburg, was received under the care of Presbytery, and on the 27th of October, ordained and installed as pastor of the congregations of Conneautville and Harmonsburg. At the same time, James Hervey Gray (104), a licentiate of the Presbytery of Alleghany City, received under the care of Presbytery the preceding day, was ordained as an evangelist. On the 26th of September, Mr. Taylor was released from the pastoral charge of Warren, Pa., and dismissed to the 2d Presbytery of Philadelphia.

In 1863, the Presbytery added one to the number of its ministers, and dismissed three to other Presbyteries. On the 26th of September, Rev. William Porter Moore (106) was received from the Presbytery of Clarion. On the 15th of April, Rev. William T. Hamilton, D. D., (105), was restored to the functions of the ministry. On the 23d of September, Mr. Sargent was dismissed to the Presbytery of Londonderry. On the 26th of September, Mr. Scott was dismissed to the Presbytery

[1] Min. vi. 201, 202.

of Steubenville, and on the 22d of December, Mr. Blackburn was released from the pastoral charge of the congregation of Park Church, Erie, and dismissed to the Presbytery of New Brunswick. On the 20th of October, the second church of Mercer was organized. This was a colony from the first church of Mercer, and consisted of forty-eight members, with three ruling elders.

During the year 1864 there was a slight gain in the membership of Presbytery. On the 23d of February, Mr. Shields was released from the pastoral charge of the congregations of Georgetown and Fairfield, and dismissed to the Presbytery of Alleghany City. On the 13th of April, Rev. George Fairies Cain (107) was received from the Presbytery of Newton, and on the 11th of May, installed as pastor of Park Church, Erie. On the 13th of April, Mr. Spelman was dismissed to the Presbytery of Washington. On the 12th of May, Dr. Hamilton was installed as pastor of the church of Warren, Pa. On the 13th of April, Mr. J. G. Condit was released from the pastoral charge of the congregation of Sandy Lake. On the 14th of June, Rev. William M. Robinson (108) was received from the Presbytery of Washington, and the next day installed as pastor of the congregation of the Second Church, Mercer. On the same day, Mr. J. R. Hamilton was released from the pastoral charge of the congregations of Sturgeonville, Girard, and Westminster, he having accepted the office of chaplain in the army of the United States. On the same day Rev. David Waggoner (54) was received from the Presbytery of Beaver, and on the 24th of June installed as pastor of the congregation of Georgetown for three fourths of his time, and on the 1st of July for the remaining fourth as pastor of Greenfield. On the 26th of September, Mr. J. G. Condit was dismissed to the

Presbytery of Fairfield, and on the 13th of December, Luther Martin Belden (109), a licentiate of the Presbytery of Redstone, was received under the care of Presbytery, and on the next day ordained and installed pastor of the congregations of Sturgeonville and Westminster.

In the year 1865, delegates were appointed to the Presbyteries of the other branch, Erie and Meadville, to convey the fraternal salutations of the Presbytery, and to endeavor to inaugurate a more friendly and sociable feeling between the bodies. The delegate to the Presbytery of Meadville, Dr. Reynolds, was prevented by ill health from fulfilling his mission. The delegate to the Erie Presbytery, Mr. Eaton, met with that Presbytery, was kindly and affectionately received, and assured of the fraternal regard of the brethren. A delegate was appointed to return the compliment. This delegate, Rev. William Grassie, met with the Presbytery, and expressed the kind wishes and Christian salutations of his brethren. The interchange was kind and feeling, and was regarded as the harbinger of better things to come.

On the 26th of April of this year, Rev. John Rice (110) was received from the Presbytery of Saltsburg, and Mr. Howey released from the pastoral charge of the congregations of Sugar Creek and Mill Creek. On the 29th of September, Mr. J. R. Hamilton was dismissed to the Presbytery of Washington. On the 8th of November, Samuel M. Glenn,[1] a member of the church of Mill Creek, was licensed to preach the gospel. Mr. Glenn was a son of Rev. Robert Glenn (44), one

---

[1] Graduate of Jefferson College; Western Theological Seminary. Dismissed to Presbytery of Columbus. Pastor of the Church of Lithopolis.

of the valued members of Presbytery, who now rested from his labors. On the 24th of September, the church of Petroleum Centre was organized. This church consisted of fourteen members with two ruling elders, and was made up of new material in a new town, in the oil region of Venango County. On the 26th of April, Dr. Hamilton was deposed from the ministry.

On the 26th of April, of this year, the following deliverance was made on the state of the country : —

"Whereas, in the great and desolating war waged to divide and destroy our government, which has continued now more than four years, during the first two or three years with varying success, often apparently to the advantage of the insurgents, our arms have in the course of the last year, and especially during the past few weeks, met with extraordinary and uninterrupted success, so that at present our government is in possession of every important harbor and seacoast city and town, from Maine to Eastern Texas, and our flag again floats over the fort, against which the first shot of the gigantic rebellion was aimed, and from which it was removed after having been lowered by its heroic garrison at the close of a gallant defense; and whereas, we are in possession of the capitol of the so-called confederate government; and whereas the general-in-chief of the rebel military forces has surrendered himself, and the principal army of the rebellion, to our armies, and the other armies of the rebellion, with few and comparatively insignificant exceptions, have surrendered and been destroyed as organized bodies ; therefore —

"*Resolved*, That our thanks and praises are due to Jehovah of Hosts, whose right-arm, we would distinctly acknowledge, has given us the victory.

"*Resolved*, That the wisdom and goodness of the

Providence of God are now clearly discernible in the light of events, in the long dark period of our disasters, in that, whilst afflicting, He has humbled us, and by tribulation, was leading us to a more full realization of what we are so slow to learn — our dependence on Him alone, the necessity of earnest prayer to Him with confession of our national sins with contrite hearts, the evil and guilt and barbarism of slavery, and the need of its utter removal from the land.

"*Resolved*, That our most hearty thanks are due to God, that through all our troubles and distresses, He has sustained the hope and confidence and courage of this great nation, so that the hearts of the people have not fainted, nor their strength failed.

"*Resolved*, That we record with deep gratitude the disposition of the loyal people of our country to see and confess the good hand of our God in our victories, and the unanimity with which, as under a common strong impulse of religious emotion, they showed forth their joy by acts and words of devout adoration.

Resolved, That we heartily rejoice at the prospect of early peace — a peace, the result of the triumph of the arms we were required by duty to God and our country to take up, in behalf and defense of right and justice and true liberty. May God, who has helped us hitherto, grant that these hopes of early peace may not be disappointed."[1]

With reference to the assassination of the President of the United States, the following paper was passed: "Whereas, in his providence, always wise, often mysterious, God has permitted the removal of our late honored Chief Magistrate, by the hand of an assassin, connected with a band of conspirators having in view the disorganization of our Federal Government: Therefore —

[1] Min. vii. 94–97.

"*Resolved*, That it becomes us as a people to bow in humble though sorrowing acquiescence under the heavy affliction, while declaring our abhorrence and condemnation of the enormous crime against the government, in which we see the spirit of barbarism, begotten out of the same iniquitous system out of which also sprang treason and rebellion, with all the cruelties inflicted on prisoners in Southern prisons, massacres of surrendered garrisons, lawless guerrilla warfare, etc.

"*Resolved*, That in the assassination of our late President, and attempted assassination of Secretary Seward, and the no-doubt purposed assassination of other high officers, we discover a legitimate fruit of the evil and dangerous tendency of the abuse of the great acknowledged American rights of the freedom of speech and of the press, showing itself in vituperation, threats, violent and intemperate denunciation, etc., of officers of the government, an evil confined to no particular time or class of persons, although of late it has been specially prevalent and intensely virulent.

"*Resolved*, In view of its tendency to demoralize and pervert the judgment and conscience, as made manifest in this rebellion, in conspiracies to burn and destroy cities and towns; to commit robberies; to put in jeopardy the lives of women and children, and other non-combatants, by attempts to hurl trains of passenger cars from railroad tracks, far away from the seat of war, and when such acts can have no possible influence in its progress favorable to the cause in the interests of which they are professedly done; and in encouraging assassinations of officers of government — a mode of warfare long since condemned by the civilized world as illegitimate and abhorrent to every human sentiment; and in view of its numerous evil effects on the white population wherever brought into contact with it, as well as in view of the monstrous wrong it is to the black race: That we rejoice in the prospect of the speedy, utter disappearance of slavery from the land; and to seek to hasten that disappearance, by all legitimate means, we regard to be the duty of all good men.

"*Resolved*, That it is the duty of all, to render a hearty support and sympathy to President Johnson, with prayers for divine counsel in his behalf, as now the head of this government.

"*Resolved*, That Presbytery recommend to all churches and church-members under our care the observance of Thursday, June the 1st (1865), next, as a day of humiliation and prayer, in compliance with the recently issued proclamation of President Johnson." [1]

In 1866, the changes were few. On the 25th of April, Mr. Gray and Mr. Howey were dismissed, the former to the Presbytery of Clarion, the latter to the Presbytery of Columbus; and on the same day Mr. Belden was released from the pastoral charge of Westminster. On the 11th of July, Mr. Lambe (111) was ordained and installed as pastor of the congregation of Milledgeville for one half of his time. On the 23d of October, Mr. Glenn, licentiate, was dismissed to put himself under the care of the Presbytery of Columbus, and Rev. James Junius Marks, D. D. (112), was received from the Presbytery of Ohio. On the 13th of December, Robert Stansbury Van Cleve (113), a licentiate of the Presbytery of New Brunswick, was received under the care of Presbytery, and ordained as an evangelist.

In the year 1867, there were not many changes. On the 8th of May, Mr. Junkin was released from the pas-

[1] Min. vii. 96–98.

toral charge of Greenville; Mr. Van Cleve was dismissed to the Presbytery of Buffalo, of the other branch; Rev. John J. Gridley (114) was received from the Methodist Episcopal Church, and Rev. J. Jones Smyth (115) from the Presbytery of Indianapolis; and on the 25th of September, Rev. David Patten (116) from the Reformed Presbyterian church. The name of the church of Mount Vernon was changed to Pleasantville, and the church of Tidioute reorganized, out of what had been the church of Deerfield. This church had been anciently called Tidioute, but had been changed to Deerfield, and now changed back to Tidioute. The church of Cochranton was also received from the Reformed Presbyterian Church.

During the last years of this period, many interesting revivals of religion have taken place. Many of the churches were very greatly refreshed and enlarged. In the year 1859, there were reported two hundred and seventy-six members as added on examination. In the next year, two hundred and forty-eight, and in 1867, three hundred and eighty-six. This latter was a year of the right-hand of the Most High, — a year when God seemed to be opening the windows of heaven in mercy to the children of men. During this year, there was a very general feeling of revival through the churches of the Presbytery, with the largest ingathering in its entire history.

CHAPTER VII.

SUPPLEMENTAL.

The roll of the Presbytery has been constantly changing. This has been owing not only to the common mortality that belongs to the human family, but chiefly to other causes. Since the origin of the Presbytery, it has been essentially missionary ground. In some sections of its territory, it is almost as destitute of the means of grace as in 1803, when "Supplications" were made for supplies. Many of its congregations are weak from the circumstances of the country and population. They have always remained weak. Some sections have been weakened by the division of Presbytery in 1838. Others, again, have been constantly depleted by emigration to the West. The consequence has been that pastoral settlements have been of short continuance, as a general rule. Some of the early fathers lived and died in the charges in which they were originally settled, but these were rare exceptions, and generally where they had procured property, when land was cheap, and drew a part of their livelihood from the soil. Ordinarily the meagreness of the salaries has induced the necessity of frequent changes, and the breaking up of pastoral relations that were otherwise pleasant, and would have been permanent.

There have been upon the roll of Presbytery, since

its organization, the names of one hundred and sixteen ministers. Of this number, forty-eight rest from their labors, and are now ministering in a higher and sublimer service in the Upper Sanctuary. It can truly be said: "Their works do follow them." The average age of these forty-eight departed brethren was sixty-five years; if we take the first thirty on the roll, the average age was seventy years, whilst the oldest three, James Satterfield, Joseph Badger, and Amos Chase, reached the patriarchal age of ninety years. Of these only eighteen actually died within the territory of the Presbytery and slumber amid the scenes of their labor in this Presbytery.

The oldest minister now living, whose name is on the roll of the Presbytery, is Daniel Washburn, of the State of New York, now in his seventy-sixth year; the next oldest is David McKinney.

It would be delightful to linger over the necrology of these deceased fathers and brethren, to speak of their labor and toil and suffering, in the Master's work; but time will not permit. Their record is on high. And when the Great Head and King in Zion makes up his jewels, and writes up the number of his people, it will be found that this and that man were born in Zion, through the instrumentality of their labors, until a mighty multitude shall stand before the throne, as the fruit of their ministry. Their record will be bright and beautiful

"When gems and crowns and monuments
Lie mouldering in the dust."

Of these one hundred and sixteen ministers, fifteen were born in foreign lands; and of these, ten were born in Ireland, two in Scotland, two in Germany, and one in England. Of those who were natives of the

United States, fifty-six were born in Pennsylvania, nine in Massachusetts, six in Ohio, five in New York, five in New Jersey, four in Connecticut, three in Vermont, two in Delaware, two in Maryland, two in Virginia, and one in Indiana, leaving three whose place of birth is unknown.

The members of this Presbytery have graduated or studied at the following institutions, namely: Cannonsburg Academy and Jefferson College, fifty-one; Washington College, Pa., six; College of New Jersey, five; Yale, four; Dickinson, three; Western University of Pennsylvania, two; and one each from the following: Alleghany, Pa.; La Fayette; Marshall; University of Pa.; Madison; Rhode Island College; Middlebury, Vt.; Amherst; Union, N. Y.; Muskingum, O.; Miamie University; Hanover, Ind.; Dartmouth; Williams, and Glasgow University. In addition to these, a few studied at academies, and of two, the place of study is unknown.

The theological education of the earlier ministers, was mainly pursued privately, under the superintendence of some laborious pastor. No less than twenty of them studied under Rev. John McMillan, D. D., one of the earliest pioneers, not only in preaching the gospel, but in lifting up the standard of education west of the Alleghany mountains. From him they received a system of theology, that they copied out laboriously, and afterwards taught to pupils who studied under them; so that the influence of Dr. McMillan's teaching did not stop with his immediate pupils, but extended to those who never saw his face or heard his voice.

After the establishment of theological seminaries, Phineas Camp, received in 1819, was the first minister in the Presbytery who had been an inmate of a seminary. He was a student of Princeton. Since that date, the Western Theological Seminary has furnished forty-one members; Princeton, nineteen; Andover, two; Union Theological Seminary, two; Oxford, one; and Auburn, one.

Of the older ministers on the roll, three at least, Joseph Badger, Johnston Eaton, and Benjamin Boyd, were regular government chaplains during the war of 1812. Of the younger members, eleven at least served as regular government chaplains during the late rebellion, and of these, three suffered imprisonment at the hands of the enemy. In addition to the regular service, nine at least were in the service of the Christian Commission for a greater or less period of time.

There is but one permanent office in the Presbytery, that of Stated Clerk. This office has been held by twelve different persons. William Wick was Stated Clerk from 1802 to 1809; Samuel Tait from 1809 to 1811; John McPherrin from 1811 to 1812; Cyrus Riggs from 1812 to 1821; Timothy Alden from 1821 to 1822; Johnston Eaton from 1822 to 1838; Wells Bushnell from 1838 to 1839; Reuben Lewis from 1839 to 1840; Absalom McCready from 1840 to 1842; John V. Reynolds from 1842 to 1851; David Waggoner from 1851 to 1853; and S. J. M. Eaton from 1853 to the present time.

The early fathers, and many of the younger brethren of the Presbytery of Erie, have passed away, and the angels are now listening to their songs; but they have left impressions behind them that will never be obliterated until the new heavens and the new earth shall take the place of those that now are. The record of their orthodoxy, their piety, their burning love for souls, and their self-denying labors, is not only written in God's great Book above, but is impressed upon the very hills and valleys that once resounded with their voices. More than this: it is written upon the green prairies of the great West; in the distant States of New England, and in the stirring region of Texas. And this record is to be gathered amid the quiet homes of many States; in the lonely military camp; amid the rush and storm and crash of the battle-field, where death holds fearful carnival; in the hospital, amid plague and pestilence and dire mutilating wounds; and amid all the varied vicissitudes of life, wherever sin has brought suffering and peril and danger. This sweet and beautiful record is to be found, wherever the breaking heart has called for comfort, and tearful eyes have looked for relief throughout all our broad land, and in other lands.

The influence of these men is felt in almost every community in Western Pennsylvania, in the peculiar type of religious faith and practice that prevails. The early fathers began their work when society was in a plastic state. The impressions they made became permanent. They have been handed down from one generation to another. They still affect the tone and character of society.

In addition to all this, their example is on record. It is a bright and luminous chapter in the history of the church of Jesus Christ. Though dead, they yet speak — speak to the churches; speak to us, their younger brethren, telling us —

"The vows
Of God are on us, and we may not stop
To play with shadows, or pluck earthly flowers,
Till we our work have done and rendered up
Account."

PART II.

BIOGRAPHICAL.

BIOGRAPHIES OF DECEASED MINISTERS.

"These all died in faith."

BIOGRAPHICAL.

(1.) THOMAS EDGAR HUGHES.
1798–1838.

Mr. Hughes, who heads the long roll of the Presbytery of Erie, was a notable man in his day. He was the first minister of the gospel who settled north of the Ohio River. He was of Welsh origin. His grandfather, William Hughes, emigrated from Wales at an early period, and died at the advanced age of one hundred years. His father, Rowland Hughes, died January 4, 1779, aged fifty-six years. Rowland Hughes was twice married. By his first wife he had two sons and one daughter. Each of these obtained a good report. His second wife was Elizabeth Smiley, daughter of Robert Smiley, long an elder in Scotland. By this marriage he had five sons and one daughter. Each of these was of good repute in the household of faith. Three were ministers of the gospel, James, Rowland, and Thomas Edgar. Two were associate judges and ruling elders, and the sister, Mrs. Isabella Anderson, was the mother of two ministers and one ruling elder.

Thomas Edgar Hughes, the fourth son of Rowland and Elizabeth (Smiley) Hughes, was born in York County, Pa., on the 7th day of April, 1769. In early youth he was not specially favored with facilities for education, except as to the principles of religion, but was occupied chiefly in the labors of the farm. About a year after his father's death, his mother with the family crossed the mountains and settled in what is now Washington County, Pa. Their home being equally distant between Chartiers and Upper Buffalo, they enjoyed the ministry of Rev. John McMillan, and at times that of Rev. Joseph Smith.

When Mr. Hughes was about twelve years of age, there were revivals of religion in both these churches. During these seasons of religious interest, deep impressions were made upon his mind, yet there seemed to be no abiding change. His seasons of thoughtfulness continued until the spring of 1787, when he was eighteen years of age. At this period, he was deeply convicted of sin and of his need of a Saviour. The more direct means of producing this state of mind he considered was an exhortation, on Monday after a communion occasion, by Dr. McMillan. This state of mind continued for several months. In deep distress he went a distance of ten miles to confer with a pious friend. This he ever afterwards regarded as a memorable visit. Whilst there his conviction of the evil and guilt of sin, especially grieving the Holy Spirit, were overpowering, well-nigh bringing him to despair. On his way home, he was led to reflect on the greatness and majesty of God, the method of salvation through Jesus Christ, until he obtained clearer views of the doctrines of the gospel than he had ever before conceived. He studied the "Assembly's Larger Catechism" closely, and was astonished that he had never before observed the truths of God's Word, so clearly set forth. Many passages of the Bible were brought to mind with an energy and grandeur before unappreciated, and he was impressed with the thought that they were the very words of God, most assuredly true and inestimably precious.

From papers left for the information of his family, the following extracts are made : —

"My mind was taken up in contemplating the amazing wisdom and love of God in providing a Saviour; but the personal glories of the Redeemer, the suitableness of his offices and work, his ability and willingness to save guilty sinners, his sufferings and death, and his present exalted state at the right hand of the throne of God, filled me with astonishment and wonder.

"Everything appeared new; the glory of God appeared to shine forth on everything around me. With intense interest I observed the change that had occurred in the frame of my mind. I dreadfully feared deception, and lifted up my heart in prayer to God to keep me from resting in any delusion. My mind, so dark and burdened before, enjoyed sweet composure and peace. The way of life appeared plain and infinitely excellent and glorious. I exclaimed : 'If I had a thousand souls, I could cheerfully trust them all in the hands of such a Saviour!'

"From this date, July 16, 1787, I humbly date my conversion to God, when I was eighteen years and three months of age."

In his handwriting, there is still extant a paper bearing date April 7, 1792, in which he enters into solemn covenant with God and consecration to his service. Not far from this date, he commenced his studies at the Cannonsburg Academy, with reference to the gospel ministry. Having made proficiency there, he repaired to Princeton and entered the College of New Jersey, where in due time he graduated, probably in 1797. There is evidence that whilst a student he maintained a godly walk and conversation. His theological studies were pursued under the direction of Rev. John McMillan, for whom he ever cherished a high degree of veneration.

He was licensed to preach the gospel by the Presbytery of Ohio, on the 17th day of October, 1798. Not long after this he began his ministerial labors in the congregation of Mount Pleasant, near Darlington, Beaver County, Pennsylvania, where he was ordained by the same Presbytery on the 28th day of August, 1799. For a time he labored in the congregation of New Salem, in connection with Mount Pleasant; but this was given up in 1808, when he devoted all his time to the latter place. Mr. Hughes' ordination was the first transaction of the kind north of the Ohio, and west of the Alleghany rivers. His pastoral relation to the church of Mount Pleasant continued until the 19th of November, 1830, a period of more than thirty years.

Leaving Mount Pleasant, he removed to Wellsville, Ohio, where, for about four years, he had charge of the Presbyterian Church in that place. He had long enjoyed a good degree of health, but at length became a great sufferer. He was afflicted with *angina pectoris*, causing him acute pain, and leading to the conclusion that his constitution was broken. He was laid aside from public labors about two years. In this time he had much tender and solemn religious exercise — penitent, humble, prayerful, hopeful, buoyant, confiding. At length his hour of death arrived. Amongst his last utterances, were these: "I feel unworthy to use such strong language as I might in truth, in speaking of the rich enjoyment the Lord permits me to experience. I am not afraid to die. My sins are all taken away through the mediation of Christ." And so he departed in peace, May 2, 1838, in the seventieth year of his age and fortieth of his ministry.

Amongst his memoranda is this : " On the 6th of May, 1799, I was married to Mary Donehey, a pious young woman. This I always regarded as one of the most happy occurrences of my life, one of the greatest gifts of God, and one received very sensibly in answer to prayer. She has been ever since, and continues yet to be, the great comfort of my life."

His wive survived him several years. They had ten children, seven sons and three daughters. Four of the sons, William, John D., Watson, and James R., are ministers of the gospel, and one an efficient ruling elder, and one of the daughters the wife of a minister. One of the ministers above mentioned has three sons in the ministry.

Mr. Hughes was a friend to education. He did much for the Greersburgh Academy. Many of the early ministers studied with him, and derived great assistance from his counsels and efforts. His charge was blessed with many revivals during his ministry. During one of these the Spirit of God was copiously poured out for several months, and upwards of one hundred persons were added to the Mount Pleasant Church. As a pastor he was faithful, being an earnest preacher, and careful in the religious training of the youth of his charge.

He was an earnest friend of missions. In the period of his vigor, he twice went, under appointment of the Synod of Pittsburgh, as a missionary amongst the Indians, for a few months. On one of these occasions he brought home with him an Indian boy to educate. This youth whilst in his family became hopefully pious, and made a public profession of religion. During one of his missionary tours,[1] he was instrumental in leading to conviction of sin, a somewhat celebrated Indian warrior called Ununqua, or Barnett, who was subsequently baptized and received into the church. He travelled as far northwest as Detroit in the work of his mission, and was with Badger (11) in the famous tour, when that veteran pioneer had such struggles with disease and cold and privation in the wilderness. But his struggles have all ceased. He rests from his labors. His ministry is now carried on where there are neither struggles, nor want, nor doubts, nor fears. He rests from his labors, and his works do follow him.

(2.) WILLIAM WICK.

1799–1815.

WILLIAM WICK was a lineal descendent of the Pilgrim Fathers. He was the son of Lemuel and Deborah (Luptein) Wick, and was born on Long Island, N. Y., on the 29th day of June, 1768. He removed to Washington County, Pa., in 1790. On the 21st day of April, 1791, he was united in marriage to Miss Elizabeth McFarland, youngest daughter of Col. Daniel McFarland, an officer of the Continental Army, in the Revolutionary War. Her mother's maiden name was Sarah Barber. Her father emigrated to Washington County at the close of the war, and settled on a large tract of land on what was called Lower Ten Mile Creek. His name is mentioned in "Old Redstone," page 146. She united with the church under the ministry of Rev. Thaddeus Dodd, and received her education chiefly from him.

There was a great call for ministers in these days,

---

[1] Dr. Elliott.

and Dr. McMillan was constantly seeking out young men of piety and gifts, and urging them to dedicate themselves to the great work of the gospel ministry. Amongst others, he sought out Mr. Wick, and urged him to abandon his farm and his cattle for this urgent work. Being of a delicate constitution, he had some doubts as to the propriety of the undertaking; but after much prayer and reflection, he felt it to be his duty to go to the Academy at Cannonsburg. Here he pursued his studies with quietness and assiduity, enjoying what facilities were there provided. His studies here were completed in 1797, before the College charter was obtained. He was one of the founders of the "Franklin Literary Society."

His theological education was obtained at Dr. McMillan's log-cabin, when he was licensed to preach the gospel by the Presbytery of Ohio, August 28, 1799. Having accepted calls to labor in the congregations of Neshannock and Hopewell, Pa., he was ordained by the Presbytery of Ohio, and installed pastor of these congregations, on the 3d day of September, 1800. During the next year he was released from the charge of the congregation of Neshannock, and installed as pastor of that of Youngstown, Ohio, for the half of his time.

Mr. Wick was one of the original members of the Presbytery of Erie. He was also an original member of the Presbytery of Beaver. His labors were confined chiefly to Youngstown and Hopewell, although he found time to engage in missionary work "in the regions beyond." He was the first permanent laborer in the Western Reserve. About three years after his settlement, he was blessed with the outpouring of God's Spirit, during which many were gathered into the church. He was aided by the Connecticut Missionary

Society, for a year or two, and was always the friend of missions. He and Joseph Badger were ever fast friends, and took missionary tours together. He was Moderator of the Synod of Pittsburgh, in 1811.

Says his daughter, Mrs. Wood, "I remember distinctly of Revs. McCurdy, Marquis, Badger, Hughes, and others meeting at my father's house, to devise plans for the spread of the gospel throughout the western wilderness."

He was a faithful minister of the Word, yet his ministry was brief. In October, 1814, he contracted a severe cold, and in a short time it became evident that his lungs were seriously affected. He was feeble through the winter, yet was generally able to preach. March 26, 1815, was the Sabbath he was to preach at Hopewell. He was not able to leave the house, and sent one of his sons to request the congregation to come to his house, and although very feeble, addressed them in a very solemn and affecting manner, and baptized a child. Being exhausted he was assisted to his bed. On Monday and Tuesday he seemed better, and walked about the house and yard, and attended to family worship as usual. On Tuesday morning he sung with his family, in worship, in a clear voice, the hymn —

"On Jordan's stormy banks I stand."

After singing, he said, "This music sounds heavenly. O, what will it be to hear the heavenly strains above!" That evening he retired without any visible change. At six o'clock on Wednesday morning, Mrs. Wick noticed that his breathing was short and labored. He was beyond the power of speech, and before his family could be summoned, his spirit had taken its flight to the land of rest and glory.

His death took place at Hopewell, Pa., on the 29th day of March, 1815, in the forty-seventh year of his age, and sixteenth of his ministry. At his own request he was buried at Youngstown, Ohio.

He was the father of eight sons and three daughters, the greatest portion of whom have gone down to the grave. One of his daughters was the wife of Rev. Thomas Anderson (37), for many years a member of the Presbytery of Erie, and the first pastor of the church of Franklin, Pa.

His sons have, several of them, occupied places of authority and trust amongst their fellow-citizens, and one of them has been in the chief council of the nation.

It is recorded on his tombstone that he preached during his ministry, one thousand five hundred and twenty-two sermons, and married fifty-six couples.

(3.) SAMUEL TAIT.

1800–1841.

SAMUEL TAIT was of Scotch descent. He was born near Shippensburg, Pa., on the 17th day of February, 1772. Although unpromising in early life, yet by the grace of God he became one of the most useful and distinguished ministers in the Presbytery. His father was engaged in the packing business. This was the transportation of goods over the mountains on horseback. Samuel Tait followed the same business with his father, and after age prevented the latter from this employment, he carried it on for himself. He was a profane lad, and gave little promise of usefulness. Whilst yet in his youth, his father removed with his family to Ligonier, Westmoreland County, Pa. Mr. Tait dated his first religious impressions to a conversation with Rev.

Elisha McCurdy. In later years whilst ploughing in the field, the conviction forced itself upon his mind that he was a poor lost sinner. At this time he would often leave his plough, and retire to the woods, and there plead for pardoning mercy, until finally light broke in upon his soul, and he was enabled to cry "Abba, Father." At this time he had no thought of seeking the ministry. He was, as he thought, settled in life, married and working on his farm. But a committee of Presbytery, much to his astonishment, waited upon him, and urged him to seek preparation for preaching the gospel.

He repaired to Cannonsburg Academy, and afterwards studied theology with Dr. McMillan, and was licensed to preach the gospel by the Presbytery of Ohio on the 25th day of June, 1800. During that summer and autumn he travelled over what is now the territory of the Presbytery of Erie. In the month of September of that year, he preached for the first time, to the people of Cool Spring, in Mercer County, Pa., from the words, "And they all with one accord began to make excuse." This sermon was blessed to the conversion of many persons. On the 19th day of November, 1800, having accepted calls from Cool Spring, and Upper Salem, he was ordained and installed their pastor by the Presbytery of Ohio, in whose bounds these churches then were.

The young pastor resided at Cool Spring, in a log-cabin that he had got raised and clapboarded. During his absence on a preaching tour, his wife chinked and daubed the cracks between the logs with mortar made by her own hands.

The pastoral relation with Cool Spring and Upper Salem continued until June 25, 1806, when he relinquished the charge of Upper Salem, and gave half his time to the newly organized church of Mercer. At the time of his coming to Mercer County, the place where Mercer now stands was an unbroken forest. Soon after the laying out of the town, a church was organized, that sought the labors of Mr. Tait. In June, 1813, the people of Cool Spring agreeing to worship at Mercer, he gave a part of his time once more to Salem, and finally in 1826, he relinquished Cool Spring, and gave all his time to Mercer. His pastorate at Mercer continued until his death; although the disease that finally terminated his life, laryngeal consumption, prevented him from engaging in active labors for a short time previous to his death. He was called to rest on the 2d day of June, 1841, in the seventieth year of his age and forty-first of his ministry. He died strong in the faith, giving glory to God. His remains are interred at the rear of the pulpit, where he had so long preached Jesus.

He was united in marriage to Miss Amelia Calvin. They had two children, one of whom died in infancy, the other was a member of the Mercer bar, and died before his father. During his entire pastorate he resided on a farm and wrought with his own hands. In his earlier years, the field was his study, and his pocket Bible his library. At intervals of rest in the labors of the field, he would turn over the leaves of his Bible, and when following the plough, his mind was busy in the great themes of the gospel. In appearance, he was most commanding. He was full six feet two inches in height, erect in his bearing, with a firm, grave cast of countenance. Many thought him austere, yet he was a kind and sympathizing friend, and had a melting tenderness, as he pointed men to the Saviour. Yet withal, he was firm and immovable when the path of duty was plain. He was the enemy of all species of vice and immorality, and sometimes exposed himself to the wrath of evil-doers, by his opposition to their evil courses.

He was most emphatically a man of prayer. His faith in the efficacy of prayer was wonderful. He had an elder, Joseph Smith, who was not one whit behind him in this respect. The prayers of these two men seem, even to the present day, to be bringing showers of mercy upon the church of Mercer. On one occasion the infant son of Mr. Smith was sick, as his physician supposed, unto death. The father, thinking the child was at the point of death, left the room. Meeting Mr. Tait at the door, he told him of his grief, and that all had been done in the power of man, and yet the child must die.

Says Mr. Tait, "Have you called the elders of the church together to pray over him?"

Another elder who was near was called in, and the three knelt down by the couch, and Mr. Tait poured forth petitions for the sick infant "with strong crying and tears," and importunity, and a wrestling with the "Angel of the Covenant," such as the elders said they had never heard equaled. He seemed as though he would not be denied. And "He had power with God, and prevailed." The child began to grow better, and recovered, and was from that time dedicated to God, for the service of the ministry. He[1] is now standing on one of the high places of Zion, in the ministry to which he was dedicated in the faith and prayer of his father.

As a man, Mr. Tait was distinguished for his strong

---

[1] Rev. J. T. Smith, D. D. (61).

common sense, discriminating judgment, and familiar acquaintance with the human heart. As a preacher he was often eloquent, and had great power over an audience, and at times could sway them with wondrous influence. As a pastor he was faithful. In dealing with "cases of conscience," as the early fathers called them, he was most judicious and successful. Sometimes to the heart almost broken with anguish, he seemed harsh, yet the result generally was that under his advice inquirers were led to forsake self, and cling to Christ alone. As a member of the ecclesiastical courts, he stood high for wisdom and good judgment. He was called to the Moderator's chair more frequently than any other member of Presbytery.

Mr. Tait had the great satisfaction of laboring in numerous revivals of religion. The first was during the "Falling Exercise," which was shared in by his churches. Again in 1831, his churches were greatly blessed. Another was in 1836. Yet in the history of his labors there was almost a constant ingathering of souls to the kingdom of Christ, the influence of which seems to remain unto this day.

Mr. Tait was for a time a missionary to the Indians at Sandusky, or on the Maumee River in Ohio. He was appointed to this charge by the Synod of Pittsburgh, on the 3d day of October, 1822. The Board of Trust of the Western Missionary Society were about organizing a mission family for this region, and recommended the Synod to appoint Mr. Tait as superintendent *pro tempore*. This appointment was accepted, and he proceeded to the field and labored faithfully for a period of seven months, when he returned home.

Mr. Tait was, when a student, one of the founders of the "Philo Literary Society," at Cannonsburg. He was also one of the original members of the Presbytery of Erie, and in 1818, Moderator of the Synod of Pittsburgh.

The following extracts are from a paper adopted by the Presbytery of Erie, on occasion of his death:[1]—

"In the death of Rev. Samuel Tait, not only is the Presbytery of which he was literally the father and founder, called to mourn, but also that the church of Christ has lost one of its most efficient ministers. For upwards of forty years, our departed father has stood as a watchman on the walls of our Zion, and has labored truly, with apostolical zeal, to advance the interest and kingdom of Jesus Christ. As a preacher of the gospel, Mr. Tait had few superiors. Having experienced in his own heart many of the blessed fruits that flow from Calvary, his soul seemed absorbed in the work of leading others to the same blessed fountain opened in the house of David for sin and uncleanness. Nor were his labors confined to the Sabbath and the pulpit. From house to house he visited the sick, cheered the mourning, comforted the disconsolate, and pointed the dying to the Lamb of God, who taketh away the sin of the world."

"On his death-bed Mr. Tait felt much for the dear people, for whose salvation he had so long labored, and literally spent his dying breath in praying for a revival of religion among them. And when his end drew nigh, a minister and friend who stood by his bed, inquired if he found comfort *now* in the doctrines he had so long preached to others, his answer was, 'All is peace, peace through the blood of Christ.'

"Blessed life! With Paul he might say, 'I have fought a good fight, I have finished my course, I have

[1] Committee: A. McCready, Cyrus Dickson, and W. M. Francis.

kept the faith; henceforth there is laid up for me a crown of righteousness, which the Lord, the righteous Judge, shall give me at that day; and not to me only, but unto all them also, that love his appearing.'"

"And now, though the tongue had ceased to discharge its functions, and the lips that but a moment before glowed with the story of a Saviour's love were sealed forever, yet when the dying saint was again asked by the same pious friend if all was well, and having made a fruitless effort to reply, he raised his hands to heaven, whilst a beam of inexpressible delight played upon his countenance. And thus he fell asleep in Jesus.

"'See where he walks, on yonder mount, that lifts
Its summit high on the right hand of bliss,
Sublime in glory, talking with his peers
Of the incarnate Saviour's love,
And, past affliction, lost in present joy.'"

(4.) JOSEPH STOCKTON.

1799–1832.

JOSEPH STOCKTON was the son of Robert and Mary (McKemy) Stockton, of Franklin County, Pa. He was born near Chambersburg, Pa., on the 25th day of February, 1779. His parents had eight children — four sons, Thomas, Robert, John, and Joseph, with four daughters, Margaret (Cotton), Frances (Stewart), Jane (Brice), and Elizabeth (Cunningham). Of these, the subject of this sketch was the youngest son and seventh child.

In the year 1784, he removed with his father's family to the neighborhood of Washington, Pa. His classical studies were prosecuted at the Cannonsburg Academy. In this institution he was also employed for a time as an instructor. He studied theology under the direction of Dr. John McMillan, and was licensed to preach the gospel on the 26th day of June, 1799, being but a few months over twenty years of age. In the next year, on the 8th day of May, 1800, he was united in marriage to Miss Esther Clark, a daughter of David Clark, Esq., who resided near his father's residence.

In the same year in which he was licensed to preach, he took a tour over the territory now constituting the Presbytery of Erie, in company with Elisha McCurdy, and preached, amongst other places, at Meadville, Pa. In the next year, late in the autumn, having received an invitation to preach statedly at this place, he set out with his wife from the paternal home on horseback, and bearing with them the few things that were to make home comfortable, and in due time pitched his tent in the new town of Meadville. Over the church in this place, in connection with that of Little Sugar Creek, now Cochranton, he was ordained as pastor on the 24th day of June, 1801, by the Presbytery of Ohio, in whose bounds these churches then were. On this occasion Elisha McCurdy preached the sermon, and Joseph Patterson delivered the charges. His relation to these churches was dissolved by the Presbytery of Erie on the 27th day of June, 1810.

During his pastorate of nine years, Mr. Stockton had charge of the Meadville Academy, and conducted it with ability and success. He was dismissed from the Presbytery of Erie on the 27th day of June, 1810, and soon after was received by the Presbytery of Redstone, from which he was transferred to that of Ohio, by act of Synod, October, 1822.

In 1809, he was elected Principal of the Pittsburgh Academy, which was subsequently merged into the

"Western University of Pennsylvania." In this position he continued to labor with great success until 1820. In connection with his labors in the Academy, he gave his attention to the preparation of school-books. He published during these years, "The Western Spelling-Book," and "The Western Calculator," both of which have been extensively used throughout the region west of the Alleghany Mountains. In addition to these educational works, he devoted much of his time to the preparation of a theological work, but his life was not spared for its completion. His scholarship was considerable, and he took a deep interest in the education of the young. In 1827, he was one of the instructors in the Western Theological Seminary.

But his labors were not confined to the Academy, after removing to Pittsburgh. He still sought and embraced opportunities of preaching the gospel, in the region around. He preached for a time to the soldiers at the United States garrison, two miles from the city, at what is now Lawrenceville. For several years he preached to the church of Pine Creek, at first devoting one third and afterwards one half of his time to this charge. Here his labors were greatly blessed to the ingathering of souls to the fold of Christ. At the time of his death, one hundred and thirty-six had been received on profession of faith. The remaining portion of his time was devoted to missionary labor, in connection with the church in Alleghany City. The last three years of his life, his ministerial labors were wholly given to the Church of Pine Creek. During this period the town of Sharpsburg took its rise, and the population increasing, on petition from the people, the Presbytery of Ohio divided the congregation, forming a new one called Sharpsburg.

Mr. Stockton was of the medium height, mild and pleasant in his manner, and was in every respect a most courteous Christian gentleman. He was always earnest in the defense of the truth. On one occasion, he met a gentleman who was skeptical in his views of divine truth. After laboring with him an entire evening in his attempts to convince him of his error, with little effect, the gentleman retired to his room. But Mr. Stockton was not satisfied and followed him to his room, and renewed the contest. "Admitting that you are right," he said, "when we pass to the world of spirits, I shall be as safe and well off as you. But if you are wrong, and I am right, you will be lost. Is not my ground then the safest?" The gentleman was forced to admit the soundness of the argument, and the untenable ground he had been occupying.

But his work upon earth was done. The Master had no longer need of his services, and he was called home to his reward. He was called suddenly to Baltimore, to see a son who was dangerously sick of fever, when he himself was attacked by cholera. After an illness, attended with extreme suffering, of twenty-four hours' continuance, he died, on the 29th day of October, 1832, in the fifty-fourth year of his age, and thirty-third of his ministry.

Although called to leave the world suddenly, and surrounded by comparative strangers, he was calm and resigned. Having requested the fifteenth chapter of John to be read, and joining in prayer with a ministerial brother, he remarked: "The battle is nearly fought — Christ is with me." He frequently expressed a longing desire to be released, and that the time might speedily come, when he should see Jesus face to face He frequently prayed, "Come, Lord Jesus, come quickly, thy servant waits." Finally, sending his love to his wife and children, and an affectionate remembrance to his congregation and all his friends, he closed his eyes and passed to the other side, to look upon the face of God.

He left a widow, four sons, and three daughters. His remains were laid to rest in the burial-grounds of the First Presbyterian Church, Baltimore, but in the year 1858 were removed to the beautiful cemetery near Alleghany city.

Mr. Stockton was one of the original members of the Presbytery of Erie, and for a period of nine years, one of its active and useful members.

(5.) ROBERT LEE.

1800–1842.

Mr. Lee was one of the original members of the Presbytery of Erie. At the time of its organization, he was settled at Amity and Big Spring (afterwards Rocky Spring). He was the son of Thomas Lee, and was born in Donegal, Ireland, in the year 1771. In the year 1787, he emigrated to the United States with his father's family, and settled in Washington County, Pa. He was thus brought within the sphere of the influence of Cannonsburg. He remained at home, assisting in the maintenance of the family, until he was of age, when he commenced for himself the struggle with the world, yet without any means save his own hands, and trusting only in Providence.

It is not now known when he made a profession of religion; yet in 1794, when he was in his twenty-third year, we find him commencing his studies, preparatory to the ministry, at the Cannonsburg Academy. He was prompted to this by the advice and persuasion of Dr.

John McMillan. From Dr. McMillan he had also the promise of aid for his support, whilst engaged in study. Then commenced the great struggle with the world, and contact with the discouraging circumstances that always surround the student of limited means; for although permitted to lean securely on the patronage of his friend, his independent spirit and sense of duty prompted him to lean on his own efforts. He had strong hands and a brave heart, and was habituated to manual labor. So he resolved to assist himself in every way possible. Accordingly he engaged in small contracts to perform labor where it was required, and even cleared at one time ten acres of land. To accomplish this without neglecting his studies, he was often obliged to work at night, fixing up his log heaps, and attending to his fires, when others were sleeping.

After the completion of his classical studies, he studied theology under the direction of his patron, Dr. McMillan, and was taken under the care of the Presbytery of Ohio, as a candidate for the gospel ministry, December 17, 1799. After passing through all his trials, he was licensed to preach the gospel, by the same Presbytery, on the 22d day of October, 1800.

After travelling through the vacancies as a missionary, he accepted calls from the congregations of Amity and Big Spring, to become their pastor, and was ordained and installed on the 26th day of June, 1801. Here he continued to labor, under great discouragements, arising from a large field and a limited support, for about six years, when, on account of failing health, he asked the Presbytery to release him from his pastoral charge. The relation was dissolved, July 14, 1807. He remained, however, within the bounds of the Presbytery for five or six years, preaching in various churches as a stated supply. In 1810, he was supplying Slate Lick and Union.

On the 7th day of April, 1813, he was dismissed from the Presbytery of Erie, and on the 20th day of the same month, was received by the Presbytery of Redstone. In the bounds of this Presbytery, he accepted calls from the congregation of Salem, in Westmoreland County, Pa., and was installed as pastor on the second Tuesday of August, 1813. Here he remained as pastor until October 20, 1819.

The West now began to attract his attention as a field of labor. He had a numerous family dependent upon him, and there was in the new field opening in northern Ohio, the prospect, not only of an interesting field of ministerial labor, but the way for the improvement of the worldly circumstances of his family. Accordingly, in November, 1821, he removed with his family to what is now Ashland County, Ohio. He was dismissed from the Presbytery of Redstone, April 17, 1822, and became connected with the Presbytery of Richland. In this new relation he became pastor of the congregation of Hopeful. This congregation afterwards became the congregation of Ashland. Here he labored for about four years. He then became the pastor of the Church of Bucyrus, Crawford County, Ohio, then under the care of Richland, but now Marion Presbytery. His pastorate in this church continued many years, and with encouraging success. After retiring from this field, he took up his residence in Leesville, Crawford County, Ohio, where he exercised the duties of a minister in various vacant churches and missionary points, until the close of his earthly labors. Sometimes he acted under the direction of the Board of Domestic Missions, sometimes under that of the Presbytery, and sometimes he used his own discretion, preaching the gospel to the poor, and laboring wherever duty called. It was a satisfaction to him, that he was able to preach where Providence opened the way, after retiring from the active duties of the pastorate.

At the age of seventy-one, a few weeks before his death, he had arranged to engage in ministerial labors in a destitute section of the country, some twelve miles from the place of his residence. But the Master had ordered otherwise. The work and the self-denial and the warfare must now cease, and instead, the crown and the palm and the sweet golden harp. He died at Leesville, Ohio, on the 9th day of February, 1842, in the seventy-first year of his age, and the forty-first of his ministry. His last words were, "Lord Jesus, if it be thy will, come quickly, that I may be at rest."

In January, 1800, Mr. Lee was united in marriage to Miss Sarah Swerngen, of Washington County, Pa., who survived him. In her youth she was a lady of great personal beauty, and throughout life a fitting helper to the pioneer missionary. Their family consisted of eight children. Four sons and one daughter are living, and are all members of the Presbyterian Church. Thus God remembers his children, and is the God of his people and of their families.

In person, Mr. Lee was tall, slender, and dignified in appearance and deportment. He was mild and conciliating, yet earnest in defense of the truth. One who knew him in youth and in old age,[1] says: "As a preacher, and in his address and manner, he was a fair model specimen of the ministers of the West, fifty or sixty years ago. He was firm in his belief of the doctrines of the Bible as set forth in the standards of the

[1] Rev. James Rowland.

Presbyterian Church, of which he was the earnest advocate, both in the pulpit and out of it. In the construction of his sermons, he never failed to present the leading points which he conceived to be contained in his text, by naming the order in which he designed to discuss each.

"In preaching, his enunciation was clear, distinct, impressive, strikingly sincere and solemn, as was also his manner. During the twenty years, the last of his ministerial life, in which he acted as a pioneer minister in the newly settled region of Northern Ohio, he aimed at doing all he could for the cause of Christ, and the good of souls. He was impeded, however, by an insufficient support, which compelled him at times to labor with his own hands, for the support of himself and family."

(6.) JAMES SATTERFIELD.

1800–1857.

James Satterfield, the son of James and Margaret (Meed) Satterfield, was born in Queen Anne County, Maryland, in August, 1767. In his father's family there were four sons and two daughters. He was the fifth child. His father dying in Maryland, his mother married Mr. Davies, and moved to Washington County, Pennsylvania, in 1786 or 1787, and settled on a farm. This brought him within the sphere of Dr. McMillan's influence, and in part accounts for the pursuits of his subsequent life. He became a professor of religion in his fourteenth year. His convictions of sin were so powerful that they influenced his views of religious experience forever afterwards.

He was a farmer in Washington County. One year

he got his wheat ground, put it on board a flat-boat, and run it to New Orleans, then under Spanish dominion. The enterprise was a most profitable one, but attended with great peril. He then took a vessel and returned by sea to Baltimore, and from thence walked over the mountains home. This profitable venture, together with the atmosphere that surrounded Dr. McMillan's log-cabin, was, under God, the means of directing him to the ministry. He went to the Cannonsburg Academy and pursued his studies there, in the meanwhile being one of the founders of the "Philo Literary Society." He of course studied theology with Dr. McMillan, and was licensed to preach the gospel by the Presbytery of Ohio, on the 3d day of September, 1800. After his licensure, he was sent as a missionary to the Indians, and travelled as far west as Detroit. In 1801, he removed to Mercer County, and on the 3d day of March, 1802, was ordained and installed as pastor of the congregations of Moorfield, Pa., and Upper Neshannock, now Neshannock, Pa., by the Presbytery of Ohio.

He was one of the original members of the Presbytery of Erie. In 1808, he was set off with others to form the Presbytery of Hartford, now Beaver. He was released from the charge of Neshannock, in the beginning of the year 1812, and from that of Moorfield in 1834. From 1812 to 1815, he had charge of the congregations of Brookfield, Ohio, in connection with Hubbard and Moorfield. He continued his connection with Hubbard, until April 6, 1831, and with Moorfield until he demitted all regular pastoral labor.

During the last years of his life he had no regular charge, but preached quite frequently to vacant churches, and assisted at communion occasions. He was always ready to preach the gospel and to bear his testimony for Christ. His remarks were always appropriate and happy on communion occasions.

He was a man of strong and robust constitution, and up to the last days of his life could mount a horse and ride to the place of worship. His last illness was brief. He complained of a sore throat after coming from church, and soon other unfavorable symptoms presented themselves. In his last act of family worship, he read the parable of the ten virgins, a favorite theme with him, and engaged in prayer. When informed by his physicians that he could not live, he replied, "My lamp is trimmed and burning." He was confined to his bed but three days. His death took place at the old homestead, near Middlesex, Mercer County, Pa., on the 20th day of November, 1857, in the ninetieth year of his age, and the fifty-eighth of his ministry.

Mr. Satterfield was thrice married. His first wife was Miss Polly Orbison of Washington County, to whom he was married October 28, 1800. She died July 23, 1802.

On the 27th of March, 1804, he was married to Miss Ann Gibson, a member of the congregation of Neshannock. She died September 12, 1815, leaving five children, two sons and three daughters.

His third marriage was with Miss Sarah Mead, a daughter of General Mead, of Meadville, Pa. This marriage took place September 3, 1816. She died May 22, 1823, leaving one son and one daughter. This son was Rev. Mead Satterfield, pastor of the churches of Harrisville and Amity, who died in 1855. The daughter, Mrs. William Mathers, now resides at New Lisbon, Ohio. Besides the latter, two children by a former marriage still survive.

As a preacher Mr. Satterfield was plain and practical.

Attempting no flights of fancy, his sermons were full of the marrow and fatness of the gospel. He was a most godly and exemplary man. The reputation he has left behind, is that of sterling integrity, unvarnished truth, and unblemished purity of heart and life. When a question of veracity would arise amongst the neighbors, it was a common remark to say, "It is just as true as though Clergy Satterfield had said it." This application "clergy," was one generally applied to him by his old neighbors.

He was most emphatically a man of prayer. During the last years of his life, he was in the habit of rising early to engage in secret prayer. Indeed, his children say that he often spent the greater portion of the day in private prayer. He walked with God here, and could well say at the last, "the lamp is trimmed and ready."

He was a systematic man. He always read the Scriptures in course, and as soon as he had read the last chapter of Revelation, commenced again at Genesis.

On occasion of the death of his son Mead, he writes to his children: "When I see an old tree standing almost alone in the field, whose limbs have fallen off one after another, till almost all have fallen, it appears a fit emblem of my condition, and I sometimes wonder that the old stock does not tumble to the earth. What the allwise and gracious God intends by it, I know not now, but I am certain I shall know hereafter."

He knows now, for he looks upon the face of God, and the lessons of life are all clear, and its mysteries all explained.

(7.) WILLIAM WYLIE, D. D.

1800–1858.

MR. WYLIE was one of the original members of the Presbytery of Erie. Although not mentioned in the act of the Synod of Virginia erecting the Presbytery, he was ordained by the Presbytery of Ohio, between this act and the time appointed for the first meeting of the Presbytery of Erie. His father was a native of Ireland, and a half brother of the Rev. Samuel Wylie, D. D., late of Philadelphia. At an early period his father removed to the West, and settled in Washington County, Pa. Here William Wylie was born on the 10th day of July, 1776. His mother was a woman of piety and prayer, and her influence was most blessed on the young mind of her son. While quite young in years he became the subject of deep religious impressions, and devoted himself to the service of the Lord. Soon after this he turned his thoughts toward preparation for the gospel ministry. After engaging for a time in study at home, he repaired to Washington, in his own county, to attend a Latin and Mathematical School, taught by Rev. Thaddeus Dodd. After this he went to Cannonsburg to attend the Academy in that place. Here he pursued his studies for some time. He was now induced to go to the State of Kentucky, with the view of teaching to replenish his treasury, and at the same time continuing his studies as opportunity might offer. In this new State, he remained for a number of years, completing his classical studies, and engaging in theological study, until in due time he was licensed to preach the gospel by the Presbytery of West Lexington.

Soon after this, and during the year 1800, he returned

to his home in Western Pennsylvania, and began to itinerate within the bounds of the Presbytery of Ohio, extending at that time from the Ohio River to Lake Erie. He was received by the Presbytery of Ohio as a licentiate from the Presbytery of West Lexington, on the 2d day of March, 1802, received calls from the congregations of Upper and Lower Sandy,[1] and Fairfield, accepted the same, and was ordained and installed their pastor on the 5th of the same month. At the same meeting he, with six other members of Presbytery, were dismissed to constitute the new Presbytery of Erie.

Mr. Wylie's field was a large one, requiring great labor in pastoral visitation, and his salary but slender, even for those times. Failure of health, and discouragement in his labor, induced him to think of seeking a new field. Although his pastorate had been one of usefulness and success, yet there were causes that led to the conviction that the path of duty led elsewhere. Accordingly at a meeting of Presbytery, held December 5, 1804, he asked for the dissolution of the pastoral relation. The reasons given were, " That said congregations had not fulfilled their contracts with him ; that he could not have a support from them for his family ; and that considering the weak state of his bodily health, he considered it to be his duty to leave them." The congregations were heard at full length, when Presbytery granted his request and the pastoral relation was dissolved. At the same meeting he received a dismission from the Presbytery, to connect himself with the Presbytery of Redstone.

On the 6th day of February, 1805, he was received as a member of the Presbytery of Redstone, and accepted calls to the pastoral charge of the congregations of

---

[1] Now Georgetown and Mill Creek.

Rehoboth and Round Hill. His ministry in these churches continued for about eleven years, with a comfortable degree of success. The congregations had, some years before, passed through a season of revival, and a reaction had taken place, throwing many obstacles in his way. Many had been received into the churches, as is usually the case at such times, who had no root in themselves, and soon withered away; and the great Adversary threw the apple of discord into the congregations, and troubled the camp.

In the spring of 1816, Mr. Wylie asked the Presbytery to dismiss him from his united charge, when he removed to Uniontown, the county-seat of Fayette County. At this time there was no actual church organization in Uniontown. The members of the Presbyterian Church were considered as belonging either to Laurel Hill or Tent churches, which had been organized in the vicinity. And during Mr. Wylie's period of labor there, there was no organization formed. The Tent Church was considered as embracing the town within its borders.

During his ministry, Mr. Wylie preached both in the Tent Church and in town, and administered the ordinances in both places. The elders lived in the country, but met as a session in both places, as it proved to be convenient and necessary. In this way the entire charge came naturally to be known as the congregation of Uniontown.[1] It was only after the lapse of two years from Mr. Wylie's departure from Uniontown, that a separate congregation was organized.

In Uniontown the labors of Mr. Wylie were eminently blessed. The state of religion when he came there was not only languishing, but there was much opposition to

[1] Dr. Joseph Smith.

religion itself. There was a practical infidelity abroad, especially amongst professional men, that was exercising a most baleful influence upon the young men of the community. The influence of Mr. Wylie was most beneficial in removing this influence, and introducing a more hopeful spirit in its stead. This very class of men rallied around him and made his cause their own. Many of them became members of his Bible-class, and eventually of the church. The tide of religious influence set in strongly, and there was an entire change in the prevailing feeling and practice. He preached in the orchards and groves, and sometimes in the Courthouse, and wrought so zealously and faithfully, that when he left the place there were the elements out of which a strong and growing church was organized

From Uniontown he removed in 1823, and took up his abode in Wheeling, Va. Here he became a member of the Presbytery of Washington, being received October 9, 1823. By this Presbytery he is reported for many years as stated supply at Wheeling and Short Creek, or West Liberty. The state of affairs at Wheeling was not favorable to successful labor. It was then but a small town, with two ministers laboring in common, in town and country. Congregations are not perfect, ministers are not infallible. Stars become pale before the rising sun. So, although there was a very strong influence exerted to induce Mr. Wylie to remain, he deemed it his duty to retire from the field.

On the 2d day of October, 1832, he was dismissed to connect himself with the Presbytery of Lancaster, now called Zanesville. Here he accepted a call to Newark, Licking County, Ohio. In this place he continued to labor during the remainder of his pastoral life. He was a useful man here, not only to the general cause of religion, but to that of Presbyterianism. In fact he had that peculiar faculty of making his impression deeply and broadly upon every community in the midst of which he had his abode. And this impression was always on the side of truth and righteousness.

In 1854, at his own request, he was dismissed from the pastoral charge of the church of Newark, although he did not remove from the place. The infirmities of age were upon him, and he felt it his duty to retire and give place for a younger and more vigorous pastor.

Mr., now Dr.[1] Wylie, was twice married. His first wife was the fourth daughter of Rev. Joseph Smith, of Redstone Presbytery, and so famous in its annals. At the age of ten she was received into the church; and after a life of earnest, consistent piety, fell asleep in Jesus, some years after her husband commenced his labors in Newark.

From this marriage there were five daughters and one son. The son, the late Rev. Joseph S. Wylie, after a ministry of usefulness and success, died in Florence, Pa. His second wife was a widow lady, Mrs. Moody, like himself, with a large family. She was from Portland, Me., and had been a member of Dr. Payson's church. This second marriage proved eminently a happy one, and added greatly to Dr. Wylie's comfort and happiness.

In the fall of 1854, Dr. Wylie went for a time to Port Gibson, Mississippi. Although this was chiefly for the benefit of Mrs. Wylie's health, yet while there she was attacked by another form of disease, and died a peaceful and happy death. This bereavement was a most distressing one to Dr. Wylie. He felt alone in his old age, and was well-nigh crushed beneath the blow.

[1] Received the degree of D. D. in 1850, from Muskingum College.

In the following spring he returned north, and took up his abode in Wheeling, where he continued to reside until called to join the church triumphant. Just before leaving Mississippi, he had fallen and fractured the bone of his thigh, which rendered him a hopeless cripple for the remainder of his life. He was, while residing in Wheeling, frequently carried to different churches, where he preached in a sitting posture, and to the satisfaction and edification of his hearers.

Although his afflictions were severe during the last years of his life, yet he bore them with exemplary patience and resignation to the Divine will. As the time of his departure approached, his faith and hope were sensibly brightened. He felt the peace of God flowing into his soul like a river, and longed to enter the rest and peace of the Good Land. The time for which he had watched and waited so patiently, came at last. It was on a Saturday morning, in the sweet month of May, that he was called to go up and spend the eternal Sabbath on Mount Zion. His death took place on the 9th day of May, 1858, just before he had completed his eighty-second year.

As a preacher, Dr. Wylie stood deservedly high amongst his contemporaries. He was a man of more than usual ability. Indeed, in his power of body and mind, he had few rivals in the faculty of stirring the deep emotions of the heart, and leading the minds of his audience captive to his subject. An eminent minister in New York testifies to his power of eloquence in these words: "He was preaching at Chartiers, on the text, 'Now have they both seen and hated both me and my father.' Now I have heard, within the last ten years, almost all our great preachers, of all denominations, but never, to this hour, have I heard a sermon comparable to that of Dr. Wylie, for overpowering grandeur and awful sublimity.

Says Dr. Joseph Smith, his relative, and perhaps better acquainted with his inner life than any other person: "His tall stature, his peculiarly solemn and expressive features and tones of voice, his perfectly inimitable tenderness and pathos, mingled with great personal dignity, gave him unwonted power. The fertility of his mind, and the rich exuberance of his thoughts, seemed, at times, to indicate an exhaustless fountain of truth and pious affections within. If any other public speaker ever rose higher in his wonderful flights, we can form no conception of it."

Dr. Wylie was eminently a social man. He excelled as a talker. In this most difficult and rare accomplishment, he shone preëminently; still he had a serious fault in the matter of conversation — he monopolized the entire time. Others were generally content to sit by and listen, and be amused and instructed and edified, as the case might be, by his exuberant flow of words and often sparkling scintillations of thought. Perhaps his chief fault in speaking and preaching and praying was indulging in strong figures and swelling hyperboles, so that there was too great a strain upon the minds of the hearers in following him. He did not excel in simplicity and plainness.

His piety was sincere and earnest. It was of the heart and outward life. It was the secret spring of action, always operative, always effectual in toning down the asperities of his nature, and impelling him to constant effort in labor and zeal in building up the kingdom of Christ.

His influence in the community where he lived was most valuable. He was a great leader of public opinion, and moulded it to his own views and convictions of right. Before him, vice in every form stood abashed. The most wicked and profane respected and reverenced him for his truth and goodness. But with all his calm dignity and solemn presence, there was nothing haughty or repulsive about him. Children were attracted to him by a kind of magnetism, that they alone understand and appreciate.

He was a kind, sympathizing pastor. In the time of affliction and distress and bereavement, he was a ministering spirit of kindness and sympathy, pointing to the sweet promises of the gospel, and pleading God's great mercy and faithfulness and love.

His correspondence shows that he was a man of prayer, and lived near to God; and that there was a gradual ripening for heaven, as well as a longing desire for its blessed rest.

The following extract of a letter from Rev. Dr. Weed to Rev. Dr. Joseph Smith, sheds light on the closing days of his life: —

1. " He spoke little of his ailments, but much of the love of God, and of the ineffable consolations flowing from the riches of Divine grace, abounding to the chief of sinners.

2. " His expressions were habitually characterized by a childlike humility, and a filial confidence in God as his Father and Redeemer. He seemed to enjoy the grace of assurance in a high degree, and without intermission.

3. " He was favored with most exalted views of the infinite perfections of God, and the transcendent glory of the Lord Jesus Christ. These were the favorite and absorbing themes of his discourse.

4. " The gospel was confirmed in his experience as a

manifestation of the mercy of God. It made him, in despite of all things else to the contrary, eminently a happy man, and a joyful sufferer. No one could be long in his presence without feeling the demonstration of the divinity of the Christian religion.

"Finally, his case was a practical refutation of the charge so often reiterated — that Calvinistic views of theology are adverse to cheerful and joyous experience, that they sour the heart and overhang the mind with gloom. Yet these were thoroughly his views, and it was from these he derived his richest and sweetest enjoyments. I will only add, that he seemed to us all as verily 'a good man, and full of the Holy Ghost and of faith.'"

(8.) JOHN BOYD.
1801–1816.

JOHN BOYD was the son of John and Mary (Fulton) Boyd, and was born in Ireland, in the year 1768. His parents emigrated to this country in the year 1772, and having settled in the bounds of Salem, Westmoreland County, Pa., his father became a ruling elder in that church. His was a priestly family, having no less than four sons in the gospel ministry — John, Abraham (9), Benjamin (17), and James (21). The eldest two were born in Ireland, the younger two in this country. But little is known of the early life of John Boyd. No doubt he worked patiently on the farm during his first years, and was content with what Providence sent him. His studies were pursued under the direction of John McPherrin (16), who was his pastor. How long these studies were prosecuted is not known. He was licensed to preach the gospel, by the Presbytery of Redstone, on the 23d day of April, 1801. For one year he preached as a licentiate, most probably within what was soon to be the bounds of the Presbytery of Erie.

At the first meeting of the Presbytery of Erie, held on the 13th of April, 1802, he presented a dismission from the Presbytery of Redstone, and was taken under the care of the new Presbytery. He had already accepted calls from the congregations of Slate Lick and Union, in what is now Armstrong County, Pa. John vi. 53, was assigned him as a subject for a trial sermon in view of ordination. His brother Abraham was received under the care of Presbytery at the same time.

Mr. Boyd's ordination took place at Union, on the 16th day of June, 1802. In the ordination exercises, William Wick (2), preached the sermon from 2 Corinthians iv. 5, and Samuel Tait (3), delivered the charges. This pastoral relation continued until April 17, 1810, when, at his own request, he was relieved.

At the meeting of the General Assembly, in May, 1809, there occurs this record in the report of the Committee on Missions, in the recommendation of the appointment of missionaries, "The Rev. John Boyd, a missionary for two months on the head-waters of Alleghany, and the borders of Lake Erie."

For a short time, Mr. Boyd supplied the churches of Amity and West Liberty, but his health having failed, he felt constrained to seek some more favorable location, and was accordingly dismissed from the Presbytery of Erie to that of Lancaster (now Zanesville), on the 4th day of October, 1810. Shortly after this he was preaching at Wills Creek, in the southeastern part of the State of Ohio. Afterwards he became pastor of the churches of Red Oak and Strait Creek, in the bounds of the Presbytery of Chilicothe. It is said that the cause of his leaving these churches, was a difficulty that grew out of the "Sunday Mail" question. He signed a petition for, and advocated the cause of, stopping the mails on the Sabbath. For this, he was branded by some of his elders and people as a traitor.

He next settled as the first pastor of the church of Bethel, in the Presbytery of Oxford, and was said to be the first Presbyterian preacher west of the Miami River. But his ministry here was brief. Five months after his settlement, he was attacked by bilious fever, and died at Indian Creek, near Hamilton, Ohio, on the 20th day of August, 1816, in the forty-eighth year of his age, and the sixteenth of his ministry. "Just before his departure," says a writer in the "Weekly Recorder," "he was blessed with a transporting view of the excellence of the gospel." His remains lie at rest in the grave-yard of the Bethel Church. On the Sabbath evening, just before his departure, some of his neighbors having gathered in to see him, he raised up on his couch and thus addressed them: "I have been in congregations where I was afraid to preach Christ, but if all the world were here, I would speak to them of the preciousness of the gospel, and the ability and willingness of Christ to save all who come to him."

Mr. Boyd left a widow and eight children, four sons and four daughters. His widow died, October 12, 1840. His eldest son James died in his twenty-sixth year, just as he was about entering the ministry.

(9.) ABRAHAM BOYD.

1800–1854.

This was the second son of John and Mary (Fulton) Boyd, and was likewise born in Ireland, in December, 1770. He was but three years of age when his parents emigrated to this country. In connection with this emigration, he frequently related the following circumstance, related by his father, as illustrating the particular providence of God towards his children : When about leaving Ireland for America, having reached the port from which they were to sail, it was discovered that the two little sons, John and Abraham, had the small-pox. The officers of the ship refused to receive them on board, and sailed without them. The ship foundered at sea. The Boyd family took the next vessel and arrived in safety.

Abraham Boyd pursued his studies at the Cannonsburg Academy, and was licensed to preach the gospel on the 25th day of June, 1800, by the Presbytery of Ohio. He was received by the Presbytery of Erie at its first meeting, April 13, 1802, and having accepted calls from the congregations of Bull Creek and Middlesex, in Armstrong County, Pa., he was assigned James iv. 17, as the subject of a sermon as part of trials for ordination. This service took place at Bull Creek, on the 17th of June, 1802. Rev. John McMillan, being present as a corresponding member of Presbytery, preached on the occasion, on Mark xvi. 15, 16, and delivered the charges. This relation continued at Middlesex until 1817, and Bull Creek until June 25, 1833. After leaving Middlesex, he gave half his time to Deer Creek, from 1817 to 1821.

An anecdote of Mr. Boyd is related in connection with his early ministry. He was passing through the woods on the Sabbath, on his way to preach. In the depth of the forest he encountered an Indian tricked out in his feathers and war paint. He saw that he was observed, and to flee would be in vain, so he knelt down at the roots of a large tree, and in full view of the savage, and began to pray, expecting each moment to be pierced by an arrow. When he arose from his knees, the Indian had departed, and he was safe.[1]

Mr. Boyd lived to a good old age, residing upon his farm, preaching the gospel when able, until the close of his life. His death took place on his farm, near Tarentum, Pa., on the 14th day of August, 1854, in the eighty-fourth year of his age, and the fifty-fifth of his ministry. The day previous to his death, he sent for his only surviving sister, saying that he expected soon to die, and wished to see her. She came the same evening. He was in his usual health, although he had been declining for some time. The next morning, appearing as well as usual, he attended to family worship, selecting from Watts' Version, Psalm 39, 2d part —

"God of my life look gently down," etc.,

and sung with a cheerful voice throughout. In half an hour from this time, as he sat conversing with his sister, he received a stroke of paralysis and never spoke afterward. He died the following night.

Mr. Boyd was twice married. His first wife was Eleanor Hallis, of Washington County, Pa. The marriage took place March 29, 1798. By her he had nine children, six daughters and three sons. Mrs. Boyd died in the year 1816. In the next year, he married Mrs. Scott. By her he had three children, two daughters and one son. The second Mrs. Boyd died in 1848.

Mr. Boyd was a plain, practical man. His aspirations were simple and limited to the one great matter — preaching the gospel of Christ, and recommending it to his people. Like nearly all of the pioneer ministers, he labored on the farm as well as in preaching the gospel. There were two reasons for this: the people

[1] Rev. R. Lea.

were poor and could not raise a sufficient salary for their ministers, and in the early days land was cheap and easily obtained.

Mr. Boyd was a spiritually minded man, an earnest preacher, and a strict disciplinarian. He was also a man of great power in prayer, and seemed to grow in grace as he grew in years.

(10.) WILLIAM WOOD.

1801–1839.

WILLIAM WOOD, son of Samuel and Isabella (Sankey) Wood, was born in York County, Pa., on the 27th day of March, 1776. Samuel Wood, his father, was born in London, England, in 1749, came to America in 1768, and married Mrs. Isabella Sankey, in York County, Pa. He died in Butler County, in 1817, leaving four children, William, Samuel, Benjamin, and Isabella. Of these, the subject of this sketch was the oldest. Of his early life little is at present known. In due course of time we find him at the Cannonsburg Academy, enjoying what advantages he might obtain there. And then, as a matter of course, he is soon seeking Dr. McMillan's log-cabin, and studying theology. From the scanty library, and the doctor's lectures, he is seeking furniture for the great work. No doubt, with others he copied, with patient labor and pains, those lectures that were the theological library of so many of the earlier ministers of the West, and which contained the very marrow of divinity. Many of those old manuscript systems have come down to our day and are worthy of being read, not only by the theological student, but by the pastor of years.

Mr. Wood was received by the Presbytery of Ohio

as a candidate for the gospel ministry, on the 26th day of December, 1800, and on the 29th day of October, 1801, licensed to preach the gospel. The field was large; the harvest inviting, and the call for laborers earnest; and having spent the winter amongst the vacant churches and missionary points, he was dismissed to put himself under the care of the Presbytery of Erie. By this Presbytery he was received on the 20th day of April, 1802. Having accepted calls from the congregations of Plaingrove and Center, in Mercer County, he was ordained and installed pastor over these churches at a meeting of Presbytery held at Plaingrove, on the 3d day of November, 1802. The trial discourse was on Titus ii. 11, 12. Rev. Robert Lee (5) preached on the occasion, on Mark xvi. 15, 16, and Dr. McMillan, a member of the Presbytery of Ohio, who was present as a corresponding member, presided and delivered the charges.

In these churches Mr. Wood labored earnestly. He was dismissed from the charge of Center on the 24th day of August, 1808, after a pastorate of six years, and from that of Plaingrove on the 7th day of October, 1816, after a pastorate of fourteen years. These pastorates terminated his labors in the Presbytery of Erie.

On the 1st day of April, 1817, he was dismissed to the Presbytery of Hartford (Beaver), being prepared to accept calls from the congregations of Hopewell and Neshannock. Over these churches he was installed pastor on the 22d day of October, 1817. At Hopewell he labored for eleven years, being dismissed on the 25th day of June, 1828.

Mr. Wood died at Utica, Licking County, Ohio, on the 31st day of July, 1839, in the sixty-fourth year of his age, and the thirty-ninth of his ministry. He was a man of more than ordinary ability, and in many a more favorable sphere of labor would have shone as a preacher; but poverty and untoward circumstances kept him down, and his light was buried up in comparative obscurity. He was united in marriage to Miss Margaret Donald, of Washington County, Pa., May 17, 1798. They had twelve children, two of whom were physicians, the elder, John D., settled in Franklin, Pa., the younger in Pulaski, Pa., both now deceased. Mrs. Wood died at Utica, Ohio, April 20, 1843.

(11.) JOSEPH BADGER.

1786–1846.

The name of Joseph Badger will long be remembered in Eastern Ohio. He was the great missionary of the Western Reserve, and one of the pioneers to regions further west. He was a most remarkable man, eminently a man for the times in which he lived. God chose him in the furnace of affliction, and prepared him as he did Israel, by wandering in the desert, for the great work that was before him.

Joseph Badger was born in Wilbraham, Mass., on the 28th day of February, 1757. He was the son of Henry and Mary (Langdon) Badger, and a descendant, in the fourth generation, of Giles Badger, who emigrated from England about the year 1635.[1] His parents were pious, and their son was carefully educated at the fireside in the principles of religion. Here, no doubt, the seed was sown, that having lain for a long time dormant, eventually germinated and produced a bountiful harvest.

When he was nine years of age, his parents removed

[1] Sprague's *Annals*, iii. 473.

to Berkshire County, Mass., a place at that time without schools or other means of intellectual culture, and so most unfavorable to the mental culture of the future pioneer missionary. The straitened circumstances of his parents too, induced the necessity of labor and toil; yet withal his natural genius was stimulated to invention, and the way was opened for a preparation most useful to him in after life.

At the age of eighteen he entered the army, just three weeks after the battle of Lexington, and received his first lessons in military life. His whole life was to be one of service. During his first two years, he was an attendant upon the chaplain of his regiment. He was present at the battle of Bunker Hill, and afterward for some time with General Arnold in Canada. In this campaign he served as usual in divers capacities. In the hospitals he was an excellent nurse; in the commissary department he was an accomplished baker; when the master of transportation required it, he could repair the broken wagons, and when the noise and shock of battle prevailed, he could handle the musket with energy and precision. In this service he was attacked with small-pox, and afterwards with chills and fever, yet through all his exposures and dangers he was mercifully preserved.

In two years from the period of his enlistment, he was discharged and returned to his friends. Here he found an expedition organizing to pursue the British troops that had two days before destroyed Danbury. Of course young Badger joined this expedition, and participated in two sharp engagements, when he returned to his friends. Shortly after this he enlisted again, and was appointed orderly sergeant. At the expiration of his term, he found that the two hundred dollars of Continental money that he had saved was so depreciated that it would not buy him a suit of clothes.[1] But this did not distress him. He at once engaged in weaving, continuing the business until he had woven sixteen hundred yards of cloth.

His mind now thirsted for knowledge, and he determined to spend some time in the acquisition of the elementary branches of study, spelling, writing, and arithmetic, intending afterward to return to the army.

There were no schools in the neighborhood, and he put himself under the instruction of Rev. Jeremiah Day, father of President Day of Yale College, and entered his family as a boarder. He studied during the winter, and resorted to the loom in the spring to recruit his exhausted finances.

But a change came over his mind here that had a most important influence on his future plans. His mind became deeply impressed with religious truth. There was no great distress or excitement, but a gradual change, that seemed to operate upon his heart, until he believed he had experienced a thorough change of heart. The light was faint at first, but continued to increase until his soul was filled with peace.

All thoughts of returning to the army were abandoned, and having made a profession of religion in the church of his patron, he entered upon a course of study preparatory to entering college. His progress was slow, and although well-nigh discouraged by the narrowness of his means, he yet persevered, sometimes weaving, and sometimes engaged in teaching school. "Yet still," he says, "I dug away like a miner after gold."

With frequent interruptions from sickness, and laboring for his livelihood, he at length entered Yale Col-

---

[1] Gillett's *History*, ii. 132.

lege in 1781, as a Freshman. During his first term he taught a singing school, and was so much discouraged that he notified President Stiles that he would be obliged to leave college. "O no, Badger," was his reply, "you must not leave. You may go and teach, study and earn, and pay your bills as well as you can."

So the earnest, patient man struggled on. Sometimes he taught school. Sometimes he rung the College bell, and performed other labors about the Hall until his Senior year. During this year he constructed a *planetarium*, that cost him three months' labor, and for which the College authorities gave him an order on the steward for one hundred dollars. He was graduated in the fall of 1783.

The next year he taught a school, and studied theology under the venerable Rev. Mark Leavenworth, and in due course was licensed to preach the gospel by the New Haven Association. During the next winter he supplied the church of Plymouth, Conn. On the 24th day of October, 1787, he was ordained pastor of the church of Blandford, Conn. He was pastor of this church thirteen years, and was dismissed October 24, 1800, to accept the commission of the Connecticut Missionary Society, to labor as a missionary in the Western Reserve of Ohio, or New Connecticut, as it was then called.

He set out on his westward journey on the 15th day of November, alone and on horseback. He was sometimes detained for days by the rain and snow. His progress was slow, from the badness of the roads, which, as he approached the close of his journey, were mere bridle-paths, and for nearly two hundred miles he was obliged to lead his horse. He was obliged to swim the Mahoning River in Ohio, but at length reached Youngstown, and found a hospitable reception with the Presbyterian pastor, Rev. William Wick[1] (2).

Here commenced a series of labors leading him in every direction, where the cabin of a settler was to be sought, or where a path was to be found through the woods. The winter was spent in the southern part of the Reserve; but in the spring he extended his travels east as far as Hudson, thence north to Cleveland. By request of the Presbytery of Ohio, he went in company with Rev. Thomas Edgar Hughes (1), as far as Maumee and Detroit, to consider the propriety of establishing a mission amongst the Indians. In this expedition he was accompanied by George Blue Jacket, the son of an Indian chief.[2] On his way he preached to the Delawares, through an interpreter. On his journey homeward, he suffered great hardships. Exposure and privation had reduced him to such a condition that he could hardly cling to his horse. Taking calomel one day and an emetic the next for five days in succession, he was finally so much reduced that he could not mount his horse without assistance. Still he pushed onward, and at length reached Hudson, Ohio, having subsisted for two days on chestnuts.

Having been absent from New England about a year, he returned to Connecticut. On his journey homeward he was taken ill at Buffalo, N. Y., with fever, and reduced to the very borders of the grave. From this he recovered partially, and after other attacks at length reached his home and family. Here he made a report of his missionary operations to the Board, and made arrangements for removing his family to the Western Reserve.

This journey was commenced on the 23d day of

[1] Gillett's *History* ii. 134.   [2] Dr. Elliott.

February, 1802. It was a most unseasonable period to undertake a journey of four or five hundred miles. Yet it was undertaken in faith and hope. The outfit was a four-horse wagon, in which were stowed his wife and six children, together with their household effects. Soon the missionary family encountered snow, that increased in depth until his wagon wheels became solid with snow and mud, and they were fain to construct a rude sled, on which the wheels were laid, having been taken from the axles, and upon these the wagon body was placed and the journey resumed. At Troy, N. Y., the snow failed, the sled was discarded, and the wagon restored to its original condition. But the mud was fearful. Onward the noble horses toiled, one accident after another happened, until finally the forward axle-tree broke, bringing them to an unwilling halt. There was no wagon-maker near, nor any other mechanic that was available. So remembering his war experience, he collected what tools were at hand, procured a piece of timber, and made a new axle with his own hands. His next accident was the breaking of his king-bolt, replaced at an expense of two dollars. He reached Austenburg, Ohio, at length, after a journey of two months. Here he had organized a church during his first tour, October 1, 1801, consisting of eight male and six female members.

At this place, he prepared to pitch his tent. He built a rude cabin of logs, found sufficient flooring for it to spread their Connecticut beds furnished by good mother Noble, but without table or chairs, or even a door or chinking between the logs.

But the missionary had not come to finish off houses or seek personal comfort, but to preach the gospel to those that were beyond. So he left his family to plant the garden and the corn-field, and set out on a missionary tour that continued three months, when he returned home. These missionary tours continued with little cessation until April, 1803. It was on April 13, 1803, that Mr. Badger became a member of the Presbytery of Erie. The minutes of the Presbytery would indicate that he was received as a Congregational minister. The minute is to this effect: "Rev. Joseph Badger, a missionary from Connecticut, having expressed a desire to join this Presbytery, and having given satisfaction of his regular standing in the body to which he formerly belonged, was received, but still retains his privilege of riding under the direction of the Connecticut Missionary Society." [1]

He is seldom found at meetings of Presbytery, during the six years he continued a member. His time was taken up in his missionary tours, and he depended on his brethren to take care of the interests of the church at home.

About this time, a letter was received from the Missionary Board in Connecticut, informing him that his salary was reduced to six dollars per week. At this Mr. Badger felt greatly aggrieved. His whole time was devoted to his missionary work, and even with this small pittance he could hardly live. He wrote repeatedly to the Home Board, reasoning and remonstrating against a policy that he denominated "injudicious and oppressive." Still he continued to labor on. A most blessed revival had been in progress for months where he was laboring, and although his family was actually suffering for many of the necessaries of life, he could not abandon the field.

The Connecticut Missionary Society have the follow-

[1] Min. Erie Pres. i. 12.

ing endorsement in their report for the year 1804:
"Mr. Badger has endured great hardships in riding in
stormy and severe weather, and in fording rivers. It
appears from his journal, that he travels in that rough,
and in some places, almost pathless country, nearly seventeen hundred miles a year; and that he preaches one
hundred and forty or fifty sermons. He attends many
conferences and meetings for prayer, catechizes the
children, and is abundant in family visits." [1]

His patience having become exhausted, he resigned
his commission from the Connecticut Missionary Society, and accepted one from the "Western Missionary
Society," located at Pittsburgh, Pa., as a missionary to
the Indians. This change took place in January, 1806.
In this work he labored amongst the Wyandotte Indians, in the region of Sandusky, Ohio, for about four
years. In the autumn of 1807, he removed his family
to Sandusky, but on account of the unhealthiness of the
climate, moved back the following year. At the close
of the year 1809, he made a journey to Boston, where
he collected nearly eleven hundred dollars in aid of his
mission. Returning, he resumed his labors amongst
the Indians, spending his time away from his family,
and heroically devoting himself to his great work. During one of these absences, he heard of the death of a
beloved daughter. Of her he makes this testimony:
"The Lord gave her to us, and continued her a comfortable child, until she was ripe for heaven. We have
reason to believe that she has, through the righteousness of the Redeemer, made a happy change." [2]

Soon after this bereavement, he received a letter
from his wife, informing him that their house had been
burned, with nearly all its contents. He immediately

[1] *Evan. Intel.* vol. i. 497.   [2] *Ibid.* vol. iii. 387.

hastened home, went to work, and with the assistance of the neighbors, erected another cabin, and placing his family in it, turned his face to the wilderness once more.

Having resigned his commission to the Western Board, he removed, in the spring of 1810, to Ashtabula, Ohio, with his family. Here and in the neighboring settlements he preached, deriving his support in part from the people and in part from the Massachusetts Missionary Society.

During the war of 1812, he was a soldier once more, in which his versatile talent was brought into active exercise. His connection with the army seems to have been providential, and without his own active agency. Perkins' brigade had been ordered westward to protect the western frontier. Many of his congregation were in the ranks, and some of them sick. Mr. Badger visited them in the camp, and without his own knowledge or solicitation, he was appointed brigade chaplain, and postmaster of the army by General Harrison. He accepted this appointment as a call to duty, and remained with the army until spring. During the winter he piloted the army across the country to Lower Sandusky, and went with it to Maumee, from which place he returned to his family in March, 1813.

Mr. Badger continued to preach in various places, without any regular support, until 1826, when, feeling the infirmities of age coming upon him, with a straitness in his means, he reported himself to the War Department as a soldier of the Revolution, and was placed upon the pension roll at ninety-six dollars a year. About the same time, he accepted an invitation to labor in Gustavus, Trumbull Co., Ohio, a small congregation of about thirty members, that had been organized by himself. Over this people he was installed as pastor by the Presbytery of Grand River, in October, 1826. Here he labored for eight years with encouraging success, but on account of declining health, he was dismissed from his charge by the Presbytery of Trumbull, June 26, 1835.[1] This dismission was at his own request, and against the wishes of his people.

In October following, he removed to Wood County, Ohio, to reside with his only surviving daughter, Mrs. Van Tassel. With her he remained until within three years of his decease, when he removed to Perrysburg, Ohio, where he died, April 5, 1846, in the ninetieth year of his age. His last sermon was preached on the day of the National Fast, appointed in consequence of the death of President Harrison, his old commander. With all his patriarchal age, "he retained his mental powers to the last moments, and died in the exercise of a triumphant faith in the Lord Jesus Christ." [2]

In his ecclesiastical relations, Mr. Badger was first a Congregationalist, but finding none of his brethren in his new field of labor, he connected himself with the Presbytery of Erie. This new relation was consummated on the 13th day of April, 1803. In 1808, the Presbytery of Hartford (Beaver) was formed, when he became one of its original members. In 1814, he became a member of the Presbytery of Grand River,[3] and lastly of the Presbytery of Trumbull.[4] It is said he always retained his preferences for Congregationalism.

"In person," says President Pierce of Western Reserve College, "he was about the medium size, of a strong and muscular frame, and yet not peculiarly cor-

---

[1] Dr. Elliott.
[2] Ibid.
[3] Formed from Hartford, 1814.
[4] Formed from Grand River, 1827.

pulent. The features of his countenance were strongly marked — bold, expressive, and manly. In his manners, he was frank, open, benevolent, and sympathetic. A stranger soon felt at home with him, and prepared to receive with confidence information on all subjects within the field of his labors."

He was a man of great versatility of genius. He could assist the farmer in manufacturing and repairing his farming utensils, or administer medicine to the sick, whilst he was equally at home in shoeing his own horse, carrying hammer and nails in his saddle-bags for that purpose.

Whilst the army lay at Lower Sandusky, during his chaplaincy, in 1812, his genius was called into requisition. Says President Pierce : —

" The settlement was small, and the army encamped in the woods was short of provisions, and suffered especially in that they had no means for grinding corn. Mr. Badger, by boring and burning, scooped out a large oak stump in the form of a mortar. In this he placed an upright shaft, fitted at the end for a pestle, and gave it motion by means of a horizontal spring-pole, fastened to the neighboring trees, and thus the corn was pounded. When he had got his machinery in operation, he called on Colonel Darrow, the commanding officer of the station, and asked him if he had ever heard of priestcraft? He replied, ' Yes.' ' Would you like to see a specimen?' ' Yes.' So he took him to the woods and showed him his contrivance."

The same authority gives us the following incident of his missionary adventures, that is well authenticated : —

" On the eve of a dark, rainy night, the streams being much raised, he came to a ford on Grand River, and crossed, intending to encamp on the bank for the night. He was prevented by the snapping and growling of some animal near. It soon became so dark that he could not see his hand holding the bridle, and he knew by the noise that a bear was continually approaching. Having a horseshoe in his hand, guided by the noise, he threw it, but without effect. He reined his horse right and left, that he might find a tree and climb from danger. Succeeding in this, he fastened the bridle to the smaller limbs, rose upon the saddle and ascended the tree. The bear came to the root and, as he supposed, began to climb. Gaining a firm footing, he drew a sharp knife and prepared for battle. But as the bear did not approach, he ascended about forty feet into the top of the tree, found a convenient place to sit upon a limb, and tied himself to the tree with his handkerchief, that he might be more safe if he should fall into a drowse. The night was most dreary, with storm and wind and heavy peals of thunder. Providentially the horse was not frightened, but remained a quiet sentinel at the foot of the tree. Being drenched with rain, he shook his saddle, and so frightened the bear that he retreated a few rods, where he remained growling and snapping his teeth until near daylight, when he left the premises, and the missionary went to his home in safety."

Mr. Badger was twice married. His first wife was Miss Lois Noble, of New Milford, Conn., a sister of the wife of his early patron, Rev. Jeremiah Day. By this marriage he had seven children, three sons and four daughters. Mrs. Badger died on the 4th of August, 1818, in the sixty-fourth year of her age. She was a most estimable woman, sharing his hardships, conducting the affairs of the house in his absence, and coöperating with him in all his missionary plans.

His second wife was Miss Abigail Ely, of Wilbraham, Mass., who was visiting her sisters in Salem, Ohio. This marriage took place in April, 1819.

And thus his record closes upon earth, but who can doubt but that it is carried forward in heaven, in higher, holier, and more exalted service, where the peace and the joy and the glory will be eternal!

(12). ALEXANDER COOK.

1802–1828.

HERE is one who led a life of vicissitudes. In his earlier years, he was familiar with the broom and the heather of Scotia's classic vales. In later life he was an artisan at Berwick-on-the-Tweed, so famous in Scottish history, and still later a missionary in the northern and southern portions of the United States.

Alexander Cook was the son of Thomas and Isabella (Ogilvie) Cook, and was born at St. Monance, Fifeshire, near Glasgow, Scotland, on the 4th day of February, 1760, and was baptized on the 6th day of the same month and year. He received a moderate English education at Glasgow, and learned the trade of a silversmith. He was at Berwick-on-the-Tweed in 1778, and emigrated to America in 1783. He lived for a time in the State of Maryland, and in 1797 was living in Cannonsburg, Pa., and working at his trade as a silversmith. In those days there seems to have been something sacred in the very atmosphere of that town. The influence of Dr. McMillan seems to have reached almost every professing Christian man, and to have drawn them, under God, into the ministry. So we find Alexander Cook working away most diligently in the fabrication of spoons and the renovating of watches; and at the same time, although nearly forty years of age, studying at the Academy, with reference to the gospel ministry. He studied theology with Dr. McMillan, and was licensed by the Presbytery of Ohio. He had been taken under the care of this Presbytery, January 21, 1802, as a suitable person to be sent to the Indians as a missionary, and for that purpose specially licensed, April 23, 1802. In the following August, it is recorded that he was commissioned by General Dearborn, then Secretary of War, as a missionary to the Indians. He had, however, an appointment of a more ecclesiastical nature, from the Synod of Pittsburgh. His history as a missionary is thus recorded: —

"Mr. Alexander Cook, a licentiate under the care of the Ohio Presbytery, was appointed to spend five months at Sandusky to instruct the Indians in the knowledge of the Gospel of Christ."

Afterwards it is recorded: "The missionaries have all fulfilled their appointments except Messrs. Joseph Patterson and Alexander Cook, who though they went to the places to which they were directed, did not meet that friendly reception they expected from the Indians, and returned in about two months."[1]

He was regularly licensed for the settlements on the 30th day of September, 1802. On the 12th day of April, 1803, he was received under the care of the Presbytery of Erie, and having accepted calls from the congregations of Slippery Rock and Lower Neshannock, (now New Castle), was assigned Rom. iii. 31, as the subject of a sermon as part of trials for ordination. He was ordained on the 22d day of June, 1803, and installed

[1] Printed *Min. Synod of Pittsburgh*, page 12.

pastor of the churches of Slippery Rock and New Castle. In these exercises John Boyd (8) preached the sermon, and Thomas Edgar Hughes (1) delivered the charges. This relation continued until June 14th, 1809, when it was dissolved by Presbytery. On the 6th day of March, 1810, he was dismissed from the Presbytery of Erie, and connected himself with the Presbytery of Hartford.

About this time Mr. Cook took a commission as a missionary to labor in the States of South Carolina and Georgia. This work continued for six months. He was also stated supply at Poland, Ohio, from 1812 to 1814. On the 3d day of January, 1815, he was received from the Presbytery of Hartford, by the Presbytery of Ohio, and installed pastor of the church of Bethany. This relation was dissolved April 1, 1820. And on the 3d day of April, 1821, he was received by the Presbytery of Alleghany, and on the 26th of June following, installed as pastor of the churches of Ebenezer and Bear Creek. This relation was dissolved on the 26th day of June, 1827. On the 19th of October following he was received by the Presbytery of Steubenville, and for a year supplied the churches of Annapolis and Bloomfield, in Jefferson County, Ohio.

In the winter of 1828, he left his home to organize a church in a Scotch settlement, in Columbiana County, Ohio. Reaching his destination on Saturday, he conversed to a late hour of the night with the family whose hospitality he was enjoying, and retired to rest. Not appearing at the usual time of rising in the morning, examination was made, when he was found dead in his bed. His death occurred at the house of Mr. Johnston, on Yellow Creek, November 30, 1828, in the sixty-ninth year of his age and the thirty-seventh of his ministry.

On the 2d day of January, 1787, Mr. Cook was united in marriage to Miss Alizannah Adams, of Abingdon, Md. They had ten children, three only of whom arrived at years of maturity. Mrs. Cook died at Slippery Rock, Beaver County, Pa., June 6, 1805. Her death took place on a Fast Day, whilst her husband was at church. He was afterwards married to Miss Clark, of Beaver County, Pa.

In person Mr. Cook was rather below the medium height, compactly built, dark complexion, dark brown eyes, with a sedate expression of countenance, generally, yet with a vein of mirth, cropping out in times of relaxation. He had a good faculty of rendering himself ageeable to the young.

(13.) ROBERT PATTERSON.

1801–1854.

ROBERT PATTERSON was the son of Rev. Joseph and Jane (Moak) Patterson. He was descended from a family illustrious for its patriotism, and what is better, for piety and zeal for the service of the Lord. The father of Robert Patterson was born in the north of Ireland, in the year 1752. His father, though but a lad at the time, was at the famous siege of Derry; and the sufferings to which the Patterson family were subjected in consequence of this siege, were most severe and distressing. This branch of the family emigrated from Scotland to Ireland, in consequence of the terrible persecutions, carried on by Claverhouse, under Charles II. The grandfather of Robert Patterson was the son of John, the founder of the Irish branch of the family.[1]

---

[1] Sprague's *Annals*.

Rev. Joseph Patterson, the father of Robert, was licensed to preach the gospel in 1788. He was a most useful and laborious minister, and died at Pittsburgh, Pa., in 1832.

Robert Patterson, the subject of this sketch, was born at Stillwater, New York, on the 1st day of April, 1773, near the spot afterwards celebrated as the field of one of the most severely contested battles of the Revolution. Not long after his birth, his parents removed to Germantown, Pa. The battle of Germantown occurred during the sojourn of the family at that place, and Mr. Patterson, then in his fifth year, distinctly remembered many of its scenes. After a brief residence in York County, the family removed to the West, and took up their abode in Washington County, Pa.

In the spring of 1791, Robert Patterson commenced his academical studies at the Cannonsburg Academy, then just opened. He recited the first lesson that was heard in connection with that institution — teacher and pupil seated under the shade of a tree, on the banks of the now classic Chartiers. After prosecuting his studies for three years in the Academy, he went east and entered the senior class of the University of Pennsylvania, where he graduated in the fall of 1795. On his way to Philadelphia, the journey there being made on horseback, he met the forces sent out by the Government to quell the Whiskey Insurrection.

Mr. Patterson had a great thirst for knowledge. He was not content with his collegiate course, and so lingered in the halls of his Alma Mater after his graduation. He was employed for nearly five years as tutor in the University, at the same time prosecuting, still further, his studies in the languages and higher mathematics. He returned to the residence of his father, who was then pastor of the Raccoon Church, in 1800, and on the 30th day of April, 1801, was licensed to preach the gospel by the Presbytery of Ohio. His theological studies had been prosecuted in part with Rev. Ashbel Green, D. D., while he was connected with the University, and in part under the direction of Dr. McMillan.

The next year after his licensure, Mr. Patterson took a tour over the destitute region of what was afterward the territory of the Presbytery of Erie. He visited the shore of Lake Erie, preached at various places, and finally was encouraged to think of settling in the congregations of Erie and Upper and Lower Greenfield. These latter churches were afterwards known as Middlebrook and North East. Rev. Elisha McCurdy had preceded him here, and soon after Mr. Patterson's first visit, he, in company with Joseph Stockton (4), James Satterfield (6), and his own famous "praying elder," Philip Jackson, organized the churches of Upper Greenfield (Middlebrook) and Lower Greenfield (North East).

At a *pro re nata* meeting of the Presbytery of Erie, held at Pittsburgh, on the 30th of September, 1802, during the sessions of the Synod of Pittsburgh, Mr. Patterson was received under its care. At the same meeting calls were presented for his pastoral labors from the congregations of Erie and Upper and Lower Greenfield, of which he declared his acceptance. Acts iii. 19 was assigned him as the subject for a sermon as part of trials for ordination. At a meeting of Presbytery held at Lower Greenfield, or North East, on the 1st day of September, 1803, the congregation of Erie, having from some cause declined entering into the arrangement, Mr. Patterson was ordained and installed as pastor of the congregations of Upper and Lower Greenfield. Here he labored faithfully and with the practice of much self-denial until the 22d day of April, 1807, when at his own request the pastoral relation was dissolved. During his labors in this field he resided at North East, and took frequent missionary tours up and down the Lake, and for a time preached a part of the time at a place called Portland. A wide-spreading fir-tree is still pointed out by an aged citizen of the neighborhood, as having been planted by Mr. Patterson's own hand.

In April, 1807, he accepted an invitation to take charge of the Pittsburgh Academy, now the Western University of Pennsylvania. During the three years he presided over this institution, he numbered among his pupils many who afterwards filled prominent public stations, and who often spoke in grateful terms of his care and faithfulness as an instructor.

In October, 1812, Mr. Patterson was dismissed from the Presbytery of Erie, to connect himself with the Presbytery of Redstone. From 1810 to 1836 he was engaged in secular business, book-selling, and at times the manufacture of paper, having been one of the proprietors of one of the first paper mills established in the West. This business was carried on extensively for nearly a quarter of a century, bringing him into extensive public notice, yet not always resulting in success. Indeed, he suffered many severe reverses, yet was always esteemed a man of most undoubted probity and honor.

During the greater portion of this time, he was stated supply of the Hilands Church, situated about seven miles from Pittsburgh, and in the bounds of the Presbytery of Ohio. The people of this charge have often remembered his faithful ministrations; and the recollection of the relationship he had sustained to them, with its many pleasing associations, was a theme of grateful acknowledgment on his part, to the latest period of his life.

In 1840, Mr. Patterson removed to the country a short distance from Pittsburgh. The infirmities of age were now upon him, and he ceased to preach regularly, yet he was always ready, when physical strength would permit, to preach in neighboring churches when they were vacant. For many years increasing spirituality seemed to characterize his mind. The things unseen of the eye of sense absorbed his attention and filled his mind, as was obvious from his reading and conversation. Scarcely a friend or even a stranger paused for a moment at his door, without having their attention called to the things of religion. Rev. Richard Lea, who knew him well, remarks that he did not remember a single conversation with him for many years, were the interview long or short, in which the subject of the soul's great interest had not been introduced. In the bosom of his own family, where he was ever the most tender of husbands, and the most affectionate of fathers, and in the enjoyment of that domestic intercourse which had for him a peculiar charm, his spirituality of character and heavenly-mindedness, shone forth with brightest lustre.

His last illness was brief. His disease was dysentery. It assumed an alarming character about a week preceding his departure. When all hope of recovery was precluded, his brother Joseph said to him, "You will soon be with that Jesus whom you have loved so long." He smiled a pleased assent. His brother then remarking that "God showed the same mercy in breaking up as in building up a family," he replied that "We are too prone to regard only one of God's attributes — his mercy; forgetting that he was infinite in them all — his justice as well as his mercy." Other remarks showed that whilst tenderly mindful of those around, his thoughts were with that Saviour he was so soon to see.

On Sabbath afternoon he lapsed into a state of almost lethargy, which continued with little interruption until Tuesday evening, September 5, 1854, when without a quivering muscle, or a heaving sigh, he passed away from earth.

There are perhaps few to whom could be applied with greater propriety the words which were the last he ever read, when he led for the last time the devotions of his family, on the Wednesday preceding his decease: "For our conversation is in heaven; from whence also we look for the Saviour, the Lord Jesus Christ, who shall change our vile body, that it may be fashioned like unto his glorious body, according to the working whereby he is able even to subdue all things unto himself." Phil. iii. 20, 21.

In August, 1801, Mr. Patterson was united in marriage to Miss Jean, daughter of Col. John Canon, the proprietor of Cannonsburg. They had seven children, five daughters, and two sons.

The following paper from the pen of Rev. Richard Lea, will throw light upon his character: "Rev. Robert Patterson, son of Joseph, was like his father in many respects: rather short and heavy, very lively and good natured. He was not a student, but a good scholar; long known in Pittsburgh as a bookseller, but preaching for twenty-five years, nearly every Sabbath, in Hilands Church. He had labored previously in Erie County, Pa. He lived many years, in a hearty old age, after his resignation as pastor.

"I never knew one so remarkable for under-valuing self. In judicatories he spoke impulsively, and if replied to *pointedly*, none enjoyed it more than himself. He would catechize a young man's performance earnestly, and ending with, 'It is too much like my own performances;' or 'It is very poor indeed, but far better than I could do myself.' The severest thing he ever said was, 'Moderator, as a performance, that is more logical and accurate than anything of my own, but I never did preach such a *Christless* thing. I never will vote for a sermon that has not the slightest perfume of the Rose of Sharon.'

"He often told with great gusto, the following, which was rather at his own expense: —

"'I was riding on horseback through the mud, seven miles to Hilands, to preach on Sabbath morning. A traveller overtook me. I told him he must be fond of violating the Sabbath to travel over such awful roads.

"'And what are you doing, friend?'

"'O, I'm going to church.'

"'Do you think it makes much difference to the horse? Couldn't you get preaching nearer?'

"The church was soon reached, and I said, 'Suppose you come and hear preaching; it will rest both you and your horse.'

"'Who is the preacher?'

"'One Patterson.'

"'Did he preach in Erie once?'

"'Yes.'

"'Then I won't stop — he is the dryest old stick I ever heard.'

"His own sermons were all extempore, and very much taken up with the relative duties of husbands and wives, parents and children. He abounded in anecdotes, sure to speak of Jesus; often, with tears, of his mother.

"The text he often *parsed* — spoke of nouns and verbs, etc., often exclaiming, 'O, the sweetness of the personal pronouns. Any one can say, a Saviour, *the* Saviour; it takes a christian to say, *my* Lord, *my* Saviour.'

"Every one wished to lodge him, at Presbytery. He would put all at ease by saying, 'What a bountiful meal God has given you for us.' 'Put as much cream into my coffee as though you kept a cow, and as much sugar as if you had a sugar camp.'

"'Make your tea strong, and weaken with cream and sugar.'

"'Madam! What a nice big boy you have! Give him to Christ, and ask him to make him a missionary.'

"To a lady who asked him what school she should send her daughter to, he replied, 'That one that has the most religion in it.'

"'Don't send your boy into the world until he has found Christ. But if he will go, follow him with prayers and tears. Give him and God no rest, until he is converted.'"

(14.) ROBERT JOHNSTON.

1802–1861.

There are many remarkable incidents connected with the life of this servant of God. His old age, his long period of active labor, and his success in winning souls to Christ, make his history interesting and instructive. There is an incident connected with his dawn of life that is worthy of record. "When he was an infant of days, his maternal grandfather died, who was a devotedly pious man. Just before his death, he was led to the door, at his own request, supported by his attendant watchers. It was night. He looked with anxious gaze towards the heavens, as though longing to fly away to God. But his work was not quite done. As he cast his eyes downward, the little babe in his mother's arms smiled upon him, at which sight he lifted his eyes again toward heaven, and poured forth a most earnest and impassioned prayer for the infant. It was his dying prayer. His work was now done, and he fell asleep in Jesus. From that hour, the parents, who had already devoted the child to God in baptism, resolved with unwavering purpose to educate him for the ministry." [1]

"Rev. Robert Johnston was of English extraction, being a lineal descendant of Oliver Cromwell, by Bridget, the eldest daughter of the Protector, who was first the wife of General Fleetwood, and afterward of General Ireton. His paternal grandfather emigrated to this country, in early manhood, and settled and married in the State of New Jersey. He had three sons — Abram, Robert, and Elisha — and one daughter. Robert, the second son, settled as a farmer on the west bank of the Juniata River, in what is called Sherman's Valley, in Cumberland (now Perry) County, Pennsylvania, where he was married to Miss Jane Graham.

"Mr. Robert Johnston had five sons, James, Edward, Robert, Francis, and William, and two daughters, Nancy and Mary. Edward obtained, when somewhat advanced in life, an education, and was licensed to preach the gospel. Robert, the third son and subject of this biographical sketch, was born on the 7th day of August, 1774." [2]

[1] Rev. Loyal Young, D. D.   [2] Dr. Swift's Sermon.

The purpose of devoting him to the gospel ministry, his parents seem to have laid up in their own hearts, for in boyhood young Robert was sent to learn the trade of a wagon-maker, which business he pursued until his twenty-second year. In the year 1792, his father crossed the mountains, and with his family settled on a place near Cannonsburg, Pa. He had become involved pecuniarily, and must seek a home in a comparatively new country. In this new location his circumstances began to prosper, and he saw the way opening for carrying out his long-cherished purpose of educating his son. In May, 1796, the parents of Robert Johnston made known to him and the rest of the family their plans and hopes, and in his twenty-second year he commenced his studies in the Cannonsburg Academy.

In the autumn of 1801, having completed his studies in the Academy, he commenced the study of theology with Dr. McMillan. His classmates were, James Carnahan, William McMillan, Robert Patterson (13), and Stephen Lindley. On the 22d of April, 1802, he was licensed to preach the gospel, by the Presbytery of Ohio.

Very providentially for the cause of history, Mr. Johnston has left behind a brief autobiography, from which a few paragraphs are selected, quoted from the discourse delivered by Rev. E. P. Swift, D. D., before the Synod of Alleghany:—

"After prosecuting the study of theology about eighteen months, I was licensed by the Presbytery of Ohio, on the 22d of April, 1802. After riding one year as a licentiate (chiefly in Ohio and Kentucky), I received a call from the united congregations of Scrubgrass and Bear Creek, and entered upon my charge on the first Sabbath of August."

BIOGRAPHICAL. 243

Mr. Johnston was ordained by the Presbytery of Erie, on the 19th day of October, 1803, at Scrubgrass. His trial sermon was on John vi. 45. In the ordination services, Rev. James Satterfield (6) preached on Matt. xvi. 26, and Rev. William Wylie (7) presided and delivered the charges.[1]

"I had become familiar with the great western revival which commenced in Kentucky, in 1802, having seen it there and in Ohio during the summer, and in Western Pennsylvania in the fall and winter following, and felt anxious to see it in my own charge. The settlement in Scrubgrass was new, and composed generally of young families, and was lamentably destitute of vital piety. So far as I knew, there were but three praying men in the congregation, and they lived in the extreme parts of it, and could not be convened for a prayer meeting."

Mr. Johnston then proceeds to relate the circumstances, already alluded to in the body of this work, connected with a powerful revival of religion, the fruits of which he states to be the hopeful conversion of more than a hundred souls within the bounds of the congregation of Scrubgrass, comprising fully one half of all its adult members.

"Not long after the revival had ceased, I resigned the charge of Bear Creek, and devoted my whole time to Scrubgrass, where I continued to labor in peace and comfort until interrupted by claims to the soil, presented by land-jobbers, which eventually drove many of my best members from their farms into the State of Ohio. This reduced the congregation so far that I was laid under the painful necessity of parting with the remains of a

[1] Min. Erie Pres. i. 21.

flock, endeared to me by every tie that could bind a pastor and his flock together in love.

"In February, 1811, I took my leave of this little flock and moved to Meadville, and took charge of that congregation, with two others, Sugar Creek and Conneaut Lake, devoting half of my time to Meadville, and the balance to the other two. Here I continued to labor until the spring of 1817, when, for causes not under my control, I felt it to be my duty to leave them and to remove to the congregations of Rehoboth and Round Hill, on the forks of the Youghiogheny River, under the care of the Presbytery of Redstone.

"In these congregations, I continued to labor in peace and comfort, and I trust not without some degree of usefulness, until December, 1822, when for various reasons that to me appeared sufficient to decide the question of duty, and which I presented to the Presbytery in writing, I took my leave of that people. I spent the following winter principally in an Agency for the Board of Domestic Missions; and in the spring I accepted an Agency in behalf of the Western Foreign Missionary Society and part of the summer and fall I acted as agent for the Western Theological Seminary.

"On the first of November, 1833, I visited Bethel congregation, Indiana County, Pa., where I spent the winter as stated supply, and in the spring accepted a call and became their pastor. Here I continued until, through the infirmities of age, I became unable to endure the fatigue and exposure necessarily connected with parochial duties, particularly family visitation, district catechising, and Bible-class and Sabbath-school instruction. Believing that in ordinary circumstances no man is justifiable in holding an office in Church or State, the duties and responsibilities of which he is unable to discharge, I asked and obtained leave to resign my pastoral charge in October, 1841, and at the request of the congregation, I continued as stated supply for six months. While I felt it my duty to resign the charge of a congregation,[1] I had no design to quit preaching, and being blessed with health and strength of lungs beyond the lot of my fellow-laborers, I had no desire to demit my beloved employment, and for six years that I have been without a charge, I have, in assisting my brethren on communion occasions, and in supplying their pulpits when they were necessarily absent, and occasionally supplying a vacant congregation, preached as many sermons as there have been Sabbaths, since my dismission in 1841 up to October, 1847. Since that time I have not been able to preach so frequently."

We have here in his own words, plain and unassuming as they are, a record of his outward life and public labors. From other sources it appears that he remained at Scrubgrass and Bear Creek about eight years; in Meadville, and the congregations attached to it, six years; in Rehoboth and Round Hill, sixteen years; in Bethel ten years, making an active pastorate of forty years.

After retiring from the pastoral office he continued to reside with his son, James W. Johnston, Esq., until his death.

Mr. Johnston was a member of the Presbytery of Erie, from the time of his ordination until February 25, 1818, when he became a member of the Presbytery of Redstone. He continued a member of this Presbytery until 1834, when he became a member of the Presbytery of Blairsville, of which he continued a

---

[1] Mr. Johnston was then in his 68th year.

member until 1851, when he became a member of the Presbytery of Beaver, continuing this connection until his death.

About the beginning of his ministry, he was united in marriage to Miss Eleanor Wright, a daughter of Judge Wright, long an eminent and valuable ruling elder in the church; and with her he lived most happily for near fifty years. This devoted woman entered most heartily into the spirit of his labors, accompanying him on horseback in his missionary work, sharing in his privations, comforting him in his discouragements, and taking such part in his labors, throughout his public ministry, as a devoted, heroic, Christian wife can, and died in New Castle, Pa., about the year 1852.

Of his family four sons received a liberal education, and are settled respectably in professional life : Rev. J. Watson Johnston, of the Presbytery of Beaver ; Hon. S. P. Johnston, President Judge of the Sixth Judicial District of Pennsylvania ; Robert Johnston, M. D., of West Middlesex, Pa.; and James W. Johnston, Esq., a member of the bar. Of his two surviving daughters, one is the wife of Rev. Loyal Young, D. D., of Butler, Pa., and the other of Alexander Ross, Esq., of New Castle, Pa.

During the last few years of his life he was much disabled by infirmity, being obliged to walk with crutches and even in this way with difficulty. The last time he appeared in Synod was at New Castle, in September, 1855 ; when, coming in on his crutches, he was cordially saluted by the venerable moderator, Dr. Swift, with inquiries for his health, he replied : "I have nothing of which to complain," but checking himself he added, — " Yes, there is the old wicked heart yet. I cannot get clear of that."

He was always punctual in his attendance at meetings of church courts. To his son-in-law, Dr. Young, he wrote in October, 1849: "My health has been so precarious for some time past, that I feel that it would not be prudent to be from home for any length of time. I have therefore concluded to be absent for the first time for the last forty-six years from the meeting of Synod."

From his early struggles in the way of life, he was eminently fitted to guide the inquiring, to comfort the desponding, and to warn those who were disposed to trust in their own works. His ministry was eminently successful. During the revivals with which his ministry was blessed, many young men were brought into the church, who afterwards became ministers of the gospel.

He was the special friend of all the benevolent operations of the church. Missionary, Educational, Bible, and Temperance Societies, always had his most hearty coöperation and encouragement.

"Mr. Johnston was an able, instructive, and impressive preacher. Without being what is familiarly called an eloquent, polished, or captivating speaker, he possessed strong lungs, a voice capable of filling with ease the largest building, and an enunciation so distinct that any in the largest assembly could easily hear him. If his voice was mighty in strength, and solemn and commanding in its utterance, it lacked melody and softness. His manner in the pulpit was grave, solemn, and often impassioned, attesting the profoundest sincerity and ardor ; and at times his appeals to the conscience were thrilling and powerful."[1]

Says Dr. Young: "His preaching was earnest, solemn, and instructive. Often was he so deeply moved by the importance of his themes, that utterance almost

[1] Dr. Swift.

failed. This was more especially the case in prayer. The unction and pathos of his prayers are well known by those who have often bowed with him at the family altar. The circle gathered there have often found the place a Bochim, while he led in penitential supplication."

With a heart overflowing with human kindness, there was yet much in his countenance and manner that reminded one of the old Puritan fathers. The blood of his old ancestors seemed to show itself in his countenance and in his speech. There was a gravity and sternness in his countenance and words that at first were almost repulsive. He used the old Anglo-Saxon language with great power, and handled the vices and follies of the times with unmitigated severity, speaking in language so strong that it seemed sometimes to amount to censoriousness and harshness. Yet withal, no one acquainted with him doubted the genuine kindness and charity that dwelt in his heart.

Says Dr. Young, in speaking of his last days: "To the doctrines and order of the Presbyterian church, Mr. Johnston was devotedly attached; and yet he loved with true Catholic charity all that bore the image of Christ. No man appreciated more than he, a good sermon or address, and he was enraptured by the power of eloquence, especially when the subject was the excellency of Christ, the glory of his coming kingdom, or the work of his grace in the hearts of men. These were themes of which he never grew weary. These themes so filled his heart during his last years that he was always happy. Never, perhaps, was an old age more cheerful. His wonder was why God should continue the life of one so useless, and he said often that he was just waiting in daily anticipation of his departure. A few years before his death, and at the last time he was at the house of the writer, while the family were gathered for worship on the evening of the Sabbath, he gave utterance to words so full of longing desire for heaven, that the pen can do no justice in attempting to record them. He said he had such an insatiable desire to know what the glory of heaven was, that he felt almost impatient for the time to come when he should be permitted to behold it; and this was said with so much pathos, and with a face so radiant with joy, that we all felt that we were communing with a man that had a foretaste of the bliss to which he was going. It was then, or at a later period, that he informed the writer that he had an *abiding* assurance of his being accepted with God and of his final happiness, and that for many years he had had no anxious doubt. In view of the Millennium, whose dawn he soon anticipated, he would sometimes say, that if it were lawful, he could wish to have been born fifty years later."

But the time of departure came at last, and with an illness of but two weeks' duration, he seemed literally to fall asleep, without a muscle indicating a departing struggle. His death occurred at New Castle, Pa., May 20, 1861, in the eighty-seventh year of his age. His remains rest in the cemetery at New Castle, near those of his departed companion in life.

(15.) NICHOLAS PITTINGER.

1803–1831.

NICHOLAS PITTINGER was born about the year 1766. Although his death took place at a comparatively late date, yet not much of his history has come down to our day. Of his parents and place of birth, we know nothing. He was educated at the Cannonsburg Academy, and studied theology in the approved way with Dr. McMillan, and was licensed by the Presbytery of Ohio on the 20th day of October, 1803. His name first appears on the records of the Presbytery of Erie, January 11, 1804, in this wise: "Mr. Pittinger, a licentiate of the Ohio Presbytery, being present and having signified his willingness to itinerate through the vacancies in this Presbytery, was appointed to preach at Poland," etc.

On the 27th day of June, in the same year, he was received under the care of Presbytery, and calls from the congregations of Westfield, Pa., and Poland, Ohio, having been presented for his pastoral labors. Rom. iii. 31, was assigned him as a subject for a sermon as part of trials for ordination.

On the 24th day of October, 1804, he was ordained to the whole work of the ministry, and installed pastor of the above churches. The meeting of Presbytery was at Westfield, the veteran Joseph Badger (11) preached the sermon, and William Wick (2) delivered the charges. He continued to serve the church of Westfield until the 13th of September, 1809, and the church of Poland until the 20th of March, 1810.

He was one of the original members of the Presbytery of Hartford, or Beaver, and from that Presbytery was dismissed to that of Washington, Ky., March 21, 1810. We cannot follow him closely now, as the footprints become indistinct. In the year 1810, he was a member of the Presbytery of Washington, Ky., and is reported as pastor of the church of Rocky Spring, near Greenfield, Ohio. Soon after, he is preaching at Nazareth and New Market, in connection with Rocky Spring. His pastorate at the latter place continued about ten years, and terminated in 1820. He is afterwards reported as stated supply at Pisgah, in the Presbytery of Chilicothe.

About the year 1821, he removed to the State of Indiana, and in 1823 was commissioned by the Board of Missions to labor in the northern part of that State.[1] This missionary work was arduous and severe. It continued but about one year, as he returned to the congregation of Rocky Spring, in Highland Co., Ohio, in April, 1824, where he continued to labor as a stated supply until his death, which occurred April 16, 1831, in the sixty-fifth year of his age, and the twenty-eighth of his ministry.

Mr. Pittinger was twice married. His first marriage took place before he entered the ministry. By this marriage he had two or three children. His second wife was from the Rocky Spring congregation. Her name was Mrs. Applegate, maiden name Taylor. She survived him until January, 1840.

Mr. Pittinger is reported as having been remarkably plain. His manner was blunt and uncompromising, exhibiting more of the spirit of John the Baptist than of John the beloved disciple.

(16.) JOHN McPHERRIN.

1789–1822.

JOHN McPHERRIN was born in Adams County, Pa., on the 17th day of November, 1757. His father's family afterwards removed to Westmoreland County, Pa. His studies, preparatory to entering College, were pursued with Rev. Robert Smith, D. D., of Pequea. He graduated at Dickinson College in 1788. His theological education was pursued under the direction of Rev. John Clark, pastor of Bethel congregation, Alleghany County, Pa. He was licensed to preach the gospel by

---

[1] Gillett's *History*.

the Presbytery of Redstone, on the 20th of August, 1789. On the 22d of September, in the year following, he was ordained by the same Presbytery, and installed as pastor of the congregations of Salem and Unity, in Westmoreland County, Pa. His labors were prosperous and successful in this field for a number of years. On the 28th of June, 1800, he was released from the charge of Unity, and on the 20th of April, 1803, from that of Salem.

On the 9th of April, 1805, he became a member of the Presbytery of Erie, having removed to Butler County, Pa., and accepted calls from the congregations of Concord and Muddy Creek. The records are not clear in regard to this period of his pastoral labor. In 1806, he is reported as pastor of Concord, Muddy Creek, and Harmony; in 1809, as pastor of Concord and Harmony. On the 7th of April, 1813, he was installed as pastor of the church of Butler, by the Presbytery of Erie. This was in connection with the church of Concord. Of this united charge he remained pastor until his death, a period of about nine years. His death took place at Butler, Pa., on the 10th day of February, 1822, in the sixty-fifth year of his age, and the thirty-third of his ministry.

The writer of his obituary notice in the "Pittsburgh Recorder,"[1] says: "He was a warm, zealous, and evangelical preacher. For some years before his death, he appeared to be remarkably weaned from the world; he indeed lived above the world. His whole heart and soul were absorbed in the love of God, and his whole aim was to promote the interests of the Redeemer's kingdom."

Mr. McPherrin appears to have been of a nervous,

[1] Quoted by Dr. Elliott, from whom many facts were received.

sensitive temperament, illy fitted for the rough contact with life. Says Dr. Loyal Young, his successor in the pastoral office at Butler: "For a few years he labored, at times, under great mental depression. A sense of his unworthiness sometimes led him to the conclusion that it was wrong for him to engage in ministerial work. Sometimes on Sabbath morning he would tell his wife that he could not preach that day, and would seem inclined not to fulfill his appointment. She would persuade him to go and conduct prayer-meeting, if he could not preach. On such occasions, he would generally preach sermons of unusual power.

"Mr. McPherrin was very faithful as a pastor. After catechising the family, he would take each of the younger members aside, and personally urge upon them the necessity of a new heart, and an interest in Christ. These private interviews were often blessed to their conversion."

The following tribute to his memory is from the pen of Hon. Walter Lowrie,[1] Secretary of the Presbyterian Board of Foreign Missions, who was his son-in-law:—

"Mr. McPherrin did not write his sermons. He used very brief but comprehensive notes, which he placed in a small pocket-Bible.

"It is no easy matter to draw a faithful likeness of Mr. McPherrin's character and appearance. He was tall in person, his hair, when I first saw him, quite gray, and his whole appearance the most venerable of any man I have ever seen. Decision and energy were the leading traits of his character. He knew not the fear of man, though sometimes his firmness degenerated into obstinacy. His natural temper was warm; hypocrisy formed no part of his character, and his heart was the

[1] Furnished to Dr. Young.

seat of friendship and good-will to man. He possessed a strong mind and strong natural abilities. At Dickinson College, under the celebrated Dr. Nesbit, he had received a thorough education, and by his studious habits, his mind was in a constant state of improvement. As a minister of the gospel, his zeal in his Master's cause never flagged, and a sincere desire to do good was his ruling passion through life. His eloquence was classically chaste, yet strong and nervous. His hearers were, in general, rather awed than charmed, more instructed than delighted, yet often did the tears of his audience flow before they were themselves aware of it. All his sermons were, in the highest degree, evangelical. Christ Jesus and him crucified was the burden of his message; and yet in every discourse he urged in the strongest manner the necessity of good works and a holy and Christian walk, not as a means or ground of acceptance with God, but as an evidence of being in the right way."

Mr. McPherrin was in early life united in marriage to Miss Mary Stevenson, daughter of John Stevenson, of Cross Creek congregation, in Washington County, Pa. Several of his descendants are, or have been, serving the church in the ministry of reconciliation. Rev. J. C. Lowrie, D. D., formerly a missionary to India, and the late Rev. Walter M. Lowrie, and Rev. Reuben P. Lowrie, missionaries to China, and Rev. Josiah McPherrin, of the Presbytery of Alleghany, are his grandsons.

The memory of Mr. McPherrin is greatly revered in the Butler congregation. Many of the older members remember, and relate with tearful interest, the record of his ministry, and his self-denying labors, and his faithful preaching of Christ, and his humble and godly walk and conversation.

(17.) BENJAMIN BOYD.

1804–1859.

THIS was the youngest of the four Boyd brothers, ordained by the Presbytery of Erie, although he entered the ministry nearly three years before his older brother James.

Benjamin Boyd, son of John and Mary (Fulton) Boyd, was born in Westmoreland County, Pa., on the 25th day of December, 1776. He probably worked on the farm with his father and brothers until near his majority, studying for a time with his good pastor, John McPherrin (16), until he went to Cannonsburg. Here he pursued his studies at the academy, and graduated after the academy had become a college. It is somewhat uncertain whether he studied theology with his pastor, or with Dr. McMillan. He was taken under the care of the Presbytery of Erie, as a candidate for the ministry, on the 22d day of June, 1803. "An Christus qua Mediator adorandus sit," was assigned him as the theme of a Latin exegesis.

He was licensed to preach the gospel by this Presbytery, on the 24th day of October, 1804. It is not on record how or where he spent his time during the next two years. But in the fall of 1806 he accepted calls from the congregations of Trumbull, Beula, and Pymatuning, on the Western Reserve, or eastern part of Ohio, and Mercer County, Pa. Rom. x. 4, was assigned him as a subject for a trial sermon. The ordination took place at Trumbull, Ohio, on the 12th day of November, 1806, Joseph Stockton (4) preached on the occasion, and Samuel Tait (3) delivered the charges. This pastoral relation continued until 1809. In 1811, he removed to Western Virginia, and in the war of 1812 served as a chaplain in the army in Virginia, under General Leftridge.[1]

In the autumn of 1814, he removed to Mason County, Ky. In 1827, he was a member of the Presbytery of Cincinnati. He preached for a time at Round Bottom, Cheviot, and Harrison, Ohio. He also preached for a time at West Liberty, Indiana, and at Dunlopsville and vicinity. At this time, he was also engaged in teaching, yet preaching as opportunity offered. In 1829, he removed to Newport, Ky., where he was engaged for a time in teaching.

In 1834 and 1835, he was a member of the Presbytery of Madison, and preached at Pleasant church, Ind. In the year 1836, he returned to Newport, Ky., where he spent the remainder of his days. He died on the 1st day of October, 1859, in the eighty-third year of his age and the fifty-sixth of his ministry. His death was the result of old age, hastened, perhaps, by a severe fall. His remains were laid to rest in the cemetery at Newport, Ky.

He was married early in life to Miss Anna Findley. They had five sons and one daughter.

Mr. Boyd's mind was probably not as well balanced as that of his other brothers, yet in many respects, he was an earnest and good man. His was a life of grievous burdens and great conflicts, and the peace and the rest of the good Land would be most grateful to his spirit.

(18.) CYRUS RIGGS.

1805–1849.

Mr. Riggs belonged to a New Jersey family. His ancestors had long resided in that State. He was the

---

[1] Wilson's *Pres. Hist. Almanac.*

son of Joseph and Hannah (Cook) Riggs, and was born in Morris County, New Jersey, on the 15th day of October, 1774. In his early years there was nothing remarkable or striking. He was a quiet, unpretending boy, intent on discharging his duty and standing in his lot. From New Jersey, Joseph Riggs removed with his family west of the Alleghany Mountains, and settled in Washington County, Pa., in the bounds of Lower Ten Mile congregation. At that time Cyrus was about twenty years of age. It is not known exactly when he became a professor of religion, but most probably soon after coming to the West, for a short time after we find him at Cannonsburg Academy, in preparation for the gospel ministry.

But circumstances seemed adverse to his plans. His father failed; his substance was sacrificed, and the son was forced to abandon his studies and give up all hope of the ministry. On the 25th day of July, 1797, Mr. Riggs was united in marriage to Miss Mary, daughter of Edward and Phebe Ross, of Washington County, Pa., who had emigrated from New Jersey about the same time with the Riggs' family. With his young wife, he removed to Mercer County, Pa., and setttled in the same congregation, where he was a few years afterward ordained as pastor. Here he commenced the laborious work of hewing himself out a home in the forest, with perhaps no thought but to spend his days in subduing the forest and cultivating the soil.

Soon, however, Dr. McMillan found him and pursuaded him to leave his axe and his plough, dispose of his little home, and return to Cannonsburg to study. He graduated in 1803 at Jefferson College, a member of the second class that graduated under the charter. After his graduation, he was employed as a tutor in the college, in the mean time commencing the study of theology under the direction of Dr. McMillan. On the 18th day of October, he was taken under the care of the Presbytery of Ohio, as a candidate for the gospel ministry, and on the 7th day of October, 1805, he was, by the same Presbytery, licensed to preach the gospel. From that time until the 23d day of October, 1806, he was engaged in supplying vacant churches within the bounds of Presbytery, when he received calls to labor in the congregations of Fairfield and Mill Creek, within the bounds of the Presbytery of Erie. In December of the same year, he declared his acceptance of these calls, and was dismissed to put himself under the care of the Presbytery of Erie.

On the 21st day of April, 1807, Mr. Riggs was received under the care of the Presbytery of Erie, and on the 21st day of October, 1807, he was ordained and installed pastor of the churches of Fairfield and Mill Creek. Mr. Riggs' trial sermon was on Psalms lxxi. 10. In the ordination services, Abraham Boyd (9) preached the sermon from Matthew xxiv. 45, and Alexander Cook (12) delivered the charges.

In this charge Mr. Riggs continued to labor until 1812, when the pastoral relation was dissolved. Having accepted calls from the congregations of Scrubgrass and West Unity (now Harrisville), he was installed pastor of this charge, on the 6th day of April, 1814. Here he continued to labor until 1834, when the pastoral relation was dissolved by the Presbytery of Alleghany. In the spring of 1821 he was dismissed with others to form the Presbytery of Alleghany, being one of its original members. In this Presbytery he remained until the autumn of 1835, when he removed with his family to the State of Illinois, and settled for a short time in the neighborhood of Macomb, McDonough County. In the summer of 1838, he removed to Washington County, in the same State, where he labored as a stated supply, in the churches of Elkhorn and Galum, up to the time of his death, which occurred on the 14th day of February, 1849, in the seventy-fifth year of his age, and forty-fifth of his ministry. His wife had died about four years previously. Their remains rest together in the cemetery of the Elkhorn church.

Mr. Riggs was a quiet, even taciturn man. He seldom made any allusion to his own life and labors. His great aim was to do good and keep his people up to the requirements of the gospel. He loved Zion and her cause dearly. Like all the early ministers of the Presbytery, he labored under great inconveniences from the smallness of his salary, and the difficulties that attend new fields of labor. He was a man of peace. He embarked in no partisan schemes, yet feeling that in congregational matters his own judgment was right, he generally managed to secure the success of his plans. This he did, not by open opposition, or dogmatic assertion of power, but by quietly removing obstacles out of the way, allaying prejudices, and meekly answering objections, until the way was open and the people satisfied.

He had the usual prejudices of the times to meet with. One of these was, that relating to the subject of psalmody. During his ministry at Scrubgrass and Unity, he passed through the transition from the psalms of Rouse, to the psalms and hymns of Watts. He was anxious for a wider range of subject than was found in the former, and for the rich, evangelic strains that were found in the latter. But it required all his tact of quiet prudence and firm resolution, to bring about the change. And in this he was eminently successful.

Mr. Riggs had eight children, five daughters and three sons. One of his sons, Cyrus Carpenter Riggs, D. D., is a member of the Presbytery of Beaver. His eldest daughter, Hannah Riggs, was long a missionary to the Indians. She was one of the company of missionaries that went to labor amongst the Ottowas, on the Maumee River. Of this company was Samuel Tait (3), pastor of the churches of Cool Spring, Salem, and Mercer, and famous in his day for missionary labor. In this missionary work did this devoted female labor, suffering hardships and privations of various kinds; now from cold, and now from a scarcity of provisions, and again from repeated attacks of fever and ague, until the mission was broken up, eleven years after its establishment. This mission was inaugurated by the Synod of Pittsburgh, but was afterwards transferred to the American Board of Missions.

It was the privilege of Mr. Riggs to labor up to the close of his pilgrimage. His last disease was paralysis. It came upon him as he sat in his study making preparation for preaching on the following Sabbath. The first shock was slight, and hardly perceptible. In the course of half an hour another shock fell upon him that prostrated him, and laid him helpless and speechless. He lingered but three days, unable to communicate his ideas or feelings, when he passed away from his labors on earth to his reward on high.

(19.) REID BRACKEN.

1805–1849.

Mr. Bracken was a fair specimen of the early pioneer ministers of the West. His early training had developed a stalwart physical constitution, and a faith and patience and self-denial that eminently adapted him to his great life-work — that of preaching the gospel to the destitute settlements.

Reid Bracken was the son of Thomas and Anne (Shannon) Bracken, and was born in York County, Pennsylvania, in the year 1778. When he was an infant of six weeks old, his father removed with his family into Washington County, in the same State, and found a home in what was soon to become the congregation of Chartiers. The same year Rev. John McMillan began to preach statedly to the people of that neighborhood. Thomas Bracken was one of the first elders elected after the organization of the church, and his little son Reid, the subject of this sketch, the first child baptized in the congregation, and indeed the first male child baptized west of the Alleghany mountains. Mrs. Bracken, the mother of Reid, was a woman of strong good sense and great decision of character, and brought up her family in the fear of God. Mr. Bracken was a farmer, and accustomed to labor, and brought up his son to the same avocation, until he was nearly of age, when finding his mind inclined to study, and with a desire for preparation for the ministry, he furnished him with a Latin Grammar, and the work of preparation commenced.

Reid Bracken graduated at Jefferson College in 1802, being a member of the first class that graduated after the College was chartered. His name stands at the head of the list, with the names of Johnston Eaton (20), William McMillan, and Israel Pickens, as classmates. Of course he studied theology with Dr. McMillan, and in due time was licensed to preach the gospel by the Presbytery of Ohio. This occurred on the 17th day of October, 1805. He travelled one year in Ohio and Virginia, preaching to vacant churches. In the year 1806, he went to Butler County, Pa., where he received calls to the pastoral charge of the congregations of Mount Nebo and Plain. On the 20th day of October, 1807, he was received under the care of the Presbytery of Erie, and Isaiah liii. 11, middle clause, assigned him as a subject of trials for ordination. On the 20th day of April, 1808, he was ordained to the whole work of the ministry, and installed pastor of these churches. In these exercises, William Wood (10) preached the sermon, and Nicholas Pittinger (15) delivered the charges. In these congregations he labored faithfully, giving one half of his time to each until October 7, 1819, when he was released from the Plain Church, and on the 28th of September, 1820, installed as pastor of Middlesex. His labors continued in the church of Middlesex until 1832, when he resigned, and became pastor of the church of Portersville. But during all these years he continued to give the half of his time to Mount Nebo, being pastor there for the period of thirty-seven years. About five years before his death he resigned his pastoral charge. He felt the infirmities of age coming upon him, and not being able to go in and out before the people as in his earlier days, give way to more vigorous laborers. Still he continued to preach, as opportunity offered, until the close of his life. His last sermon to his old charge at Mount Nebo, was from the words of the Apostle, 1 Cor. xii. 27, " Now ye are the body of Christ, and members in particular." This discourse will long be remembered by that people. One week before his death, he rode ten miles and preached to one of his old congregations from the words, "They shall be mine, saith the Lord of Hosts, in that day when I make up my jewels." It was his last sermon, and so strong was the impression made upon the minds of his friends, that after he was laid in his last sleep, these words were engraved upon his tombstone.

He was confined to his couch but a few days during his last illness. Three days previous to his decease, he was asked whether he had anything to say to his family previous to his departure. He addressed them as follows, the words being taken down by one of the family at the time: —

"My children, you are all here. It is a solemn time. From present appearances I am about to leave you, having served my generation, and am going to render up my account to my Judge. I have a comfortable hope of meeting my Savior in peace, and spending eternity in happiness. It is of the greatest consequence to have a hope that maketh not ashamed. It is my sincere desire that all my children should be prepared.[1] . . . . Give all diligence to make your calling and election sure. . . . . Rely upon the merits of Christ as the only foundation of hope. . . . . Now is the accepted time, now is the day of salvation. Salvation is free to all that will accept. Come unto me all ye that labor and are heavy laden, and I will give you rest."

This address was followed by a short and feeling prayer. And so he went down into the valley, leaning on the rod and staff of the Good Shepherd, and passed over

[1] Some of his words were inaudible.

the river to dwell with God. He died on his farm in Butler County, Pa., on the 29th day of July, 1849, in the seventy-second year of his age and the forty-fourth of his ministry.

Mr. Bracken was united in marriage to Miss Mary Graham, of Lexington, Va., on the 1st day of May, 1806. She was the youngest daughter of that distinguished servant of God, Rev. William Graham, founder of Washington College, Virginia, to whom frequent reference is made in the life of Dr. Archibald Alexander. After a long and useful life, she went to rejoin her husband in eternal union, December 30, 1863, in the seventy-eighth year of her age. They had eight children.

Mr. Bracken moved to Butler County when it was new and the people poor. Like his people, he commenced in the woods, and by the labor of his own hands cut down the forest, and opened for himself a farm, which he afterwards cultivated with his own hands, to assist in the support of his family. His sons well remember the time when his practice was, to labor in the fields five days in the week, and devote the Saturday to the work of preparation for the pulpit. He was a stalwart man, and could excel most able-bodied men in laboring with an axe, or in the harvest-field. His physical health was almost uniformly good; and with all his labor on his farm his mind did not become secularized.

He labored faithfully in the Master's field. Many churches were built up through the instrumentality of his labors. He was not a fluent speaker. He knew nothing of the eloquence that holds an audience spellbound through the beauty of tropes, and the grand flow of fitly chosen words. Yet he could set forth Christ crucified with love and zeal and effect. He stood high in the estimation of his brethren, as a sound and earnest preacher of the New Testament.

As a member of ecclesiastical courts, he was punctual and attentive. He seldom spoke, yet when he did, it was to the point, and his remarks always had great weight.

He was one of the original members of the Presbytery of Alleghany, and continued a member until his death.

(20.) JOHNSTON EATON.

1805-1847.

JOHNSTON EATON, son of John Eaton, was born in Rocky Spring Congregation, Franklin County, Pa., on the 7th day of February, 1776. His ancestors had long been dwellers in Pennsylvania. An old patriarch, now deceased, related that he had seen five generations of the Eatons in that congregation. Little is now known of his early years, for he was quiet and reticent in regard to anything that concerned himself. In 1801, he entered the Junior class of the College of New Jersey, where he remained one year, at the close of which, the college building being burned, he repaired to Cannonsburg, and entered the Senior class of Jefferson College, at which institution he graduated in the autumn of 1802, a member of the first class that graduated under the charter. His classmates were, Rev. Reid Bracken (19), Rev. William McMillan, D. D., President of Jefferson College, Israel Pickens, Governor of Alabama, and Rev. John Rhea.

His theological education was completed under the direction of Dr. John McMillan, when he was licensed to preach the gospel by the Presbytery of Ohio, on the 22d day of August, 1805. His constitution, naturally delicate and sensitive, being much broken, and his energies weakened by laborious application, he determined to spend some time in travelling and visiting the destitutions of the West. After visiting Erie County, which was to be the scene of his future life-labors, he spent a year in the southern part of Ohio. In 1806 he returned to Erie County, and took up his abode there. His first sermon there was preached in a small log tavern at the mouth of Walnut Creek, kept by Captain Swan. The country at this time was literally a wilderness. The mighty, grand old forest, was hardly broken by the woodman's axe. There were not more than two or three churches in the county, and at the period of his coming, not a minister of any denomination.

He was ordained by the Presbytery of Erie on the 30th day of June, 1808. The services were held in William Sturgeon's barn, near the present site of the village of Fairview. Mr. Johnston (14) preached on the occasion, and Mr. Stockton (4) delivered the charges. He was installed at the same time pastor of the congregations of Fairview and Springfield, a relation he sustained to the former during the remainder of his life, a period of forty years. He was released from the charge of Springfield on the 8th of November, 1814. He then divided his time between Fairview, Erie, and North East. This arrangement continued until 1818, when North East was dropped, and his time divided between Erie and Fairview, until 1823.

The fragment of an old journal recites something of his early experience : " Preached three months in the congregations of Fairview, Springfield, and Mill Creek (probably near Erie), beginning July, 1806, at ninety dollars per quarter."

In the year 1813, during the war with Great Britain,

he was employed as a government chaplain, and ministered to the troops stationed at Erie. He also preached for a portion of his time at Harbor Creek, Waterford, Washington, and McKean, in Erie County, Pa. He continued to labor in the congregation of Fairview until the close of his earthly toils. He met with his people for the last time in December, 1846, when feeling that it was the last time, he committed them to God and the word of his grace, when his people separated, not to meet again until they met to mingle their tears over his grave.

His death took place, at what had been his earthly home for nearly forty years, on the 17th day of June, 1847, in the seventy-second year of his age, and the forty-third of his ministry. His disease was paralysis, which not only prostrated his physical powers but greatly obscured his mental faculties. Yet he was not without the comforting presence of God. He who has said, " When thou passest through the waters, I will be with thee, and through the rivers, they shall not overflow thee," was with him in the darkest hour of his pain and languishing. At times when the veil seemed lifted, his mind was full of peace and tranquillity. And so he passed away : a meek, quiet, humble, faithful minister of Jesus Christ.

On the 30th of September, 1807, Mr. Eaton was united in marriage to Miss Eliza Canon, of Fayette County, Pa., a niece of Colonel John Canon, the founder of Cannonsburg. They had nine children : six sons and three daughters. One of the daughters died in childhood, the other children are living and members of the visible church.

In person, Mr. Eaton was below the ordinary stature, about five feet seven in height, and always light and slender. He had a mild blue eye, with a tinge of sadness in its cast, nose approaching the aquiline, with thin brown hair, that did not become entirely gray in his old age. There was a nervous sensitiveness about him that rendered him particularly averse to anything like display or outward show of any kind. He had naturally quick sensibilities, that would have led many a man into occasional exhibitions of temper, but he possessed most admirable control over his feelings and could rule his own spirit in every emergency.

He did not write his sermons, but preached from a brief skeleton, which was carefully drawn out and systematized, and generally kept in his pocket-Bible whilst preaching. His sermons were all digested thoroughly before delivery, and presented with freedom and unction.

The Record of Presbytery, on occasion of his death, is in part, in these words: "He was uniformly meek, gentle, and forbearing, generous and hospitable. As a preacher, he was clear, logical, instructive, and evangelical, and eminently sound in the faith. In his death the Boards of our church, and the cause of benevolent effort for the salvation of a perishing world, have lost a devoted friend."

One of his pupils [1] says of him: "He was one of the most conscientious persons I ever knew. He was highly esteemed by all who knew him for his suavity of manners and Christian consistency. He was a careful reader, an able theologian, and a correct thinker, and his mind, to work, must have arrangement. I owe more to him than to all other men for my place in the ministry, and my success too. The interest he took in me is to me unacountable. When a boy, he sought me out and

---

[1] Rev. G. W. Hampson (43).

gave me the course. I hope to meet him again. Till then *no more*. He rests from his labors."

Says another correspondent,[1] who knew and appreciated him:" "In some respects Mr. Eaton and Mr. Doolittle were alike. They were both zealous ministers of Christ, uncompromising where duty was concerned, both determined to know nothing but Jesus Christ and him crucified, and both had great dignity of ministerial character. But I think there was a certain genial humor about Mr. Eaton that Mr. Doolittle did not possess. He knew how to unbend without letting himself down, and could be, occasionally, both merry and witty. I think he was a man of great delicacy of feeling, and had a reverence almost sacred for the personality and consciousness of others. He possessed that manly attribute, a strong will, and was sometimes what people call set in his way, but at the same time his great kindness, his generosity and disinterestedness were more than an offset to that. I never knew a more honorable, just, generous, unselfish man. How well his people loved and reverenced him, you must know. I think the Scotch-Irish characteristics were strongly developed in him. He lived at a time when the church was in a transition state, or was becoming Americanized, and held firmly to the fathers."

His mortal remains await the resurrection near the spot on which he was ordained nearly forty years before his death.

(21.) JAMES BOYD.

1807–1813.

JAMES BOYD, son of John and Mary (Fulton) Boyd, was the last of the four brothers to enter the ministry.

[1] Miss Jacks.

He was born in Westmoreland County, Pa., in 1774. After studying with his pastor for a time, he went to Cannonsburg, and completed his classical studies at Jefferson College. He then studied theology with Dr. McMillan. He was taken under the care of the Presbytery of Erie, as a candidate for the ministry, on the 10th of April, 1806, and assigned as a theme for a Latin exegesis, "*An angeli per mortem Christi benefacti sint?*"

He was licensed to preach the gospel by the same Presbytery on the 22d day of April, 1807. He labored as a supply in various portions of the Presbytery, and in the autumn of 1808, having accepted calls from the churches of Newton and Warren, Ohio, was ordained and installed as their pastor at Warren, Ohio, on the 19th day of October, 1808. In these services William Wick (2) preached the sermon, and Thomas Edgar Hughes (1) delivered the charges. On the next day he was dismissed to become one of the original members of the Presbytery of Hartford, now Beaver, which had been created that fall by the Synod of Pittsburgh.

The congregations of Newton and Warren were his only charge. His ministry was brief. His labors were short. The purpose of his heart and the work of his hands were accepted, and he was called to a higher sphere of service above. He died at Warren, Ohio, on the 8th day of March, 1813, in the thirty-ninth year of his age, and the sixth of his ministry. His dust slumbers with that of his people.

Mr. Boyd was united in marriage to Miss Isabella Craig. They had three children, two sons and one daughter.

A lady in Tarentum, Pa., still living, relates that she has seen all four of the Boyd brothers in the pulpit at the same time.

(22.) JOHN MATTHEWS.

1809–1861.

This old patriarch could say with one of old, " I am a stranger and a sojourner with you." His was essentially a missionary life. From youth to extreme old age, the lot ordained for him by Providence, was to labor in new settlements, found churches, and travel from place to place. Difficulties never seemed to be in the way, so as to discourage him. Hardships seemed to be his familiar friends, and to urge him on to labor. Yet withal, he lived to a good old age, and has left behind him a beautiful record of labor and self-denial, and sacrifice in the Master's service.

John Matthews was the son of James and Prudence (Gordon) Matthews, and was born in Franklin County, Pa., on the 7th day of February, 1778. His parents were of the good old Scotch-Irish blood, and had brought their notions of duty and religion with them across the waters. And from such stock, ideas of faith and duty and practice do not readily change or run out. So we find the subject of this sketch carefully brought up and educated in the principles of our holy religion.

He entered Jefferson College in the year 1805, and graduated in 1807, when he was nearly thirty years of age. After this he entered the only theological seminary that was then known west of the Alleghany mountains, namely, the little log-cabin of Rev. John McMillan, D. D. Here he studied patiently and perseveringly, writing out at full length a system of theology, taken from the Doctor's lectures. This system is still extant, and may be found amongst his papers.

He was licensed to preach the gospel by the Presbytery of Ohio, on the 22d day of June, 1809. On the 26th of June, 1810, he presented a certificate of dismission from the Presbytery of Ohio, and was received under the care of the Presbytery of Erie. At the same time calls were presented for his pastoral labors from the congregations of Waterford and Gravel Run. These calls were accepted, and on the 17th of October following, he was ordained and installed as their pastor. Robert Johnston (14) preached on the occasion, and Samuel Tait (3) presided and delivered the charges. On the 8th of November, 1814, he was released from his charge at Gravel Run, and employed the portion of his time appropriated there to the congregations of Conneautee and Union. On the 2d of April, 1817, his pastoral relation to Waterford was dissolved, and on the 15th of February following, he was dismissed from the Presbytery of Erie, to seek a connection with the Presbytery of Missouri.[1]

The missionary spirit abounded in the heart of Mr. Matthews, even at that early day, and he sought the release from his charges in Erie Presbytery, with the view of itinerating in the great West. Many people from Western Pennsylvania were emigrating to the new regions of Illinois and Missouri, and the prospect seemed most inviting to go with them and assist in building up churches, and thus keep abreast with the swelling tide of emigration that was rolling thither.

We quote from Wilson's "Pres. Historical Almanac," vol. iv. 102, 103 : " He started on his journey West, going down the Ohio River on a flat-boat as far as Louisville, Ky., then on horseback through Indiana by way of Vincennes, then through the territory of Illinois

[1] Old Minutes.

to St. Louis, Mo., where he met with Rev. Salmon Giddings, who was one of the first Presbyterian ministers who crossed the Mississippi River. From St. Louis he went up the Missouri River to St. Charles, and took charge of the church at Louisiana, Pike County, Mo., where he continued preaching and itinerating amongst the destitutions of that vicinity, until 1825."

"In the fall of 1825 he settled at Apple Creek Church, in Cape Girardeau County, Missouri. After remaining there about two years, he removed to Kaskaskia, Randolph County, Ill. At that place he served the church, and itinerated eight or ten years (sometimes teaching and farming, to eke out a meagre support, as some ministers have to do yet in the West). He then served the Sugar Creek Church in Madison County, Illinois, about two years, and then returned to Missouri.

"He spent one year in Missouri, and received a call to a church in Ohio, which he served four or five years, but which he was compelled to give up in consequence of the failure of his health. He then spent some time in Greenville, Mercer County, Pa., with his friends, preaching as occasion might offer, and his health permit.

"After a few years' sojourn in Pennsylvania, his health having improved to some extent, he again returned to Missouri, where he rode and preached until his health again gave way. About ten or eleven years ago, he moved to Georgetown, Randolph County, Ill., where he ended his days. For several years he preached but seldom, in consequence of the infirmities of age, and of a worn-out constitution."

Mr. Matthews was one of the first ministers of the Presbyterian church in Missouri, and is justly regarded as one of the pioneers. At this time there was a noble trio of men, Giddings, Matthews, and Flint, who were bending all their energies in order to build up the Redeemer's kingdom in this new region. Of Matthews, a valued historian[1] says : "He was a workman that needed not to be ashamed, in labors most abundant, and, with all his itinerancy, a thorough student of theology."

The labors of these men were most arduous. For several years after their arrival, there was but a single settled pastor in the territory. Says Gillett, "The burden, devolved upon Messrs. Giddings, Matthews, and Flint, was almost crushing. But the calm, resolute energy and self-possession of the first, and the untiring energies of the others did not give way."

Mr. Matthews preached the opening sermon of the first Presbytery formed west of the Mississippi River; also the opening sermon of Kaskaskia Presbytery in Illinois.

But the Messenger came at last, and summoned him to his rest — "being old and full of days."

A brother in the ministry [2] thus sums up his character: "Father Matthews, as he was usually called, was a kind and affectionate husband, a warm-hearted and cheerful Christian, and was kind and obliging to his neighbors. He enjoyed the company of his brethren and friends very much. He was punctual in the discharge of every known duty. He was a man of prayer, labored hard, and went through many hardships, trials, and privations which he endured with patience and Christian fortitude. 'And now his labors are ended, and we trust he is at rest in heaven.'"

His death was the result of the decay of his vital

---

[1] Gillett's *History of the Presbyterian Church*, ii. 430, 431.
[2] Rev. D. A. Wallace, in *Pres. Hist. Almanac.*

powers, through old age, and the wearing out of his system by the labors of more than fourscore years. His death occurred at Georgetown, Ill., on the 12th day of May, 1861, in the eighty-fourth year of his age.

He was twice married. His first wife was Miss Nancy Bracken, of Cannonsburg, Pa. His second wife was Miss Anna Smith, of Missouri, who survives him. He had no children.

(23.) ROBERT McGARRAUGH.

1803–1839.

ROBERT McGARRAUGH, the son of Joseph and Jane McGarraugh, was born in Westmoreland County, Pa., on the 9th day of January, 1771. It is not known here how his early life was passed; most probably in the quiet pursuits of agriculture. For a time he studied with Dr. James Dunlap, afterwards President of Jefferson College; and for a time with Rev. David Smith, in the "forks of Yough." After this he was at the Cannonsburg Academy. He pursued his theological studies with Dr. McMillan, and was licensed to preach the gospel by the Presbytery of Redstone, October 19, 1803.

In the same year he visited the region that is now Clarion County, Pennsylvania, and preached for some time to the families that were settled there, and then returned to his family, then in Fayette County, Pa. Being invited to settle in the Clarion region, he gathered together his household effects, and with his family set out for the wilderness home, which he reached on the 1st of June, 1804. They were seven or eight days making the journey, which was performed on horseback. The mother and two of the children rode on one horse.

All the kitchen furniture was packed upon another, "Old Dick," and the oldest son, John, mounted upon the top of this. Thus accoutred, Mr. McGarraugh sought the field of his labor. They were detained one day at Mahoning, and another at Red Bank Creek, as they were obliged to make canoes to get across, in the meanwhile swimming their horses. The first year the family lived in a log-cabin, twelve or sixteen feet square, having a door made of chestnut bark.

Mr. McGarraugh was the first Presbyterian minister who preached the gospel east of the Alleghany River, in what is now Clarion County. He was ordained by the Presbytery of Redstone on the 12th of November, 1807, and installed pastor of the churches of New Rehoboth and Licking.

On the 4th of October, 1811, he was, with his congregations, detached from the Presbytery of Redstone, by the Synod of Pittsburgh, and connected with the Presbytery of Erie. On the 3d of April, 1822, his pastoral relation was dissolved with New Rehoboth and Licking. He labored after this time at Calensburg, Concord, and some other places to the time of his death. He was one of the original members of the Presbytery of Alleghany.

Mr. McGarraugh died in Perry Township, Clarion County (then Armstrong), Pa., on the 17th day of July, 1839, in the sixty-ninth year of his age, and the thirty-sixth of his ministry. Of him his successor [1] in the pastoral work says, "He was an humble, faithful, godly, self-denying, and laborious minister of the gospel; who labored long and well, and laid deep the foundations of Presbyterianism in this region of country."

He was not a man of remarkable ability, nor was he

[1] Rev. James Montgomery.

blessed with the gift of eloquence. But he had at heart the good of immortal souls, and the glory of the kingdom of Christ. He was not afraid of hardships; he did not love money; he sought not human applause. And so he was adapted to his field of labor. He pleased the people, and God was with him. He was a plain, unassuming man, intent only on this one thing — to stand in his lot and do his duty. And thus he lived, and to-day his memory is fragrant, whilst that of more highly gifted men is a by-word. To-day his record is higher than the stars, for it is written in God's great book of remembrance.

On the 10th of December, 1795, he was united in marriage to Miss Levina Stille. She was born March 30, 1773, and brought up in Washington County, Pa. Her father was from New Jersey. They had seven children, four daughters, and three sons; some of whom have passed away from earth.

(24.) IRA CONDIT.

1811–1836.

IRA CONDIT was a native of New Jersey. He was born near Morristown, and in the same county with Cyrus Riggs (18) and John Munson (28), on the 6th day of March, 1772. Of his early life little is preserved. He was a modest, unassuming man, and thinking that there was little of interest in his early life, has left nothing on record. But he is known to have been an earnest, conscientious Christian, as well as a devoted minister of Christ, and we may well suppose that his early life was passed in quietness and peace, standing in his lot as best he could.

His early life was that of a farmer, and even before

entering upon the preparation for the ministry had had experience of the rough life of the new settlements, and of the hardships of the frontier. In the year 1798 he emigrated to Mercer County, Pa., and settled within a mile of where the Fairfield church now stands, little knowing that there was to be the scene of his future labors in the Lord's spiritual vineyard. He does not seem at that time to have thought of the ministry, for his great work appears to have been to open up a farm and erect for himself a home and a fireside, where he might spend his life comfortably and usefully.

About the year 1800 he went to Washington County, Pa., where he was united in marriage to Miss Mary Miller, whose father was afterwards a member of Amity church. With his wife he returned to his farm on Sandy Creek, settling down to the peaceful life of a farmer, but no doubt oppressed with the destitution and want of spiritual privileges that characterized the country. He made a profession of religion May 10, 1802, and became a member of the church of Fairfield, of which he was afterwards pastor. For three years after his marriage he continued to cultivate his modest acres, when a voice that perhaps for some time had been heard in the deep chambers of his heart, constrained him to resolve to begin at once preparation for the gospel ministry.

For him to resolve, was to act. So in 1803 he leaves his little farm, moves his family to Cannonsburg, and commences his studies, where he graduated in 1808, After graduation he moved with his family to a farm belonging to his brother, about seven miles from Washington, where he commenced the study of theology under the direction of Dr. McMillan, and his pastor, Rev. George M. Scott, supporting his family in the mean time by teaching a school in the neighborhood. His eldest son remembers distinctly a well-beaten path on a knoll near the house, where the divinity student was in the habit of walking back and forth whilst engaged in his studies. A church was afterwards built on the same spot.

After completing his studies, he was licensed to preach the gospel by the Presbytery of Ohio, on the 17th day of October, 1811. The first year of his labor was spent as a missionary, itinerating amongst the vacant churches and destitute settlements of Washington County. An incident that occurred during this missionary work, illustrates the character of the man. When returning home from a tour, he was about crossing the Monongahela River in a ferry boat. There was a stranger wishing to cross at the same time, but being without money, the ferryman refused to take him over. Mr. Condit gave him all the money he had in his possession, and trusted to Providence for the supply of his wants on his way home. He had not proceeded far on his way before he met a man who owed him some money, but which he never expected to receive. The man voluntarily paid him the debt.

In 1812, Mr. Condit moved back to Sandy Creek, where he had first erected his home in the wilderness, and after preaching for some time in the vacant churches, accepted calls from the congregations of Fairfield and Big Sugar Creek. His ordination took place at Big Sugar Creek, on the 8th day of November, 1814. Rev. Robert Johnston (14) preached on the occasion, and Rev. Samuel Tait (3) delivered the charges. Fairfield church had been organized near the place where Mr. Condit had originally settled as a farmer, and Sugar Creek was perhaps fifteen miles distant.

In April, 1827, he accepted calls to the congregation of Georgetown, or Upper Sandy as it was then called. This call is still in existence, and is a curiosity in its way. It is for one third of the minister's time, and proceeds in the ordinary orthodox way: "And that you may be free from worldly cares and avocations, we hereby promise and oblige ourselves to pay to you the sum of one hundred dollars, in regular half-yearly payments, one third in cash and two thirds in produce, during the time of your being and continuing the regular pastor of this church."

He was afterwards installed for a portion of his time over the congregation of Amity. This charge was relinquished April 22, 1829. In June of the same year, he accepted a call to the congregation of Cool Spring, for one third of his time, and was installed June 24, 1829. In this united charge, Fairfield, one of his original charges, Georgetown, and Cool Spring, he labored until he was released by death.

Mr. Condit was a man of robust health. During his whole ministry of twenty-five years, he lost but two Sabbaths by sickness. In person he was tall and erect, being over six feet in height, of a sanguine temperament, and with a grave and solemn countenance. He was always extremely diffident, particularly in the earlier years of his ministry. He was not gifted in conversation, although of a social nature and domestic habits. Still he always had a word for Christ on all proper occasions. He has left behind him a name that is like precious ointment, and his memory is dearly cherished by all who knew him.

As a preacher he was not eloquent. Nor was he gifted in the art of sermonizing. He was, however, very solemn and impressive in his manner, which gave great weight to his words. His people loved to hear him preach, for he broke to them the Bread of Life, with all sincerity and solemnity and love. He has left behind him a few manuscripts of sermons, but he did not often, nor perhaps ever, after the first few years of his ministry, write out his discourses. Several hundred skeletons of sermons remain amongst his papers, giving an idea of his taste in sermonizing. He always preached from notes, holding a small Bible in his hand, containing the heads of his discourse. He used little action, nor had he much variety in tone of voice, but simply delivered the message, and trusted to no meretricious adornment of style or manner to enforce the truth.

Mr. Condit was the father of thirteen children. Two of these died in infancy, and one at the age of thirteen, and ten grew up to maturity. About a year previous to his death, he removed to Georgetown, and lived in a house that was under the same roof with that of his eldest son. His death was sudden, and occurred October 24, 1836, from typhoid fever. This disease entered his and his son's families together. Eight members of the two households lay sick together, of whom four died. Mr. Condit was sick but eight days. He and his son Samuel, who was studying for the ministry, both died the same day and were buried in the same grave. His wife died soon after.

His remains find rest in the cemetery connected with the Fairfield church. His monument is seen facing the edifice in which he preached so many years, bearing the usual inscription, with the following homely yet terse lines, composed by a Rev. Mr. Smith, —

> "In yonder sacred house I spent my breath;
> Now slumbering here I lie in death.
> This sleeping dust shall rise and yet declare,
> A dread Amen to doctrines published there."

Mr. Condit was the grandfather of Rev. Ira M. Condit, a missionary of the Presbyterian Board to China.

(25.) AMOS CHASE.

1786–1849.

AMOS CHASE was a native of New England. He was born in Sutton, near Boston, Mass., on the 12th day of May, 1760. When he was four years of age, his father moved to Cornish, N. H., and settled in the valley of the Connecticut River, at that time a dense wilderness. At the age of sixteen, he entered Dartmouth College, with the view of preparing himself for the life of a physician. But there was a different course marked out for him by the hand of Providence. The training that was begun in the wilderness of New Hampshire, must be put into practice in the wilderness of Northwestern Pennsylvania.

He became a subject of a revival that occurred in the College and surrounding country, in connection with the labors of Rev. Mr. Whitefield. His thoughts now ran in a different channel. He devoted himself to the service of God, and listening to the earnest call for laborers in the great vineyard, made a solemn consecration of himself to the work of the gospel ministry.

After taking his first degree in the arts in 1780, he commenced the study of theology, under the direction of Dr. Nathaniel Emmons, of Boston. His theological studies were completed under the direction of Levi Hart, D. D., of Preston, Connecticut. He was licensed to preach the gospel by the South Association of Connecticut, and after some time spent in proving his gifts, was ordained by the same association at Litchfield, Connecticut, on the 27th day of June, 1787. In these services, his preceptor, Dr. Hart, preached the sermon.[1] Here he commenced his work as pastor of the church at Litchfield South Farms, which continued for twenty-six years. In this field he was content to labor and practice self-denial, striving to live and educate a growing family upon a meagre salary, until forced to look for a different place of labor. The temporal interests of his family as well as the spiritual interests of his people, were a part of his burden, and he began to look to the West as an inviting field of labor.

The great Holland Land Company, at that time, were in possession of vast quantities of land, in Northwestern Pennsylvania, that they were anxious to have brought into market. To this end they offered inducements to clergymen to go out and settle in the territory they were opening up. Worldly prudence and a desire for the spiritual welfare of the people were mingled together in unequal proportions, and so some of the agents of the company made overtures to Mr. Chase looking to the removal of his family and the establishment of himself in the wilds of Pennsylvania. The motives held forth were, the wide field of usefulness in a new country and in the midst of a destitute people, the founding of churches, and general missionary work; together with the prospect of bettering his worldly circumstances. It was not kept out of view, however, that the company were to be benefited by the minister's removal, by inducing others to accompany or to follow him to the new country. And so the minister went to the new country, found the wide, rough field of labor, a loud call for the preaching of the gospel, and earnest toil in building up Zion, but not the pecuniary advantages that had been promised. Still he labored and was content.

[1] Sprague's *Annals*.

The people of his old charge were much attached to him, and were unwilling to part with him. They proposed raising his salary, feeling that under his pastorate they had been most abundantly prospered. But the path of duty seemed plain, and at his own request, he was dismissed from his pastoral charge in 1814, and in the month of February, 1815, with his family, he set his face toward the West.

The association that dismissed him reported that he "had proved himself a workman that need not be ashamed: that the parish from a low estate of morality and religion, had become, under his ministrations, as a city set on a hill."

To the same effect is the testimony of an old parishioner, after his removal westward: "How much good, under God, Mr. Chase did, the world will never know. Think of South Farms, a place, when he went there, of comparative ignorance and vice, addicted to all kinds of vulgarity, debasing amusements, and dissipation; but raised during his residence there to respectability and intelligence, and what is still better, become the devoted worshippers of the living God."

The land of promise to which Mr. Chase had resolved to emigrate was the northeastern part of Crawford County, Pa., in the neighborhood of what is now the city of Titusville. It was not a promising region then. On his first visit, the preceding summer, he found partially improved farms, with forsaken habitations, fields on which crops had been raised, but of which nothing now remained but decaying fences, and girdled trees standing in their nakedness, as monuments of wasted strength and disappointed hopes. Many who yet remained were preparing to leave the country as an accursed place. But Mr. Chase encouraged them to remain, by assuring them that many families were on their way to the country; and as the want of schools was very much complained of, assured them that his daughters had signified their willingness to teach, if in that way they could be useful. With these assurances many were deterred from leaving, and a new impulse was given to the growth and prosperity of the country.

Here he pitched his tent and girded himself for labor. The whole country round was a spiritual desert. To one of his brethren in the East who had written him for a particular account of his circumstances and labors, he writes: "Take a map and stand with me a moment at Centerville, at the upper forks (navigable by law) of Oil Creek, and look an hundred miles to the east, northeast, and southeast, and there is no minister of Jesus Christ. Look again southwest, west, and northwest, and there are three ministers of our order, each ministering to three or four congregations. Who would not be ready to say, 'Who is sufficient for these things?' Being thus set down in the valley of dry bones, in the open valley and very dry, who would not tremble? My poor, feeble labors were, during the past year, distributed to encourage churches, congregations, and schools over an extent of country not less than one hundred miles between Buffalo and the Alleghany River. They were very general and without much effect save that of furnishing myself with an extensive knowledge of men and things in this region. My labors since have been more particular and their effects more evident."

On the 27th day of June, 1815, Mr. Chase was received into the Presbytery of Erie, as a member. For eleven years he took no regular pastoral charge, but acted as the missionary of Presbytery, particularly in portions of Crawford, Warren, and Venango counties.

In the year 1815, he organized the churches of Oil Creek and Centerville. Of the first of these churches, he says: "A church was gathered, elders and trustees selected, and the sealing ordinances administered. The congregation, about two hundred, have continued to appear solemn as well as punctual. The place I speak of is ten miles below Centerville (the present site of Titusville), at which place I have also gathered a congregation, where there never was a meeting of any Protestant denomination before."

The labors of Mr. Chase, during these long years of watching and toil, were most exhausting. With his numerous family in the midst of the forest, his sons yet in their minority and needing his care and supervision, and the people scattered and poor, so that they could do little for his support, no wonder that his brave heart was well-nigh crushed. He had hoped for encouragement and support from his brethren in Connecticut, but a change in his church relations had abated their zeal. He writes: "The appeal in my behalf to the missionary society of Connecticut, was not encouraged. . . . If not much deceived, I have taken possession of this extensive field of missionary labor, in the name of the Lord, without the support of a missionary, but still remembering that the silver and the gold are the Lord's." Subsequently he received a commission from the Assembly's Board of Missions for one year.

In the year 1820, Mr. Chase represented the Presbytery of Erie in the General Assembly, and in 1825, was its moderator. On the 24th day of May, 1826, he was installed as pastor of the church of Oil Creek for one half his time, and on the 27th of April, 1827, he was installed at Centerville for one fourth of his time, leaving a remaining fourth for missionary labor. These relations were dissolved in 1830.

He was now in his seventieth year, and the infirmities of age were coming upon him. Still his frame was erect and massive, and he felt that much missionary labor might yet be accomplished. The remainder of his days was spent in those itinerating labors to which he had devoted the strength of his manhood.

Mr. Chase was a social, friendly man, and his Christian character always above reproach. As a preacher, he abounded in aphorisms. His discourses were rich and full of thought, but often like Proverbs, abounding in short sententious utterances that sparkled with truth, drawn from the mine of sacred writ. Perhaps this style of speaking became more prominent during his labors as a missionary. The people were not accustomed to labored disquisitions, or elaborately written discourses, and preferred to have a preacher come to the point at once.

In figure and bearing Mr. Chase was noble and commanding. Tall and stout without being corpulent, in his missionary tours he sat his horse like a cavalier of old. In his old age he presented a peculiarly patriarchal appearance. He was a useful man in his day, and the now celebrated oil regions are yet reaping the benefit of his self-denying labors.

Mr. Chase was twice married. He was first married to Rebecca, daughter of Rev. Levi Hart, D. D., his old preceptor at Preston, Connecticut. She was also a granddaughter of the celebrated Dr. Bellamy of Bethlehem, Connecticut. This marriage took place on the 30th day of November, 1788. Mrs. Chase died on the 25th day of February, 1791, in the 26th year of her age. He was married the second time to Joanna, daughter of Peter Lanman, Esq., Norwich, Connecticut, June 10, 1792. Mrs. Chase was his companion for more than half a century, comforting him in his sorrows and encouraging him in his labors, until August, 1848, when she was called to rest. The children consisted of six sons and six daughters, who were a comfort to them in their old age and are useful in their day and generation. Mr. Chase survived his wife but little over a year, when he too fell asleep. His death occurred at Centerville, Crawford County, Pa., December 23, 1849, in the ninetieth year of his age, and sixty-third year of his ministry.

At the division of the Presbytery of Erie, in 1838, Mr. Chase chose his membership, in connection with the New School portion of the church.

(26.) JOHN REDICK.

1813–1850.

JOHN REDICK, son of John and Elizabeth (Sorrell) Redick, was born in Westmoreland County, Pa., about the year 1787. His father's family resided near Hannastown at the time of the Indian troubles, and with his neighbors suffered grievously from their depredations. On one occasion, when the neighborhood had been alarmed, and the people taken refuge in the fort, his father was wounded in the arm and permanently disabled, whilst crossing a fence near the fort. This was at the time Hannastown was burned. After this his father sold his farm and removed to Butler County, Pa., near the line of Venango County, and about one and a half miles from the Alleghany River. Here John Redick was raised, working on the farm and assisting in the support of the family. After he had attained to years of manhood, a circumstance of a providential kind took place, that was the means of bringing him into the ministry. He with others were about crossing the Alleghany River on a hunting excursion. His companions had seated themselves in the canoe, when young Redick placed his gun in the canoe, took hold of the bow, and was in the act of pushing it from the shore, when the gun went off and wounded him severely in the limb. His father, supposing he would never be able to labor, proposed educating him as well as his means would permit.

The probabilities are, that before this he had made a profession of religion. He commenced his studies with Robert Johnston (14), who was then pastor of the church of Scrubgrass. This was in company with several other students — Hon. Walter Lowrie, Rev. James Wright, Rev. Alexander Crawford, and others. He afterwards went to the academy at Greersburg, now Darlington, Beaver County, Pa. His theological studies were pursued under the direction of Mr. Johnston, who was probably his pastor. No doubt a part of the training consisted in copying the system of theology, or lectures of Rev. Dr. McMillan, that was the chief staple with the early fathers of the Presbytery of Erie.

Having preached a trial discourse on John iv. 18, as well as passed other usual trials, he was licensed to preach the gospel by the Presbytery of Erie at its sessions at Meadville, Pa., on the 20th day of October, 1813. He was ordained by the same Presbytery on the 28th day of September, 1815, and installed as pastor of the united congregations of Slate Lick and Union, in Armstrong County, Pa. This meeting was at the former place. On the occasion, his old preceptor, Robert Johnston (14), preached the sermon, and John McPherrin (16) delivered the charges.

He continued the beloved faithful pastor of these churches until the autumn of 1848, when he resigned his charge on account of the infirmities of age and inability to discharge the duties of the pastoral office. He did not continue long upon earth after the resignation of his charge. Growing infirmities pressed upon him, until on the 11th day of July, 1850, he fell asleep in Jesus, in the seventy-third year of his age, and thirty-seventh of his ministry. His mortal remains await the resurrection in the little graveyard attached to the Slate Lick Church.

About the year 1812, Mr. Redick was united in marriage to Miss Betsey Coulter, a sister of Rev. John Coulter, of the Presbytery of Alleghany. They had five sons and four daughters. Mrs. Redick was a model wife for a minister, and was throughout their journey together a most useful helpmeet to her husband. Mr. Redick was a plain, practical preacher, and a pious, godly man. His great aim was to do the Master's work and win souls to Christ. Through his instrumentality, the churches of his charge were greatly strengthened and built up. He spent his entire pastoral life in their service, and was entirely devoted to their welfare. His memory will long be fragrant in their midst.

(27.) TIMOTHY ALDEN.

1798–1839.

TIMOTHY ALDEN was of Puritan ancestry. He was a descendant of John Alden, of Duxbury, who came in the "Mayflower," to seek his fortune on the bleak shores of New England. He was the son of Rev. Timothy and Sarah Weld Alden. Rev. Timothy Alden, his father, was born November 24, 1736, old style, graduated at Harvard, 1762, ordained pastor of the

Congregational Church of Yarmouth, Mass., December 15, 1769, and died November 13, 1828. His mother was Sarah, daughter of Rev. Habijah Weld, of Attleboro', Mass., lineally descended, according to Guillim, from Edrich Igloaticus, Anglicized Wild or Weld, and in the maternal line, from John Fox, the Martyrologist. Rev. Habijah Weld was graduated at Harvard, 1723. He was the son of Rev. Thomas Weld, graduated at Harvard, 1671. Timothy Alden, the subject of this sketch, was also great-grandson of Rev. John Fox, who graduated at Harvard, 1698, who was the son of Rev. Jabez Fox, who graduated at Harvard, 1665.

Timothy Alden, the subject of this sketch, was born at Yarmouth, Mass., on the 28th day of August, 1771. At the age of eight years, he left the paternal home, and went to reside with an uncle, where he continued until his fifteenth year. The design was to train him to the business of farming, his uncle being engaged in that pursuit. His uncle had made him the promise that his valuable farm should be his inheritance if he would remain with him. But young Alden thought of a different avocation from that of cultivating the soil. Even in boyhood he was resolutely bent on securing a liberal education. When sent into the fields to work, he would carry his Latin grammar with him, and in the midst of declensions and conjugations, forget all about his corn and his oxen. Under these circumstances, his uncle wrote to the father of the lad, telling him that the project of making a farmer of him was vain, and advising to send him to college.

His preparatory course commenced when he was about fifteen, first with his father, and afterwards at Philips' Academy, at Andover. It is supposed that his mind took a religious direction whilst he was at

Andover. He entered Harvard in 1790, and graduated in 1794. Whilst at college, he took and maintained a very high position as a linguist. He was particularly fond of the Oriental languages, and carried this taste beyond the ordinary *curriculum* of the institution. At the Commencement, his graduating oration was written in the Syriac language. It is said, that when he submitted this oration to the President for his approval, the President, being altogether ignorant of the language, said, "Come Alden, sit down and construe it for me." When reduced to the form of good Anglo-Saxon, it was heartily approved.

The probabilities are that he engaged somewhat in the study of theology during his collegiate course, and that he remained at Cambridge for a short time after graduating. We next find him teaching at Marblehead, Mass., and whilst there, he was licensed to preach the gospel. In the year 1799, he preached with the view of settlement at Portsmouth, N. H., and on the 20th of November of that year, was ordained as co-pastor with Dr. Haven, over the church of that place.

The church was not strong, and the salary being inadequate, he commenced teaching a young ladies' school in the spring of 1800, in connection with his pastoral labors. Wearied with this double burden, and discouraged with the prospects before him in Portsmouth, he resigned his charge, and was dismissed July 31, 1805. He still continued his labors as a teacher, however, until 1808, when he left Portsmouth, and opened a ladies' school in Boston. Here he was highly appreciated and his efforts liberally sustained. In this city, his learned and antiquarian tastes had a fine field for their exercise and cultivation, and he rendered some very important services to the cause of science.

In 1809, Mr. Alden resigned his position in Boston, and in the beginning of the following year, took charge of the young ladies' department in the academy at Newark, N. J. After continuing there some years, he opened a school for young ladies in the city of New York.

About the year 1815, the project was agitated of founding a college at Meadville, Pa. In this enterprise, Mr. Alden enlisted with great zeal and earnestness. He gave up his school in New York, and became the agent for the new institution. During the many journeys taken in behalf of Alleghany College, he was offered the presidency of the college at Cincinnati, Ohio, with liberal pecuniary inducements. These were declined, as he was for the present at least pledged to Alleghany. Having accepted the offices both of President and Professor in the Faculty, he was inaugurated on the 28th day of July, 1817.

Mr. Alden became a member of the Presbytery of Erie on the 2d day of April, 1816. During the period of his membership in the Presbytery of Erie, he had no regular charge. He preached to the Presbyterian congregation of Meadville at times when they were vacant, and often supplied vacant congregations in the neighborhood. He delighted in missionary work, and for many successive years labored for a time among the Seneca and Munsee Indians, who had reservations in northwestern Pennsylvania and southwestern New York. These labors were at first performed on his own account, but afterwards he received an appointment from an eastern society, organized for the purpose of sending the gospel to the Indians. He enjoyed these labors very much. During his tours he became acquainted with the celebrated chief Cornplanter, and enjoyed his protection and friendship. This was in Warren County, Pa.

Mr. Alden's last missionary tour among the Indians, was in 1820. He had a great admiration for their character, and enjoyed his labors among them, not only from the opportunities of doing good, but from studying their character in their forest homes.

Mr. Alden was a valuable friend to Alleghany College. It was mainly through his instrumentality that its valuable library and chemical apparatus was collected. Through his acquaintance in New England, one or two private libraries of great value were obtained and added to the catalogue. Many of these volumes are rare and valuable. His connection with the college terminated in November, 1831. He retired from the position he had so long occupied, with the grateful acknowledgments of the Board of Trustees, and others interested in the institution, as well as the kindest feelings of the community.

In the month of April, 1832, he was dismissed from the Presbytery of Erie to connect with the Presbytery of Cincinnati. He removed his family to Cincinnati in June, 1832, and opened a boarding-school. The health of some of the members of his family suffering at this place, he removed to East Liberty, near Pittsburgh, Pa., in the autumn of 1833, and the next spring took charge of the academy at that place. Here, as at other places, he embraced every opportunity of preaching the gospel in vacant churches. In the year 1838, he became stated supply to the congregation of Pine Creek, about five miles from Pittsburgh. Being of a vigorous constitution, he was able to perform as much labor as many who were his juniors in years, and enjoyed good health up to within a few months of his death, when he was attacked by rheumatism. His last sermon was preached from the words, " The end of all things is at hand."

During his last illness, when the prospect of recovery seemed to fade away, " a dark cloud for some time rested over his mind, and he looked forward with awful apprehensions to the change that awaited him. That cloud, however, soon passed off, and those apprehensions yielded to an humble confidence in his Redeemer, which quickly became so strong as to cast out all fear, and even to fill his mind with the most intense rapture. In this state he continued until the moment of his departure." [1]

He died at the house of his daughter, Mrs. J. B. McFadden, in Pittsburgh, Pa., on the 5th day of July, 1839, in the sixty-eighth year of his age, and the forty-first of his ministry. His remains were laid to rest in the cemetery connected with the Pine Creek Church, where his last pastoral labors were performed.

As a teacher and professor, Mr. Alden stood deservedly high, not only in the extent of his knowledge, but in the faculty of communicating it to others. As a preacher, his appearance in the pulpit was imposing, his manner of delivery on the whole pleasing, yet rather monotonous, and at times rather rapid. " As a man, he was affable and social, his conversation agreeable and instructive. As a minister, his public ministrations were respectable, but lacking in earnestness and energy. His prayers were beautiful in construction, but without variety. His sermons were written with care, but read with little action, and monotonous in tone. He was a good man." [2]

Besides many occasional sermons and addresses, Mr.

[1] Sprague's *Annals*. [2] John Reynolds, Esq.

Alden published, in 1814, " A Collection of American Epitaphs," in five volumes, 18mo., and in 1827, a " History of Sundry Missions," and in 1821, a " Hebrew Catechism."

Mr. Alden was twice married: first to Miss Elizabeth Shepard Wormsted, of Marblehead, Mass. She died at Meadville, Pa., April, 1820. She was the mother of five children, three daughters and two sons. The sons were educated at Meadville. One was supposed to have been lost at sea, the other, T. J. Fox Alden, was a lawyer of eminence at the Pittsburgh bar. In 1822, he was married the second time, to Sophia Louisa L. Mulcock, of Philadelphia. By her he had one daughter.

(28.) JOHN MUNSON.

1816–1866.

JOHN MUNSON, son of Daniel and Susanna (Drake) Munson, was born in Morris County, New Jersey, on the 22d day of February, 1784. His father died in 1790, when John was but six years of age. His father's death took place in Herkimer County, New York, where his mother was left a widow among strangers. After some time his mother married again, and with her husband and family removed to Lycoming County, Pa. This was when John was eleven years of age. His mother was a pious woman, and hearing what the Lord was doing in the outpouring of his Spirit in Western Pennsylvania, felt a great desire to place her family within the sphere of religious influence. Accordingly the family removed to Beaver County in 1806. His mother lived to see her husband and seven children received into the communion of the church, and one of her sons a minister of the gospel. She died in 1838, in the seventy-ninth year of her age. John Munson did not make a profession of religion until perhaps his twenty-fifth year.

He pursued his literary studies at the Greersburg Academy, under the direction of Rev. Thomas Edgar Hughes (1), with whom he also studied theology. He was licensed to preach the gospel by the Presbytery of Hartford (now Beaver), on the 16th day of October, 1816. From this Presbytery, he was received by that of Erie in 1817. Having accepted calls from the congregations of Plaingrove and Center, he was ordained at Plaingrove, by the Presbytery of Erie, on the 25th of February, 1818, and installed as pastor of these churches. In these services Amos Chase (25) preached the sermon, and John McPherrin (16) delivered the charges. He was set off with others to form the new Presbytery of Alleghany in 1820. His pastoral relation to Plaingrove was dissolved February 6, 1838, when he gave all his time to Center. The latter charge he resigned June 28, 1859, after a pastorate of forty-one years.

Soon after this, growing infirmities prevented him from engaging in much public labor. His last sufferings were protracted and severe. Says a co-presbyter:[1] "He was for months paralyzed so as to be almost entirely helpless. His mind, however, kept bright and vigorous. His conversation was very much about Christ and heavenly things. He spoke to those who called to see him about their eternal interests; sent messages to his old parishioners and acquaintances, telling them of his peace, and giving them his love and blessing. To ministers he would say, 'Preach Christ.' 'Tell the brethren to preach Christ crucified more and more!' For

[1] Rev. R. B. Walker, D. D.

months he had not a doubt as to his acceptance with God, and his mind was full of sweet, heavenly peace. On one occasion he spoke to a ministerial brother of his circumstances rather despondingly, but in a moment added, 'But I am a rich man. O, what a rich man I am! I am a joint-heir with Christ to an inheritance uncorrupted and undefiled.' He died in the full possession of all his mental faculties, full of peace and in the joyful hope of a blessed immortality."

His death took place at his residence, London, Mercer County, Pa., on the 18th day of December, 1866, in the eighty-third year of his age and fifty-first of his ministry. Mr. Munson was thrice married. His first wife was Miss Jane, daughter of George Allen, who died in less than a year after their marriage. Her death took place in 1809. His second wife was Elizabeth Clark, to whom he was married in 1815, and who died in 1836, at the age of fifty-five. His third wife was Mrs. Abby S., widow of Thomas Branden, and daughter of Adam Black. They were married in 1837, Mrs. Munson died in 1862. Mr. Munson had but one child, which died in infancy.

In personal appearance he was, in his prime, robust and rough-hewn, with strongly marked features and little claim to personal beauty. He was able to endure great labor, and was never backward in undertaking any amount of self-denial and privation in the Master's work, that seemed to be called for. In his earlier ministry he travelled much through the destitute settlements, preaching day after day, forcing his way through snow-storms and swollen streams, rarely failing to meet his appointments and always ready to expose himself, rather than disappoint his hearers.

Few Christians have had a richer experience than he.

Says the same co-presbyter already quoted: "When first awakened his convictions were deep and pungent. He felt himself to be the chief of sinners. We have often heard him say that he did not see how it was possible for God to save him, and that after him no anxious sinner need despair of finding mercy. But when the light came, his peace was as a river. The principles of the gospel were deeply fixed in his heart. He lived out and adorned the doctrines which he preached. During his long ministerial life, there was not a single stain upon his character."

As a theologian, he was accurate and discriminating. His reading was not extensive, yet valuable, for he retained and appropriated what he read. In the religious controversies of his day he was well versed, and able at all times to defend his views of right.

As a preacher his great aim was to unfold the truths of God's Word, so as to convince his hearers and lead them to God and his service. His great themes were, God's great love and mercy — of Christ and his cross. He was a good minister of the Lord Jesus, and labored faithfully for his cause, and so his rest must be sweet and his reward glorious.

(29.) PHINEAS CAMP.

1816–1868.

PHINEAS CAMP, the son of Phineas and Martha (Hall) Camp, was born in Durham County, N. Y., on the 18th day of February, 1788. At the age of eight years, he removed with his father's family to Oneida County, in the same State. His classical studies commenced at an academy at Whitestown, N. Y. Afterwards he entered Union College, where he graduated in

1811. For two years after this, he taught a classical school in Orange County, N. Y. His theological studies were pursued at Princeton. Having completed a full course at that institution, he was licensed to preach the gospel by the Presbytery of North River in 1816. The first two years of his ministry were spent in itinerant labors. He was ordained as an evangelist by the Presbytery of North River, on the 15th day of July, 1817. He came into the bounds of the Presbytery of Erie in 1817, and was received from the Presbytery of Hudson, as a member, on the 29th day of June, 1819.

In connection with Johnston Eaton, he reorganized the churches of Westfield and Ripley, N. Y. His first pastoral settlement was at Westfield, where he was installed on the 8th day of September, 1819. Cyrus Riggs (18), preached the sermon, and Samuel Tait delivered the charges. This pastorate continued for two and a half years, when, on account of ill-health in his family, the relation was dissolved. After two years of labor as an evangelist, he was installed pastor of the church of Lowville, N. Y., having been dismissed from the Presbytery of Erie to that of St. Lawrence, February 9, 1825. Here he continued for four years, when the pastoral relation was dissolved. From this time Mr. Camp devoted himself to missionary labors in various portions of the church, being particularly active in revivals of religion. These labors extended over northwestern Pennsylvania, New York, and portions of Ohio. Being of a warm, fervid frame of mind, he was particularly adapted to missionary work, and to efforts in times of refreshing. He delighted in these labors. It seemed to be his meat and his drink to direct inquiring souls to Christ. During his labors, the "bodily exercise," spoken of elsewhere, prevailed, and was treated by him as of great importance as a manifestation of the Spirit of God. Many of the churches along the shore of Lake Erie, at Westfield, North East, Fairview, and Springfield, enjoyed his revival labors, and some of the aged fathers and mothers in Israel yet speak of his unction and zeal in the Lord's cause. His last years were spent in connection with "the other branch."

Mr. Camp was twice married. His first wife was Miss Mary A. Leeworthy. His second was Miss Anna Spalding. He had three children, two sons and a daughter, all of whom profess to be the followers of the God of their father.

About four years ago he removed to Dixon, Illinois, to spend his declining years with his children. Yet although laid aside in a great degree from the active labors of preaching the gospel, he continued to seek opportunities of doing good, in distributing tracts, and personal religious intercourse. These labors continued until within two days of his death.

A short time before his departure, he wrote in his diary: "I desire to possess dying grace for the present hour. I am dying: declining with age daily, that is dying. Shall I be overwhelmed with surprise and awe on entering the celestial world? How can a stranger from earth endure it? Even the holy evangelist John, who had so often conversed with his mighty Saviour, had well-nigh fainted and died at the sight of the angel of the Apocalypse. I apprehend believers on entering that state will be gently dealt with; will be gradually made familiar with the grand and fearful things that shall in turn be unfolded and explained. But be this as it may, let me have 'perfect holiness' in the fear of the Lord, and be ready when called to go."

His last illness was short, and without suffering. It

was rather the wearing out of life's machinery than positive disease. To his children and friends who gathered around his couch, he commended Christ as the only hope. When asked if he felt prepared for the journey, he replied, " Yes, yes, I settled that question long before this. This trying hour would be insupportable were it not for my hope in Christ." After taking leave of his children one by one, with the expression on his lips, " Farewell, world, farewell," he sweetly fell asleep.

He died on the 30th day of January, 1868, having nearly completed his eightieth year, and in the fifty-second year of his ministry. He was an old man, full of years and labors, and has gone to reap the reward of those who " turn many to righteousness."

(31.) BRADFORD MARCY.

1809–1845.

Mr. Marcy was a native of Berkshire County, Mass. He was the son of Smith and Patience (Lawton) Marcy, and was born at Otis, Mass., on the 9th day of March, 1774. Of his early life little can now be learned, as he was a quiet man, leaving little behind that would throw light upon his history. His classical studies were pursued at the college of Rhode Island, where he graduated in 1798. From a paper left behind originating from the college authorities, it is evident that his standing as a scholar was very good. The probabilities are that he studied theology privately, and was licensed to preach by some of the New England associations. From a note attached to his ordination sermon, it appears that he was ordained by the Eastern Connecticut Association. His name is found in the records of the General Association, as a missionary laboring in Delaware in 1805.[1] After this he became a member of the Presbytery of Long Island, and was pastor of the churches of Smithtown and Islip, from 1811 to 1814.

Mr. Marcy removed into the bounds of the Presbytery of Erie, sometime about the year 1820. He was received from the Presbytery of Long Island, on the 13th of April, 1824. He took no active charge in the Presbytery, although he preached frequently in the vacant congregations in the neighborhood where he resided. He settled down upon a farm in Crawford County, Pa., and was very successful in the cultivation of the soil.

As a preacher he had more learning than faculty in bringing forth the treasures of his mind in sermonizing. He seemed anxious to do good, yet his peculiarities were often in the way of his accomplishing it. His infirmities prevented his preaching during the last three years of his life. He died near Venango, Crawford County, Pa., on the 6th day of April, 1845, in the seventy-second year of his age.

He was united in marriage to Miss Catherine Evans, of Crawford County, Pa., on the 22d day of June, 1824. They had no children.

(33). GILES DOOLITTLE.

1823–1842.

GILES DOOLITTLE was the son of Elisaph and Ruth (Potter) Doolittle of the State of Connecticut. His father was born in Wallingford, Conn., June 1, 1750. Giles, his son, was born in Plymouth, Conn., on the 22d day of May, 1794. His first years were spent in the quiet ways of a Connecticut home, and under the instructions and prayers of a pious mother. When

---

[1] Gillett's *History*, ii. 1.

about six or seven years of age, he was the subject of deep religious impressions, that were never afterwards obliterated. He had then such views of the evil of sin, and the holiness of God, as influenced the remainder of his life. Later in life he was inclined to believe that at this time God's saving grace commenced its work in his soul.

Early in life an incident occurred that seems to have influenced all his subsequent years. He read in the Connecticut Magazine an account of the labors and privations of the missionaries in the West. The account so moved him that he secretly resolved that he would devote himself to the ministry and the missionary work. But circumstances seemed for a long time to be in the way of his preparation for this great work. His parents were dependent upon his care, and he could not leave them. In his eighteenth year he made a public profession of religion, and connected himself with the Congregational church in his native town. About this time his mother died; and in his twenty-third year his father was called away, leaving him free to follow his inclination and conviction of duty by commencing preparations for the work of the ministry.

After studying for a few months, he became discouraged, as he looked at his age and the long years that must elapse before he could enter upon the work. The narrowness of his own means also added to this discouragement.

He now removed to Oneida County, New York, and engaged in teaching. Here, through the advice and encouragement of friends, he once more resumed his studies, and entered Hamilton College in his twenty-fourth year. Graduating in 1822, he returned to his native town and commenced the study of theology with his old friend and pastor, Rev. Luther Hart, and in due time was licensed to preach the gospel by the South Association of Litchfield County, Conn., June 3, 1823. After preaching for a time in Connecticut, he journeyed westward, and tarried for a time in Oneida County, New York. But his desire to carry out his youthful plans soon induced him to move still further west, and in the year 1824 he came to Chautauque County, New York. Whilst in Oneida County, he placed himself under the care of the Presbytery of Oneida, and on coming into the bounds of the Presbytery of Erie, he put himself under the care of that Presbytery, being received March 2, 1825. Accepting calls from the united churches of North East and Ripley, he was ordained and installed at the former place, on the 14th day of April, 1825. In these exercises Johnston Eaton (20) preached the sermon, and Samuel Tait (3) delivered the charges. This relation continued for five years, when, on the 14th day of April, 1830, he was at his own request dismissed from Ripley, and gave the whole of his time to North East. In the latter church his labors continued until September 12, 1832, when at his own request he was dismissed. His labors were greatly blessed at North East, and many were gathered into the fold of the Redeemer. It is said that he afterwards regretted having sundered his connection with this church. He left it, however, strong and flourishing.

On the 10th day of April, 1833, Mr. Doolittle was dismissed from the Presbytery of Erie, and connected himself with that of Portage, having entered upon pastoral labor in Hudson, Ohio. He was soon afterwards installed as pastor of the Presbyterian church at that place. This relation continued until the spring of 1840, when his declining health obliged him to withdraw from all the duties and labors of the ministry. His disease was pulmonary consumption, and with all its flattering voices, the invalid felt that his work upon earth was almost done. Although he had relinquished all pastoral cares, he yet continued in a very feeble condition. For the last few months of his life, he went down rapidly to the grave. Under all his afflictions, he was uniformly patient, calm, and hopeful. God was his stay and his helper. His mind was clear and untroubled to the last. In view of leaving his children portionless, he said he left them with a covenant-keeping God, whose promises were a more sure and blessed inheritance than millions of gold.

As the light of earth grew dim, and the splendors of the heavenly world were bursting upon his vision, raising both hands he exclaimed, —

"O death! where is thy sting? O grave! where is thy victory?"

And these were his last words. His spirit departed on the morning of September 22, 1842, in the forty-ninth year of his age, and the twentieth of his ministry.

Mr. Doolittle was twice married. His first marriage was in Oneida County, New York, to Miss Bethena Brooks, September, 1823. Her death took place at North East, Pa., in June, 1831. He was married the second time to Miss Electa Upham, of Jamestown, New York, November 8, 1831. He was the father of eight children, five of whom have gone to rest. Three daughters with his widow yet survive.

"As a pastor he was faithful, prayerful, and watchful, laboring for the good of souls, to the extent of his physical health and strength. As a preacher he was plain, evangelical, and solemn, applying the truth rather to the intellect and conscience, than to the emotions of the hearer. His natural temperament was sedate and calm; his disposition was serious but kind, amiable, and affectionate." [1]

He left the following message for the church of which he had been pastor: —

"Tell them to remember their solemn covenant with God, and with one another. . . . . Tell them to rally round their pastor and sustain his hands and uphold him in every good work, and beware of all influences that divide and destroy the peace of Zion."

His message to the impenitent was, —

"Tell them I thank them deeply and cordially, for their kindness. May the Lord richly reward them. . . . . My last prayers are for their salvation. Bid them delay not to seek and find that peace and joy in believing, without which they cannot possess the reward of the righteous."

One who knew him well,[2] and who was brought into the church at North East through his ministry, thus speaks of him: —

"He was a good preacher, with a pleasant voice and delivery, talents above the average; of medium size, spare, gray eyes, sallow complexion, with a mild, benignant countenance, and such a heavenly smile! I never heard him converse on any other subject than that of religion. He was a Puritan of the Puritans. He seemed to be always faithful, always zealous, always at the post of duty. He never unbent, was very reticent, and had remarkable control over his feelings; so much so that he preached one Sabbath, when one of his children lay dead at home. He was cheerful under all trials; nothing seemed to disturb him, except the wrongdoing of his people. Then he would weep over them,

[1] Prof. Hickok.   [2] Miss Jacks.

and be moved as no bereavements of his own could move him. Yet he was not a stern man, but kind and gentle to all. When his wife died, whilst attending the funeral, he announced the hymn —

"Unvail thy bosom, faithful tomb,"

and preached her funeral sermon himself the following Sabbath. In this sermon, his manner was calm, and with apparent impassiveness he depicted her character, speaking of her many excellences, without exaggerating them.

(34.) NATHAN HARNED.

1822-1854.

The subject of this sketch led a life of vicissitudes. Being of a delicate constitution, his health suffered during his preparatory studies, and throughout the remainder of his life he was unable to enter with vigor upon the active labors of the ministry. But he seems to have been active and diligent according to his measure of strength, and has left behind him the testimony that he was an earnest, faithful minister of the New Testament.

Nathan Harned, the son of David and Hannah (Walker) Harned, was born in Rockingham County, Va., on the 4th day of February, 1789. Of his early life and struggles, previous to entering the household of faith and dedicating himself to the work of the gospel ministry, nothing can here be said. It would be a valuable contribution to the history of the church, if this important chapter on the lives of its ministers could be written, setting forth the struggles and the resolutions, the doubts and the fears, that agitate their minds previous to commencing the great work.

Mr. Harned's academical studies were pursued in the

city of New York. He was at this time in religious creed and profession a Baptist, and commenced the study of theology in the Theological Institution of the Baptist General Convention, in the city of Philadelphia. Here he continued for three years, and completing his course, received a certificate of the same, July 25, 1821.

He was regularly licensed to preach the gospel by a Baptist association, and soon after received a call from a Baptist church in Northern Pennsylvania. But his mind was not at ease. He entertained grave doubts in regard to the peculiar tenets held by his church, that made him hesitate in regard to accepting this call. He took time to review the whole ground in relation to the subject of baptism and ecclesiastical polity, as entertained by his church. The call to the church in Pennsylvania was declined. After a thorough examination of the whole subject, with earnest prayer for guidance and direction, he renounced the doctrinal peculiarities of his Baptist brethren, and placed himself under the care of the Presbytery of Philadelphia, and was by that Presbytery licensed at a meeting held at Doylestown, on the 16th day of October, 1822.

His name first appears on the records of Erie Presbytery in 1824. He was regularly received under its care on the 2d day of March, 1825, having preached for some time previous to this in Warren County, Pa. At the same meeting at which he was received, calls were placed in his hands by Presbytery, from the congregations of Warren, Sugar Grove, Great Brokenstraw, and Lottsville. These calls were accepted, and arrangements made for his ordination and installation. This took place at a meeting of Presbytery held at Warren on the 20th day of April, 1825. In these exercises, Mr.

Tait (3) preached the sermon, and Mr. Chase (25) offered the ordaining prayer and delivered the charges.

This was a large field for the young pastor, and involved a large amount of labor. The labor was performed, however, in these four churches for nearly a year, when leave was asked to resign the charge of Brokenstraw, and probably Lottsville. The relation appears to have been a harmonious one, as an elder White from the former church declared, " that the congregation thought it was a matter of regret that Mr. Harned should leave them," yet under the circumstances, could not object to the dissolution of the pastoral relation. It was accordingly dissolved. In the month of May following, the relation with the churches of Warren and Sugar Grove was dissolved.

On the 22d of June, 1826, Mr. Harned asked and received a dismission to connect himself with the Presbytery of Hartford (now Beaver).

In the fall of 1826, the honorary degree of A. M. was conferred on him by Alleghany College.

His next field of labor was Youngstown, Ohio, at that time under the care of the Presbytery of Hartford, or Beaver. Here he labored about three years, when failing health compelled him once more to resign his charge. He then spent some time in the South and Southwest, hoping that a more genial climate might restore his wasted energies. From Hartford Presbytery, he received a dismission, October 5, 1830, and connected himself with the Presbytery of Philadelphia. His next field was Ridley, Delaware County, Pa., where he labored for a time under appointment by the Board of Missions. This appointment dates January 1, 1831.

After this, health failing, and suffering from an affection of the throat,[1] precluding for the time the idea of

[1] Dr. John McDowell.

preaching, with the consent and advice of Presbytery, he engaged in secular business. We find him next at New Orleans, probably engaged in secular employment, yet with improving health, for he was able in part to supply the pulpit of the Second Presbyterian Church during the temporary absence of the pastor, Rev. R. L. Stanton, D. D. He also supplied, occasionally, the Presbyterian Church in the third municipality, then vacant. This was in 1850.

About this time he returned to Philadelphia, and was connected with the Penn Presbyterian Church, which he served as a ruling elder and superintendent of a Sabbath-school of five hundred scholars.

Mr. Harned's labors on earth closed on the 9th day of October, 1854. He died in the city of New York, of disease of the heart, cancer of the stomach, and hydrothorax. His remains were interred in the Presbyterian Cemetery at Abington, Montgomery County, Pa.

(35.) WELLS BUSHNELL.

1825–1863.

WELLS BUSHNELL, the son of Alexander and Sarah (Wells) Bushnell, was born in Hartford, Conn., in the month of April, 1799. His mother was a pious woman, and by a godly example and earnest precept, strove to bring up her family in the fear of God. At the age of seventeen, Wells Bushnell was living in the city of Pittsburgh, Pa., and there, and at that time, made a public profession of religion, and connected himself with the First Presbyterian Church, then under the pastoral care of Rev. Francis Herron, D. D.

After some preparatory study, he became a student of Jefferson College, where he graduated in due course.

His theological education was completed at Princeton Theological Seminary. He was taken under the care of the Presbytery of New Brunswick, and licensed probably in the year 1825.

His name first appears on the minutes of the Presbytery of Erie, on May 24, 1826, when, as a licentiate, he presented a certificate of dismission from the Presbytery of New Brunswick, and asked to be taken under its care. Calls having been presented from the church of Meadville, Pa., for his pastoral labors, Luke ii. 11 was assigned him as part of trials for ordination. The ordination took place on the 22d day of June, 1826. In these exercises, Joseph Stockton (4), of the Presbytery of Ohio, preached the sermon, Samuel Tait (3) delivered the charge to the pastor, and Johnston Eaton (20) the charge to the people.

This relation continued until June 26, 1833, when, at his own request, it was dissolved, in order that he might go as a missionary to the Wea Indians. The "Western Board of Foreign Missions" had been recently established at Pittsburgh, and as missions were about to be organized for different points in heathen lands, Mr. Bushnell felt impelled to offer himself for the work. His warm, impulsive heart was stirred to its depths with a longing desire to engage in the great work. His firm and earnest conviction was, that the voice of the Master was calling him to the work, and he resolved to sunder the tie that bound him to an attached people, and labor and toil as best he might for the welfare of the benighted and the dying. And so, with his family, he entered the wilds of the West. But he had overestimated his constitution and power of endurance. With all his self-denial and earnestness, he experienced little but excessive fatigue, and prolonged sickness of himself and family, until he was worn out and discouraged. His labors continued in the Indian country for one year and a half, when he felt it his duty to return to the East. No doubt his labor and self-sacrifice were accepted of the Master, even though he was permitted to see but little fruit of his labor. No doubt it was said of him as of one of old, " He hath done what he could."

After leaving the Indian country, he returned to New Albany, Ind., where his parents resided. After a season of rest, he received an invitation to supply the First Presbyterian church in Louisville, Ky., in the absence of the regular pastor. He was also earnestly solicited to take charge of a new church enterprise in that city. But his views on the subject of slavery were even at that day so strongly in opposition to this institution, that he could not consistently accept. He then accepted a call to the congregation at Greensburg, Ind., in connection with one at Shelbyville, in the same State. After laboring here for one year and a half, his health failed, and he returned to New Albany. Soon after this, he returned to Pittsburgh, for the purpose of rest and recruiting his health.

Whilst in Pittsburgh, he accepted an invitation to supply the churches of Gravel Run and Cambridge, in Crawford County, Pa.

On the 3d of February, 1836, he had been dismissed from the Presbytery of Erie to that of Indianapolis. On the 11th day of April, 1838, he was received again into the Presbytery of Erie.

On the 18th day of April, 1839, he was dismissed to the Presbytery of Beaver, having accepted calls to the church of New Castle, Pa. Here he continued to labor for fifteen years and a half, with much success.

At the close of this period, a change took place in

Mr. Bushnell's views, in regard to his church relation. He was not satisfied with the position of the church on the question of slavery. In this matter he was honest and sincere, and felt that he could no longer remain in the Presbyterian church. He accordingly severed his connection with the Presbytery of Beaver, and united with the "Free Presbyterian Church." In this new relation, he ministered to the congregations of Mount Jackson, Lawrence County, and New Bedford, Mercer County, until the close of his earthly labors. The disease that terminated in his death was cholera morbus. He died at Mount Jackson, on the 16th day of July, 1863, in the sixty-fifth year of his age and thirty-eighth of his ministry.

On the 25th of April, 1826, he was united in marriage to Miss Eleanor Hannen, a daughter of Dr. John Hannen, of Pittsburgh, Pa. Five children survived him, four daughters and one son.

Mr. Bushnell was a successful minister of Jesus Christ. His heart was warm, and sometimes his zeal bore down his judgment. Says one who was a co-presbyter: "He was a good minister of Jesus Christ, a very good preacher, and a good pastor. During his stay at Meadville, his labors were much blessed, and no man in these parts was more popular than he. A ready mind and a determined will rendered his conclusions often premature, but he was a dear brother and devoted to his Master's work."

Says one of his session at his first field of labor: "He was courteous, familiar, and pleasant in general intercourse. As a Christian, he was esteemed as sincere and zealous; as a minister, his sermons were well written, and delivered with unction, and with us his ministry was much blessed."

His end was peace. He failed rapidly at the last, but expressed his prospects as "all glorious."

(37.) THOMAS ANDERSON.

1825–1853.

THOMAS ANDERSON, the son of John and ——— (Laughlin) Anderson, was born in Cumberland County, Pa., on the first day of the new year, 1791. His ancestors were Irish. His parents removed to this country from Tyrone County, Ireland, in 1787. Thomas was raised a farmer, and at twelve years of age was talked of in the family, as the prospective student of college. Difficulties were in the way, however, and it was not until the age of twenty-one, that the way was opened up for the commencement of his studies. At the age of eighteen he became a member of the Presbyterian church of Neshannock, Mercer County, Pa., then under the pastoral charge of Rev. William Wick. His is the old story of the early ministers — poverty, struggles, discouragements: and yet over all he triumphed. He studied Latin and Greek partly at home, partly at Greersburg Academy, sometimes teaching, sometimes laboring with his hands, until he was fitted for college. He graduated at Washington College, Pa., in 1820. In his early struggles he walked several miles to the home of Mr. Wick, to borrow a Latin grammar. Here he first saw the lady who eight years afterwards became his wife.

After graduating, he was united in marriage, on the 11th of October, 1820, to Miss Phebe, daughter of Rev. William Wick (2), and removing to the town of Mercer, took charge of the academy in that place. Here he taught for five years, paying off the balance of his college debts, purchased a little home in Mercer, and at the same time pursued his theological studies under the direction of Mr. Tait (3), pastor of the church in Mercer, copying out carefully and neatly Dr. McMillan's system of divinity, which was the *sine qua non* of all the earlier ministers.

He was licensed to preach the gospel by the Presbytery of Erie, on the 28th day of December, 1825. His first sermon after licensure, was delivered January 1, 1826 ; he was that day thirty-four years of age, and had a wife and two children.

He commenced his ministerial labors regularly at Concord, May 7, 1826; at Big Sugar Creek, the Sabbath following; and at Franklin, June 11, 1826. All these places are in Venango County, Pa. He was ordained by the Presbytery of Erie, September 19, 1826, and installed as pastor of the above congregations. In these exercises, Mr. Bushnell preached the sermon, Mr. Chase delivered the charge to the pastor, and Mr. McKinney the charge to the people.

He lived near the Sugar Creek Church at this time, rode seven miles to Franklin, and over twenty to Concord. In addition to these places he performed a large amount of missionary work through Venango and the neighboring counties.

On the 13th of April, 1831, he was released from the charge of the congregation of Concord, and gave all his time to Franklin and Big Sugar Creek, living at the former place. He was released from the charge of Franklin on the 12th of September, 1837, and probably from Big Sugar Creek about the same time.

At the division of the Presbytery, in 1838, Mr. Anderson adhered to the New School. He labored for a time after this in Beaverdam and Union, in Erie County, and in 1843 removed to Huntington, Indiana. Here he organized a Presbyterian church in November, 1843, consisting of nine members. It was the first evangelical church organized in the place, and the first point of Presbyterian preaching in the county. Here he labored faithfully for five years, when growing infirmities compelled him to think of resigning. He was released from his charge of Huntington, January 9, 1848. In relation to this resignation he says, " I feel sad to think I cannot stay and work in the harvest. I have the heart but not the strength ; but what little strength I have I expect to use for missionary ends. I am not afraid of poverty and want.

"'My Shepherd will supply my need,
Jehovah is his name.'"

Mr. Anderson records that whilst laboring in the Erie Presbytery for sixteen years, he preached two thousand five hundred and eighty-two sermons. On one occasion he rode twenty miles, preached, and then rode four miles further before eating. He loved to speak of his old charge in Venango County, Pennsylvania.

" My heart clings," he writes, " to my native land, my boyhood's home, my first field of ministerial labor. The impressions there made, the friendships there formed, and the associations that cluster around the phrase 'pastor and people,' are too sacred to be trifled with and too precious to be forgotten."

So he continued to labor whilst he had strength, preaching Christ to the poor and destitute, until the Master called him to his rest and his reward.

His death was sudden. The circumstances attending it are furnished by his daughter.[1] " After family worship he retired to rest. Mother spent the night with a sick

[1] Mrs. B. A. Moore.

grand-daughter up-stairs. At the hour father usually arose, she heard him uttering a groan, and hastened to him. He remarked that he had not slept well; that just now he had such a dreadful pain about his heart; if he had another such attack it would kill him. She hastened to prepare warm stimulants, and send for a physician, but before she returned to his bedside, 'he was not, for God took him.' If there were fears and anguish during the long watches of that night, they were known only to Him, who 'neither slumbers nor sleeps.'

> "He laid aside his raiment for the night,
> And angels clothed him in the coming light:
> So like his life, he passed from earth away,
> Quiet and peaceful — God alone his stay."

He died at Huntington, Indiana, on the 22d day of December, 1853, a few days before he had completed his sixty-third year, and in the twenty-ninth year of his ministry.

Mrs. Anderson has since rejoined him in rest. They had eight children, five of whom survive them. The eldest son, Rev. Philander Anderson, is a member of the Presbytery of Indianapolis.

Rev. A. W. Freeman, a co-presbyter, says of Mr. Anderson, "His piety was humble and child-like. His manner of conducting devotional meetings was exceedingly happy. As a preacher he was clear, logical, earnest, forcible, and striking; and had not his health been impaired, he would have been well qualified to minister to any congregation to the end of his life."

A plain stone, erected to his memory, bears the following inscription: —

REV. THOMAS ANDERSON,

Died December 22, 1853, aged 63 years.
Graduated at Washington College, in 1819.

Ordained at Franklin, Pa., in 1826.
Removed to Huntington, Ind., in 1843.
The first pastor of the Presbyterian church in this place.

"Thy sun shall no more go down; neither shall thy moon withdraw itself; for the Lord shall be thine everlasting light, and the days of thy mourning shall be ended."

(38.) PIERCE CHAMBERLAIN.

1822–1850.

The subject of this sketch was born on the 11th day of June, 1790, in Newark, Delaware. He was the son of Joseph and Martha Chamberlain, respectable and worthy members of the Society of Friends. In this faith he was nurtured and brought up. The grace of God, free and sovereign, was most signally manifested in his life history. For years he was tossed upon a sea of doubts and fears, with struggles and conflicts innumerable, yet safely anchoring in the quiet harbor at last.

About the time of arriving at maturity, he became thoughtful and anxious about the interests of salvation. He read much in Quaker books of devotion, but obtained little satisfactory light. So great was his internal distress and agitation, that his health suffered in consequence. His mind became morbid, and doubts were entertained in regard to a future state. He was driven almost to the verge of insanity, induced by despair. In this condition of doubt and mental distraction, the great Adversary tempted him to take his own life, and he actually repaired to the bank of a creek for that purpose. But the grace of God prevented. He reflected that this would be folly and wickedness, and lying down beneath an apple-tree, gave himself up to the most terrible struggle through which he had ever passed. Foiled in his attempt to lead him to self-destruction, the great enemy tried a new system of tactics. He suggested a doubt of the being of God. This was accepted at once, and the young man sprang to his feet and returned home full of a deceptive joy, for now he felt there was no accountability hereafter. His joy was manifest to his friends, and he seemed to be from this time completely in the Devil's toils.

But all this time the grace of God was following him. His atheism soon forsook him, and he found himself in the depths of darkness and wretchedness. Going to Philadelphia, he heard the Rev. Dr. Skinner preach on the Divine Decrees. This sermon was ordered in the providence of God, for his special benefit and enlightenment. It produced a great change in his views. He now beheld the Lord Jesus Christ, as the Saviour of the guilty, and the hope of the helpless. Comfort came to his mind. Peace filled his heart. The love of Christ seemed to him so great and so wonderful that he not only gave himself up to his service, but resolved to devote himself to the gospel ministry.

He attended the Academy at Andover for a short period, but health failing, he returned to his home, and worked at his trade for a time. After this he was engaged as clerk in a store, engaging in study at the Newark Academy, as health and strength would permit. Thus he advanced from one degree to another in his studies, until he commenced that of theology. This study was pursued with Rev. Dr. Skinner and others, until the 4th day of April, 1822, when he was licensed to preach the gospel by the Presbytery of New Castle. The Presbytery was induced to relax the usual rule in regard to a full course of classical study, because of the age, delicacy of health, and apparent maturity of judgment, prudence, and zeal of the candidate.

Mr. Chamberlain preached for some time in his own Presbytery, the vacancies of which were numerous. He had much of the missionary spirit, and for a time labored in the almshouses and prisons in the city of Philadelphia, preaching the gospel to the lowly and the wretched. After continuing these labors for some few years, he was ordained as an evangelist by the Presbytery of New Castle, and received a commission from the Board of Missions to labor within the bounds of the Presbytery of Erie.

Mr. Chamberlain first visited the shore of Lake Erie in 1826, and labored for some time in the vacant churches with much acceptance. On the 12th day of April, he accepted calls from the church of Springfield, in Erie County, and on the 16th of January, 1828, was installed as pastor of that church. But his pastoral labors were brief here. Ill health, that had stood in his way ever since he commenced his preparatory studies, compelled him to ask the Presbytery to dissolve the pastoral relation. This was done on the 1st day of October, 1828.

From this time, until the spring of 1836, he labored as a missionary throughout the bounds of the Presbytery, preaching in school-houses and private dwellings, whenever and wherever he could collect a congregation to hear him. For this kind of labor he was eminently fitted, for although usually a taciturn man, he had a wonderful faculty of attracting children to him, and was always well provided with books and tracts to distribute, and had a word of kindness and advice for all classes of people. In these labors in the highways and hedges, the people hung upon his words. There was a solemnity and unction in his preaching that, in that day, was most persuasive and attractive. Through these missionary labors many people were turned to the Lord.

In the spring of 1836 he received and accepted calls from the congregations of Waterford and Union. He was installed as pastor on the 15th day of September, 1836. After this, having given up the charge of Union, he labored at Gravel Run in connection with Waterford for a number of years. Here his health again failed, and he was released from his pastoral charge. He soon after left the bounds of Erie Presbytery, and returned to his old home in Newark, Delaware.

At the time of the division in the Presbyterian church, in 1838, Mr. Chamberlain identified himself with that branch popularly known as the New School.

On his return to Newark, the state of his health precluding the idea of a pastoral charge, he took charge of a Female Seminary, in the labors connected with which he employed himself until called to his rest and reward. His disease was cholera. He died on the 23d day of August, 1850, in the sixty-first year of his age, and twenty-ninth of his ministry.

Mr. Chamberlain was a man of medium size, light, thin hair, mild, blue eyes, and regular features, with an expression of great solemnity and earnest thought constantly manifested in his countenance. He was a good man, and full of faith. He loved the cause of Zion. As a preacher, he was most solemn and impressive. He dealt not so much in logic and attempts to convince the reason, as in earnest appeals to the heart and conscience. He did not so much point his hearers to Sinai as to Calvary; nor did he so much dwell upon the justice and righteousness of God, as upon his love and mercy, as set forth in the work of Jesus Christ. He had many warmly attached friends, all over his missionary field, and men went long distances to hear him, where he had appointments to preach. He was a man of prayer. Although not without his weaknesses of temper, yet he preserved an admirable government over himself through the grace of God.

Mr. Chamberlain was united in marriage to Miss Christiana B. Whitehill, of Strasburg, Pa. He left four or five children with the precious legacy of a father's prayers, and the memory of a father's usefulness and devotion and unselfish labor in the Master's cause, to stimulate them to duty and diligence and labor. One of these children is Rev. George Chamberlain, missionary to Brazil.

(42.) EDSON HART.
—— 1867.

Mr. Hart most probably came from New England. He was received into the Presbytery of Erie, September 22, 1830, on certificate from the Presbytery of Trumbull. He labored for a few years at Springfield and Girard, as a stated supply. After removing from the bounds of Presbytery, he acted as agent for some educational project in Kentucky. He was dismissed to the Presbytery of Muhlenburg, January 21, 1843. After this he removed to New Orleans, and was there engaged in secular business in connection with the Bible agency, until the beginning of the war, when he came north and stopped in Oldham County, Kentucky, where he died on the 19th day of September, 1867.

(44.) ROBERT GLENN.

1831–1857.

This brother was in a peculiar sense a child of the Presbytery of Erie. He was born within its boundaries. He was gathered into the fold of the Good Shepherd through the ministry of its members. He was licensed and ordained by it. All his ministerial labors were confined to its field; and within its bounds his sleeping dust awaits the Master's call on the morning of the Resurrection.

Robert Glenn was born on the 2d day of March, 1802, in Wolfcreek Township, Mercer County, Pa. It is believed that his deepest convictions of sin, and most triumphant hopes in Christ, were received under the ministrations of Rev. Samuel Tait (3), late of Mercer, Pa. To him he was in the habit of going in his time of conflict and trouble, seeking instruction and advice. Often the mistake was made that is so common in all religious experience, of expecting too much from the minister in the way of light and comfort. The rugged experience and matter-of-fact mind of Mr. Tait often left the young inquirer to labor and struggle and wait until he was ready to conclude that his spiritual adviser was without sympathy or interest in his welfare. But he afterwards found that the discipline was most salutary, and that in those days of trial he was but preparing for the solemn work of dealing with immortal souls, in the labors of the ministry. Throughout his entire Christian course he was not a sanguine Christian. He was oftener in the Valley of Humiliation than on the Delectable Mountains. Yet withal, he felt that his feet were planted on the Rock, and whilst trembling at times as the billows dashed around him, he felt safe.

After some preparatory study, Mr. Glenn became a student of Jefferson College, where he graduated in 1828. One of his classmates [1] at College, says, " While at College, he was one of the most sedate and circumspect of the students; and although cheerful, free from all the levities so characteristic of youth."

Mr. Glenn was for two years a student of the Western Theological Seminary. He also studied for some time under the advice and direction of his old pastor, Rev. Samuel Tait. He was licensed to preach the gospel, at a meeting of the Presbytery of Erie, held at Mercer, Pa., on the 2d day of February, 1831.

The intervening year and a half was spent chiefly in preaching to the vacant congregations of Amity, Mill Creek, and Sandy Lake, where, at a meeting of Presbytery held at Mill Creek on the 12th day of September, 1832, he was ordained to the whole work of the ministry, and installed as pastor of the congregations of Mill Creek and Amity for two thirds of his time. The remaining third was spent as a stated supply in the church of Sandy Lake. The relation to the church of Amity continued until April 3, 1850; that to Mill Creek until it was dissolved by death.

About the time he was released from Amity, the relation to the church of Sandy Lake was suspended, and Mr. Glenn accepted calls from the congregation of Big Sugar Creek, and was installed as pastor there on the 18th day of June, 1850, spending half his time in each of the congregations of Mill Creek and Big Sugar Creek. This was his charge during the remainder of his ministry, making at Mill Creek a ministry of over twenty-five years.

Mr. Glenn was a laborious and most faithful pastor. He was instant in season and out of season, and liter-

[1] Rev. Loyal Young, D. D.

ally wore himself out in preaching the gospel. He was not a great man, but he was a good man. He was not an orator, but he was a faithful preacher of the Word. He labored for the souls of men as one that must give account. He labored and toiled over his sermons as the miner does in his quest for gold. It is not strange then that his preaching was accompanied with the demonstration of the Spirit and with power. If he did not excel in the power of logic, or in that intense grappling of mind with great subjects that exhibits peculiar powers of intellect, he could relate the simple story of the Cross with most persuasive power and unction. And, like Jacob of old, he had peculiar power in wrestling with the Angel of the Covenant. He was mighty in prayer. Those who heard him felt that to him the mercy-seat was a familiar place, and that reverence and boldness and faith were all prominent in his addresses to the Most High. As a man he was uniformly meek, humble, diffident of his own judgment and abilities, yet firm in his adherence to principle and conscience. He was a power for good in the community where he dwelt, and had fewer enemies than many who are less zealous for the cause of truth and righteousness. As a Christian he was simple and childlike in his piety, shrinking from any allusion to his own attainments; yet most evidently bearing about with him the glow of ardent love to God and the souls of men. His ministry was characterized by regular, systematic, conscientious effort, and its fruits were a gradual growth, and a steady, constant adding to the church not only from the families already connected with it, but from the families of the world.

The last hours of such a man were of course peaceful. Constant labor and frequent exposure gradually undermined a constitution that must have been originally of great power and endurance. The disease to which he ultimately succumbed was consumption. He saw the end approaching, and commenced setting his house in order. His religious exercises were most delightful and comforting to those who witnessed them. Yet there was nothing of presumption or mere sentiment connected with them. When the deep waters were approaching his footsteps, a ministerial brother inquired if he felt that he was on the Rock. He replied, "Yes; but as a poor guilty sinner, with no hope but in precious, atoning blood." He looked across the dark valley, not with the presumption of the sentimentalist, or the feigned calmness of the philosopher, but with the earnest, humble faith of the believer in Jesus. And thus, in sublime faith and childlike confidence in God, he passed through the valley, and entered the City of Gold, to "see the King in his beauty."

His death occurred on the morning of the Sabbath, September 6, 1857; and he was laid to rest in the burial ground of the church of Mill Creek, just in the rear of the pulpit from which he had preached the gospel for more than a quarter of a century. A simple marble shaft marks the place of his burial, on which was inscribed, by the direction of Presbytery, the following words: —

(First Side of the Die.)

ROBERT GLENN:

A MINISTER OF JESUS CHRIST, AND FOR TWENTY-FIVE YEARS PASTOR OF THE PRESBYTERIAN CHURCH OF MILL CREEK.

(Second Side.)

BORN MARCH 2, 1802,
DIED SEPT. 6, 1857,
"HE GIVETH HIS BELOVED SLEEP."
Ps. cxxvii. 2.

(Third Side.)

THEY THAT TURN MANY TO RIGHTEOUSNESS
SHALL SHINE AS THE STARS, FOREVER AND EVER.
Dan. xii. 3.

(Fourth Side.)

HE LOVED TO PREACH CHRIST,
AND WITH A BURNING ZEAL FOR SOULS,
HE WORE HIMSELF OUT IN THE
MASTER'S SERVICE.

Mr. Glenn was thrice married. His first wife was Miss Rebecca Wycoff, of Mercer County, Pa., with whom he lived fifteen years, when she was called away from earth. By her he had three sons and two daughters. One of these sons, Samuel M., was licensed to preach the gospel by the Presbytery of Erie, and afterwards ordained and installed within the bounds of the Presbytery of Columbus. His second wife was Miss Mary Ann McCracken, a member of the congregation of Mill Creek, and daughter of one of his elders. She died eight months after marriage. His third wife was Miss Harriet Finley of Evansburg, Crawford County, Pa., with whom he lived eight years, until his death, and by whom he had three children.

(45.) JOHN McNAIR, D. D.

1831–1867.

JOHN McNAIR was the third son of Solomon and Sarah (McMasters) McNair. He was born near Newtown, Bucks County, Pa., on the 28th day of May, 1806. His mother was a great grand-daughter of a French gentleman named De la Plaine, who emigrated at an early day to New Jersey. From him Dr. McNair inherited that peculiar vibratory motion of the eye, so familiar to his friends. He had the advantage of a careful religious training in his childhood and youth, and at an early age became a member of the church. He owed much to his mother, who was eminently pious and a lady of great decision of character.

He received his academical education at Newtown academy. In 1825, he entered the Sophomore Class at Jefferson College, and graduated in 1828. His theological studies were pursued at Princeton, and he was licensed to preach the gospel by the Presbytery of Philadelphia, in 1831, and soon after set out to Western Pennsylvania, to labor as a domestic missionary. His first field was in Warren County, Pa., in the bounds of the Presbytery of Erie. By this Presbytery he was ordained as an evangelist on the 7th day of November, 1833. Johnston Eaton (20) preached the sermon, and James Alexander (40) delivered the charge. He was a member of the Presbytery of Erie about three years, and from it was transferred to that of Vincennes in 1836.

Dr. McNair labored as an evangelist about eight years ; one year in Warren, Pa., one in Fairmount near Philadelphia, one in Vincennes, Iowa, one in Milford, N. J., one in Stroudsburg, Pa., and more than three in the Musconetcong Valley, N. J. His first permanent settlement was in Lancaster City, Pa., where he continued eleven years. He was obliged to resign this charge on account of ill health, when he removed to Clinton, N. J., amongst his wife's relatives. Here he purchased a farm and commenced farming in connection with ministerial labors, very greatly to the benefit of his health. He preached at Clinton for six or eight years.

During the war, he received a commission as Chaplain of the 31st Regiment of New Jersey Volunteers, and went to the field to share the hardships and dangers of the army. He was a model chaplain; always faithful, always at the post of duty, and always earnest in his great work. When his army labors closed, he returned to Lancaster, where he resided until his death, which took place on Sabbath, January 27, 1867, in the sixty-first year of his age and the thirtieth of his ministry. His illness was very brief. He had been studying and laboring hard during the winter and overtaxed his brain; in this condition of mind and body, he took a violent cold whilst laboring during the "week of prayer." This brought on congestion of the brain and lungs, and in one week's time he sunk to the grave. His remains were carried to Clarksville, N. J., and laid to rest beside those of his son, who had died a few months before.

An appreciative friend thus speaks of him: "Those who knew him best will ever cherish his memory, while they do but simple justice to the characteristics of his head and his heart. Retiring in his manner and deportment, he was ever cheerful and kind, possessing however a firmness and integrity of purpose which made itself felt in his expressed opinions, together with a sincerity unquestioned, which gave a high tone to the doctrines he inculcated. His sermons evinced a high order of talent; eloquent, yet plain and unaffected, lucid and easily comprehended. As a logician he was unsurpassed, and he was consequently an able debater. One could readily ' Look through the crystal waters of his style, down to the golden sands of his thoughts,' and this it was that rendered his discourses so interesting, truthful, and impressive. His arguments were ever clear and concise, and it was impossible to listen to them without feeling convinced that his belief was sincere and that his opinions were the honest and firm convictions of a man who loved God and kept his commandments.

> ' His lips taught virtue, which his life confess'd.'

"As a husband and father, he was what might have been expected from so pure a man."

About the year 1838, Dr. McNair was united in marriage to Miss Susan Adaline Hunt, daughter of Dr. William A. A. Hunt, and grand-daughter of Rev. Holloway W. Hunt. They had two children; the elder a daughter named Lizzie (now Mrs. Lizzie Day); the younger a son named Alfred, who was killed by a railroad accident but a few months before his father's departure.

(47.) NATHANIEL WEST, D. D.

1820–1864.

Dr. West was born in the province of Ulster, Ireland,[1] although to all intents and purposes he was as much a Scotchman as though he had taken his first lease of life amid the mountain fastnesses of Scotland. It is probable that his early life was passed in Scotland. He was born in the year 1794. He was at one time a chaplain in the army. His theological studies were pursued in Edinburgh. He entered the ministry in the year 1820, in the Independent connection.

He emigrated to this country in 1834, bearing letters with him from many of the distinguished ministers of Scotland, amongst them one from Dr. Chalmers.

In the month of September, 1834, he came to Meadville, Pa. He had been taken on trial as a foreign minister, by the Second Presbytery of Philadelphia, and was by that body dismissed to the Presbytery of Erie, by which he was received on further trial, April 15,

---

[1] Wilson's *Presbyterian Historical Almanac.*

1835. On the 8th of October following, he was approved and accepted as a member of Presbytery, subject to the approval of Synod. The action was afterwards approved by Synod. Having accepted calls to the church of Meadville, Pa., he was installed on the 11th day of May, 1836. This relation continued until the 26th day of June, 1838, when at his own request it was dissolved. He subsequently labored at North East, Pa., Monroe, Mich., Pittsburgh, McKeesport, Belmont, and Hestonville (united), Pa. At the time of his death he was the senior chaplain of the Satterlee U. S. Hospital, West Philadelphia.

Dr. West was a remarkable man. His history was crowded with incident and anecdote, that were interesting and almost romantic. He was endowed by nature with a stalwart frame, great powers of endurance, and an energy that was almost invincible under ordinary difficulties. In mind, he was gifted above the ordinary range of men, although his mental characteristics were peculiar. His powers of analysis and his strength of memory were astonishing. His knowledge of the Scriptures was such, that he could not only quote at any length verbatim, but give chapter and verse. In this respect he was almost literally a living Concordance. He was accustomed to draw from the Word of God the rules that governed his daily life and action, so that at times it seemed to strangers almost as though he used the Word of God in too light and trifling a manner. He was never at a loss for Scripture language in any reply or retort he thought necessary to make. On occasion of coming into the bounds of the Presbytery of Erie, and before he had become acquainted with the members, he was preaching at a small town near where two of the brethren were stopping. They went to hear him, and after the service was concluded, made themselves known to him. His instantaneous remark was —

"Had I but known you were here, sure my text should have been Gen. xlii. 16. 'By the life of Pharoah, surely ye are spies.'"

During his chaplaincy at Satterlee Hospital, he felt the need of a small chapel for the use of the sick and wounded soldiers, and opened a subscription for the purpose of erecting one. Among others he called upon an acquaintance, a member of the Society of Friends, with the remark —

"Friend John, I have called to ask thee to subscribe to an important enterprise."

"Very well, friend Nathaniel, what is it?" The Doctor proceeded to describe the need of a chapel for the hospital, when his friend replied, —

"Well, that is a good object, and I think I will subscribe twenty-five dollars."

"But, friend John, I can prove to thee from the Scriptures, that thee should subscribe fifty."

"Well, friend Nathaniel, if thee can do that I will even subscribe fifty."

"And sure, and does it not say in Luke xvi. 6: 'Take thy bill, and sit down quickly, and write fifty.'"

As a preacher Dr. West was original, fluent, and eminently Scriptural. His divisions were usually textual, and drawn out in the old style of many divisions and sub-divisions, yet all based upon the text and rigidly drawn from it. In the Old Testament Scriptures, in every tree and shrub, in every nail and stone of the Temple, he saw something that pointed to the gospel and the work of Christ. He was an eminently instructive preacher, bringing from his treasure things new and old.

He published many sermons and tracts. The "Analysis of the Bible" was, however, his great work. Although based on the work of Talbot, yet the work of compiling and arranging it for the press was herculean.

At the division of the Church in 1838, Dr. West went with the New School, but after the lapse of some ten or twelve years became connected with the Old School.

His disease was paralysis. He died at Philadelphia, on the 2d day of September, 1864, in the seventieth year of his age and the forty-fourth of his ministry. His remains rest in the Oakland Cemetery.

(53.) CHARLES DANFORTH.

1829–1867.

CHARLES DANFORTH, the son of Samuel and Lucy (Auger) Danforth, was born at Rupert, Bennington County, Vermont, on the 23d day of August, 1800. His father was son of Jonathan Danforth, of Hardwick, Mass. His mother, Lucy Auger, was a native of New Haven, Conn. He was fitted for college by Rev. Moses Hallock, of Plainfield, Mass. He graduated at Williams College in 1826.

His was a life of struggles and vicissitudes. With a desire to work for the cause of Christ, and for the good of souls, he found the way often full of obstacles and sore discouragements. There was to his inner ear the voice, "Go work to-day in my vineyard," and the discouraging thought, that weakness of constitution and narrowness of means would be in his way; so he pressed on in study and resolution, possibly one of the martyrs of the church militant.

His theological education was obtained at Auburn Theological Seminary, where he was licensed to preach the gospel by the Presbytery of Cayuga, in 1829 ; and, at the same meeting, ordained to do the work of an evangelist. He soon after went out to labor in the States of Ohio and Indiana. He afterwards labored several years in the bounds of the Presbyteries of Miami and Chilicothe. On the 11th of April, 1838, he became a member of the Presbytery of Erie, and removed from its bounds in 1840. He labored for a time in Springfield, Pa.

In April, 1830, Mr. Danforth was united in marriage to Miss Cornelia F. Sadd, daughter of Harry Sadd, of Austinburg, Ohio. They have had five children, three daughters and two sons. The second daughter went as a missionary to Africa, and was connected with the Mendi Mission. Whilst there she became the wife of Rev. S. J. Whiton, of the same mission. After laboring a little more than a year in that benighted land, she was called to rest in Jesus. Her departure was greatly lamented by all who knew her. Mr. Danforth adhered to the New School branch at the division.

During the last years of Mr. Danforth's life, he suffered greatly from ill health. In fact, for several years he had no pastoral charge, but resided at Oberlin, Ohio, preaching occasionally as opportunity offered and strength permitted. In the spring of 1867, he was greatly afflicted with lameness, and other symptoms of failing health. His liver became complicated with disease of the lungs, when he rapidly sunk. He died at Oberlin, Ohio, on the 29th day of April, 1867, in the sixty-seventh year of his age, and the thirty-eighth of his ministry.

In the last weeks of his life, he made a thorough re-examination of his hope, and felt that he could trust all in Christ. The Rock seemed firmer under his feet,

and he could trust confidently in the merits of Jesus
Christ. And to the last Christ was with him, sustain-
ing, comforting, and cheering him, until he went up to be
"Forever with the Lord."

(66.) JOHN LIMBER.

1843–1849.

JOHN LIMBER was the son of John and Mary (Long)
Limber, and was born in Crawford County, Pa., on the
22d day of April, 1814. Both his father's and mother's
families came from Northumberland County, Pa., and
settled in Crawford County, about the year 1795. His
mother died when he was but four years of age. The
family was then broken up, and John was raised amongst
his friends until the age of fourteen, when he was sent
to Meadville, to learn a mechanical occupation. Whilst
at his trade, with other boys of his age, he formed
a literary society for mutual improvement; and as he
grew older, manifested a very earnest desire for a better
education than he had yet been able to obtain. Through
the influence of friends he was released from his ap-
prenticeship, when he went to Greenville, Pa., worked
at his trade, and studied with Rev. James Alexander
(40), who was pastor of the church at that place.
Whilst there he made a profession of religion. From
this place he went to Zelienople, Pa., and pursued his
studies under great difficulties, but with considerable
success. He was also tutor in the family of Judge
Derickson, at Meadville, Pa. Studying at the same
time with Rev. Nathaniel West (47), pastor of the
church there. He also studied for a time at Alleghany
College. Finally he became a student at Amherst
College, Mass., pursuing his studies under great and

pressing difficulties, yet with a calm heroism that was well-nigh sublime. Sometimes he would teach in the neighborhood of the college, and recruit his finances. On one occasion, he went to North Carolina and taught for a time. He finally graduated. After this he taught for a time in the academies of Meadville and Erie, meanwhile pursuing his theological studies privately.

He was licensed to preach the gospel by the Presbytery of Erie, on the 4th day of October, 1843. For a year or two, he was engaged in preaching in vacant churches in the bounds of the Presbytery, to the great satisfaction of those who heard him. But there was a nervous diffidence that oppressed him like a great shadow resting upon his heart, and often filling him with distress amounting to agony. Under this feeling of oppression, he would sometimes walk his room wringing his hands in his distress, yet he felt at the same time, "Woe is me, if I preach not the gospel."

In the autumn of 1844, he was designated by the Presbyterian Board of Foreign Missions, as a missionary to the Indians. In view of this, he was ordained by the Presbytery of Erie, on the 16th day of October, 1844. John V. Reynolds (56) preached on the occasion, David Waggoner (54) presided, and Cyrus Dickson (58) delivered the charge to the missionary.

He labored amongst the Indians for a year or two, and then went as a missionary to Texas. He preached at Houston, Galveston, Austin, and Washington. He finally concluded to settle at Washington, Texas, and was dismissed from the Presbytery of Erie to that of Brazos, on the 25th day of April, 1846.

Previous to going to the Indian country, he had formed the acquaintance of Miss Emily S. Messenger, of Wrentham, Mass., but who was then teaching at Meadville, Pa. To this lady, Mr. Limber was married on the 18th day of January, 1849. The marriage took place at Louisville, Ky., where Miss Messenger was then teaching. The same day they left on board a steamboat for New Orleans. On the 29th of January, the boat lay to at the Lafayette landing. Then he went down to the city, took passage on another boat to Texas, and returned to his wife. After tea, and about dark, he remarked that he wished to procure a few Bibles to take with him, took an omnibus, went down to the city. At the Bible House he purchased his books, placed them in a satchel, and finding that the carriages had ceased running, started to walk to the boat, a distance of two miles, through the dark and stormy night. Here his record ceases. He never returned to the boat. Alone in that dark, tempestuous night, and in that city of great wickedness, he disappeared. Who shall finish the record? Who tell how he passed away? The completed history will be found only in God's great book above. Whose voice did he hear? That of the midnight robber? that of the wildly surging river? Did some " horror of great darkness " envelop him as in a cloud from which there was no escape? Great are the mysteries of time. Eternity will reveal them all.

The stricken, widowed wife went on to Texas, and resumed her old employment. From boyhood, Mr. Limber was of a quiet, shrinking temperament, fond of reading, seldom playing, most inoffensive in his disposition, and exemplary in his life. After the age of fifteen, his burning desire was to receive a liberal education, and after all his difficulties, he accomplished this, becoming a good, critical scholar.

The following tribute, written at the time of his disappearance, by one [1] who knew him well, is so beautiful and just, that it is here reproduced : " He was gentle as a woman, tender and kind as a mother, generous almost to a fault, often to his own injury, sympathetic as a sister. His heart was deep as woman's, and he added the mental qualities and discipline and worth of a man. He covered up great stores of wealth, that none but his intimate friends ever knew, under a modesty and diffidence very rare. His life was full of troubles. Poor from a boy, he struggled without aid through school and college, and became a superior scholar. His fears were great, and he was doomed to a constant strife. He was driven to and fro, and tossed by buffetings. He came, one scarcely knew whence, nor whither, how, nor where. He would hail you from Brokenstraw, from the Creek Indians, from Texas. He married, and has gone, none knows how, nor under what circumstances. As a mist he has faded from our sight."

(68.) ALEXANDER BOYD.

1825–1864.

ALEXANDER BOYD was the son of William and Margaret (McCann) Boyd, and was born in the city of Dublin, Ireland, about the year 1796. His father was a merchant of Armagh, Ireland, but about the year 1825, removed to Paisley, Scotland. Alexander Boyd had one brother named William, a printer, and two sisters, who married and settled in Scotland.

The subject of this sketch was taken in childhood, and raised by his grandfather, who was a pious and devoted man. He was designed for the ministry; and after some preparatory education, was sent to Queen's

[1] Rev. J. V. Reynolds, D. D.

College, Belfast. Dr. Edgar was at that time a professor, and the late Dr. Edgar, son of the professor, was his fellow-student. He completed his course about the year 1825, and was licensed to preach the gospel by the Presbytery of Donegan, now Londonderry. Before the Union, he was a seceder.

Intending to emigrate to America, he declined all calls to a pastoral settlement, although he remained some years, preaching in various vacant churches as opportunity offered. Amongst other places, he supplied the congregation of Stranorlar, near his grandfather's.

In April, 1829, he was united in marriage to Miss Ann Dickey, daughter of Rev. Wm. Dickey, of Carnom, Ireland, at which place her brother, Rev. John Dickey, is now settled, as successor to his father. Her father's ministry in that congregation extended over a period of fifty years. Her brother, Rev. Joseph Dickey, is settled at Kilrea, in the County of Londonderry, Ireland, and her remaining brother Robert, is a ruling elder in the U. P. Church, at Greenville, Pa.

Mr. Boyd emigrated to America in the year 1831, and landed in Philadelphia, where he tarried for a time, but declined all overtures looking toward a settlement, as he wished to explore the country, and particularly to visit the great West. Soon after this, he removed to Alleghany County, and spent some time within the bounds of the Presbytery of Alleghany. He was, at this time, in connection with the Associate Presbyterian Church. About the year 1835, he accepted calls to the Associate Presbyterian Church of New Castle, Pa., where he was ordained and installed as pastor by the Presbytery of Shenango. He also preached a portion of his time at Wilmington and Mount Prospect, in connection with New Castle. He continued in these charges some ten years.

His views having changed in some matters, Mr. Boyd proposed changing his ecclesiastical relation, and on the 22d day of October, 1845, he was received as a member into the Presbytery of Erie. From this he passed by certificate to the Presbytery of Steubenville.

He preached for a time at Beech Woods, but declining a call there, passed into the bounds of the Presbytery of Huntington, and became pastor of the churches of Fruit Hill and Mount Pleasant. In this charge he labored pleasantly and successfully for five or six years. It was with great reluctance that the people of these congregations consented to part with him; but he felt that there were reasons why he should remove further westward. He removed to the State of Iowa about the year 1853, and settled in Solon, of which church he was elected pastor. After laboring here for some years, he resigned his pastoral charge, though he labored in various places in the region until his death, which occurred at Newport Centre, Iowa, December 9, 1864, in the sixty-ninth year of his age and the thirty-ninth of his ministry. He left a widow and six children, three sons and three daughters. From the beginning of his last illness, he had no hope or desire of recovery, but was patient and resigned, and longed to depart and be with Christ.

(70.) JOHN KINKEAD CORNYN.

1845–1853.

John K. Cornyn was a native of Cumberland County, Pa. He was born at Carlisle, Pa., on the 16th day of August, 1815. His earlier life was spent in the acquisition and practice of a mechanical trade. He was a student of Jefferson College, where he graduated in the autumn of 1842. Soon after graduation, he became a student of theology in the Western Theological Seminary. Here he remained the full term of three years, when he was licensed by the Presbytery of Alleghany on the 3d day of April, 1845.

For two years after his licensure, he was employed in supplying vacant churches in the bounds of Alleghany and neighboring presbyteries, having his head-quarters mainly at the Western Theological Seminary, which he considered as his home. About the beginning of the year 1847, he came into the bounds of the Presbytery of Erie, where he preached to the congregations of Sturgeonville, Girard, and Harbor Creek. Having accepted calls from these congregations, he was ordained and installed as their pastor by the Presbytery of Erie, on the 11th day of August, 1847. In these services, Rev. Alexander Cunningham (65) preached the sermon, Rev. Robert Glenn presided, Rev. Cyrus Dickson (58) delivered the charge to the pastor, and Rev. James Coulter (62) the charge to the people.

On the 4th day of April, 1850, the pastoral relation was dissolved between Mr. Cornyn and the congregations of Girard and Harbor Creek, and on June 19, 1850, between him and Sturgeonville.

During the interval of a year, Mr. Cornyn was employed in preaching in vacant churches, when, at his own request, he was dismissed from the Presbytery of Erie, with the view of connecting himself with the Presbytery of Wyoming. After this, Mr. Cornyn labored for a time in Troy, Pa., but failing health soon obliged him to retire from the active duties of the ministry. His disease developed into consumption, and he lingered until the 22d day of December, 1853, when he passed away from earth.

On the 21st day of March, 1848, Mr. Cornyn was united in marriage to Miss Eliza J. Frost, who, with two or three children, still survives him.

During his period of ill health, Mr. Cornyn prepared and published a work called "Dick Wilson, or the Rumseller's Victim," that was designed to illustrate the evils of intemperance. There were many noble traits in his character. Although not possessing that just balance that constitutes the fully rounded outline of a desirable character, he was yet generous, sympathizing, and kind. With an exuberant flow of beautiful language, and nice taste in the choice of words, he was well calculated to be an attractive public speaker. Yet withal there was a sluggishness of mind that kept him back from the highest excellence in his profession.

(71.) LEWIS W. WILLIAMS.

1840–1857.

Lewis W. Williams was descended from an old Pennsylvania family. He was the son of Hudson and Agnes (Gray) Williams. The name of his paternal grandfather was Lewis Williams, that of his maternal grandfather, William Gray. He was one of a family of five children, a son and daughter being older, and a son and daughter younger than himself. His father was a brother of the late Rev. Joshua Williams, D. D., of Newville, Pa.

Lewis W. Williams was born at Bellefonte, Centre County, Pa., on the 29th day of January, 1807. During his infancy, his parents removed from Bellefonte to the neighborhood of Milton, Pa. Here his father died in March, 1814. His mother survived until March 27, 1850. Lewis made a profession of religion in his nineteenth year, and united with the Presbyterian church of Milton.

The matter of the gospel ministry seems to have occupied his mind even before he made a public profession of religion. An older brother writes: "To my certain knowledge, it was his earnest wish, early in life, that Providence would open up the way for his receiving an education. From the time he commenced his studies, his mind was entirely set on preaching the gospel."

The means of accomplishing this desire were furnished by his brothers. After spending a number of years in teaching in the district schools, he commenced his classical studies in the Milton Academy. Here he prepared for the sophomore class, which he entered at Princeton College, in the fall of 1833. He was graduated in 1836, standing, in point of scholarship, among the first in his class. His theological studies were pursued in the Princeton Theological Seminary. He was licensed to preach the gospel by the Presbytery of Philadelphia, on the 21st day of April, 1840.

His first pastoral charge was at Indiana, Pa. The opening to that field seemed providential. He had been advised to spend a year in travelling as a missionary, for the purpose of recuperating his health, and was putting the advice to the practical test, when he stopped at Indiana to spend the Sabbath. The Presbyterian church at that place being vacant, he was invited to preach. He did so, and the congregation were so favorably impressed in regard to him, that they prevailed on him to abandon the idea of travelling and remain with them. The way seemed so plain, that their call was accepted, and he was ordained by the Presbytery of Blairsville, on the 12th day of May, 1841, as pastor of the church of Indiana, Pa.

During the early part of the following winter, his health became so much enfeebled that he was prevailed upon to take a tour to the South. His health not improving materially, his stay was protracted, and some misunderstanding having arisen, his pastoral relation was dissolved. On his return to Pennsylvania, the attachment was so strong between Mr. Williams and his people, that new calls were prepared for him. These calls were accepted, and on the 12th day of July, 1843, he was reinstalled.

But the new relation was not as pleasant as he had anticipated. His prospects of usefulness did not seem as good as before. On the 4th day of March, 1844, at his own request, the pastoral relation was again dissolved. This was perhaps an imprudent step. It is said that Mr. Williams ever afterwards regretted it himself.

About this time he was tendered a professorship in Washington College, Tennessee. This professorship was accepted, and he at once entered upon the discharge of its duties.

On the 20th day of October, 1844, he was united in marriage to Miss Mary Thompson, daughter of Mr. Samuel Thompson of Pittsburgh, Pa.

Owing chiefly to the delicate health of his wife, he resigned his professorship and returned to Pittsburgh, Pa., in the fall of 1845, and on the 8th day of January following, was called to mourn over the early death of his wife. She died at Pittsburgh, leaving an infant daughter, who afterwards received her own name — Mary Thompson.

During the summer following, he received an invitation to visit Greenville, Mercer County, Pa., within the bounds of the Presbytery of Erie. He became a member of the Presbytery of Erie on the 27th day of October, 1847, and labored in the congregation of Greenville as a stated supply for about two years.

The summer of 1848 was spent in supplying the churches of Rock Island and Camden, Ill.

On the 20th February, 1849, he was again united in marriage to Miss Caroline Larimore, daughter of Robert Larimore, Esq., of Columbus, Ohio.

His next field of labor was in Holidaysburg, Pa., where, assisted by his wife, who was an accomplished and successful teacher, he opened a male and female academy, which was carried forward with encouraging success for about two years. During this time he preached every third Sabbath at Martinsburg, a neighboring village.

But teaching, although to his taste, and pursued with profit, was not preaching the gospel, and he came to the conclusion that he must give up teaching at any sacrifice, even though but a bare pittance might be the consequence. It was the soul cry of the Apostle repeated, "Woe is me if I preach not the gospel."

In the fall of 1851, he received and accepted calls from the united congregations of Lower Path Valley and Burnt Cabins, in the Presbytery of Carlisle, where he was installed the following summer. He had previously been dismissed from the Presbytery of Erie on the 26th day of June, 1849, to the Presbytery of Huntington. In this new charge he continued for three years and a half, laboring faithfully and earnestly, and with much acceptance.

In the spring of 1855, he resigned his pastoral charge, and accepted calls to become the pastor of the united congregations of Landisburg, Center, and Upper, in Perry County, Pa. This was his last charge. Here he was greatly encouraged by the promises of usefulness that opened before him, and commenced his labors with great zeal and energy. After the death of a beloved little son in October, 1856, he was greatly depressed and discouraged, and in this state of mind, went to the Upper church to administer the Lord's Supper. The means of grace were accompanied by the gracious influences of the Holy Spirit, and a revival of religion was commenced that extended throughout his entire charge. The services were protracted for ten days. Then followed the usual exercises at Center, and the following week appointments were made for Landisburg. These labors were a severe tax on his physical system, but they greatly refreshed his own soul. He labored not only in his own charges, but assisted his brethren in other churches in the Presbytery. It is believed that his exhausting labors, performed under such exciting circumstances, during that winter, were the principal cause of the giving way of his physical constitution and his rapid decline, the following spring.

His last labor in the sanctuary was performed Sabbath, April 26, when he preached three times, at different places. His last text was peculiarly fitting for the closing work of the ministry, "Without holiness no man shall see the Lord." His discourse from these words was deeply solemn and impressive.

He returned home on Monday evening with a severe cold and sick headache. On Tuesday evening a physician was called, but for several days his symptoms were not considered alarming. But there was a voice that warned him that his life was ebbing. On the next Sabbath he remarked to his wife, " My feelings are not very fervent, but my faith is strong. I have no righteousness of my own to recommend me to the favor of God; but I will tell you what I have that is far better. I have a Saviour! His righteousness will give me a sure passport. How sweet the name of Jesus sounds! Jesus my Saviour!"

On Tuesday he was informed by his physician that he could not recover. "Yes, yes," he replied, "the Lord's will be done." The next evening, being that of the prayer-meeting, he remarked to a gentleman present, "Remember your pastor in your prayers. He has often prayed for you; now you must pray for him." He would frequently say, "My work is done. His service was my delight; but the Lord has nothing more for me to do. O that I could sing his praise; but my harp is all unstrung!"

His lips were moving until almost the last. He whispered of those who had gone before, that he expected soon to meet, and of those he was about to leave behind, with words of comfort for their cheer; and then the great work occupied his mind, — "an outpouring of the Spirit of God," he feebly articulated, and then closed his lips, until they were to be opened in singing the "new song" in the upper sanctuary.

He died of pneumonia, on the 7th day of May, 1857, in the fifty-first year of his age and seventeenth of his ministry. His remains rest in the little cemetery of the Center church.

Mr. Williams left a widow and four children. Mary T., daughter of his first wife, and three little boys, sons of his second wife, — Louis L., Hudson R., and Walter Lowrie.

He was of a nervous, sanguine temperament, subject at times to great depression of spirits, but always active and diligent in labor for Christ's cause. He was a fine writer, and always commanded attention in the pulpit, not only for the substance of the truth uttered, but for the manner of its delivery. His last days were his best days, for God set the seal of his Spirit to his work, and he passed away just at the close of a most precious revival.

(72.) LEMUEL P. BATES.

1820–1860.

LEMUEL P. BATES was the son of Lemuel and Lucy (Wait) Bates. He was born at Blandford, Mass., in December, 1791. His parents removed to Southampton, Mass., when he was quite young. His classical course was completed at Williams College, Mass., his theological at Princeton, N. J., where he graduated in 1822. In 1820, he was licensed to preach the gospel by the Hampshire Congregational Association of Massachusetts. In the year 1823, he was ordained by a council of Congregational ministers as pastor of the churches of Whately and Templeton, Mass.

In 1846, he removed to the West and became pastor of the Presbyterian church of Pontiac, Michigan, within the bounds of the Presbytery of Michigan. After laboring here for about one year, he went to Crawford County, Pennsylvania, and became a member of the Presbytery of Erie, on the 16th day of March, 1848, on certificate from the Presbytery of Michigan. In this Presbytery he became stated supply of the churches of Conneautville and Harmonsburg. This relation continued until 1850. On the 11th day of September, of that year he was dismissed from the Presbytery of Erie to connect himself with the Presbytery of Michigan.

Sometime after this, he connected himself with the Presbytery of New Lisbon, and labored in Utica, Ohio. After this he removed with some relatives to Illinois, and was for some time without charge, yet frequently preached as opportunity offered. In 1859, he took charge of the church at Edwardsville, Illinois, where he was laboring at the time of his last illness.

In 1823, Mr. Bates was united in marriage to Miss Eunice Edwards, daughter of Deacon Elisha Edwards of Southampton, Mass. Mrs. Bates died at Southampton in 1854. They had no children.

Mr. Bates excelled as a preacher. His theology was that of the older New England divines, and to this he adhered to the last. He was a fine writer, and generally had his sermons wrought out to a great degree of elegance. His ministry was successful, and many revivals occurred during his pastoral labors.

In his outward appearance there was much to attract the attention. He possessed great dignity of manners, rather solemn countenance, and mild expressive eye. He was withal of a cheerful, even genial disposition, and at all times a most welcome guest. He was remarkable for physical endurance. During his labors at Edwardsville, he spent much of his time at the home of his nephew, Rev. Dr. Taylor of Alton, Illinois. He would frequently walk the whole distance, twelve miles, and still not complain of fatigue. An incident, illustrating his physical strength and jovial, sunshiny disposition, is related by his friends. A young minister who was in the pulpit with him had prayed for the "aged brother, now in the decline of life." Some allusion being afterwards made to it, Mr. Bates replied, "I could whip *him* any day."

In regard to his last days upon earth, one [1] who watched

[1] Mrs. C. H. Taylor.

over him to the last is best qualified to speak: "His powers of physical endurance were remarkable, and when his last illness came upon him, he was wholly indisposed to yield to it; and did not give up the hope and expectation of recovery, until the day of his death. A partial unconsciousness came upon him unawares, and when aroused to answer an inquiry whether Jesus was near, he replied humbly but hopefully. He sang no note of triumph. As the spirit left the body, those of us who stood by him were electrified by the sudden illumination of his face. A radiant smile broke over every feature, as if a vision of delights unutterable had opened before him, and we felt that the golden gates were opened, and he had heard the plaudit — 'Well done, good and faithful servant.'"

His death took place at Alton, Illinois, of fever complicated with other diseases, on the 7th day of March, 1860, in the sixty-ninth year of his age, and fortieth of his ministry. The same loving pen quoted above relates further: "We have erected a stone to his memory in the cemetery in Alton, where his body lies. On it are inscribed these familiar and appropriate lines: —

> "Servant of God well done —
> Rest from thy sweet employ,
> The battle fought, the victory won,
> Enter thy Master's joy."

(74.) CHARLES V. STRUVÈ.

Mr. Struvè, was a native of Germany, and was a man of considerable scholarship. Soon after coming to the United States, he became connected with the Baptist Church. He had previously been a minister in some of the German churches of the Fatherland. He was received into membership of the Presbyterian church of Franklin in 1847, and on the 23d of June, 1848, he was received as a minister into the Presbytery of Erie. He labored for a time amongst the Germans in the bounds of the Presbytery, and in the autumn of 1849, removed to Saint Louis, Mo., where he died in the month of October, 1849. He left a wife and several children.

(77.) NATHANIEL MARCUS CRANE.
1836–1859.

NATHANIEL M. CRANE was the son of Oliver and Susannah Crane, and was born in West Bloomfield, New Jersey, on the 12th day of December, 1805. He was the child of pious parents, and was early instructed in the truths and practice of religion. He was designed for a tradesman by his parents, and was apprenticed at the age of fifteen. Making a profession of religion soon after this, his mind was directed to the ministry. He devoted himself to the work and employed the little means he had acquired by his industry in quiet preparation for it.

Having spent two years in Bloomfield Academy, he entered Williams College, Mass. Remaining here several sessions, his health gave way, when he travelled westward, and finding his health restored, entered Washington College, Pa., where he graduated in 1832. His theological studies were pursued in the Western Theological Seminary, Alleghany, Pa., and at Auburn, N. Y. During the progress of these studies, he decided to become a foreign missionary. He was licensed to preach the gospel, by the Presbytery of Cayuga, on the 13th day of April, 1836, and on the 6th day of July following was ordained by the same Presbytery, as a foreign missionary.

Soon after this he was married to Miss Julia A. Ostrander, and on the 13th day of November, 1836, in company with six other missionaries and their wives, set sail from Boston, to Southern India, to labor amongst the Hindoos. He was under the care of the American Board, and his point of labor Madura. Here he continued to labor for upwards of seven years, until his health failed under the enervating influences of the climate. His physician giving it as his opinion that he was beyond the hope of recovery in that climate, he reluctantly severed his connection with the mission and in December, 1844, set sail for home. He landed in Boston early in May, 1845.

After spending about two years in New Jersey amongst his friends, he removed with his family to Warren County, Pa., and engaged in agriculture. Continuing in this avocation for about two years, his health was so far restored that he was able to engage in preaching. On the 26th day of June, 1849, he was received as a member by the Presbytery of Erie, and preached as a stated supply to the congregations of Sugar Grove and Irvine. Here he labored for six years, with great self-denial, and in the face of many discouragements. His support was very inadequate, and the field one that would have severely taxed the energies of a minister in full health.

On the 27th day of June, 1854, he was dismissed from the Presbytery of Erie and connected himself with that of Clarion. He removed his family to Reimersburgh, Clarion County, Pa., and labored in the churches of Bethesda, New Bethlehem and Middle Creek. Over the former of these churches he was installed pastor in 1855, serving the others as stated supply.

In the autumn of 1857, he removed to the West, and spent the following winter in Illinois. The next spring he removed to Indian Town, Tama County, Iowa. This was his last field of labor. He preached here for eighteen months, when he was attacked by typhoid fever, and died September 21, 1859, in the fifty-fourth year of his age, and twenty-fourth of his ministry. His last words were, "I die in the faith of Jesus Christ. 'Tis sweet to die in Jesus."[1]

Mr. Crane was one of the purest of men. His character was a model of excellence in all the characteristics that adorn humanity. There was a meekness and quietness and humility about him that won the hearts of all that came in contact with him. He was at the same time dignified in person and polished in manners. He was throughout his whole life a missionary. In the destitute regions of Pennsylvania and on the prairies of the great West, he was a missionary, as well as under the burning sun of India. And in all places, and under all circumstances, he was distinguished for his sincere and earnest devotion to the gospel and the welfare of his fellow-men.

In person Mr. Crane was of medium stature, complexion rather dark, yet with a mild blue eye that kindled with animation in conversation and in public discourse. He was not fluent in discourse, nor was he free in the use of words even in conversation; yet he was social, friendly, and even genial as a companion.

One who was his companion on the ocean voyage and his associate for six years in the Madura mission, and who knew him most intimately, thus speaks of him :[2] "You have brought to my attention the name of the

---

[1] Wilson's *Presbyterian Historical Almanac*.
[2] Rev. F. De W. Ward, D. D.

purest, most symmetrical, and most excellent of men: one of whom it is difficult to speak as I would, without apparent exaggeration. My acquaintance with Mr. Crane covered more than six years, during which time our relations were intimate, as associates in the same missionary circle. He was, in its true meaning and strictest sense of the term, a gentleman. He was so innately, and without much artificial culture. I cannot recall the word or the act, that was aside from perfect propriety and good taste. As a Christian he was intelligent, thoughtful, calm, with no fitfulness, and little demonstration. What he believed to be right, he did with few words, and no parade of sacrifice. As a minister of the gospel, he was well informed in doctrine and ecclesiastics, with no claim to a mastery of theological and exegetical science. His discourses were written with a slow pen and carefulness of expression, were clear in style, instructive in matter, pious in spirit, and calculated to benefit the thoughtful hearer. As a missionary, he was fraternal in all his feelings towards his associates, ready to go to any place, and engage in any service assigned him. Though slow in acquiring the language, yet through catechists he did what he could for the parish placed under his care. He was greatly esteemed by all around him.

"Among the many who have gone to India in the service of the American Board, there have been persons of more masterly intellect, profounder scholarship, bolder enterprise, more effective oratory, and wider reputation at home; but for kindness of spirit, suavity of manner, singleness of purpose, true-hearted piety, and sincere desire to be and do right at all times and in all ways, Mr. Crane had no superiors, and few equals. I recall with greatest satisfaction, the days passed with him in traversing the villages of Southern India, on itinerating tours, with Bibles and Tracts, doing what we could in making known the name and claims of Messiah, the Saviour King.

"In Mrs. Crane, was found the faithful wife and mother, the endeared friend, and the useful missionary assistant."

Mr. Crane left a widow and six children, four daughters and two sons.

(85.) WILLIAM McCULLOUGH.

1852–1858.

DEATH came to this young brother in the very prime of life. He was younger in years, at the time of his departure, than any whose names had preceded his on the roll of the Presbytery of Erie.

William McCullough, the son of Alexander and ———— McCullough, was born near the town of Mercer, on the 15th day of October, 1824. He was probably baptized by Rev. Samuel Tait (3), the pastor of the church of which his parents were members, at the date of his birth. He was a child of the Covenant. And so we find him in early youth seeking the fold of the Good Shepherd, and consecrating himself to the service of the God of his fathers.

After preliminary studies at home, he entered Jefferson College, at which institution he graduated in 1849, with a reputation and a record that would be creditable to any young man in the land.

His theological studies were pursued at the Western Theological Seminary, where, at a meeting of the Presbytery of Erie, held at Evansburg, Pa., on the 15th day of September, 1852, he was licensed to preach the gospel. The trial exercises on this occasion were, first, a popular lecture on Heb. xii. 25–28; and second, a popular sermon on Phil. ii. 12, 13.

The numerous vacancies within the bounds of Presbytery, afforded a fine field of labor for the young licentiate during the next year, when, at a meeting of the Presbytery of Erie at Conneautville, Pa., on the 7th day of September, 1853, he was ordained as an evangelist, with the view of laboring as a missionary near the outlet of Lake Superior.

In these services, Mr. Sailor (79) preached the sermon, Mr. Eaton (76) presided, proposed the constitutional questions, and offered the ordaining prayer, and Mr. Reynolds (56) delivered the charge to the evangelist.

On the 15th of October, 1853, Mr. McCullough reached his contemplated field of labor. This was Saut Ste. Marie, at the outlet of Lake Superior. Here he continued to labor under many and sore difficulties, until a church was organized, and a house of worship erected for its accommodation.

In this remote place his faith and confidence in God kept him from despondency under his many discouragements. In one of his reports, he speaks of some of these discouragements: "Besides the general indifference and Catholicism which prevail here, I meet with various other errors, such as Universalism, Unitarianism, Swedenborgianism, etc." As to the "indifference," he mentions that some of the Board of Trustees of his church, had never even been out to hear him preach. But there was a brighter side to the picture. One of the first persons received into the church, on examination, was a man who had been long years before a member of the Presbyterian Church in Scotland. For thirty years he had been in the employ of the Hudson

Bay Fur Company, married to an Indian woman, and had had his home amongst the savages. But all these years, and under all these disadvantages, he had kept religion alive in his own soul, and like Abraham of old, had erected his altar and had bowed at its side wherever he had wandered, and wherever he had sojourned. Feeling the weight of years coming upon him, this strange man who had in youth wandered amid the heather and broom of old Scotia's hills, and in his manhood amid the bleak hills and eternal snows of Northwestern America, gathers together his household, and makes a journey of sixteen hundred miles, with a view of ending his days and leaving his family in the midst of Christian society. So grace reigns, and thus will it ultimately triumph.

But the missionary's health failed under the rigors of this inclement region, and with a sad heart he was forced to leave his little flock in the wilderness, and return to his home. Here he labored for some time with much acceptance in the congregations of Fairview, Sturgeonville, and Girard, although the state of his health precluded the idea of a permanent settlement. Sometimes, under these labors, he was ready to despond, and write bitter things against himself, as an unprofitable servant, but on receiving a member to the communion of the church of Fairview, who traced his religious convictions to his ministry, he rejoiced greatly, and said that this amply compensated him for all his labor for Christ.

His last labor upon earth was in collecting funds for the erection of Park Presbyterian Church, Erie, Pa. His disease was consumption, and when forced to retire from all labor by increasing weakness, he returned to his native home, and in the arms of his parents, he sweetly fell asleep in Jesus on the 1st day of February, 1858, in the thirty-fourth year of his age and sixth of his ministry.

Throughout his entire preparatory course, as well as during the years of his ministry, this young brother was subject to ill health, which paralyzed his energies, and filled him oftentimes with deep discouragement. In spirit, he was eminently peaceful and quiet; in personal faith strong, although his heart was often sad, as he looked out upon the fields white for the harvest, without the physical strength to enter upon the work. But the will, and the heart to labor, were accepted by the Master, and so he was called early to the rest and the reward, where the heart is never sad, and where "the inhabitant shall no more say, I am sick."

The subjoined faithful and loving tribute, is from the hand of an intimate friend and ministerial brother:[1] —

"It has been my privilege to walk hand in hand with William McCullough through every stage, from the commencement of his Christian journey. In the same social circle, the same preparatory studies, and the same ministerial labors, I have known him, not as companion knows companion, but as heart mingles with familiar heart. And everywhere I have witnessed from him a precious and beautiful lesson, which his life has furnished to all his acquaintance, — that of a character moulded by the truths which he professed. A distinguished Professor has portrayed 'Our Theology in its Developments,' by an intellectual view, which renders our system clearer to every human heart. But it was given to brother McCullough to illustrate that theology in the conformation of a personal Christian

[1] Rev. J. I. Smith.

character, which displayed the symmetry, completeness, and gospel likeness of the same system wrought out into actual life.

"His theological views seemed to be but the acceptance and transfer of Scriptural statements, without any trace of doctrinal formularies. He knew nothing of the intervention of human questionings between God's utterances and his implicit belief. Though familiar with the range of discussions, when he came to apply for wisdom to the Holy Scriptures, he appeared unconscious that there were opinions of others recorded. He drew near to listen only to the voice of the Most High. Nothing for a moment found respect with him, unless it was on the inspired pages of the Bible. If he saw it there, he transferred it at once to its appropriate place in his system, or applied it to its proper use upon the heart.

"It was truth prevailed so distinguishingly to form a complete religious character. No veil of distrust hung between God's utterances and his heart. Consequently his habits of devotion were the responsive feelings of his heart to truths so close and real to him. None could overhear his exercises in private, or join his prayers in public, without being impressed and profited by the freedom and directness of his intercourse with God. It was the language of a fully confiding soul, speaking to a present God and Father. Many who have heard him, have longed to attain his holy intimacy in prayer; but it was only the result of his habit of accepting every word at once from God's mouth, cherished by practice and baptized by the Holy Ghost.

"His entire character seemed to present a beautiful miniature of the gospel. Each truth which he embraced, seemed to germinate and grow into its corresponding trait, so forming the harmonious completeness of the Christian. In his work, he knew but one object and one degree of consecration to it — the measure of his life. He sustained uninterrupted cheerfulness, beneath the languor and discouragements of a most dispiriting form of disease. His work was speedily closed. His welcome, his rest, his reward soon reached."

(102.) ROBERT TAYLOR.

1861–1864.

ROBERT TAYLOR was a native of Ireland. He was born in Ballynarig, County Derry, on the 12th day of August, 1830. His parents moved in the humbler walks of life, yet were devotedly pious. In his infancy, his parents emigrated to this country and settled in Philadelphia. Here Robert enjoyed the careful religious training of a mother who, although often sorely afflicted, yet sedulously endeavored to discharge her whole duty to her household. To this son she was peculiarly attached; and for him her faith was unbounded. As he approached manhood, and at times seemed light and wayward and unpromising, her prophetic saying was, "My boy will live and yet be a minister of the precious One, who loved me and gave Himself for me."

He became a communicant in the Second Associate Reformed Church of Philadelphia, and by that church was enabled to prosecute his studies until he entered the University of Pennsylvania.

In this institution he gave promise of great excellence as a scholar and public speaker. There was a brilliancy and polish that shone out from his mind that was most attractive. But there was a change that came over him that filled his friends with apprehension and fear. The world became very attractive to him. The voice of pleasure was in his ear. The song of the siren attracted him until it seemed that he must be wrecked upon the rocks and devoured by the sea-monsters. He left the University in his junior year and engaged in business for a time; married, moved to Cincinnati, Ohio,[1] studied law, and was admitted to the bar. After this he removed to Mercer, Pennsylvania, and commenced practice, with eminent qualifications for success. But the voice of the siren still followed him, and although he knew her song was luring him to ruin, he could not break away from her influence. With surpassing gifts of reason and eloquence, he yet wasted his noble powers and threw away his influence. Others would undertake causes, engage his services before the jury, where he would appear with most persuasive eloquence and power, and themselves reap all the substantial benefits. Says one [2] who was a fellow member of the bar of Mercer, "I well remember the first time I met him as an antagonist. It was before a justice, and on the trial of a trifling case. Not over a dozen persons were present. The case was a plain one, and I was surprised that he spoke at all; much more so that he spoke as he did. I had never before heard a better argument, nor so much eloquence and beauty of diction in any trial, and before any court. His closing words were, 'Surely I ask nothing wrong when I only ask for justice!'

"He had accidentally left a manuscript in one of my books used at the trial. It contained the substance of his argument and the finest passages of his speech. I returned it to him with the remark, that he had made

---

[1] Wilson's *Presbyterian Historical Almanac*, 1865.
[2] Judge Trunkey.

too good an effort for such an occasion, 'No,' said he, 'when a man speaks, he should always try to speak well.' The preparation for this small case is an index to his character. I never knew him to speak without preparation when he had opportunity to prepare.

"When he closed his brief career at the bar, he stood in this community first for eloquence, among the first for power as an advocate and ability to arrive at correct conclusions on legal questions; and for beauty and finish of his legal papers and reports he had no peer. He loved study. He loved to write. He delighted in the classics and higher order of literature. Before he left the bar, I often thought how much nature and culture had done to fit him for a preacher of the gospel. His style of speaking seemed to me well adapted to the ministry — grave, earnest, and impressive. His mind was well stored with classical learning, and he seldom spoke without drawing therefrom to beautify and adorn his subject. His knowledge of English literature was very great.

"He reasoned much by analogy. No man could better illustrate his subject by appropriate comparisons. His imagination seemed to be boundless. His temperament was such that when composing he would write as though his audience were before him, thereby giving to his written addresses that spirit seldom reached in studied orations. His erudition and learning, always adorning and illustrating his theme, never rendered him pedantic."

But all this time the mercy and grace of God were following him. His waywardness and folly were always obvious to him; yet he began at last to see his danger, and resolve for better things. He was made to trace with an overflowing heart, the influence of a mother's prayers and the rich grace of a covenant-keeping God. The path of duty seemed plain. He sought once more the fold of the Church, and was received as a member of the First Presbyterian church of Mercer. The profession of law was relinquished, and he became a student of the Western Theological Seminary. On the 8th day of May, 1861, he was licensed to preach the gospel by the Presbytery of Erie.

Anxious to labor, as he remarked to a friend, where he could do the most good during his short life, he accepted an invitation to labor in Warren, Pa., and preached his first sermon to that people from the words: "Glory to God in the highest, and on earth peace, good will towards men." On the 13th of the following November, he was ordained and installed by the same Presbytery as pastor of the church of Warren. In these services John V. Reynolds, D. D., (56), preached the sermon, John R. Findley (92) delivered the charge to the pastor, and James M. Shields (88) the charge to the people. Here he continued to labor earnestly and with great acceptance, until September 26, 1862, when at his own request the pastoral relation was dissolved, and he dismissed to connect himself with the Second Presbytery of Philadelphia. He had resolved to accept a call to the Second Presbyterian Church of Germantown, Pa. He labored there with fidelity and earnestness. But he was not to continue long in that field. The North Presbyterian Church, Philadelphia, sought him for their pastor. The pressure was great. He loved his present charge. But the new field was large, and after earnest inquiry and prayer he determined to accept the new call. Accordingly arrangements were made to preach, on the following Sabbath, his farewell sermon in the one congregation in the morning and his introductory to the other in the evening.

But man's ways are not God's ways. Before the Sabbath dawned Mr. Taylor was upon a sick couch. From this couch he never rose. He gradually declined, until after a brief illness, in which he manifested eminent composure of mind and a calm and loving confidence in the Saviour whom he had preached and in whom he gloried as the Lord his righteousness, he gently entered into rest, April 15, 1864, in the thirty-fourth year of his age and third of his ministry. Life closed peacefully and calmly when he passed up to be with God.

Mr. Taylor was an eloquent preacher. People hung upon his lips with breathless attention from the opening sentence of his discourses until the close. Yet there was a humility and a meekness about him that were most beautiful and attractive. The same friend,[1] whose language is quoted above, says: "I did not often have the pleasure of hearing him preach. His sermons were all that I expected. I thought he appeared meek and humble, if not embarrassed. He could not have been unconscious of his ability and eloquence, but to me his manner betrayed a diffidence far beyond what I expected to see."

There is no doubt but that constant application and study wore out Mr. Taylor's life. He would never preach without the most elaborate preparation. His discourses must be wrought out with the most scrupulous care and attention. In Germantown he commenced lecturing on the Pilgrim's Progress, at his Wednesday evening prayer meetings. At first he took but little pains with the preparation of these lectures,

[1] Judge Trunkey.

but their fame soon spread, and people came to hear. Thus encouraged, he began to write out these lectures in full, thus increasing a burden that was already too great for his physical system. The mind and the body were illy mated, and the latter gave way under the nervous pressure of the former. It was the bright Damascus blade wearing away and cutting in sunder the scabbard that was illy adapted to its power.

In person Mr. Taylor was about the medium stature, dark complexion, dark brilliant eye, and generally manifested an abstracted air, as though his thoughts were far away. He was most unselfish in his disposition, and in his intercourse with others gentle, magnanimous, and forgiving. This was true even amid the bustle and excitement of trials and the confusion of courts. He always maintained the "suaviter in modo."

Early in life he was united in marriage to Miss Christiana, daughter of Thomas Pearson of Mercer, Pa., who survives him. They had no children.

NOTICES OF LIVING MINISTERS.

(30.) JOHN VAN LIEW, D. D.

1820 ——.

Dr. Van Liew is of Holland origin. He is the son of Dennis and Maria (Suidam) Van Liew, and was born in Neshannick, Somerville County, N. J., on the 30th day of September, 1798. His ancestors emigrated to this country with the early settlement of New York. His parents were married in 1789. John Van Liew's education, both classical and theological, was acquired in New Brunswick, N. J. He graduated at Queen's (now Rutger's) College in 1816, and studied theology at the Theological Seminary of the Reformed Protestant Dutch Church. He was licensed to preach the gospel by the Classis of New Brunswick, in June, 1820. In the summer of that year, he came to Meadville, and commenced his labors in the Presbyterian Church at that place. Here he was ordained by the Presbytery of Erie on the 22d day of August, 1821. In these exercises, Johnston Eaton (20) preached the sermon, and Amos Chase (25) delivered the charges. This relation continued until June 21, 1824, when, on account of impaired health, it was dissolved, and the next day Mr. Van Liew was dismissed to the Presbytery of Jersey.

In the spring of the next year, his health having improved, he accepted a call to the Presbyterian Church of Mendham, N. J. In the autumn of 1825, his health again failing, he took a tour to the Southern States, going as far as Georgia. After spending six months in the South, he returned, and soon accepted a call to the pastorate of the Reformed Protestant Dutch Church, in Readington, N. J. In this church he has labored faithfully and successfully for upwards of forty years.

On the 20th of June, 1827, he was united in marriage to Miss Ann M. Woodruff, daughter of Dr. H. S. Woodruff, of Mendham, N. J. They have three children.

Mr. Van Liew is of medium height, light hair and complexion, blue eyes, and rather slender form. His ecclesiastical connection is now with the Classis of Philadelphia, the most southern of any Classis in the Reformed Protestant Dutch Church.

(32.) DAVID McKINNEY, D. D.

1824 ——.

DAVID McKINNEY, the son of Isaac and Jane McKinney, was born in Mifflin County, Pa., October 22, 1795. In his infancy his parents removed to Center County, Pa., where he grew up to manhood. He graduated at Jefferson College in 1821, pursued his theological studies at Princeton, and was licensed to preach the gospel by the Presbytery of Philadelphia, in April, 1824. Soon after he went to Erie, Pa., where accepting calls from the church of that place, he was ordained and installed by the Presbytery of Erie, April 13, 1825. In these exercises, Timothy Alden (27) preached the sermon, and Samuel Tait (3) delivered the charges. This relation continued until April 22, 1829, when, at his own request, it was dissolved, and on the 21st of September, 1830, he was dismissed to the Presbytery of Huntington. Dr. McKinney resided eleven years in Center County, Pa. Seven of these years, from 1834 to 1841, he was pastor of the churches of Sinking Creek and Spring Creek. From 1841 to 1852, he was pastor of the church of Hollidaysburg, Pa. In 1852, he removed to Philadelphia, and established the " Presbyterian Banner." In 1855, he removed the "Banner" to Pittsburgh, Pa., and conducted it until 1864, when he established the "Family Treasure." He is at the present time Librarian and Treasurer of the Synodical Board of Colportage.

(36.) ABSALOM McCREADY.

1825 ——.

ABSALOM McCREADY was born in Washington County, Pa., on the 6th day of June, 1796. He graduated at Jefferson College, in 1824. His theological studies were pursued under the direction of Samuel Tait (3). He was licensed to preach the gospel by the Presbytery of Erie, on the 28th day of December, 1825. Having accepted calls from the churches of Middlebrook (formerly Upper Greenfield), Union, and Beaverdam, in Erie County, Pa., he was ordained by the Presbytery on the 14th day of September, 1826, and installed as pastor. In these exercises, David McKinney (32) preached the sermon, Samuel Tait (3) delivered the charge to the pastor, and Giles Doolittle (33) to the people. He was released from Middlebrook in 1833, and from Beaverdam and Union in 1835. In 1837, he was installed pastor of the church of Warren, Pa. This relation was dissolved in 1838. In 1839, he was installed pastor of the church of Neshannock. In 1845, he, with his church, was attached to the Presbytery of Beaver. The pastoral relation with the church of Neshannock was dissolved in 1858.

(39.) PETER HASSINGER.

1827 ——.

PETER HASSINGER, son of Peter and Jane Hassinger, was born near Newark, Delaware, on the 24th day of November, 1801. He is one of twins. His early life was spent in agricultural and mechanical pursuits. Always serious and thoughtful on the subject of religion, he made a public profession in his eighteenth year, and some months afterward began to consider the matter of the gospel ministry. He commenced his classical studies in his twentieth year at the Newark Academy. His theological studies were pursued at Princeton, after which he was licensed to preach the gospel by the Presbytery of New Castle, in April, 1827. He preached for a few months in the vacancies around Philadelphia, when he received a commission from the Board of missions to labor in Crawford and Erie counties, within the bounds of the Presbytery of Erie. On the first day of October, 1828, he was ordained and installed as pastor of the congregation of Gravel Run. Giles Doolittle (33) preached the sermon, Amos Chase (25) delivered the charge to the pastor, and David McKinney (32) the charge to the people. He preached in Waterford one third of the time in connection with Gravel Run. This relation was dissolved in 1832, when he preached for a time to the churches of Evansburg, Harmonsburg, and North Bank in Crawford County, Pa. In September, 1836, he was dismissed from the Presbytery of Erie to that of Washington, when he settled in Claysville, Pa. He resigned this charge in 1839, and settled in the church of Unity, in Blairsville Presbytery. He was afterwards settled at McVeytown, Huntingdon

Presbytery. In 1849, he removed to the West. In the West he has been preaching, distributing Bibles and Tracts, and engaged in other enterprises, looking to the welfare of Zion.

About the year 1831, Mr. Hassinger was united in marriage to Miss Anna S. Hyde, daughter of John and Mary Hyde, of New York city. She died on the 28th of March, 1855, uttering as her last words, " All will fail but Jesus." They had three children.

(40.) JAMES ALEXANDER, D. D.

1828 ——.

JAMES ALEXANDER, the son of William and Elizabeth Alexander, was born in Mercer County, Pa., on the 25th day of September, 1798. He was the first young man born in Mercer County, who was licensed to preach the gospel by the Presbytery of Erie. He made a profession of religion in his twenty-second year. Soon after, he began to think of the gospel ministry but was deterred by lack of means. Without a knowledge of this, a Ladies' Missionary Society in Mercer offered to assist him, when he commenced his studies. Having studied for a time at Mercer Academy, he repaired to Jefferson College, where he graduated in 1826. His theological studies were prosecuted under the direction of Samuel Tait (3), his pastor. He was licensed to preach the gospel by the Presbytery of Erie on the 9th day of April, 1828, and on the 13th of October, in the same year, was ordained and installed pastor of the churches of Greenville, Salem, and Big Bend. Johnston Eaton (20) delivered the charge, and Pierce Chamberlain (38) preached the sermon. This relation was dissolved June 25, 1834, and in the following January, he was dismissed to the Presbytery of Ohio. Dr. Alexander has labored with fidelity since that time in churches in Ohio and Virginia.

(41.) GEORGE A. LYON, D. D.

1828 ——.

Dr. Lyon was born in Baltimore, Md. He graduated at Dickinson College in 1824. His theological education was pursued at Princeton. He was licensed to preach the gospel by the Presbytery of Carlisle, on the 9th day of April, 1828. In December of the same year, he was invited to preach at Erie, Pa., in the First Presbyterian Church, where he was ordained and installed by the Presbytery of Erie on the 9th day of September, 1829. Giles Doolittle (33) preached the sermon, Wells Bushnell (35) and Thomas Anderson (37) delivered the charges. Dr. Lyon is still the pastor of this church. At the division of the Presbytery in 1838, he cast his lot with the New School branch.

(43.) GEORGE W. HAMPSON.

1830 ——.

Mr. Hampson was born in Huntingdon County, Pa. In early life his father, Robert Hampson, removed, with his family, to Harbor Creek, Erie County, Pa. George W. Hampson commenced his classical studies with Johnston Eaton (20), graduated at Jefferson College in 1827, and pursued his theological studies at Princeton. He was licensed to preach the gospel by the Presbytery of Erie, April 4, 1830. He was ordained by the same body, and installed pastor of the churches of Oil Creek (now Titusville) and Concord June 27, 1832. In these services, Giles Doolittle (33) preached the sermon, Johnston Eaton (20) and Thomas Anderson (37) delivered the charges. He was relieved of the charge of Concord in 1837. He also labored for a time at Cherrytree, and for many years has been pastor of the churches of Gravel Run and Cambridge, in Crawford County, Pa. At the division of the church in 1838, he adhered to the New School branch.

(46.) WILLIAM A. ADAIR.
1833 ——.

William A. Adair, the son of James and Mary (McCord) Adair, was born at Poland, Ohio. He graduated at Jefferson College in 1827. His theological studies were pursued in the Western Theological Seminary. He was licensed by the Presbytery of Hartford (now Beaver) on the 9th day of January, 1833. Having accepted calls from the congregations of North East and Harbor Creek within the bounds of the Presbytery of Erie, he was ordained and installed as their pastor by that Presbytery on the 7th day of November, 1833. In these exercises Johnston Eaton (20) preached the sermon, and James Alexander (40) and Pierce Chamberlain (38) delivered the charges. He was released from Harbor Creek in 1834, and from North East about 1837. After leaving Erie Presbytery he labored for a time in Alleghany City. He adhered to the New School branch at the division of the church in 1838.

(48.) SIMEON PECK.

1830 ——.

SIMEON PECK, son of Ebba and Margaret (Taggart) Peck, was born in Lebanon, Grafton County, N. H., on the 16th day of October, 1799. His literary studies were pursued at Hamilton College, N. Y., and his theological at Princeton. He was licensed to preach the gospel by the Presbytery of Oneida, in June, 1830. He was ordained by the Presbytery of Buffalo, at Carrol, Chautauque County, N. Y., in 1834. Mr. Peck's life has been a stormy one, owing to the times and circumstances under which he has exercised his ministry. He has labored successfully at Alden, Penfield, and Big Flats, N. Y., Salem, Ohio, Carrol and Otto, N. Y. On the 11th of May, 1836, he was received into the Presbytery of Erie, from that of Buffalo. In this Presbytery he labored at Harbor Creek, Evansburg, and Neshannock. In 1839, he was dismissed to the Presbytery of Philadelphia. There he labored in Milford and Millville, Pa., also along the Atlantic Coast in New Jersey.

In 1841, he turned his face towards the great West, laboring for a time at Findley, Lykens, Eden, Caroline, and Waynesburg, Ohio. In 1857, he removed again to the West, and pitched his tent at Omaha City, Nebraska. Here he has been laboring in the midst of poverty and sickness and self-denial, as few of the Lord's ministers are called to labor.

Mr. Peck has been twice married. His first wife was Miss Christiana Hollinshead, who died in 1845. His second wife was Miss Eliza Clark. Their children were thirteen in number, several of whom were called away in childhood. At two different periods in Mr. Peck's life, his house was burned, leaving him in poverty and suffering. His whole life in fact has been one of struggles and hardships. Yet withal, he has endured hardness as a good soldier of Jesus Christ, content with labor and toil and suffering here, in the Master's work, with the hope of rest and peace and triumph hereafter.

(49.) JAMES G. WILSON.

1833 ——.

Mr. Wilson was born in Dublin, Bucks County, Pa., January, 1806. His classical studies were pursued for a time at Doylestown and Newtown, where he entered Alleghany College, and graduated in 1829. He studied theology at the Western Theological Seminary, and was licensed to preach the gospel by the Presbytery of Erie, June 26, 1833. He preached for two years at Randolph, Crawford County, Pa. On the 12th day of October, 1836, he was ordained and installed pastor of the churches of Greenville and Salem, in Mercer County, Pa. In these services, Thomas Anderson (37) preached the sermon, and Samuel Tait (3) and Nathaniel West (47) delivered the charges. He was released from this charge of Greenville in 1841, and of Salem in 1851. He was also pastor of Cool Spring for a portion of his time, from 1842 to 1850. On the 1st day of October, 1850, he was dismissed from the Presbytery of Erie to that of Iowa, since which time he has been laboring in that Presbytery.

(50.) ROBINSON S. LOCKWOOD.

1834——.

R. S. LOCKWOOD, son of Nathan Lockwood, was born in Springfield, Windsor County, Vt. When he was twelve years of age, his father moved with his family to St. Lawrence County, N. Y. Here he commenced his classical studies. He graduated at Middlebury College in 1832. His theological studies were pursued in part privately, and in part at the Auburn Theological Seminary. He was licensed to preach the gospel by the Presbytery of St. Lawrence, in September, 1834. He was ordained by the Presbytery of Erie, and installed as pastor of the church of Girard, Pa., January 11, 1837. In these exercises, Nathaniel West (47) preached the sermon, and Johnston Eaton (20), and George A. Lyon (41), delivered the charges. He was released from this pastoral charge in 1841. Mr. Lockwood adhered to the New School branch, at the time of the division of the Church.

(51.) REUBEN LEWIS.

1836 ——.

MR. LEWIS was born in Indiana County, January 1, 1807. He graduated at the Western University, at Pittsburgh, in 1835. His theological education was completed at the Western Theological Seminary, and he was licensed to preach the gospel by the Presbytery of Blairsville, October 6, 1836. He was ordained by the Presbytery of Erie, November 1, 1837, and installed pastor of the church of Harbor Creek. He had labored previously as a missionary in the churches of Harmonsburg, Conneautville, and Big Conneaut, in Crawford County, Pa. He was released from the charge of Harbor Creek in 1840, and dismissed to the Presbytery of Ohio. He labored afterwards for a time at Fairmount, Va. He is now in connection with the Southern General Assembly.

(52.) WILLIAM FULLER.

1827 ——.

WILLIAM FULLER, son of Samuel and Mary (Huntington) Fuller, was born at Hampton, Conn., January 28, 1801. He graduated at Yale College in 1825. His theological studies were pursued in part at Yale, and completed at Princeton. He was licensed to preach the gospel by the Windham County Association, October 5, 1827. He was ordained by the same association, October 19, 1830. Much of his life and labors have been of a missionary kind. He labored at Bristol and Weston, R. I., and at Southhold, Long Island. In 1833, he took a tour west, as far as Louisville, Ky., preaching by the way. For the five succeeding years, he preached in different churches in New York and New England, when he settled in Conneaut, Ohio. In 1838, he became a member of the Presbytery of Erie. In 1842, he was connected with the Erie "Ladies' Seminary." In 1844, he removed to Michigan, where he has labored in various churches with considerable success.

In August, 1837, Mr. Fuller was united in marriage to Miss Margaretta Knox, of Carlisle, Pa. They have two sons.

(54.) DAVID WAGGONER.

1838 ——.

DAVID WAGGONER was born in Dauphin County, Pa. His literary studies were pursued in part at Jefferson College, and in part at the Western University of Pennsylvania, where he graduated. His theological studies were pursued at the Western Theological Seminary. He was licensed to preach the gospel by the Presbytery of Ohio, in 1838. Having accepted calls from the congregations of Georgetown and Fairfield, within the bounds of the Presbytery of Erie, he was ordained by that body on the 11th day of July, 1838. In these exercises, Wells Bushnell (35) preached the sermon, and Absalom McCready (36) and Robert Glenn (44) delivered the charges. He was released from these charges in 1853, when he became pastor of the church of Pulaski, in the Presbytery of Beaver. In 1864, he returned to the Presbytery of Erie, and was installed pastor of the churches of Georgetown and Greenfield.

(55.) DANIEL WASHBURN.

1825 ——.

DANIEL WASHBURN was born in South Brimfield, Mass., in the year 1792; graduated at Middlebury College in 1818, and was licensed to preach the gospel by the Presbytery of Bath, in 1825. He was ordained as an evangelist in 1831, by the same Presbytery. He was received by the Presbytery of Erie in 1839, and labored for a time at Evansburg, and was, in 1841, dismissed to the Presbytery of Wooster; thence he removed and became connected with the Presbytery of Zanesville.

In 1823 Mr. Washburn was united in marriage to Miss Elizabeth Diven.

(56.) JOHN VAN LIEW REYNOLDS, D. D.
1838 ——.

John V. Reynolds, son of John and Jane (Ellicott) Reynolds, was born in Meadville, Pa. He graduated at Jefferson College in 1834, studied theology at Princeton, and was licensed to preach the gospel by the Presbytery of Erie, April 18, 1838, and was ordained by the same body, and installed as pastor of the church of Meadville, November 13, 1839. Absalom McCready (36) preached the sermon, Samuel Tait (3) and Johnston Eaton (20) delivered the charges. Dr. Reynolds' charge has not changed to the present time.

(57.) EDMUND McKINNEY.

Mr. McKinney is a graduate of Washington College, and was licensed to preach the gospel by the Presbytery of Carlisle. He was received under the care of the Presbytery of Erie, October 12, 1839, and ordained by that body as an evangelist, November 13, of the same year. He was dismissed from the Presbytery of Erie, to that of Carlisle, September 15, 1841. He was a government chaplain during the war.

(58.) CYRUS DICKSON, D. D.
1839 ——.

Cyrus Dickson, son of William and Christiana (Moorhead) Dickson, was born in Harbor Creek, Erie County, Pa. He graduated at Jefferson College in 1837.

His theological studies were pursued privately. He was licensed to preach the gospel by the Presbytery of Erie, October 13, 1839, and ordained by the same Presbytery, June 24, 1840, and installed as pastor of the churches of Franklin and Sugar Creek. From the latter church, he was dismissed January 1, 1846, and from the former, March, 1848. At the latter date, he was dismissed from the Presbytery of Erie, to that of Washington. From 1848 to 1856, he was pastor of the Second Church, Wheeling, West Virginia, when he was transferred to the pastorate of Westminster Church, Baltimore, Md.

(59.) EDWARD SPENCER BLAKE.

1839 ——.

E. S. BLAKE was born in Westborough, Worcester County, Mass. He was graduated at Yale in 1835, studied theology at the Western Theological Seminary, and at Andover, and was licensed to preach the gospel by the Woburn Association in 1839. He was ordained by the Presbytery of Erie, April 14, 1841, and installed pastor of the churches of Gravel Run and Evansburg. Ill health compelled him to resign his charge at the close of one year, since which time he has been teaching, and engaged in secular business.

(60.) HIRAM EDDY.

1839 ——.

HIRAM EDDY was born in Pittsfield, Vt., in 1813. His literary studies were pursued at Hamilton College, N. Y., theological studies pursued privately. He was licensed and ordained by the Western New York Association; the former date was January 17, 1839, the latter May, 1840. He became a member of the Presbytery of Erie, in June, 1841, and was dismissed to Buffalo City in 1845. During the late rebellion, he served as a chaplain, and suffered imprisonment in Libby Prison.

(61.) JOSEPH T. SMITH, D. D.

1841 ——.

JOSEPH T. SMITH, son of Joseph Smith, was born at Mercer, Pa. He graduated at Jefferson College in 1837, studied theology privately, and was licensed to preach the gospel by the Presbytery of Erie, April 14, 1841. He was ordained by the same Presbytery, April 20, 1842, and installed pastor of the church of Mercer. He was released from this charge in April, 1849. At the same time, he was dismissed from the Presbytery of Erie, to that of Baltimore, where he became pastor of the Central Presbyterian Church, Baltimore.

(62.) JAMES COULTER.

1842 ——.

JAMES COULTER was born in Mercer County, Pa. He graduated at Jefferson College in 1839, studied theology at the Western Theological Seminary, and was licensed to preach the gospel by the Presbytery of Alleghany, in April, 1842. He was ordained by the Presbytery of Erie, September 14, 1842, and installed as pastor of the churches of Concord and Deerfield, in Venango and Warren counties. He was afterwards pastor of the churches of Sugar Creek, Harmonsburg, and Evansburg. On the 15th day of June, 1852, he was dismissed from the Presbytery of Erie to that of Alleghany, where he is still laboring.

(63.) HENRY WEBBER.

1843 ——.

HENRY WEBBER was born in Chester County, Pa. He graduated at Princeton, pursued his theological studies at the same place, and was licensed to preach the gospel by the Presbytery of Elizabethtown, in April, 1843. He was ordained by the Presbytery of Erie on the 20th day of January, 1843, and installed as pastor of the church of Greenville, Pa. He was released from this charge, October 16, 1844, and on the 22d of January following, dismissed from the Presbytery to that of Beaver. In this Presbytery, he labored for many years in the church of North Sewickley.

(64.) JAMES W. DICKEY.

1842 ——.

MR. DICKEY was born in Zanesville, Ohio. His literary studies were pursued at Hopewell Academy, and his theological under the supervision of Rev. Wm. Neill, D. D. He was licensed to preach the gospel by the Second Presbytery of Philadelphia, April 20, 1842, and ordained by the Presbytery of Erie, October 4, 1843, and installed as pastor of the churches of Conneautville, Harmonsburg, and Evansburg. In 1847, he was dismissed to the Presbytery of Richland, and became pastor of the church of Mansfield, Ohio. In 1854, he returned to the Presbytery of Erie, and has since been pastor of the churches of Gravel Run and Washington.

(65.) ALEXANDER CUNNINGHAM.

Mr. Cunningham, son of Thomas S. Cunningham, was born in Mercer, Pa., January 21, 1815, graduated at Washington College, Pa., in 1840, studied theology at the Western Theological Seminary, and was licensed to preach the gospel by the Presbytery of Erie, September 4, 1842, and ordained by the same, October 5, 1843, and installed as the pastor of the churches of Gravel Run and Washington. He was released from this charge in 1851, and dismissed to the Presbytery of Alleghany.

(67.) JOHN M. SMITH.

1837 ——.

Mr. Smith was born in Cannonsburg, Pa. He was for a time a student at Jefferson, but graduated at Washington College, in 1835. His theological studies were pursued at the Western Theological Seminary; licensed by the Presbytery of Redstone, June, 1837; ordained by the Presbytery of Ohio, in 1840, and installed pastor of the church of Mingo. In October, 1845, he became a member of the Presbytery of Erie, and on the 28th of January following, was installed as pastor of the church of Warren, Pa.; released from his charge August 11, 1847. He was dismissed from the Presbytery of Erie to that of Muhlenburg in March, 1848. Since that time he has been mainly engaged in teaching, although preaching as opportunity offers.

(69.) MILES T. MERWIN.

1841 ——.

Mr. Merwin was born in Milford, Conn., and graduated at Yale in 1828. His theological studies were pursued in part with the late Ichabod S. Spencer, D. D., and in part at Princeton. He was licensed October 13, 1841, by the Presbytery of New York; ordained by the Presbytery of Erie, June 24, 1846, and installed as pastor of the church of Irvine, Warren County, Pa., laboring at the same time at Sugar Grove and Warren. He was dismissed from the Presbytery of Erie to that of Huntington, October 28, 1848. Here he labored for a time. Afterwards he visited Florida, and remained for a time, travelling into Alabama, and preaching at vacant points. Of late years he has labored as a domestic missionary, wherever the field has opened before him.

(73.) LEMUEL GREGORY OLMSTEAD, LL. D.

1837 ——.

Dr. Olmstead was born in Saratoga County, N. Y., graduated at Union College, and pursued his theological studies at the Western Theological Seminary. He was licensed to preach the gospel by the Presbytery of Beaver, about the year 1837, and ordained by the Presbytery of Erie, April 20, 1848. He then visited Europe, sojourning in Rome for several years. His principal business has been teaching. During the War of the Rebellion he acted as chaplain for some three years. As a scientific scholar and antiquarian, Dr. Olmstead has had few equals amongst his brethren of the Presbytery.

(75.) JAMES HENRY CALLEN.

1848 ——.

Mr. Callen was born at Raphoe, Ireland, and emigrated to this country February 28, 1843. He graduated at La Fayette College, Pa., and pursued his theological studies at the Western Theological Seminary. He was licensed to preach the gospel by the Presbytery of Washington, April 19, 1848, and ordained by the Presbytery of Erie, October 25, of the same year, and installed as pastor of the church of Greenville. He was released from this charge June 23, 1852, and on the 12th of January following, dismissed from the Presbytery of Erie to that of Redstone. He was for a time pastor of the church of Uniontown, Pa.; thence he removed to New Jersey, thence to Brooklyn, L. I.

(76.) SAMUEL J. MILLS EATON.

1848 ——.

S. J. M. Eaton, son of Rev. Johnston and Eliza (Canon) Eaton, was born in Fairview, Erie County, Pa. He graduated at Jefferson College, in 1845, pursued his theological studies at the Western Theological Seminary, and was licensed to preach the gospel by the Presbytery of Erie on the 16th day of March, 1848. He was ordained by the same Presbytery on the 7th day of February, 1849, and installed as pastor of the churches of Franklin and Mount Pleasant, one third of the time in the latter place. He was released from the charge of Mount Pleasant, August 29, 1855, giving his entire time to Franklin. He was a member of the Christian Commission.

(78.) MICHAEL A. PARKINSON.

1849 ——.

Mr. Parkinson was born in Washington County, Pa. He graduated at Jefferson College in 1846; studied theology at the Western Theological Seminary; licensed to preach the gospel by the Presbytery of Ohio April 18, 1849, and ordained by the Presbytery of Erie, September 11, 1850, and installed as pastor of the congregations of Concord and Deerfield, the former in Venango County, and the latter in Warren County, Pa. He was released from this charge October 20, 1854, and dismissed to the Presbytery of Steubenville, in whose bounds he became pastor of the church of Island Creek. Lately he has been transferred to the church of Bloomfield in the same Presbytery.

(79.) JOHN SAILOR.

1847 ——.

Mr. Sailor was born in Carlisle, Pa., graduated at Dickinson College; studied theology at the Union Theological Seminary; licensed to preach the gospel by the Presbytery of Harrisburg, April 12, 1847, and ordained by the Presbytery of Pennsylvania, in June, 1848. He was received from that Presbytery into that of Erie, September 10, 1850. On the 4th of May, 1853, he was installed as pastor of the congregation of Warren, Pa., released from his charge August 29, 1855, and on the next day dismissed to the Presbytery of St. Joseph. Here he took charge of the Congregational Church of Michigan City. He is at present pastor of the church of Allegan, Michigan.

(80.) ROBERT SLEMMONS MORTON.

1848 ——.

Mr. Morton was born in Beaver County, Pa., graduated at Jefferson College in 1845; studied theology at the Western Theological Seminary; licensed to preach the gospel by the Presbytery of Beaver, June 14, 1848, and ordained by the same Presbytery, June 10, 1851, and installed as pastor of Mount Pleasant. On the 10th of June, 1851, he was received into the Presbytery of Erie, and on the 10th of September following, was installed as pastor of the congregation of Mercer. He was released from this charge September 14, 1852, and on the day following, dismissed to the Presbytery of Blairsville.

Since that time he has been pastor of the churches of Ebensburg, Mill Creek and Hookstown, and Slippery Rock and Newport, Pa.

For a time during the War of the Rebellion he was Chaplain of the 140th Pennsylvania Volunteers, having been previously in the Christian Commission.

(81.) WILLIAM WILLSON.

1850 ——.

Mr. Willson was born in Alleghany County, Pa.; graduated at Muskingum College, Ohio; studied theology at the Western Theological Seminary; licensed by the Presbytery of Ohio, June 19, 1850; ordained by the Presbytery of Erie, June 11, 1851, and installed as pastor of the congregations of Girard, Sturgeonville, and Fairview. He was released from this charge May 2, 1855, and on the 26th of September, 1857, dismissed to the Presbytery of Kansas; since which time he has been laboring successfully to build up the kingdom of Christ in that new State. For a part of the time during the War of the Rebellion he was an army chaplain.

(82.) JOHN WESLEY McCUNE.

1851 ——.

Mr. McCune was born in Mercersburg, Pa.; graduated at Marshall College in 1846; studied theology at the Western Theological Seminary; was licensed by the Presbytery of Carlisle, June 11, 1851; ordained by the Presbytery of Erie, June 23, 1852, and installed as pastor of the churches of Cool Spring and Sandy Lake, in Mercer County, Pa. He was released from the latter charge, February 7, 1855, and at the present time labors a third of his time in the congregation of Salem, in connection with Cool Spring. He was a delegate of the Christian Commission.

(83.) DAVID GRIER.

Mr. Grier is a native of Ireland. He was received from the Presbytery of Wyoming, September 7, 1853; installed as pastor of the congregation of Greenville, January 18, 1854; released April 13, 1859; dismissed to the Presbytery of Carlisle, September 28, 1860. Here he was pastor for a time of the congregation of Dickinson, but finally returned to Ireland.

(84.) GEORGE WRIGHT ZAHNISER.

1851 ——.

Mr. Zahniser was born in Mercer, Pa.; graduated at Jefferson College in 1846; studied theology at

Princeton; licensed to preach the gospel by the Presbytery of Erie April 10, 1851; ordained by the same Presbytery, September 7, 1853, and installed as pastor of the congregation of Conneautville, in Crawford County, Pa. He was released from this charge on the 13th of April, 1859, and dismissed to the Presbytery of Huntington, when he became pastor of the church of Huntington.

(86.) ROBERT F. SAMPLE.
1852 ——.

Mr. Sample was born at Painted Post, N. Y.; graduated at Jefferson College in 1849; studied theology at the Western Theological Seminary; licensed to preach the gospel by the Presbytery of Northumberland, June 8, 1852; ordained by the Presbytery of Erie, October 18, 1853, and installed as pastor of the church of Mercer; released from his charge May 7, 1856, and dismissed the same day to the Presbytery of Carlisle; pastor of the church of Bedford, Pa., until 1857; at present pastor at St. Anthony, Minn.

(87.) JAMES IRWIN SMITH.
1853 ——.

Mr. Smith was born in Mercer County, Pa.; graduated at Jefferson College in 1851; studied theology at the Western Theological Seminary; licensed to preach the gospel by the Presbytery of Erie, September 8, 1853; ordained by the same Presbytery, as an evangelist, August 29, 1854. He labored as a missionary at Ontonagon on Lake Superior, for upwards of ten years. He is at the present time a domestic missionary, located at La Crosse, Wisconsin.

(88.) JAMES M. SHIELDS.

1854 ——.

Mr. Shields was born in Indiana, Pa.; graduated at Washington College; studied theology at the Western Theological Seminary; licensed by the Presbytery of Blairsville, April 11, 1854; ordained by the Presbytery of Erie, August 29, 1855, and installed as pastor of the congregations of Georgetown and Fairfield; released from his charge February 23, 1864, and dismissed to the Presbytery of Alleghany City, where he became pastor of the congregation of Bridgewater.

(88.) WILLIAM J. ALEXANDER.

1854 ——.

Mr. Alexander was born in Mercer County, Pa.; graduated at Jefferson College in 1852. Studied theology at the Western Theological Seminary; licensed to preach the gospel by the Presbytery of Erie, January 18, 1854; ordained by the same Presbytery December 19, 1855; and installed as pastor of Concord and Deerfield, in Venango and Warren Counties; released from his charge January 7, 1857; on the 13th of April, 1858, dismissed to the Presbytery of Washington, where he became pastor of the congregation of West Union. Mr. Alexander is a nephew of Rev. James Alexander, D. D. (40), a former member of Erie Presbytery. He was a delegate of the Christian Commission.

(90.) CHARLES A. BEHRENDS.

Mr. Behrends is a native of Germany. He was received into the Presbytery August 13, 1856, on papers setting forth that he was in connection with a German Synod. These papers being found defective, his name was stricken from the roll August 12, 1857.

(91.) WILLIAM M. BLACKBURN.

1854 ——.

Mr. Blackburn was born in Carlisle, Indiana; graduated at Hanover College, Indiana, in 1850; studied theology at Princeton; licensed to preach the gospel by the Presbytery of New Brunswick, April, 1854; ordained by the Presbytery of Lake, in 1855; received by the Presbytery of Erie, January 7, 1857; installed as pastor of Park Church, Erie, on the 25th of May following; released from his charge December 22, 1863, and dismissed to the Presbytery of New Brunswick, where he became pastor of the Fourth Church, Trenton, N. J. Mr. Blackburn is the author of numerous Sabbath-school books.

(92.) JOHN ROSS FINDLEY.

1852 ——.

Mr. Findley was born in Washington, Ohio; graduated at Madison College; studied theology at Oxford, Ohio; licensed to preach the gospel by the Associate Reformed Presbytery of Chilicothe, April 9, 1852; ordained by the Associate Reformed Presbytery of Springfield, August, 1853; received into the Presbytery of Erie, April 29, 1857, from the Presbytery of Sydney;

and installed the same day as pastor of the First church of Mercer. Mr. Findley is son of Rev. Dr. Findley, of the United Presbyterian Church, and has three brothers in the ministry. He was a delegate of the Christian Commission.

(93.) JOHN R. HAMILTON.

1858 ——.

Mr. Hamilton was born in Westmoreland County, Pa.; graduated at Washington College in 1853; studied theology at the Western Theological Seminary; licensed to preach by the Presbytery of Blairsville, April 15, 1858; ordained by the Presbytery of Erie, June 15, 1859, and installed as pastor of the congregations of Fairview and Sturgeonville; released from his charge June 15, 1864; September 28, 1865, dismissed to the Presbytery of Washington. He is at present pastor of the congregation of Newark, Del. During the War of the Rebellion, Mr. Hamilton was for a time chaplain of the 145th Regiment Penn. Vols.

(94.) JOHN DAGG HOWEY.

1858 ——.

Mr. Howey was born at Carrollton, Ohio; graduated at Jefferson College in 1856; studied theology at the Western Theological Seminary; licensed by the Presbytery of Steubenville, April 14, 1858; ordained by the Presbytery of Erie, September 21, 1859, and installed as pastor of the congregations of Mill Creek and Sugar Creek, in Venango County, Pa.; released from his pastoral charge April 26, 1865; dismissed to the Presbytery of Columbus, April 25, 1866.

(95.) IRA MILLER CONDIT.

1858 ——.

Mr. Condit is the son of John and Mary (Zahniser) Condit, and was born at Georgetown, Pa.; graduated at Jefferson College in 1855; studied theology at the Western Theological Seminary; licensed to preach the gospel by the Presbytery of Erie, April 14, 1858; ordained by the same Presbytery, September 24, 1859, as an evangelist. In the autumn of the same year, he sailed to China, as a missionary of the Presbyterian Board. He is at the present time in this country. He is a grandson of Rev. Ira Condit (24), one of the fathers of the Presbytery.

(96.) ANTHONY CANON JUNKIN.

1854 ——.

Mr. Junkin was born in Green County, Ohio; graduated at Miami University in 1852; studied theology at Oxford, Ohio; licensed by the First Associate Reformed Presbytery of Ohio, April 5, 1854; ordained by the Associate Reformed Presbytery of Boston, May 7, 1856; received into the Presbytery of Erie, April 10, 1860, from the Presbytery of Baltimore; installed as pastor of the congregation of Greenville, June 10, 1862, and released from his charge May 8, 1867. He was a delegate of the Christian Commission.

(97.) HUEY NEWELL.

1848 ——.

Mr. Newell was born in Centre County, Pa.; pursued his studies at Jefferson College, and the Western Theological Seminary; licensed to preach the gospel by the Presbytery of Clarion, April, 1848; ordained by the same Presbytery in April, 1849. He labored for a time in Clarion County, Pa.; afterwards in Iowa. He was received into the Presbytery of Erie, April 11, 1860, from the Presbytery of Iowa.

(98.) GEORGE SCOTT.

1859 ——.

Mr. Scott was born in Hancock County, West Virginia; graduated at Jefferson College in 1856, studied theology at the Western Theological Seminary; licensed to preach the gospel by the Presbytery of Washington, in April, 1859; ordained by the Presbytery of Erie, June 27, 1860, and installed as pastor of the congregations of Greenfield, Evansburg, and Harmonsburg; released from his charge, June 10, 1862; dismissed to the Presbytery of Steubenville, September 26, 1863.

(99.) JAMES HILLIAR SPELMAN.

1850 ——.

Mr. Spelman was born at East Granville, Mass.; graduated at Williams' College; studied theology privately; licensed to preach the gospel by the Presbytery of North River, April 17, 1850; ordained by the Presbytery of Franklin, June 2, 1852; received into the Presbytery of Erie, April 8, 1861, from the Presbytery of Hudson; dismissed to the Presbytery of Washington, April 13, 1864.

(100.) JOHN GORDEN CONDIT.

1860 ——.

Mr. Condit is the son of William Condit, and the nephew of Rev. Ira Condit (24), and was born in Mercer County, Pa.; graduated at Jefferson College; studied theology at the Western Theological Seminary; licensed to preach the gospel by the Presbytery of Erie, April 11, 1860; ordained by the same Presbytery, June 26, 1861; installed pastor at Sandy Lake, and stated supply at Mount Pleasant, 1863; released 1864; dismissed September 26, 1864, to the Presbytery of Fairfield; stated supply at Salina, Iowa.

(101.) JOHN HASKELL SARGENT.

1856 ——.

Mr. Sargent is the son of Winthrop Sargent, of Philadelphia; born in Gloucester, Mass.; graduated at Dartmouth in 1852; studied theology at Princeton; licensed to preach the gospel by the Presbytery of Philadelphia, April, 1856; ordained by the Presbytery of Erie, June 26, 1861; stated supply at Concord and Deerfield; dismissed to the Presbytery of Londonderry, September 23, 1863.

(103.) NEWELL SAMUEL LOWRIE.

1861 ——.

Mr. Lowrie was born in Montour County, Pa. ; studied theology at the Western Theological Seminary ; licensed to preach the gospel by the Presbytery of Saltsburg in 1861 ; ordained by the Presbytery of Erie, October 22, 1862, and installed as pastor of the congregations of Conneautville and Harmonsburg. He was a delegate of the Christian Commission.

(104.) JAMES HERVEY GRAY.

1861 ——.

Mr. Gray was born in Ross County, Ohio ; studied theology at the Western Theological Seminary ; licensed to preach the gospel by the Presbytery of Alleghany City, April, 1861 ; ordained by the Presbytery of Erie, October 22, 1862 ; dismissed to the Presbytery of Clarion, April 25, 1866.

(105.) WILLIAM T. HAMILTON, D. D.

1823 ——.

Dr. Hamilton is a native of England ; licensed to preach the gospel by the Presbytery of Philadelphia, October, 1823 ; ordained by the Presbytery of Jersey July 24, 1824 ; restored to the ministry by the Presbytery of Erie, April 15, 1863 ; name removed from the roll, April 26, 1865. He was for a time pastor of the church of Warren, Pa.

(106.) WILLIAM PORTER MOORE.

1857 ——.

Mr. Moore was born at Tarentum, Pa.; graduated at Jefferson College in 1855; studied theology at the Western Theological Seminary; licensed to preach the gospel by the Presbytery of Blairsville, October 8, 1857; ordained by the Presbytery of Clarion; received into the Presbytery of Erie, from that of Clarion, September 26, 1863; stated supply at Oil City, Pa. During a portion of the War of the Rebellion, Mr. Moore was chaplain of the 142d Regiment, Penn. Volunteers.

(107.) GEORGE FAIRES CAIN.

1861 ——.

Mr. Cain is the son of George Faires and Rebecca (McCaffrey) Cain, and was born in Cumberland County, Pa. He was a student of Dickinson College, Pa., and for seven years a member of the Carlisle Bar. He was licensed to preach the gospel by the Presbytery of Carlisle, November 9, 1861; ordained by the Presbytery of Newton, and installed as pastor at Stroudsburg, Pa., May 28, 1863; received into Erie Presbytery from that of Newton, April 13, 1864; installed as pastor of Park Church, Erie, on the 11th of May following.

(108.) WILLIAM MARSHALL ROBINSON.

Mr. Robinson, son of John and Jane Scott (Marshall) Robinson, was born in Indiana County, Pa.; graduated at Jefferson College in 1841; studied theology at the Western Theological Seminary; licensed to preach the gospel by the Presbytery of Blairsville, June 19, 1844; ordained by the Presbytery of Zanesville, January, 1846; stated supply for ten years at Hebron and Brownsville, Ohio; pastor at Newark, Ohio, for seven years; stated supply at Wellsburg, West Virginia; received into the Presbytery of Erie, from that of Washington, June 14, 1864; installed pastor of the Second Church, Mercer, June 15, 1864. He was a delegate of the Christian Commission.

(109.) LUTHER MARTIN BELDEN.

1863 ——.

Mr. Belden was born at Sandisfield, Mass.; graduated at Washington College, in 1861; studied theology at the Western Theological Seminary; licensed to preach the gospel by the Presbytery of Redstone, April, 1863; ordained by the Presbytery of Erie, December 14, 1864; installed pastor of Sturgeonville and Westminster.

(110.) JOHN RICE.

1849 ——.

Mr. Rice was born at Paisley, Scotland; graduated at Glasgow; studied theology at the Seminary of the Associate Reformed Church, Scotland; licensed to preach the gospel by the Presbytery of Paisley, August, 1849; received into the Presbytery of Erie from that of Saltsburg, April 26, 1865; stated supply of Fairfield and Sandy Lake.

(111.) HENRY BRUIN LAMBE.

1860 ——.

Mr. Lambe is a native of Ireland; licensed to preach the gospel by the Presbytery of Alleghany City, September, 1860; ordained by the Presbytery of Erie, July 11, 1866, and installed as pastor of the church of Milledgeville, Pa.; released from his charge May 8, 1867; dismissed to the Presbytery of Blairsville, June 26, 1867. Mr. Lambe was a chaplain during the War of the Rebellion, and suffered imprisonment at the hands of the enemy in Texas.

(112.) JAMES JUNIUS MARKS, D. D.

1835 ——.

Dr. Marks is the son of the late General William and Alice Anna (Hanson) Marks, of Alleghany County, Pa.; graduated at Jefferson College in 1831; studied theology at the Western Theological Seminary; licensed to preach the gospel by the Presbytery of Ohio, May, 1835; ordained by the Presbytery of Palmyra, February, 1838; received into the Presbytery of Erie, October 23, 1866, from the Presbytery of Ohio. Dr. Marks was chaplain of the 63d Regiment Pennsylvania Volunteers during the War, and was for a time a prisoner of war in the hands of the enemy.

(113.) ROBERT STANSBURY VAN CLEVE.

1865 ——.

Mr. Van Cleve was born at Beaver Meadow, Pa.; graduated at Princeton College in 1863, and Princeton

Seminary in 1866; licensed to preach the gospel by the Presbytery of New Brunswick, April, 1865; ordained by the Presbytery of Erie, December 14, 1866; dismissed to the Presbytery of Buffalo, May 8, 1867; pastor of the congregation of Westfield, New York.

(114.) JOHN J. GRIDLEY.

1837 ——.

Mr. Gridley was born at Chesterfield, N. H.; graduated at the Wesleyan University; licensed to preach the gospel by the Methodist Episcopal Church, January 14, 1837; ordained by the same, June, 1840; received into the Presbytery of Erie, May 8, 1867.

(115.) JAMES JONES SMYTH.

1844 ——.

Mr. Smyth was born in Londonderry, Ireland. He is the son of William and Jane (Crawford) Smyth. He was graduated A. B., at Trinity College, Dublin, in 1839, and A. M., at Glasgow University in 1840, and pursued his theological studies at Glasgow and Edinburgh. He was licensed to preach by the Presbytery of Winchester, April 21, 1844; ordained by the Presbytery of East Hanover, April 15, 1849. He was principal of Winchester Academy, and of Petersburg Institute in Virginia, for many years. Afterwards was pastor at Sussex Court House, Virginia; stated supply in North Carolina; also pastor at Greensboro, North Carolina. Afterwards was stated supply at Shelbyville, Indiana; at the present time stated supply at Pleasantville and Concord, Erie Presbytery.

(116.) DAVID PATTON.
1865 ——.

Mr. Patton is the son of Archibald and Elizabeth S. Patton, and was born in Mercer County, Pa. He graduated at Jefferson College in 1860, was a student for a time at the Western Theological Seminary, and completed his theological course at the Reformed Seminary at Philadelphia. After this he was in the Army of the United States for upwards of three years, when he was licensed to preach the gospel by the Pittsburgh Reformed Presbytery, on the 19th day of May, 1865. On the 27th day of June, 1866, he was ordained by the same Presbytery, and installed as pastor of Cochranton and Shenango congregations. On the 25th day of September, 1867, Mr. Patton, together with his congregation, Cochranton, were received under the care of the Presbytery of Erie.

PART III.

HISTORICAL NOTICES OF CHURCHES.

CHURCHES.

MOUNT PLEASANT.

This church is in Beaver County, Pa., near to the present town of Darlington. It was probably organized by Rev. Thomas Edgar Hughes (1), in the year 1798 or 1799. It is, moreover, probably the first church that was organized within the ancient bounds of the Presbytery of Erie. Its first pastor was Mr. Hughes, installed August 28, 1799, in connection with New Salem. He was released from his charge of Mount Pleasant, November 19, 1840. He was succeeded by Rev. William D. Smith. The next pastor was Rev. Arthur B. Bradford, who was released from his charge in 1845, or 1846. The next pastor was Rev. R. S. Morton (80), ordained and installed June 14, 1848; released from his charge in 1851. The next pastor was Rev. J. Watson Johnston, installed in 1853, released from his charge in 1856 or 1857. He was succeeded by Rev. A. W. Boyd. The present pastor elect is Rev. Albert Dilworth. It is now under the care of Beaver Presbytery.

NEW SALEM.

This was one of the early churches. Rev. Thomas Edgar Hughes was pastor from 1799 to 1808. After this, it was long vacant. Rev. Ezekiel Glasgow was installed August 31, 1813; died, April 23, 1814. The next pastor was Rev. William Reed, ordained and installed April 11, 1821; released in 1860. Rev. D. L. Dickey is now pastor.

YOUNGSTOWN, OHIO.

This is one of the oldest churches within what was anciently the Presbytery of Erie. The early records are lost. It is probable that it was organized about the year 1800. The first pastor was Rev. William Wick (2), who was ordained September 3, 1800. He was installed at Youngstown, Ohio, in the summer of 1801, having been settled for a time at Neshannock. He labored at Youngstown, Ohio, and Hopewell, then in Mercer County, Pa. He continued to be pastor of these churches until his death, March 29, 1815. The second pastor was Rev. John Core,[1] installed pastor, June 25, 1817, in connection with Brookfield, Ohio. He was released, April 10, 1823, after a successful pastorate of six years, during which over one hundred were added to the church.

After Mr. Core's removal, Rev. Enoch Bouton supplied the church until 1826. He was succeeded by Rev. Nathan Harned (34), who labored there until 1826. In 1830, Rev. Ward Stafford was installed as pastor. He was released in 1837. Rev. C. A. Boardman succeeded Mr. Stafford, and commenced his labors in 1838 or 1839. He terminated his labors in October, 1854. He was succeeded by Rev. Frederick H. Brown, who supplied the church until 1859, but was not regu-

---

[1] Afterwards in Clarion Presbytery; born, 1785; licensed, 1816; died, May 17, 1854.

larly installed. On November 9, 1859, the present pastor, Rev. Levi B. Wilson, was installed as pastor. The old people of the church speak of revivals of religion in the years of the past. In later years, 1858, 1862, and 1866, were years of the power of the Most High.

Previous to 1831, the congregation worshipped in a log building. In 1826, or 1827, a brick building was commenced, but never finished. In 1831, a frame building of modest pretensions was completed and occupied. During the year 1866, a large, commodious brick structure was commenced, that will soon be completed. The congregation, at the division of the church, adhered to the branch popularly known as the New School.

HOPEWELL.

THIS church is in Lawrence County, Pa., and is one of the earliest churches organized in the bounds of the old Presbytery of Erie. The date of its organization is not now known, but it was toward the close of the last century. The first pastor was Rev. William Wick (2), who was ordained and installed by the Presbytery of Ohio, September 3, 1800, in connection with Neshannock. Mr. Wick was pastor until his death, March 29, 1815. The next pastor was Rev. William Wood (10), who commenced his pastorate, in connection with Neshannock, March 11, 1816; released, June 25, 1829. He was succeeded by Rev. William Nesbit, who was ordained and installed, October 7, 1829; released, October 6, 1840. The next pastor was Rev. Henry Webber (63); installed, April 11, 1849; released, June 29, 1853. Rev. William Nesbit was again installed in May, 1854; released, April 6, 1858. The present pastor, Rev. James P. Fulton, was installed

May 28, 1867. This church is under the care of the Presbytery of Beaver.

BEAVER.

This congregation was under the care of the Presbytery of Erie, at a very early day. In 1808, it passed to that of Beaver, and in 1854, to that of Alleghany City. The first pastor was Rev. Ezekiel Glasgow;[1] ordained and installed, August 31, 1813; died, April 23, 1814. He was succeeded by Rev. William McLain, who was installed April 7, 1824. It has been served successively by Rev. A. B. Quay, Rev. B. C. Critchlow, Rev. W. G. Taylor, and others, as stated supplies. The present pastor is Rev. D. P. Lowary.

COOL SPRING.

This church is in Mercer County, Pa., and was organized by Rev. Samuel Tait (3), most probably in the year 1800, as he was ordained its first pastor, November 19, of that year. This was in connection with the church of Salem. Mr. Tait continued to preach a portion of his time at Cool Spring, until 1813, when, by some arrangement between that congregation and Mercer, the people of Cool Spring agreed to worship at Mercer, and Cool Spring became practically disbanded. This arrangement continued until 1827, when, on petition of the people of Cool Spring, the church was reorganized.[2] On the 24th day of June, 1829, Rev. Ira Condit (24) was installed pastor for the one third of his time. This relation continued until his death, October 24, 1836.

[1] Born in Beaver County, 1788: Jefferson College, theology with Dr. McMillan; licensed, October 17, 1810.
[2] Min. ii. 227.

Rev. David Waggoner (54) then supplied the church for a short time, giving them one third of his time. The next pastor was Rev. James G. Wilson (49), installed in 1842, in connection with Salem, one half his time at each. This pastorate continued until 1850. The present pastor, Rev. John W. McCune (82) was ordained and installed June 23, 1852, in connection with Sandy Lake; one half his time to each. At the present time, he gives two thirds of his time to Cool Spring. The church edifices have manifested a gradual improvement in architecture. The account of the first building has been given. The people now occupy the third church edifice, a comfortable and neat structure. This church has been blessed with many revivals.

SALEM.

This church is also in Mercer County, Pa., and is first known as Upper Salem. It was organized in 1800. The first sermon in this congregation was preached on the banks of the Shenango, near where Greenville now stands. Mr. Tait preached the first Sabbath, and Mr. Stockton (4) the next. After this, preaching was enjoyed at a tent near the site of the present Salem church. At the organization, J. Stinson, Robert Mann, and Samuel Williamson, were the first ruling elders. Mr. Tait was ordained the first pastor, November 19, 1800, in connection with Cool Spring.

This arrangement continued until the 28th of June, when Mr. Tait was released, giving half his time to Mercer. In June, 1813, Mr. Tait relinquished Cool Spring, and gave a portion of his time to Salem, until the year 1826, when he gave the whole of his time to Mercer. On the 13th of October, 1828, Rev. James

Alexander (40) was ordained and installed as pastor of Salem, in connection with Greenville and Big Bend. He was released from this charge, June 25, 1834.

On the 12th of April, 1836, Rev. James G. Wilson (49) was ordained and installed as pastor, in connection with Greenville. He was released in 1851. Rev. James H. Callen (75) supplied the church for a short time, also, Rev. T. P. Johnston, until 1857. In 1858, Rev. James Coulter (62) supplied it, and in 1859, Rev. David Grier (83). It is supplied at the present time by Rev. John W. McCune (82).

MERCER, FIRST.

The church of Mercer was organized in 1804, with twenty members. Rev. Samuel Tait was the first pastor. He preached but a portion of his time here, until January, 1826, when he gave Mercer the whole of his time. He continued the pastor until his death, June 2, 1841.

The second pastor was Joseph T. Smith (67). He was born and raised in Mercer, and ordained and installed April 20, 1842. He was released, April 18, 1849, after a pastorate of seven years. The third pastor was Rev. Robert S. Morton (80). He was installed, September 10, 1851, and released, September 14, 1852. The fourth pastor was Rev. Robert F. Sample (86). He was ordained and installed, October 18, 1853; released, May 7, 1856. The present pastor, Rev. John Ross Findley (92), was installed April 29, 1857. Many revivals of religion have rendered beautiful the history of this church.

The first place of worship was in a room over the jail. After some time a brick house was erected, but being considered unsafe, was abandoned after some years. The present structure was erected in 1830, but has since been remodeled and greatly improved.

MEADVILLE.

This church is in Crawford County, and was probably organized in 1800. Elisha Macurdy and Joseph Stockton (4) had preached here the year before. The first elders were John Cotton, Robert Stockton, and a third, whose name has passed away. Mr. Stockton, then in his twenty-first year, was called to be the first pastor. He was ordained by the Presbytery of Ohio, on the 24th of June, 1801, and installed as pastor of the congregations of Meadville and Little Sugar Creek [1] (now Cochranton). One half his time was given to each. He was released from these charges June 27, 1810.

The second pastor was Rev. Robert Johnston (14). He was installed, October 15, 1811, as pastor of Meadville, Little Sugar Creek, and Conneaut (now Evansburg). This relation was dissolved April 2, 1817. The third pastor was Rev. John Van Liew (30). He was ordained and installed August 22, 1821. He gave the whole of his time to Meadville, and was released from his charge, June 21, 1824. The fourth pastor was Rev. Wells Bushnell (35). He was ordained and installed June 22, 1826. The pastoral relation was dissolved June 26, 1833. The fifth pastor was Nathaniel West (47), installed May 11, 1836; released from his pastoral charge, June 26, 1838. The present pastor is John Van Liew Reynolds, D. D. (56); ordained and installed November 13, 1839. Of those who have sus-

---

[1] This church connected itself with the Associate Reformed Church about 1820.

tained the pastoral relation to this church, besides the present incumbent, one only survives — Dr. Van Liew.

From the installation of Dr. Reynolds in 1839, the session remained unbroken for twenty-five years, without increase or diminution. At the division of the church in 1838, the Meadville church was divided, forming a second church, of the other branch. Of this church, Rev. Richard Craighead has long been the pastor.

AMITY.

This church is in Venango and Mercer Counties, and was organized probably about 1800. The first pastor was Rev. Robert Lee (5); ordained and installed, June 26, 1801, in connection with Rocky Spring.[1] He was released from his pastoral charge, July 14, 1807. After this, Rev. John Boyd (11) supplied Amity for a short time, and the second regular pastor was Rev. Ira Condit (24). His pastorate extended from the close of 1825 to April 22, 1829, when he was released. His salary was at the rate of three hundred dollars a year. He served this church for the one third of his time. After this, Rev. Hezekiah May supplied the church for one year; after him, Rev. Nathaniel R. Snowden for a year.

The next regular pastor was Rev. Robert Glenn (44). He was ordained and installed as pastor of Amity and Mill Creek, one third of his time at each, on the 12th day of September, 1832. He was released from the charge of Amity, April 3, 1850, after a pastorate of eighteen years.

The next pastor was Rev. Meade Satterfield, son of

[1] This church connected itself, at an early day, with the Associate, or Associate Reformed Church.

Rev. James Satterfield (6), one of the original members of the Presbytery of Erie. He was ordained and installed about the year 1850, in connection with Harrisville. He preached at Amity about six years, when he was called to his rest above. The next pastor was Rev. John F. Boyd. He was installed about the year 1856, and continued pastor ten years, being released June 26, 1866. The present pastor is Rev. W. D. Patton, commencing his labors about the close of the year 1866.

This church has had an exciting history. Always in advance on the subject of slavery, they hesitated not to enter their protest against the acts of Presbytery and General Assembly, when not sufficiently awake to the subject.

This congregation worshipped at first in the green wood, with a simple tent for the minister. They would sit in the beating rain and even snow, during the time of service and not become impatient. On one occasion during communion services, a rain-storm commenced that bid defiance to umbrellas, and literally flooded the ground until the water was several inches deep. The first house of worship was of round logs, about twenty-two feet square, and built in a day. The next was of hewn logs, thirty feet square. This house burned down. It was the work of an incendiary. The present house is a frame forty-five by fifty-five feet, built at a cost of $1,300.

This church has been blessed with numerous revivals. In the early days they had the "falling exercise," when the people could hardly be persuaded to leave the church or go to their homes. Within the past few years it has been greatly blessed. Amity is now under the care of the Presbytery of Alleghany.

NESHANNOCK.

This congregation is in Mercer and Lawrence counties, Pa. It was organized about the year 1800. The first pastor was Rev. William Wick (2), ordained September 3, 1800, in connection with Hopewell. He was released from his charge June 30, 1801. The next pastor was Rev. James Satterfield (6), an original member of Erie Presbytery. He was ordained and installed by the Presbytery of Ohio, on the 3d of March, 1802, and installed as pastor of this congregation in connection with that of Moorfield. The first elders were William Jackson, Thomas Scott and Robert Stevenson. Mr. Satterfield was the pastor until the beginning of the year 1813. In July of that year, Rev. William Matthews took charge of the church and continued to serve it until 1815. He was succeeded by Rev. William Wood (10). Mr. Wood commenced his labors March 11, 1816. He labored at Hopewell in connection with Neshannock, until July 1, 1828, when he give all his time to the latter. He was released January 1, 1837, after a pastorate of twenty-one years.

The next pastor was Rev. Absalom McCready (36). He was installed October 14, 1839, and released from his charge in 1857. The next pastor was Rev. Robert Dickson, installed 1858, released from his charge 1867. The present pastor is Rev. John M. Mealy.

The first house of worship was of round logs, thirty feet square, with a hole in the centre of the roof through which the smoke ascended. The next building was of hewn logs, thirty feet by seventy. In 1839, the present fine frame building was erected. Many revivals have blessed this church, the most important in the winter of 1866–67.

FAIRFIELD.

This congregation is in Mercer County, Pa., and is one of the oldest in the Presbytery. It was organized in September, 1799, by Elisha Macurdy and Joseph Stockton. The first elders were Daniel Axtell, David Condit, and Ithiel Dodd. These men came from Washington County, Pa., and arrived with their families at the place of their destination on Saturday evening. They camped out, and on the Sabbath morning held the first prayer-meeting, read a sermon, and catechized the children. That prayer-meeting has been kept up to the present day, and is blessing that congregation still. The first pastor was Rev. William Wylie (7). He was ordained by the Presbytery of Ohio, April 13, 1802. He was released from his pastoral charge, December 5, 1804. He had preached at Upper and Lower Sandy,[1] in connection with Fairfield. In 1804, the number of communicants was twenty-six. The next pastor was Rev. Cyrus Riggs (18). He was ordained and installed pastor of Fairfield and Mill Creek, October 21, 1807. He was released from this charge April 8, 1812.

The next pastor was Rev. Ira Condit (24). He was ordained and installed, November 8, 1814, in connection with Big Sugar Creek. He was released by death, October 24, 1836, after a pastorate of twenty-two years.

The next pastor was Rev. David Waggoner (54). He was ordained and installed, July 11, 1838, in connection with Georgetown. He was released from his charge, May 4, 1853. The next pastor was Rev. James M. Shields (88), ordained August 9, 1855. He was

---

[1] Now Georgetown and Mill Creek.

released February 23, 1864. Rev. John Rice (110) is at present stated supply.

The "falling exercise" was experienced in the early days of this church. Many revivals of religion were enjoyed. On one occasion at a singing-school, the singing was abandoned, Mr. Condit sent for, and the whole night spent in prayer. A church of the other branch was at one time organized from this congregation and that of Georgetown.

UPPER SANDY, now GEORGETOWN.

This church is also in Mercer County, Pa. It was organized by Elisha Macurdy and Joseph Stockton in 1799. The first elders were William Byers and Alexander McCracken. The first pastor was Rev. William Wylie, settled April 13, 1802, released December 5, 1804. After this Mr. Stockton, pastor at Meadville, supplied them one third of the time for one year; Mr. Johnston also supplied them for one year. The elders removing about this time, the organization became extinct. About the year 1814, it was reorganized under the name of Georgetown, when Mr. Condit became their pastor, ordained and installed, in connection with Fairfield, November 8, 1814. Mr. Condit was released by the Master, and entered into rest, October 24, 1836. Mr. Waggoner was the next pastor. He was installed July 11, 1838; released from his charge, May 4, 1853. The next pastor was Rev. James M. Shields, ordained and installed, August 9, 1855; released from his charge, February 28, 1864. In May, 1864, Mr. Waggoner returned, and was installed again as pastor, for two thirds of his time, Greenfield taking the remaining third.

In Mr. Condit's time this church was blessed with an interesting revival of religion. At a later day there was a revival in 1841, another in 1843, and a much more extensive one in 1848. During the last year there were added to the church about fifty persons.

LOWER SANDY, now MILL CREEK.

This congregation is in Venango County, Pa. It was organized about the same time with Upper Sandy and Fairfield, namely, about 1800. Mr. Wylie was the first pastor: ordained and installed, April 13, 1802; released from his charge of the united congregations of Upper and Lower Sandy and Fairfield, December 5, 1804. At the first organization of the churches, the same session was appointed for both, but on the 11th of March, 1802, it was resolved to have a separate session for each.

Mr. Riggs was the second pastor: ordained and installed pastor of Mill Creek (Lower Sandy) and Fairfield, October 21, 1807; released from his charge, April 8, 1812. About the beginning of his pastorate the name of the congregation was changed to Mill Creek, the present name. In 1810, there were nineteen members.

There is a chasm in the history of this church, that cannot be filled up. It seems to have become disorganized, the members probably worshipping at Fairfield and Sugar Creek. The late Rev. Robert Glenn records, that "The church of Mill Creek was organized in the fall of 1827, by Rev. Ira Condit and Ezekiel Condit,[1] Elder, at the house of John Gorden, there being as yet no meeting-house. By a vote of the congrega-

---

[1] Brother of the former.

tion, the two oldest members were chosen elders, namely, John Gorden and James Adams. In a short time after, the congregation feeling the necessity of having a house to worship in, and not being able to hire a workman to build one, resolved to build a house with their own hands, there being several of them acquainted with the use of tools." The work was accomplished with little expense save their own labor.

Under its reorganization, Robert Glenn (44) was the first pastor. He was ordained September 12, 1832, in connection with Amity and Sandy Lake, giving one third of his time to each. He served Mill Creek for one third of his time until September, 1850, and one half his time during the remainder of his life. He died September 6, 1857, after a pastorate of twenty-five years.

The next pastor was John Dagg Howey (94). He was ordained and installed as pastor in connection with Sugar Creek, September 21, 1859; released from his charge April 26, 1865.

SLATE LICK.

This congregation is in Armstrong County, Pa. When it was organized is now uncertain. Its first pastor was Rev. John Boyd (8). He was ordained and installed as pastor, in connection with Union, on the 26th day of June, 1802; released from his charge, April 17, 1810. For nearly five years, the church was dependent on supplies. The second pastor was Rev. John Redick (26). He was ordained and installed over the same charge as his predecessor, September 28, 1815, and labored in the same field until the close of the year 1848, when he resigned on account of old age. He died July 11, 1850, after a pastorate of thirty-three years in Slate Lick and Union. He was succeeded in Slate Lick by Rev. William F. Kean, who was ordained and installed as pastor of Slate Lick and Freeport, in the spring of 1849. He was released from the charge of Slate Lick in June, 1864. The present pastor, Rev. Thomas C. Anderson, was ordained and installed October 17, 1865.

UNION (Armstrong County).

The history of this church is almost identical with that of Slate Lick. Probably organized about the same time, it continued to enjoy the labors of the same pastor, until the close of Father Redick's ministry. About the year 1857, Rev. David Hall became the pastor in connection with Brady's Bend. He was released from his charge in 1867.

PYMATUNING, BEULA, AND TRUMBULL.

These congregations constituted the original charge of Rev. Benjamin Boyd, and all seem to have become extinct. They were situated near the boundary line of Ohio and Pennsylvania. Mr. Boyd was installed over them November 12, 1806, and was dismissed in 1809. These churches seem to have declined soon after. The names of Beula and Trumbull do not appear on the roll after the year 1810; and Pymatuning is not mentioned after 1813. The membership was probably drawn to churches springing up in more favorable localities in the neighborhood.

BULL CREEK.

This congregation was a portion of the original charge of Rev. Abraham Boyd (9), who was its first pastor. There is a tradition amongst the old members of the church, that it was organized as early as 1793 or 1794. Mr. Boyd himself believed it to be the oldest church west of the Alleghany River. It is located in the neighborhood of Tarentum, Pa. Mr. Boyd was ordained and installed as pastor of this church, in connection with Middlesex, on the 17th of June, 1802. Dr. McMillan was present, and preached the sermon on the occasion. Mr. Boyd continued to be the pastor until the spring of 1833, preaching his farewell sermon June 30 of that year. This congregation has furnished four ministers of the gospel.

The next pastor was Rev. Samuel Caldwell, installed October, 1834. The next minister was Rev. J. Watson Johnston, who was stated supply for one year. In the fall of 1840, Rev. Thomas W. Kerr was installed as pastor. He was released by death, October 29, 1847. The next pastor was Rev. James M. Smith. The next was Rev. William G. Taylor, installed January 19, 1857; released from his charge, May 1, 1861.

Rev. G. W. Jackson was the next pastor, ordained and installed June 23, 1863. Mr. Jackson was pastor but a short time. The present pastor, Rev. John Fulton Boyd, a relative of the first pastor, was installed November 19, 1866, for two thirds of his time. This congregation worshipped for several of the first years of its existence in a grove. The first house of worship was erected in 1801.

MIDDLESEX.

This too is one of the early churches in the history of the Erie Presbytery. Abraham Boyd was installed as its first pastor June 17, 1802; released from his charge in 1817. The next pastor was Rev. Reid Bracken (19), installed September 28, 1820; released from his charge in 1832. Rev. J. W. Johnston was pastor three or four years. Rev. Thomas W. Kerr was pastor until his death, October 29, 1847, after a pastorate of seven years. Rev. Ephraim Ogden, the present pastor, was installed in 1848 or 1849.

MOUNT NEBO.

The name of this church first appears on the minutes in 1805. The first pastor was Rev. Reid Bracken (19). He was ordained and installed by the Presbytery of Erie, April 20, 1808. He continued to minister to this charge until 1844, nearly thirty-seven years, and only resigned through infirmity. Rev. Lemuel F. Leake was pastor in 1847 and 1848. Rev. Alexander Cunningham (65) was pastor from 1853 to 1861. The present pastor, Rev. William P. Harvison, commenced his labors in 1864. The church is now under the care of the Presbytery of Alleghany.

PLAIN.

This church was long connected with Mount Nebo, in the support of a pastor. The first pastor was Rev. Reid Bracken (19): ordained and installed by the Presbytery of Erie, April 20, 1808; released from his charge, November 7, 1819. The next pastor was Rev.

John Moore, installed in 1828; released from his charge, April 5, 1831. Rev. L. R. McAboy was pastor until 1859. The last pastor, Rev. John W. Potter, was ordained and installed in 1864; died, 1866. The church is now under the care of the Presbytery of Alleghany City.

POLAND, OHIO.

This church is in Mahoning County, Ohio, and under the care of the Presbytery of New Lisbon, Synod of Wheeling. It is said to have been organized May 21, 1802, by Rev. Wm. Wick, by direction of the Presbytery of Erie. The first pastor was Rev. Nicholas Pittinger (15), ordained, October 24, 1824, and installed as pastor, in connection with Westfield, Pa., one half his time in each congregation. He was released from his charge, March 20, 1810.

The next pastor was Rev. James Wright, ordained and installed, June 26, 1816, in connection with Westfield. He was released from his pastoral charge, January 10, 1832. The next pastor was Rev. John W. Scott,[1] ordained and installed, April 3, 1834, by the Presbytery of Beaver; released from his charge, April 13, 1836. The next pastor was Rev. Edwin H. Nevin, installed, June 25, 1839; released, April 20, 1841. The next pastor was Rev. Joseph Kerr, installed November 27, 1843; released, 1854. The present pastor, Rev. Algernon Sydney MacMaster, D. D., was installed November, 1854.

The people worshipped first in the grove, then in a log-house, then in a frame. In 1857, a fine brick edifice was erected. The church has had its troubles, yet can say, "Hitherto hath the Lord helped us."

[1] Rev. J. W. Scott, D. D., late President of Washington College, Pa.

WESTFIELD.

This church is in Lawrence County, Pa., and at present under the care of the Presbytery of Beaver. It was organized in the former part of the year 1803,[1] by Rev. Thomas E. Hughes, by direction of the Presbytery of Erie. The first elders were George Baird, John Hunter, and John Clark. The first communion service was held in 1803, by Mr. Hughes and Mr. Wick (2). The first pastor was Rev. Nicholas Pittinger (15). He first began to preach in this congregation in the autumn of 1803, and brought his family out the following spring. He was ordained and installed by the Presbytery of Erie on the 24th day of October, 1804, in connection with Poland, Ohio, one half his time in each. Difficulties having arisen in the congregation, he was released from his charge, September 13, 1809. The church was then vacant for nearly six years. The next pastor was Rev. James Wright, ordained and installed June 26, 1816, in connection with Poland. This connection continued until 1831, when Westfield called Mr. Wright the whole of his time. He served Westfield until January 12, 1842, when, on account of infirmity, he resigned his charge. On the 30th of March, 1843, he entered into his rest, and was interred near the church where he had preached the Word for so many years.

The next pastor was Rev. Algernon Sydney MacMaster, D. D. He was installed, April 12, 1843, for the whole of his time. At his own request, he was released from his pastoral charge, November 9, 1854.

The next pastor was Rev. Thomas G. Scott. He was ordained and installed by the Presbytery of Beaver,

[1] Dr. Dilworth.

September 8, 1857; released from his charge, June 19, 1860.

The present pastor, Rev. William M. Taylor, was raised in the bounds of the congregation, and was ordained and installed June 12, 1861.

At the time of its organization, there were but twenty-two members; there were, in 1867, two hundred and thirty-six. Numerous revivals have been enjoyed. The "falling exercise" was noticed to some extent. The first place of preaching was the grove. Walter and George Clark gave each an acre of ground for church purposes. Here a log-house was erected. Afterwards a frame building was erected, that served until 1830, when a substantial brick edifice was erected. This gave place recently to the fine structure in which the people now worship. To this people the lines have fallen in pleasant places. It was under the care of the Presbytery of Erie until 1808, when the Presbytery of Beaver was erected.

PLAINGROVE.

This congregation is in Mercer County, Pa., and was probably organized between 1796 and 1800. The first elders were William McNeel and Joseph Campbell.

The first pastor was Rev. William Wood (10). He was ordained and installed as pastor of Plaingrove and Center, November 3, 1802, by the Presbytery of Erie. Dr. McMillan was present, and by invitation, delivered the charges to the pastor and people. He was released from the pastoral charge of Plaingrove, October 7, 1816. During his pastorate, there were cases of the "falling exercise."

The next pastor was Rev. John Munson (28). He was ordained and installed as pastor, February 28,

1818. He was released February 5, 1818. The present pastor, Rev. Robert B. Walker, D. D., was ordained and installed April 2, 1839. The church had at that time a membership of one hundred and seventy-six. This church has been blessed with many revivals. It is now under the care of the Presbytery of Alleghany.

CENTER.

THIS church has much the same history as Plaingrove. First pastor, Rev. Wm. Wood; installed, November 3, 1802; released from his charge, August 24, 1808.

The second pastor was Rev. John Munson, ordained and installed February 25, 1818; released, June 28, 1859, after a pastorate of forty-one years. He was succeeded by Rev. W. W. McKinney, who was installed in 1861; pastoral relation dissolved in June, 1865. The present pastor is Rev. S. A. Hughes, installed on Tuesday preceding the first Sabbath of November, 1866. It is also under the care of the Presbytery of Alleghany.

UPPER GREENFIELD, afterwards MIDDLEBROOK.

THIS was one of the earliest churches organized in Erie County, Pa., and had the first church edifice erected in the county.[1] It was organized in the year 1801, by Elisha Macurdy and Joseph Stockton. The first pastor was Rev. Robert Patterson (13). He was ordained and installed pastor, in connection with Lower Greenfield, or North East, by the Presbytery of Erie, on the 1st September, 1803. The pastoral relation was dissolved April 22, 1807. The next year it appears on the minutes as Middlebrook.

[1] Miss Sanford's *History*, 171.

For the next twenty years, this congregation appears to have been dependent on supplies sent by the Presbytery. The next pastor was Rev. Absalom McCready (36), who was ordained and installed on the 14th of September, 1826, serving this church in connection with Union and Beaverdam. He was released from the charge of Middlebrook, September 11, 1833.

In the mean time, the village of Wattsburg had sprung up in the neighborhood, and in the year 1833 a church was organized there from the membership of Middlebrook, and from that time it began to decline. From 1846 to 1848, Rev. Pierce Chamberlain (38) frequently preached there ; but it continued to decline, until April 30, 1859, when a committee of Presbytery of the other branch dissolved the church and attached its members to Wattsburg. It was the second church organized in Erie County, and the first to erect a church edifice. An account of this edifice is given in another place. It was standing a few years ago, but in the last stages of dilapidation. The church organization and the old building decayed together, and soon the very place where the people worshipped God for sixty years, will have been forgotten. Thus the rushing hosts of the present trample over the sacred memorials of the past.

HILANDS.

This church, in the neighborhood of Pittsburgh, once owed allegiance to the Presbytery of Erie. At the beginning of the present century, Rev. John Andrews, editor of the "Pittsburgh Recorder," and Rev. N. R. Snowden, preached there. It was probably organized in 1800. Rev. Robert Patterson (13) acted as stated supply from 1807 to 1833. The first regular pastor was Rev. Joseph Reed, who was installed in 1834; released in 1839. In 1840, Rev. J. Watson Johnston was installed as pastor; released in 1849. Rev. James R. Smith was installed as pastor in October, 1851; released in 1854. The present pastor, Rev. M. L. Wortman, was ordained and installed as pastor in January, 1859, in connection with the church of Long Island. At the present time, the whole of Mr. Wortman's time is given to the Hilands church. The name is derived from Robert Hilands, one of the prominent elders of the church, now gone to rest. It is now under the care of the Presbytery of Alleghany City.

LOWER GREENFIELD, now NORTH EAST.

This congregation is on the Lake Shore, in Erie County, Pa. It was organized by Elisha Macurdy and Joseph Stockton, in 1801. The church was organized in the woods, and this continued to be the place of worship for some time. The first pastor was Robert Patterson (13), ordained and installed by the Presbytery of Erie, September 1, 1803, for one third of his time; released from his pastoral charge, April 22, 1807. There was a long period succeeding this without a pastor. Rev. John McPherrin (16) supplied them for six months in 1812. Then Rev. Johnston Eaton (20) supplied them one fourth of his time in 1815–16. In 1818, Rev. Phineas Camp (29) supplied for a time; then Judah Ely, a licentiate, for a time.

The next pastor was Rev. Giles Doolittle (33). He was ordained and installed by the Presbytery of Erie, April 14, 1825; released from his charge September 14, 1832. The next pastor was Rev. W. A. Adair (46). He was ordained November 7, 1863; released from his charge in 1837. The next pastor was Rev. Nathaniel West (47). His pastorate extended from June, 1838, to July 17, 1841. Rev. Miles Doolittle served from 1842 to 1844. Then Rev. Samuel Montgomery in 1844; then Rev. Mr. Paine in 1848; then Rev. Mr. Cochran in 1850; then Rev. D. D. Gregory in 1852; then Rev. A. H. Carrier in 1859. Mr. Carrier was succeeded by the present pastor, Rev. T. B. Hudson. At the division of the church in 1838, this church adhered to " the other branch."

SCRUBGRASS.

This church is in Venango County, Pa., and at present under the care of the Presbytery of Alleghany. It was organized in 1802 or 1803. The first elders were John Lowrie, father of Hon. Walter Lowrie, senior Secretary of the Board of Foreign Missions, John Crawford, and another, whose name is illegible on the manuscript. The first pastor was Rev. Robert Johnston (14). He was ordained and installed by the Presbytery of Erie, October 19, 1803. His charge was Scrubgrass and Bear Creek.[1] This was a most successful pastorate. A wonderful work of Divine grace attended Mr. Johnston's labors. He was released from his pastoral charge January 2, 1811.

Mr. Johnston was succeeded by Rev. Cyrus Riggs (18), who was installed April 6, 1814; released from his pastoral charge April 2, 1834.

The next pastor was Rev. John R. Agnew. He was installed April 3, 1838; pastoral relation dissolved October 21, 1845. The next pastor was Rev. Ebenezer Henry. He was ordained and installed November 10,

[1] Bear Creek many years ago became connected with the Associate Reformed Church.

1847; relation dissolved, November 5, 1856. The present pastor is Rev. J. R. Coulter, who was ordained and installed August 25, 1857. This church has been under the care of the Presbytery of Alleghany since the year 1820. It has furnished ten ministers of the gospel:[1] namely, John Redick (26), John Coulter, Cyrus C. Riggs, D. D. (son of one of its pastors), Thomas W. Kerr, Thomas S. Leason, William B. Stewart, Samuel McAnderson, D. D., Samuel Williams, Thomas C. Anderson, and M. L. Anderson. Another member of the church, James F. Craig, died whilst a theological student.

The first church edifice was of logs, afterwards enlarged by cutting out one side and adding a shed. Afterwards a frame building was erected, and at a late date the present edifice, which is of stone.

SLIPPERY ROCK.

This congregation is in Beaver County, and was probably organized in 1801 or 1802. In the records of Presbytery in 1802, it is reported as able to support a pastor, in connection with New Castle.

The first pastor was Rev. Alexander Cook (12). He was ordained and installed by the Presbytery of Erie, June 22, 1803. This relation was dissolved June 14, 1809. The next pastor was Rev. Robert Sample, ordained and installed October 23, 1810; released, 1834. The next pastor was Rev. B. C. Critchlow, ordained and installed September 5, 1838; released from his charge, February 18, 1845. Rev. James S. Henderson, ordained and installed October 22, 1845; released, October 1, 1850. Rev. A. S. Biblingsley, installed second

[1] Dr. Young states that twenty ministers have been licensed, who were brought up in this church.

Tuesday of January, 1854; released, December 24, 1856; Rev. Henry Webber (83), installed June 10, 1862; released, January 11, 1865. The present pastor, Rev. R. S. Morton (80), was installed February 21, 1862. It is now under the care of the Presbytery of Beaver.

LOWER NESHANNOCK, now NEW CASTLE.

This congregation is in Lawrence County, Pa. It was organized about the same time as Slippery Rock, and with it constituted a pastoral charge for nearly forty years. Rev. Alexander Cook was the first pastor, ordained and installed by the Presbytery of Erie, June 22, 1803; released from his charge, June 14, 1809. The second pastor was Rev. Robert Sample, ordained and installed October 23, 1810; released from his charge, 1837. The next pastor was Rev. Wells Bushnell, installed 1839; pastoral relation dissolved, June 29, 1853. The next pastor was Rev. E. E. Swift, installed, September 27, 1854; pastoral relation dissolved, February 19, 1861. The next pastor was Rev. Joseph S. Grimes, installed July 9, 1861; released from his charge, September 27, 1865. The present pastor, Rev. D. X. Junkin, D. D., was installed September 13, 1866.

The ground on which New Castle now stands was originally occupied by John Wilson, Joseph, Isaac, and John Thompson, and J. C. Stewart. This was about the year 1800. The town was laid out in 1802, by John Carlisle Stewart. The church was organized either that year or the following, as the first pastor was installed in 1803. The congregation at first worshipped in the woods, around a tent that stood in the northwest corner of the present town-plot, but then outside the original plot. They afterwards built a small log-house near to the tent, but in a thicket through which paths had to be mown, in the midst of the thick bushes. This cabin was burned down, when a hewed log-house was erected near the old site. This was occupied until a brick house was built, that is now occupied as a brewery. Finally, the present comfortable structure was erected. The church is now under the care of the Presbytery of Beaver.

CONCORD (Butler County, Pa.).

This church was organized somewhere between 1803 and 1805. The first pastor was Rev. John McPherrin (16). He continued his pastorate until his death, February 10, 1822. The next pastor was Rev. John Coulter, ordained and installed by the Presbytery of Alleghany, September 10, 1823, in connection with Butler and Muddy Creek. He was released from his charge in the spring of 1864, after a pastorate of nearly forty-one years. The present pastor, Rev. J. H. Marshall, was installed in October, 1865.

The congregation worshipped first in a small log-house, with earthen floor and split log seats, with an old-fashioned wood fire. The second church edifice was also of logs, and was thirty feet square. It was afterwards enlarged by the addition of thirty feet to its length. In 1838, the present brick structure was erected. During Mr. Coulter's ministry, many seasons of refreshing were enjoyed. The most remarkable of these was in the winter of 1857 and 1858, when sixty were added to the church. It is under the care of the Presbytery of Alleghany.

MUDDY CREEK.

This church is also in Butler County, Pa., in the Presbytery of Alleghany. In 1803, Muddy Creek is reported to Synod by the Presbytery of Erie, as able to support a pastor in connection with Concord. In 1806, Mr. McPherrin is reported as pastor of Concord, Muddy Creek, and Harmony.[1] At the organization of the church of Butler in 1813, Muddy Creek became disbanded. The church was reorganized in 1823, when Rev. John Coulter became pastor. He was released from his charge in 1850. In 1853, Rev. Alexander Cunningham (65) became pastor; released from his charge, August, 1855. The present pastor is Rev. Samuel Williams, ordained and installed by the Presbytery of Alleghany in 1857.

During the first two years of Mr. Coulter's ministry, the people worshipped in the woods in summer, and in the dwellings in winter. During that whole period, the congregation were not once interrupted at divine service by rain or storm. But the first Sabbath they entered the new log church, there was a rain-storm.

BUTLER.

This church was organized in 1813. Several congregations mentioned in the minutes of the Presbytery of Erie, were component parts of the organization. Thorn's Tent, Salt Spring, and Harmony, with portions of Muddy Creek, were merged into one, and constituted the present flourishing church of Butler. The first pastor was Rev. John McPherrin (16). He was in-

---

[1] Merged in Butler in 1813.

stalled April 7, 1813, and continued his pastoral relation until his death, February 10, 1822.

The present pastor, Rev. Loyal Young, D. D., was ordained and installed by the Presbytery of Alleghany,[1] December 4, 1833. In 1815 a stone edifice was erected as a house of worship, which in 1833 gave place to a commodious one of brick; this again gave place to the present fine structure in 1865. This church has enjoyed many precious revival scenes; the most important of which have been in 1836, 1843, and 1853. It has also furnished many ministers of the gospel, who are laboring in the great field, and some who now rest from their labors. It is in the Presbytery of Alleghany.

FAIRVIEW, now WESTMINSTER.

This church was gathered and organized by Rev. Johnston Eaton (20), who was its first pastor. It is somewhat uncertain as to the precise date of its organization, perhaps 1806. The first elders were Andrew Caughey, George Reed, and William Arbuckle. At its organization, it consisted of but twenty-five members; all, with two exceptions, have now passed away. Mr. Eaton was ordained and installed pastor of this church by the Presbytery of Erie, in connection with Springfield, on the 30th of June, 1808. He continued its pastor until the time of his death, June 17, 1847, a period of nearly forty years.

The second pastor was Rev. William Willson (81), who was ordained and installed June 11, 1851, in connection with Sturgeonville and Girard. He was released from his charge, May 2, 1855. The next pastor was Rev. John R. Hamilton (93), ordained and installed June 15, 1859; released, June 15, 1864. The next pas-

---
[1] Erected 1820.

tor was Rev. L. M. Belden (109), ordained and installed December 14, 1864; released, April 25, 1866.

In the year 1847, this church sent off a colony to form the church of Sturgeonville, that reduced its numbers considerably. Soon after, the church edifice was removed to a more central locality. Its name was afterwards changed to Westminster, inasmuch as it was now removed from Fairview Township, where it had been originally located.

The first church edifice was of hewn logs, on a beautiful site, overlooking Lake Erie. This was afterwards enlarged by cutting out two or three logs, and building an open shed against the side. The next edifice was of frame, on a new site. This was afterwards removed to the position it now occupies.

About the time of the organization of the church of Sturgeonville, the church of Fairview (New School), was organized, mainly from the elements of the old Fairview church. This church is now under the pastoral care of Rev. A. Dunn. The influence of this old Fairview church, and its first pastor, in moulding and forming the character of the community along the Lake Shore, cannot be fully appreciated. It has been the mother of churches.

SPRINGFIELD.

THIS church is in Erie County, Pa., on the shore of Lake Erie, and is at the present time in connection with "the other branch." It was organized as a preaching point, in the year 1804, by Rev. Robert Patterson (13), and regularly organized as a church in 1806, by Rev. Johnston Eaton (20). The first elders were Isaac Miller, James Blair, and James Bruce. There were at this time thirty members. The first pastor was Rev. Johnston Eaton, ordained and installed by the Presbytery of Erie, June 30, 1808; pastoral relation dissolved November 8, 1814. In 1817, Rev. Phineas Camp (29), conducted a series of meetings, that were accompanied by the bodily exercise. In 1818, Rev. Michael Law preached for a time. The house of worship being but about twenty or twenty-five feet square, and unable to contain the people, Mr. Law preached in the grove, having for a pulpit a single slab knocked in between two trees endwise. At this time Cornelius Aten, Robert Porter, and Allen Law were elected elders.

From this time until 1827, the church was dependent on supplies. In this latter year a call was made out for the pastoral labors of Rev. Pierce Chamberlain (38). This call was accepted, and he was installed as pastor by the Presbytery of Erie, on the 16th of January, 1828. This relation was dissolved on the 1st of October of the same year, on account of the ill health of the pastor.

In the year 1837, Rev. Charles Danforth (53), preached as a stated supply. From 1841 to 1843, Rev. Richard Craighead labored in this field. From 1844 to 1850, Rev. John M. Williams; in 1854, Rev. James F. Reed; in 1860, Rev. O. W. Norton; afterwards Rev. J. D. Barstow; and at the present time, Rev. E. B. Chamberlain.

WARREN, OHIO.

This church was organized on the 19th of November, 1803, under the name of "The Church of Christ in Warren," by Rev. Joseph Badger (11), assisted by Mr. Tait (3), and Mr. Wick (2). It was at the first composed of but six members. Rev. Thomas Robbins and Rev. Jonathan Leslie supplied the church for the first five years.

The first pastor was Rev. James Boyd (21). He was ordained and installed as pastor of Warren and Newton, October 19, 1808, by the Presbytery of Erie. He was removed by death on the 8th of March, 1813.

Rev. James Duncan then supplied the church for two years. The next pastor was Rev. Joseph W. Curtis; installed February 4, 1820, by the Presbytery of Grand River; released from his charge in June, 1831. Rev. G. W. Hulin and Rev. J. A. Woodruff were stated supplies for a time. The next pastor was Rev. Nathan B. Purinton, installed May, 1840, by the Presbytery of Trumbull; released, April 12, 1848. The next pastor was Rev. William C. Clark, installed November 15, 1848, by the Presbytery of Trumbull; released, April 22, 1863. The next pastor was Rev. Henry Richard Hoisington, installed December 14, 1864; released, April 16, 1867.

At the first, this church was congregational. The Presbyterian form of government was adopted February 1, 1838. It is now in connection with the other branch, and is in a flourishing condition, having at the present time two hundred and forty-one communicants. It is under the care of the Presbytery of Trumbull.

MOORFIELD.

This church was a portion of Mr. Satterfield's first charge. It was situated in Hickory Township, Mercer County, about two miles east of Sharon. It was probably organized about 1800 or 1801. Mr. Satterfield was installed as pastor, March 3, 1802, in connection with

Neshannock. He continued the pastor of Moorfield, until he demitted the active duties of the ministry in 1834. At this time villages and churches had sprung up all around Moorfield, — Sharon, Middlesex, and Clarksville, — which gradually absorbed its membership, when it became extinct. It was dissolved soon after Mr. Satterfield's resignation.

BROOKFIELD, OHIO.

This church is in the Western Reserve. Its name first appears on the minutes in 1809. Rev. John Core was the first pastor, installed in 1817, in connection with Youngstown and Vienna. The pastoral relation was dissolved October 21, 1824. Rev. James Satterfield was pastor from 1812 to 1814. After this it was long vacant and dependent on supplies. In 1851 Rev. Jacob Coon was pastor. Rev. George S. Rice is now pastor elect.

HUBBARD, OHIO.

This congregation was first enrolled in 1809. In 1812 Rev. James Satterfield became pastor in connection with Moorfield and Brookfield. This relation continued until April 6, 1831. In 1852, Rev. A. O. Rockwell was pastor. Rev. George S. Rice is now pastor elect.

FIRST CHURCH, ERIE, PA.

Although not the first of the churches planted on the shore of Lake Erie, yet this church has always, since its organization, held a prominent place. It is first spoken of in the old minutes as Presque Isle, and afterwards Erietown. It is mentioned as seeking supplies in 1802, though it was not regularly organized until September, 1815. In 1803 it united with Middlebrook and North East, then called Upper and Lower Greenfield, in extending a call to Rev. Robert Patterson (13), although the call was not prosecuted. The church was supplied by Rev. Johnston Eaton (20), from 1814 to 1823; the first four years of this period, one third of the time was given to Erie, and the remaining five years one half. The first pastor was Rev. David McKinney (32). He was ordained and installed by the Presbytery of Erie, April 13, 1825; released April 21, 1829. The present pastor is Rev. George A. Lyon, D. D. He was ordained and installed September 9, 1829. Next to that of Mr. Eaton, Dr. Lyon's pastorate has been the longest in the history of the Presbytery of Erie.

The first regular place of worship was a frame building called "the Yellow Meeting-house." In 1824 a comfortable brick house was erected, and in June, 1859, the corner-stone of the present elaborate and beautiful church was laid.[1] One of the most prominent members of the session was Judah Colt. He came to Erie in 1795. He made a profession of religion in the days of Elisha Macurdy, and was ever afterwards a generous, consistent, and useful man. At the great division, this church adhered to the other branch. It has sent out two colonies: Belle Valley, of which Rev. Joseph Vance is pastor, and the Park Church, noticed elsewhere.

UNITY, now HARRISVILLE.

This church is in Butler County, and now under the care of the Presbytery of Alleghany. The organization took place in 1807. It first appears on the min-

---
[1] Miss Sanford's *History*.

utes in 1808. Sometimes is called West Unity. The first pastor was Rev. Cyrus Riggs (18). He was installed April 6, 1814; released, April 2, 1834. The next pastor was Rev. John R. Agnew; installed April 3, 1838; released, October 21, 1845 or 1846. Rev. John Moore was pastor from 1847 to 1849. Rev. Meade Satterfield, son of Rev. James Satterfield (5), one of the original members of Presbytery, was pastor from 1850 to the time of his death, a period of six years. He was succeeded by Rev. J. F. Boyd, who was installed in 1856; released, June 26, 1866. The present pastor is Rev. W. D. Patton, who was installed in 1866.

NEWTON.

THIS church is in Ohio, and was a portion of the original charge of Rev. James Boyd (21), in connection with Warren, Ohio. Mr. Boyd was ordained and installed by the Presbytery of Erie, October 19, 1808. He was released by death, March 8, 1813. It was then vacant, until Rev. Joshua Beer, a former licentiate of the Presbytery of Erie, was installed, June 24, 1818; released, January, 1822. After this it was long vacant. Rev. William O. Stratton was pastor from 1844 to 1855. Rev. John B. Miller from 1857 to 1858. The present pastor, Rev. T. P. Speer, was installed in 1860. It is now under the care of the Presbytery of New Lisbon.

NEW REHOBOTH AND LICKING.

THESE congregations are in Clarion County, Pa. They were gathered and organized by Rev. Robert McGarraugh (23), about the year 1806 or 1807. Mr. McGarraugh was installed as their pastor by the Presbytery of Redstone, November 12, 1807. On the 4th of October, 1811, they were detached from the Presbytery of Redstone by Synod, and connected with the Presbytery of Erie. At the organization of the Presbytery of Alleghany in 1820, they fell within its territory; and at the organization of the Presbytery of Clarion, in 1841, they became connected with that body.

On the 3d of April, 1822, Mr. McGarraugh was released from the charge of these churches. The next pastor was Rev. John Core, installed September 16, 1824. He was released from the pastoral charge of the church of New Rehoboth in 1844, and from that of Licking by death, May 7, 1854.

The present pastor of the church of New Rehoboth is Rev. James Montgomery, who commenced his pastorate in 1844. The present pastor of the church of Licking is Rev. Joseph Mateer, installed 1855.

BIG SUGAR CREEK.

This church is in Venango County, Pa., and was organized in 1813 or 1814. The first pastor was Rev. Ira Condit (24), ordained November 8, 1814, by the Presbytery of Erie, in connection with Fairfield; released from the charge of the former, December 28, 1825. The next pastor was Rev. Thomas Anderson (37). He was ordained and installed by the Presbytery of Erie, September 19, 1826, in connection with Concord and Franklin; released from the pastoral charge of the former in 1837. The next pastor was Rev. Cyrus Dickson (58). He was ordained and installed by the Presbytery of Erie, June 24, 1840, in connection with Franklin; released from the former, January 1, 1846. The next pastor was Rev. James Coulter (62), installed September, 1848; released, January 16, 1850.

CHURCHES. 443

The next pastor was Rev. Robert Glenn (44), installed June 18, 1850; released by death, September 6, 1857. The next pastor was Rev. J. D. Howey (94), ordained and installed September 21, 1859; released, April 26, 1865. The congregation, since that time, has been dependent on supplies. It is now supplied by Rev. D. Patton.

WATERFORD.

This church is in Erie County, and at present in connection with the other branch. It was probably organized about the year 1809 or 1810. The first pastor was Rev. John Matthews (22). He was ordained and installed in connection with Gravel Run, October 17, 1810; released from Waterford April 2, 1817. From this date until 1828, the church was dependent on supplies. Rev. Phineas Camp (29), and Mr. Judah Ely, preached for a time. Rev. Peter Hassinger (39) was stated supply from 1828 to 1833. Rev. B. J. Wallace supplied in 1833, and the next year Rev. J. Watson Johnston. On the 15th of September, 1836, Rev. Pierce Chamberlain (38) was installed as pastor, in connection with Union. He was released from the charge of Waterford in 1844. Rev. G. W. Cleveland supplied until 1849. The church was subsequently supplied by Rev. C. F. Diver, and perhaps others. The present pastor is Rev. T. T. Bradford. The congregation had no regular place of worship until 1835, when the present house was erected. The church is now in a prosperous condition.

GRAVEL RUN.

This church is in Crawford County, and was probably organized in 1809 or 1810. The first pastor was

Rev. John Matthews (22), installed in connection with Waterford, October 17, 1810. He was released from the charge of Gravel Run, November 8, 1814. The next pastor was Rev. Peter Hassinger (39). He was ordained and installed, October 1, 1828; released from his charge in 1832.

Rev. Alexander Cunningham (65) was ordained and installed as pastor, October 5, 1843; released from his charge in 1851. The present pastor is Rev. James W. Dickey (64), installed April 19, 1854.

At the division in 1838, this church was divided, a portion adhering to each branch. The New School branch is called also Gravel Run; Rev. G. W. Hampson is the pastor.

WASHINGTON.

This church is in Edinboro', Erie County. For the last quarter of a century its history has been identified with that of Gravel Run, having been united in the same pastoral charge. Mr. Cunningham was installed pastor, October 5, 1853; released from his charge in 1851. Mr. Dickey, the present pastor, was installed April 19, 1854. This church was also divided in 1838. The New School branch is called Edinboro'; Rev. William Grassie is the pastor.

WARREN, PA.

This is an old congregation, yet the records are dim and misty that relate to its history. Its name first appears on the minutes in 1810. Probably the first pastor was Rev. Nathan Harned (34). He was ordained and installed, April 20, 1825; released in March, 1826. The next pastor was Rev. Absalom McCready (36); installed,

September 13, 1837; released, June 27, 1838. For a few years from 1841, Rev. Hiram Eddy (60) supplied the church. The next pastor was Rev. John M. Smith (67), installed January 28, 1846; released, August 11, 1847. The next pastor was Rev. John Sailor (79), installed May 4, 1853; released, August 29, 1855. After this Mr. Hequembourg supplied for a time. The next pastor was Rev. Robert Taylor (102); ordained and installed November 13, 1861; released, September 26, 1862. The next pastor was Rev. W. T. Hamilton, D. D. (105); installed in May, 1864; released, April 26, 1865. The present stated supply is Rev. William Rankin. This congregation has recently completed a fine church edifice.

OIL CREEK, now TITUSVILLE.

This church was gathered and organized by Rev. Amos Chase (25) about the year 1815. Mr. Chase supplied it until the 24th day of May, 1826, when he was installed as its first pastor for one half of his time. The pastoral relation was dissolved in 1830. The next pastor was Rev. G. W. Hampson (43), who was ordained and installed as pastor by the Presbytery of Erie, June 27, 1832. He continued his relation for some ten years, when the relation was dissolved. Owing to peculiar circumstances, the church gradually became disorganized, and its individuality lost. A few years ago it was reorganized under the name of the First Presbyterian Church of Titusville, Rev. William Howell Taylor, pastor. It is situated in Crawford County, Pa., and in connection with the other branch.

CENTERVILLE.

This church is situated about ten miles from Titusville. It was gathered by Mr. Chase in 1815. He was its first, and perhaps only pastor. He was installed in 1827, and released from his charge in 1830.

UNION (Erie County, Pa.).

This church was organized in April, 1811, with eight members, and one elder, Matthew Gray. It was long dependent on supplies. In 1820, Rev. Amos Chase supplied it for one fourth of his time. Previous to this or about 1814, Rev. John Matthews (22) supplied it. The first pastor was Rev. Absalom McCready (36), who was ordained and installed by the Presbytery of Erie, September 14, 1826. He was released from his charge in 1835. In May, 1836, Rev. Pierce Chamberlain (38) began to supply, and continued until November, 1840. In 1841, Rev. Thomas Anderson (37), was installed pastor; released from his charge in 1843. The church has been successively supplied by Rev. G. W. Cleveland, Rev. C. F. Diver, Rev. T. T. Bradford, Rev. G. H. Hammer, and Rev. William Grassie. On the 8th of February, 1862, Rev. J. F. Reed, D. D., was installed as pastor; released April 10, 1866. Rev. F. V. Warren is the present stated supply. It is in connection with the other branch.

WESTFIELD, N. Y.

This church was first organized by Rev. John Lindsey, in 1808, under the name of " Chatauque." It soon lost its organization. On the 7th day of November,

1817, it was reorganized by Rev. Johnston Eaton (20) and Rev. Phineas Camp (29). The latter was its first pastor, installed September 8, 1819; released, September, 1821. On the 1st of July, 1819, the name was changed to Westfield. About the year 1824, the church was transferred to Buffalo Presbytery. The next pastor was Rev. Isaac Oakes. In 1835, Rev. D. O. Gregory was pastor. From 1840 to 1845 Rev. T. M. Hopkins was pastor. From 1845 to 1854 Rev. Reuben Tinker was pastor. Rev. C. F. Muzzy was pastor in 1855. Rev. J. P. Fisher was pastor from 1863 to 1865. The present pastor is Rev. R. S. Van Cleve (113), installed in 1867. It is now in connection with the other branch.

FRANKLIN.

This church was organized July 28, 1817, by Rev. Ira Condit. John Broadfoot and James Gilleland were chosen as elders. In July, 1821, the church was reorganized by Rev. Alexander Cook and Rev. Cyrus Riggs. It was then taken under the care of the Presbytery of Alleghany. At this time it consisted of nine members. The next elders were Andrew Bowman and Levi Dodd. The first pastor was Rev. Thomas Anderson (37). He was ordained and installed by the Presbytery of Erie, September 19, 1826, about which time the church was transferred to the Presbytery of Erie. He was released from his charge September 12, 1837.

The next pastor was Rev. Cyrus Dickson; ordained and installed by the Presbytery of Erie, June 24, 1840, released from his charge, March, 1848. The present pastor, Rev. S. J. M. Eaton (76), was ordained and installed February 7, 1849. Some precious revivals have characterized the history of this church. In the winter of 1867, one hundred and eleven were added to it.

The first house of worship was erected in 1830. The corner-stone of the present edifice was laid July 9, 1867.

CONCORD (Venango County, Pa.).

The name of this church first appears on the minutes of Presbytery in 1826, when it became a part of the charge of Rev. Thomas Anderson. He was installed as its pastor, September 19 of that year. He was released from the pastoral charge of this congregation on the 13th of April, 1831. The next pastor was Rev. G. W. Hampson (43). He was ordained and installed as pastor by the Presbytery of Erie, June 27, 1832; released in 1837. The next pastor was Rev. James Coulter (62). He was ordained and installed by the Presbytery of Erie as pastor, in connection with Deerfield, September 14, 1842; released about the year 1846. The next pastor was Rev. M. A. Parkinson (78), ordained and installed September 11, 1850; released, October 20, 1854. The next pastor was Rev. W. J. Alexander (89). He was ordained and installed December 19, 1855; released, January 7, 1857. From 1860 to 1863, the church was supplied by Rev. J. H. Sargent (101). It was afterward supplied by Rev. H. Newell (97), and Rev. John McKean, and at present by Rev. J. J. Smyth (115).

TIDIOUTE (formerly DEERFIELD).

This church is in Warren County, Pa. It was anciently known as Tidioute; the name was afterwards changed to Deerfield. It was received under the care of Presbytery as a regularly organized church in 1827. Its first pastor was probably Rev. James Coulter, installed September 14, 1842; released about 1846. The next was Rev. M. A. Parkinson, installed September 11, 1850; released, October 20, 1854. The next, Rev. W. J. Alexander, installed December 19, 1855; released, January 7, 1857. The church was afterwards supplied by Mr. Sargent, Mr. Newell, and Mr. McKean. Having fallen into dilapidation, it was reorganized in 1867, under the name of Tidioute.

HARBOR CREEK.

This church is in Erie County, Pa., and was a colony from the church of North East. It was organized on the 26th of May, 1832, with fifty-eight members. The first elders were Myron Bacchus, Samuel Kingsbury, and J. M. Moorhead. It was supplied for one year by Rev. Giles Doolittle (33), pastor of North East. The first pastor was Rev. William A. Adair (46), ordained and installed November 7, 1833, in connection with North East. The pastoral relation was dissolved October 9, 1834. After this Rev. Simeon Peck (48) supplied for one year. The next pastor was Rev. Reuben Lewis (51), ordained and installed November 1, 1837; released, June 28, 1838. At this time the great division took place, when this church was divided. The old school branch was supplied by Mr. J. H. Townley, and on the 11th day of August, 1847, Rev. J. K. Cornyn (70) was installed as pastor. He was released April 4, 1850. On the 4th day of June, 1866, the two divisions of the church were merged in one, under the care of the other branch.

In the mean time, of the other branch, Rev. N.

West was pastor from 1838 to 1842. The church was next supplied by Rev. Miles Doolittle, and Rev. M. T. Smith, until 1848. The present pastor is Rev. G. W. Cleveland. He was installed September, 1852. The church edifice was erected in 1836.

GIRARD.

This church was a colony from Springfield. It is in Erie County, Pa., and was organized May 16, 1835. The first elders were Robert Porter and Philip Bristol. At the first, Rev. Edson Hart (42), who was preaching at Springfield, supplied them. The first pastor was Rev. R. S. Lockwood (52), ordained and installed January 11, 1837; released in 1841. Afterwards Rev. William Fuller (52), and Rev. Mr. Root, supplied. The next pastor was Rev. Joseph Vance, installed in 1846; released in 1854. From this date to 1863, Rev. Alexander Porter was stated supply. In September, 1864, Rev. H. O. Howland was installed as pastor; released, 1866. Rev. Ira M. Condit (95) is at present stated supply. It is in connection with the other branch.

SANDY LAKE.

This church is in Mercer County, Pa., and was organized October 3, 1835, with thirteen members. The first elders were Alexander Brown, Homer Bailey, and Eli Butler. Rev. Robert Glenn labored in this church as stated supply for one third of his time, for eleven years. Rev. J. W. McCune was installed pastor, June 23, 1852; released, February 7, 1855. Rev. John G. Condit (100) was pastor nearly two years. Rev. John Rice (110) is the present stated supply.

The present church edifice was erected in 1846, and greatly improved in 1867.

HARMONSBURG.

THIS church is in Crawford County, Pa., and was organized in 1829. It was dependent on supplies for many years. In the year 1832, Rev. Peter Hassinger (39) supplied it. On the 4th day of October, 1843, Rev. J. W. Dickey (64) was ordained and installed as its pastor; released in 1847. After this Rev. L. P. Bates (72) supplied for a time. On the 14th of September, 1852, Rev. James Coulter was installed as pastor; released, 1857 or 1858. Rev. George Scott was installed June 27, 1860; released, June 10, 1862. The present pastor is Rev. N. S. Lowrie (103), who was ordained and installed October 22, 1862.

CONNEAUTVILLE.

THIS church is in Crawford County, Pa. It was organized, October 31, 1835, by Rev. P. Hassinger. One elder, John Craven, was elected. It was supplied by Rev. R. Lewis, Rev. D. Waggoner, and others. The first pastor was Rev. J. W. Dickey (64), ordained and installed, October 4, 1843, in connection with Harmonsburg and Evansburg. He was released in 1847. Rev. L. P. Bates (72) supplied for a time in 1847. Rev. James Coulter supplied the church for a time in 1853. Rev. George W. Zahniser (84) was ordained and installed as pastor September 7, 1853; released, April 13, 1859. The present pastor, Rev. N. S. Lowrie (103) was ordained and installed, October 22, 1862. This church was for eleven years divided into two branches, but became united in 1865.

EVANSBURG.

This church was formerly known as Conneaut, or the Outlet of Conneaut. In 1811 to 1817, it constituted a part of the charge of Rev. Robert Johnston, in connection with Meadville and Little Sugar Creek. It was probably dependent on supplies from that time to April 14, 1841, when Rev. Edward S. Blake (59) was ordained and installed as pastor, in connection with Gravel Run. His pastorate continued for one year. On the 4th of October, 1843, Rev. J. W. Dickey was installed as pastor; released in 1847. In September, 1852, Rev. James Coulter was installed as pastor; released in 1857 or 1858. Rev. George Scott (98) was ordained and installed as pastor, June 27, 1860; released, June 10, 1862.

CHERRY TREE.

This church is in Venango County, Pa., and was organized, February 1, 1837, with thirteen members. The first elders were John Irwin and John Rynd. The first pastor was Rev. G. W. Hampson (43). At the division, this church went with the other branch. The present stated supply is Rev. W. C. Birchard.

GREENVILLE.

This church is in Mercer County, and was probably formed from elements drawn from the church of Salem. It was organized in 1825. The first pastor was Rev. James Alexander (40), who was ordained and installed October 13, 1828; released, June 25, 1834. The next pastor was Rev. J. G. Wilson (49), ordained and installed, October 12, 1836; released, 1841. The next pastor was Rev. Henry Webber (63), ordained and installed January 20, 1843; released, October 16, 1844. In 1847 and 1848, the church was supplied by Rev. L. W. Williams (71). The next pastor was Rev. J. H. Callen (75), ordained and installed October 25, 1848; released, June 23, 1852. The next pastor was Rev. David Grier (83); installed, January 18, 1854; released, April 13, 1859. The next pastor was Rev. A. C. Junkin, installed June 10, 1862; released, May 8, 1867.

BIG BEND.

This congregation was organized in 1825, and was for a time associated with Greenville. In the course of events, it has become disorganized. Its name was removed from the roll in 1842.

STURGEONVILLE.

This church was a colony from the old church of Fairview, Erie County, Pa. It was organized in 1845. It was first supplied by Mr. Kean, a licentiate of the Presbytery of Blairsville. The first pastor was Rev. J. K. Cornyn (70), ordained and installed August 11, 1847; released, June 19, 1850. The next pastor was Rev. William Wilson (18), ordained and installed June 11, 1851; released, May 2, 1855. The next pastor was Rev. J. R. Hamilton (93), ordained and installed June 15, 1859; released, June 15, 1864. The present pastor is Rev. L. M. Belden (109), who was ordained and installed December 14, 1864.

WATERLOO.

This church is in Venango County, Pa., and was organized, March 5, 1854, from the membership of

Franklin and Mill Creek. It has depended chiefly on supplies. Mr. Coulter, Mr. Condit, and Mr. Newell have supplied it. The church edifice was erected by James Gilleland, one of the first elders, at his individual expense.

SUGAR GROVE.

This is an old church in Warren County, Pa. From the peculiar circumstances of its position, it has been mainly dependent on supplies.

IRVINE.

This church is also in Warren County, and has not always enjoyed the labors of a pastor. It was organized in 1844.

MOUNT PLEASANT.

This church is in Venango County, Pa., and was organized in 1842. Its first pastor was Rev. S. J. M. Eaton (76), installed February 7, 1849, for one third of his time; released August 29, 1855. It has since been supplied by Rev. James Coulter, Rev. J. G. Condit, and Rev. John McKean.

PARK CHURCH, ERIE, PA.

This church was organized, June 28, 1855. The first pastor was Rev. William M. Blackburn (91), installed May 25, 1857; released, December 22, 1863. The present pastor, Rev. George F. Cain (107), was installed May 11, 1864.

MILLEDGEVILLE.

This church is in Mercer County, and was organized in 1856. It has been mainly dependent on supplies.

Henry B. Lambe (111) was installed as pastor July 11, 1866; released, May 9, 1867. The present supply is Mr. Patton.

OIL CITY, PA.

This church was organized, December, 1861, with twelve members and two ruling elders, Adam Turner and C. C. Waldo. Rev. W. P. Moore (106), has been stated supply since 1863.

GREENFIELD.

This church is in Crawford County, Pa. It was a colony from the church of Georgetown, and was organized on the 22d of June, 1854, with twenty members. The first pastor was Rev. George Scott (98), having been previously supplied by Rev. James Coulter. Mr. Scott was ordained and installed June 27, 1860; released, June 10, 1862. The present pastor is Rev. David Waggoner, who was installed July 1, 1864.

VENANGO.

This church is in Crawford County, Pa., and was organized, by act of Presbytery, October 24, 1866. It was a colony from the Gravel Run Church. It takes its name from the borough where the church is located.

COCHRANTON.

This church was received from the care of the Pittsburgh Reformed Presbytery, September 26, 1867. It was originally a colony from the United Presbyterian Church of the same place. This latter church was anciently under the care of the Presbytery of Erie, under the name of "Little Sugar Creek." It was a portion of

Mr. Johnston's (14) charge, from 1811 to 1817, and passed to the connection of the Associate Reformed Church about the year 1819 or 1820. Mr. Patton is the present pastor of this church.

SECOND PRESBYTERIAN CHURCH, MERCER, PA.

THIS church is a colony from the First Church, Mercer. It was organized, October 20, 1863, with forty-eight members and three ruling elders, Elias Alexander, Joseph Fleming, and R. M. J. Zahniser. The pastor, Rev. W. M. Robinson (108), was installed June 15, 1864. At first the congregation worshipped in the Court House, but have recently completed a substantial brick edifice.

MOUNT VERNON, now PLEASANTVILLE.

THIS church is in Venango County, and was organized June 19, 1860, as a colony from the church of Concord. It contained at its organization twelve members. On the 9th of May, 1867, the name was changed to Pleasantville. It is at present supplied by Rev. J. J. Smyth (115).

PETROLEUM CENTER.

THIS church was gathered by Dr. Marks (112), and was organized September 24, 1865, with fourteen members. The first elders were A. D. Cotton and J. M. Dickey. It was at first supplied by Dr. Marks. Mr. J. T. Oxtoby is pastor elect.

INDEX.

Ability Question, 125.
Act of Synod, 28, 139.
Act and Testimony, 129.
Adair, W. A., notice of, 375, 128.
Adventure of Badger, 228.
Alden, Timothy, biography of, 290, 83, 91, 124.
Agnew, J. R., 430.
Alexander, Dr. Archibald, 108.
Alexander, James, D. D., notice of, 373.
Alexander, Wm. J., notice of, 392, 155.
Amity, history of, 414.
Anderson, T. C., 421.
Anderson, Thomas, biography of, 315, 110, 112.
Anecdote of Patterson, 239.
    " Porter, 86.
    " Rice, 28.
    " Wood, 12.
    " West, 333.
    " Wilson, 115.
Anxious seat, 121.
Appeal to Synod, 141.
Badger, Joseph, biography of, 218, 42, 52.
Bans of marriage, 75.
Baptism, question of, 124.
Barns, worship in, 67.
Barrett, John, 106.
Bates, L. P., biography of, 349, 152.
Beaver Church, history of, 410.
Beer, Joshua, 441, 54.
Behrends, C. A., notice of, 392, 157.
Belden, L. M., notice of, 400, 163.
Billingsley, A. S., 431.

BIOGRAPHY OF DECEASED MINISTERS: —

  Alden, Timothy, 290.

Anderson, Thomas, 315.
Badger, Joseph, 218.
Bates, Lemuel P., 349.
Boyd, Abraham, 213.
  " Benjamin, 255.
  " James, 269.
  " John, 211.
  " Alexander, 339.
Bracken, Reid, 261.
Bushnell, Wells, 311.
Camp, Phineas, 299.
Chamberlain, Pierce, 319.
Chase, Amos, 282.
Condit, Ira, 277.
Cook, Alexander, 230.
Cornyn, John K., 341.
Crane, N. M., 352.
Danforth, Charles, 334.
Doolittle, Giles, 303.
Eaton, Johnston, 265.
Glenn, Robert, 324.
Harned, Nathan, 308.
Hart, Edson, 323.
Hughes, Thomas E., 177.
Johnston, Robert, 240.
Lee, Robert, 195.
Limber, John, 336.
Marcy, Bradford, 302.
Matthews, John, 271.
McCullough, William, 356.
McGarraugh, Robert, 275.
McNair, John, D. D., 328.
McPherrin, John, 251.
Munson, John, 296.
Patterson, Robert, 233.
Pittinger, Nicholas, 249.
Redick, John, 288.
Riggs, Cyrus, 256.
Satterfield, James, 199.
Stockton, Joseph, 191.
Struve, Charles V., 351.
Tait, Samuel, 185.

INDEX.

Taylor, Robert, 361.
West, Nathaniel, D. D., 331.
Wick, William, 182.
Williams, Lewis W., 343.
Wood, William, 216.
Wylie, William, D. D., 203.

Big Bend, history of, 453.
Blake, E. S., notice of, 382, 147.
Blackburn, W. M., notice of, 393, 157.
Boardman, C. A., 408.
Bodily Exercise, 59.
Bodily Exercise, described, 60.
Bodily Exercise, Mr. Johnston's account of, 62.
Books sought, 41.
Boundaries of Presbytery, 56.
Boundaries, new, 98.
Bouton, E., 408.
Boyd, Abraham, biography of, 213.
" Benjamin, biography of, 255.
" James, biography of, 269, 57.
" John, biography of, 211.
" Alex., biography of, 339.
" J. F., 415.
Bracken, Reid, biography of, 261, 52, 53.
Bradford, A. B., 407.
" T. T., 443.
Brookfield, history of, 439.
Bull Creek, history of, 422.
Butler, history of, 434.
Bushnell, Wells, biography of, 311, 111.

Cain, George F., notice of, 399, 162.
Callen, J. H., notice of, 387.
Caldwell, S., 422.
Camp, Phineas, biography of, 299, 96.
Candidates, 94.
Carrier, A. H., 430.
Catechism, 25.
Chamberlain, P., biography of, 319.
Chaplains, 79, 172.
Charcoal fire, 74.
Chase, Amos, biography of, 282, 81, 118.
Cherry Tree, history of, 452.
Cholera, 125.
Center, history of, 427.
Centerville, history of, 446.
Cleveland, G. W., 442.

Cochranton, history of, 455.
Cochran, Mr., 430.
Commissioners, first, 35.
Commission, Christian, 172.
Committees, 49.
Complaint, 136.
Concord, history of, 433.
Concord, (Venango Co.) history of, 448.
Conneautville, history of, 451.
Confession of Faith, 117.
Condit, Ira, biography of, 277, 80, 114.
Condit, Ira M., notice of, 395, 158.
Condit, J. G., notice of, 397, 159.
Colt, Judah, 440, 108.
Core, John, 408.
Cornplanter, 92.
Cornyn, J. K., biography of, 341.
Cook, Alex., biography of, 230, 42, 70.
Cool Spring, history of, 410, 31, 113.
Coulter, John, 433.
Coulter, James, notice of, 383, 148.
" J. R., 431.
Country, state of the, 160, 164.
Craighead, R., 414, 437.
Crane, N. M., biography of, 352, 153.
Critchlow, B. C., 470.

Danforth, Charles, biography of, 334, 133.
Delegates to New School, 163.
Dickson, William, 54.
" " his Journal, 74.
Dickson, Cyrus, D. D., notice of, 381, 149.
Dickson, Robert, 416.
Dickey, D. L., 408.
" J. W., notice of, 384.
Dilworth, Dr. R., 425.
" Albert, 407.
Division of Presbytery, 51, 140.
Diver, C. F., 442.
Doolittle, Giles, biography of, 303, 109, 126.
Dunn, Ambrose, 436.

Eaton, Johnston, biography of, 265, 51, 53, 78.
Eaton, S. J. M., notice of, 387.
Eddy, Hiram, notice of, 382, 147.
Education, 34.
Elder question, 79.
Ely, Judah, 106.

INDEX. 459

Enterprise, 3.
Erie, First Church, 439.
" Park Church, 454.
" Presbytery erected, 29.
Evansburg, history of, 452.
Excision acts, 135.
Exegesis, 107.

Fairfield Church, history of, 417.
Fairview Church, history of, 435.
Fairview Church, name changed, 160.
Fasting, 91.
Fencing tables, 24.
Findley, J. R., notice of, 393.
Fire in churches, 72.
Fisher, J. P., 447.
Forest worship, 68.
Franklin Church, history of, 447, 113.
Fuller, William, notice of, 379, 133.
Fulton, J. P., 409.

General Assembly rule, 140.
Georgetown Church, history of, 418.
Girard Church, history of, 450.
Gray, J. H., notice of, 398, 161.
Gravel Run Church, history of, 443.
Greenville Church, history of, 452.
Greenfield Church, history of, 455.
Greenfield Upper Church, history of, 437.
Greenfield Lower Church, history of, 429.
Glenn, Robert, biography of, 324, 126, 157.
Glenn, S. M., 163.
Glasgow, Ezekiel, 410.
Grassie, William, 444.
Gridley, J. J., notice of, 402, 168.
Grier, David, notice of, 390, 155.
Grimes, W. M., 432.
Greersburgh Academy, 34, 52.

Hall, David, 421.
Hamilton, W. T., D. D., notice of, 398, 161.
Hamilton, J. R., notice of, 394, 158.
Hammer, G. H., 446.
Hampson, George W., notice of, 374, 118.
Harbor Creek Church, history of, 449, 124.
Harmonsburg Church, history of, 451, 117.
Harned, Nathan, biography of, 308.

Harrisville, history of, 440.
Harvest year, 123.
Harvison, W. P., 423.
Hassinger, P., notice of, 372, 118.
Hart, Edson, biography of, 323.
Hearers, 9.
Hequembourg, C. L., 445.
Henry, Ebenezer, 430.
Heydon, Daniel, 54.
Hilands Church, history of, 428, 17.

HISTORIES OF CHURCHES:—
Amity, 414.
Beaver, 410.
Beula, 421.
Brookfield, 439.
Bull Creek, 422.
Big Bend, 453.
Butler, 434.
Cherry Tree, 452.
Center, 427.
Centreville, 446.
Cochranton, 455.
Concord (Butler Co.), 433.
Concord (Venango Co.), 448.
Conneautville, 451.
Cool Spring, 410.
Deerfield, 448.
Erie, First Church, 439.
Erie, Park Church, 454.
Evansburg, 452.
Fairfield, 417.
Fairview, 435.
Franklin, 447.
Gravel Run, 443.
Georgetown, 418.
Girard, 450.
Greenville, 452.
Greenfield, 455.
Greenfield, Upper, 427.
" Lower, 429.
Harbor Creek, 449.
Harmonsburg, 451.
Harrisville, 440.
Hilands, 428.
Hopewell, 409.
Hubbard, 439.
Irvine, 454.
Licking, 441.
Meadville, 413.
Mercer, First, 412.
" Second, 456.
Middlesex, 423.
Middlebrook, 427.
Mill Creek, 419.
Milledgeville, 454.
Moorfield, 438.

460   INDEX.

Mt. Pleasant (Beaver Co.), 407.
Mt. Pleasant (Venango Co.), 454.
Mt. Nebo, 423.
Muddy Creek, 434.
Neshannock, 416.
Newton, 441.
New Castle, 432.
New Rehoboth, 441.
New Salem, 407.
North East, 429.
Oil Creek, 445.
Oil City, 455.
Park Church, Erie, 454.
Petroleum Center, 456.
Plain, 423.
Plaingrove, 426.
Pymatuning, 421.
Poland, 424.
Sandy, Upper, 418.
" Lower, 419.
Sandy Lake, 450.
Salem, 411.
Scrubgrass, 430.
Slate Lick, 420.
Sturgeonville, 453.
Slippery Rock, 431.
Springfield, 436.
Sugar Grove, 454.
Sugar Creek, 442.
Tidioute, 448.
Titusville, 445.
Trumbull, 421.
Union, Armstrong Co., 421.
Union, Erie Co., 446.
Unity, 440.
Venango, 455.
Washington, 444.
Warren (O.), 437.
" (Pa.), 444.
Waterford, 443.
Waterloo, 453.
Westfield, (Pa.) 425.
" (N. Y.) 446.
Westminster, 435.
Youngstown, 408.

History of Presbytery, 50, 110.
Hoisington, H. R., 438.
Hopewell Church, history of, 409.
Houses, 17.
Howland, H. O., 450.
Howey, J. D., notice of, 394, 161.
Hubbard, 439.
Hudson, T. B., 430.
Hughes, T. E., biography of, 177, 30.
Hughes, S.A., 427.

Hulin, G. W., 438.

Indian Missions, 49.
Irvine, history of, 454.
Influence of Presbytery, 179.

Jacks, Miss Eliza, 305.
Jackson, G. W., 422.
Johnston, Robert, biography of, 240, 46, 71.
" Edward, 54.
" J. W., 407.
" T. P., 412.
Jones, Dr. J. H., 108.
Journal of William Dickson, 37.
" Robert Patterson, 43.
Junkin, A. C., notice of, 395, 159.
" Capt., 80.
" Dr. George, 80.
" Dr. D. X., 80, 432.

Kean, John F., 151.
" William F., 421.
Kerr, T. W., 422.
" Joseph, 424.

Labors of early ministers, 10, 49.
Lake shore troubles, 80.
Lambe, H. B., notice of, 401.
Law, M., 437.
Lectures, McMillan's, 10.
Lee, Robert, biography of, 195, 33, 51.
Leake, L. F., 423.
Letter, Munson's, 5.
Lewis, R., notice of, 378, 132.
Licentiates, first, 34.
Licking Church, history of, 441.
Limber, John, biography of, 336.
Lining out, 57.
Lockwood, R. S., notice of, 378, 132.
Longevity of ministers, 170.
Lowrie family, 71.
" N. S., notice of, 398, 161.
Lowary, D. P., 410.
Lyon, G. A., D. D., notice of, 374.

Manufactures, 19.
Mateer, J., 442.
May, Hezekiah, 414.
McAboy, L. R., D. D., 424.
McCullough, W., biography of, 356, 154.
McCready, A., notice of, 371, 110.
McCune, J. W., notice of, 390, 154.
McGarraugh, R., biography of, 275, 76.

INDEX. 463

Shields, J. M., notice of, 392, 156.
Singing, 21
Slavery, 131, 132, 150.
" petition on, 149.
Smith, J. T., D. D., notice of, 383.
" John M., notice of, 385.
" James R., 429.
" J. Irwin, notice of, 391, 155.
" Joseph, 188.
" W. D., 407.
Smoking accommodations, 70.
Smyth, J. Jones, notice of, 402, 163.
Slate Lick, history of, 420.
Slippery Rock, history of, 431.
Snowden, N. R., 414.
Speer, T. P., 441.
Spelman, J. H., notice of, 396.
Springfield, history of, 436, 134.
Stated Clerks, 172.
Stated Clerk's Bill, 52.
Stockton, Joseph, biography of, 191, 33.
Stratton, W. O., 441.
Struve, C. V., biography of, 351, 152.
Sturgeonville, history of, 453.
Sugar Creek, history of, 442.
Sugar Grove, history of, 454.
Supplies, 42, 53.
Swift, Dr. E. P., 159.
" E. E., 432.
Synod of Western Pennsylvania, 142.

Tait, Samuel, biography of, 185, 31.
Taylor, Robert, biography of, 361, 159.
" William G., 410.
" William M., 426.
" William Howell, 445.
Temperance, 81, 116.
Territory, 5.
Times, 3.
Tinker, Reuben, 446.
Titusville, history of, 445.
Tokens, 23.
Tour of Macurdy, 36.
Travelling, 13, 20.
Townley, J. H., 148.
Trunkey, Judge, 363.

Union, Armstrong Co., history of, 421.
Union, Erie Co., history of, 446.
Vacancies, 56, 100.
Vance, Joseph, 440.
Vance's Fort, 4.
Van Cleve, R. S., notice of, 401, 167.
Van Liew, John, D. D., notice of, 369, 101.
Venango, history of, 455.
Vote of Presbytery, 139.

Waggoner, D., notice of, 380, 145, 162.
Walker, R. B., D. D., 427.
Wallace, B. J., D. D., 127.
Warren, F. V., 446.
" Pa., history of, 444.
" O., history of, 437.
Washington, history of, 446.
Washburn, D., notice of, 380, 146.
Waterford, history of, 443.
Waterloo, history of, 453.
Webber, H., history of, 384, 148.
West, N., D. D., biography of, 331.
Westfield, Pa., history of, 425.
" N. Y., history of, 446.
Wick, William, biography of, 182.
Williams, L. W., biography of, 343, 152.
Williams, Samuel, 434.
Willson, William, notice of, 389.
Wilson, J. G., notice of, 377, 132.
" L. B., 409.
Wilson's Presbyterian Historical Almanac, 272.
Wood, William, biography of, 216.
Wortman, M. L., 429.
Wright, James, 424.
Wylie, William, D. D., biography of, 203, 33, 48.

Young, Loyal, D D., 435.
Young, James, 154.
Youngstown, history of, 408.

Zahniser, G. W. notice of, 390, 154.

www.ingramcontent.com/pod-product-compliance
Lightning Source LLC
Chambersburg PA
CBHW050133240426
43673CB00043B/1646